Ilyushin IL-76

Russia's Versatile Airlifter

Dmitriy Komissarov and Yefim Gordon

Ilyushin IL-76:
Russia's Versatile Airlifter

© 2001 Dmitriy Komissarov and Yefim Gordon

ISBN 1 85780 106 7

Published by Midland Publishing
4 Watling Drive, Hinckley, LE10 3EY, England
Tel: 01455 254 490   Fax: 01455 254 495
E-mail: midlandbooks@compuserve.com

Midland Publishing is an imprint of
Ian Allan Publishing Ltd

Worldwide distribution (except North America):
Midland Counties Publications
4 Watling Drive, Hinckley, LE10 3EY, England
Telephone: 01455 254 450   Fax: 01455 233 737
E-mail: midlandbooks@compuserve.com
www.midlandcountiessuperstore.com

North American trade distribution:
Specialty Press Publishers & Wholesalers Inc.
11605 Kost Dam Road, North Branch, MN 55056
Tel: 651 583 3239   Fax: 651 583 2023
Toll free telephone: 800 895 4585

Design concept and layout
© 2001 Midland Publishing and
Stephen Thompson Associates

Printed in England by
Ian Allan Printing Ltd
Riverdene Business Park, Molesey Road,
Hersham, Surrey, KT12 4RG

Contents

Title page: **This view of the IL-76MF prototype
emphasises the large diameter of the new
engine nacelles.** Yefim Gordon

Below: **An apron shot of A-50s; apparently this
variant of the IL-76 took a lot of punishment in
operational conditions; the very battered
rotodomes are noteworthy.** Yefim Gordon

Introduction

Soviet and Russian aviation always attracted considerable interest in the West. Whilst combat aircraft always attracted the limelight, many transport aircraft also deserve close attention, both because of their considerable capabilities and notable design features and because they have seen no less action than some fighters or strike aircraft.

One such aircraft is the now familiar and ubiquitous Ilyushin IL-76. This was the Soviet Union's first jet transport to be designed from scratch, the first to enter production – and the most prolific, with some 930 built to date and production still continuing. Originally dismissed as a 'Starlifter clone', it has earned worldwide recognition as a competent freighter. It has made its mark in such noteworthy conflicts as Afghanistan and Chechnya and found a stable niche on the civil air transport market.

Carrying cargo was one of the principal tasks of aviation from the outset. Yet specialised transport aircraft took some time coming. In the early days of aviation aircraft had to be jacks of

The Antonov An-8 was the Soviet Air Force's first tactical airlifter designed with modern requirements in mind (soft-field capability, rear loading door etc). Though produced in extremely small numbers (a mere 150 were built for the VVS), the *Camp* is still around, serving with the more obscure operators in the Middle East and Africa. Yefim Gordon

all trades, and freight and mail was often carried by converted airliners – an idea which evolved into the quick-change concept – and even 'demilitarised' bombers withdrawn from active duty. The Soviet Union was no exception; for instance, the Polar Aviation Directorate used Tupolev TB-3 (ANT-6) bombers in the 1930s and briefly operated converted Tupolev Tu-4 bombers (reverse-engineered Boeing B-29 Superfortress, NATO code name *Bull*) in the late 1950s.

The Second World War demonstrated the efficiency of airborne assault during offensive operations, which is why increasing importance was attached to airborne troops after the war both sides of the newly-erected Iron Curtain. In the Soviet Union the airborne troops (VDV – voz*dooshn*o-de*sahnt*nyye voy*skah*) became an independent arm of the armed forces in 1946. In the same year the assault transport branch was created within the framework of the Soviet Air Force (VVS – *voyenno*-voz*dooshn*yye **see***ly*); this was eventually reorganised into the military transport aviation (VTA – *voyenno*-**trahns**portnaya avi**ah**tsiya), the Soviet equivalent to the USAF's Military Airlift Command.

It soon became obvious that new transport aircraft capable of carrying more troops and/or heavy military equipment were required to bolster the combat potential of the VDV and VTA. Hence in 1947 the Soviet government launched a major new hardware development

programme for the VDV. The Ministry of Aircraft Industry (MAP – *Ministerstvo aviatseeonnoy promyshlennosti*) was responsible for transport aircraft with paradrop capability and assault gliders. The general operational requirement (GOR) called for aircraft capable of transporting 30 to 60 fully equipped troops and vehicles such as self-propelled howitzers.

Three renowned Soviet aircraft design bureaux led by Andrey Nikolayevich Tupolev (OKB-156), Sergey Vladimirovich Ilyushin (OKB-240) and Aleksandr Sergeyevich Yakovlev (OKB-115)[1] were tasked with developing transport aircraft, even though they had other equally important military programmes to work on. The Tupolev OKB (*opytno-konstrooktorskoye byuro* – experimental design bureau) came up with the Tu-75, a four-engined freighter with rear loading ramp based on the Tu-70 *Cart* experimental airliner, itself a spinoff of the Tu-4. The Tu-75 had a 10-ton (22,045 lb) payload and performed well but did not enter production.

Ilyushin produced a 4-ton (8,818 lb) tactical airlift, troopship and glider towing version of the IL-12 *Coach* airliner developed in 1943-46 as a DC-3 replacement. This aircraft, the IL-12D (for *desahntnyy* – paratroop), fared better, making up the backbone of the VTA until the late 1950s together with its derivative IL-14T *Crate*.

Assault gliders were then considered the only means of delivering heavy vehicles to the landing zone, since most transport aircraft of the time had side loading which precluded the

paradropping of bulky items. Thus the OKBs led by Ilyushin, Yakovlev and Pyotr V Tsybin developed the IL-32, Yak-14 *Mare* and Ts-30 respectively. Of these only the Yak-14 entered production, complementing the earlier Ts-25 *Mist*.

Operational experience with these aircraft, however, showed that dedicated airlifters and paradropping systems were the way to go (though this was found out by trial and error, as will be evident). From the mid-50s onwards Soviet design bureaux started working in that direction. In 1956 the young OKB led by Oleg Konstantinovich Antonov produced the An-8 *Camp* twin-turboprop tactical transport. This was followed three years later by the broadly similar four-turboprop An-12 *Cub* – a Lockheed C-130 look-alike which, though derived from the An-10 Ookraina (The Ukraine)/*Cat* airliner, had all the features a modern military freighter should have, including a rear loading door and the ability to operate from semi-prepared tactical airstrips. The An-12 turned out to be a successful aircraft, and though production ended in 1972 it still soldiers on with the VVS and some other air forces, as well as civil operators, as of this writing.

Yet as early as 17th June 1955 Soviet civil aviation entered the jet age with the Tu-104 *Camel* twinjet medium-range airliner. Compared to this, the Antonov turboprops seemed slow and the military started clamouring for a jet transport aircraft. MAP chimed in, too. As Pyotr V Dement'yev (then Minister of Aircraft Industry) put it in a conversation with one of Ilyushin's aides, 'I've had enough of those windmills (as he disparagingly called propeller-driven aircraft – *Author*). They're history. The military airlift command needs fast aircraft as much as everybody else. What we need is an aircraft combining the design culture of a (state-of-the-art jet) airliner and the qualities of a mil-

itary airlifter – reliability, ease of operation and maintenance, self-contained operation and the ability to use dirt strips. In a nutshell, a real workhorse. I think your OKB can do it.'

Tupolev were the first to react: the Tu-107 entered flight test in 1957. This was a straightforward derivative of the Tu-104A with a rear loading ramp and a tail gun barbette with twin 23mm (.90 calibre) Afanas'yev/Makarov AM-23 cannons and PRS-1[2] Argon gun-laying radar.

However, the Tu-107 had two major shortcomings. First, it could only operate from paved airstrips; second, the rather stalky undercarriage precluded straight-in loading from a truck bed. This was because the low-wing Tu-104/Tu-107 was a spinoff of the mid-wing Tu-16 *Badger* bomber. In the end the 'bad news' outweighed the 'good news' and the Tu-107 did not progress beyond the prototype stage.

Still, the need for an An-12 replacement grew increasingly acute as time passed. The VVS needed a jet transport with equally good field performance (including rough-field capability) and the ability to operate independently from ground support equipment but with much higher speed and a bigger payload. So did the sole Soviet airline, Aeroflot, which had to haul heavy equipment to oil and gas fields in Siberia and goods coming in via seaports in the Far East. Enter the Ilyushin IL-76.

Dmitriy Komissarov
Yefim Gordon

January 2001

The An-12 was the mainstay of the Soviet Air Force's transport element until the advent of the IL-76. This particular example based at Kubinka (17 Red, c/n 5342810) was even built at the same factory which later built the *Candid*. Yefim Gordon

Acknowledgements

The authors wish to thank the following persons who assisted in the making of this book: Viktor G Kravchenko, Sergey Yu Panov and Dmitriy A Petrochenko who provided valuable information on fleet lists;

Rudolf A Teymurazov, Ivan G Faleyev, Lydia N Anghelova and Natal'ya I Titova at the CIS Interstate Aviation Committee who provided access to the official records of civil IL-76s;

Yevgeniy D Izotov, Anatoliy A Pozdnyakov, Yelena Ye Vorob'yova and Yevgenia V Khamkova at the Bykovo Air Services Company who provided insight into how the IL-76 is overhauled;

East Line Aviation Security which provided access to the apron at Domodedovo, allowing some valuable photos to be taken;

Vladimir Petrov at LII;

Andrey Yurgenson, who prepared all of the line drawings included in the book;

and, last but not least, Dmitriy Makovenko who printed most of the photos included in this book with excellent quality.

Russian Language and Transliteration

The Russian language is phonetic – pronounced as written, or 'as seen'. Translating into English gives rise to many problems and the vast majority of these arise because English is not a straightforward language, with many pitfalls of pronunciation!

Accordingly, Russian words must be translated through into a *phonetic* form of English and this can lead to different ways of helping the reader pronounce what he sees. Every effort has been made to standardise this, but inevitably variations will occur. While reading from source to source this might seem confusing and/or inaccurate but it is the name as *pronounced* that is the constancy, not the *spelling* of that pronunciation!

The 20th letter of the Russian (Cyrillic) alphabet looks very much like a 'Y' but is pronounced as a 'U' as in the word 'rule'.

Another example is the train of thought that Russian words ending in 'y' are perhaps better spelt out as 'yi' to underline the pronunciation, but it is felt that most Western speakers would have problems getting their tongues around this!

This is a good example of the sort of problem that some Western sources have suffered from in the past (and occasionally even today) when they make the mental leap about what they see approximating to an English letter.

Chapter One

A New Machine

The Ilyushin OKB had made the same mistake as Tupolev, in trying to adapt the 1957-vintage IL-18 *Coot* four-turboprop airliner to the military transport role: the IL-18TD troop transport (CCCP-74296, c/n 187010603) remained a one-off and was later reconverted to a standard IL-18D. Experience showed that a dedicated freighter, not a warmed-over airliner, was the correct approach. The specific operational requirement (SOR) for such an aircraft was drawn up on 28th June 1966; on 27th November 1967 the Soviet Council of Ministers issued a directive tasking the Ilyushin OKB with developing a four-jet freighter designated IL-76.

This was the first Ilyushin aircraft to be designed under someone other than the bureau's founder. Sergey V Ilyushin's health had been failing and he retired in 1970; thus his deputy, Ghenrikh Vasil'yevich Novozhilov, was the IL-76's chief project engineer. Soon after Novozhilov had succeeded Ilyushin as General Designer (the official title of Soviet OKB chiefs), Radiy Petrovich Papkovskiy was appointed IL-76 project chief in 1975.

The freighter's design specifications were perhaps the most stringent of the time. The IL-76 had to carry a 40-ton (88,183 lb) payload over 5,000km (2,700nm) – twice the payload and range of the An-12 – in less than six hours with lower operating costs. It had to be capable of using dirt or snow strips with a bearing strength of no more than of $6kg/cm^2$ (85.35 lb/in^2) and operating away from maintenance bases for up to 90 days at ambient temperatures ranging from -70°C to +45°C (-94 to +113°F). Takeoff and landing run at normal take-off and landing weight was not to exceed 900m (2,952ft) and 500m (1,640ft) respectively.

The general arrangement was identical to the Lockheed L-300-50A (C-141 Starlifter), with a circular-section fuselage, shoulder-mounted anhedral wings with moderate sweepback, a T-tail and four turbofans in separate underwing nacelles. Since the Starlifter had been around for quite some time by then (the YC-141A prototype, 61-2775, had entered flight test on 17th December 1963), Western analysts inevitably started comparing the IL-76 to the C-141 as soon as they had seen it – with the customary

allegations that the Soviets had once again copied a Western design. Such accusations were often unfounded, since the similarity in many cases was purely superficial; moreover, critics on this point often choose to forget the similarity between, for instance, the Douglas DC-9, BAC One-Eleven and Fokker F.28 Fellowship.

Well, during the Cold War years the East and the West never missed an opportunity to sting each other. As for the apparent similarity between the C-141 and the IL-76, engineers in different countries facing the same problem often come to similar solutions; we will elaborate on this later.

At the preliminary development (PD) stage aircraft often change beyond recognition, and the IL-76 was a case in point. The elegant airlifter we know today was presaged by two rather ungainly PD projects. Version 1 had an An-12-style nose with glazed navigator's station and undernose ground mapping radar, albeit with a much longer and deeper fairing. The aft fuselage originally *did* resemble the C-141 with its rather plump contours, and the fin had a prominent fillet.

The cargo door design, however, was rather different. The IL-76 featured three cargo door segments; the narrow outer segments opened outwards and the wide centre segment upwards to lie flat against the cargo bay roof, propped up by the flat rear pressure bulkhead which swung backwards and up. This arrangement developed jointly with TsAGI (*Tsentrahl'nyy aero- i ghidrodinameecheskiy institoot* – Central Aerodynamics & Hydrodynamics Institute named after Nikolay V Zhukovskiy) minimised drag when opened in

flight for paradropping. By comparison, the C-141 had clamshell cargo doors which protruded far beyond the fuselage contour when opened, causing considerable drag.

The landing gear originally also was quite similar to that of the C-141, with a forward-retracting twin-wheel nose unit and four-wheel main bogies retracting upwards into lateral fairings. The latter were quite large because the IL-76 had fat low-pressure tyres for rough-field capability; still, having the main units retract inwards would have necessitated raising the cargo cabin floor, which was undesirable. This was important because the IL-76 sat fairly high off the ground (unlike the C-141 which was designed for paved runways and had a rather short undercarriage). The extra drag of the bulky main gear fairings could be compensated by fitting more powerful engines.

The IL-76 was powered by four 12,000kgp (26,455 lbst) D-30KP two-shaft turbofans – an uprated version of the 11,000kgp (24,250 lbst) D-30KU developed for the IL-62M *Classic* long-range airliner by Pavel Aleksandrovich Solov'yov's OKB[1] in Perm'. Despite the similar designation, the D-30KU/KP has only some 15% commonality (in the core) with the 6,800kgp (14,991 lbst) Solov'yov D-30 developed for the Tu-134 *Crusty* short/medium-range airliner. Bypass ratio is 2.42 compared to 1.0 for the D-30; besides, the D-30KP has a clamshell thrust reverser (optional on the D-30KU) whereas the D-30 Srs II/Srs III has a cascade thrust reverser and the D-30 Srs I has none. Incidentally, the higher bypass ratio resulted in a much more agreeable sound. Believe it or not, the four-engined IL-62M and IL-76 appear less noisy than the twin-engined

The C-141A Starlifter was the nearest Western equivalent of the future IL-76 with which it shared the general arrangement. Thus, inevitably, the Ilyushin design bureau was accused of 'copying the Starlifter', an allegation often heard in the Cold War years. Bob Archer

Tu-134 which earned the disdainful nickname of *svistok* (whistle) for the high-pitched screech of its D-30 engines.

As a point of interest, the original project evolved into a 250-seat airliner in January 1967. This project incorporated several unusual features. First, it was one of the very few high-wing airliners to have a double-deck fuselage (the only other known aircraft of the kind is a 720-seat monster based on the An-22 *Cock* which likewise never got off the drawing board). The top floor seated 184 in six- or seven-abreast economy-class seating and the lower floor 66 three-abreast. Second, the lower floor was divided lengthwise into a port side baggage compartment and a starboard side passenger cabin (!). For the first time in Soviet practice the baggage was containerised. Third, the aircraft had three integral airstairs – two on the lower deck on the port side and a third under the aft fuselage *à la* Boeing 727 with direct access to the upper deck.

A massive redesign was made in February 1967. The avionics suite was updated to include the Koopol ground mapping radar (cupola – or rather, in this context, parachute canopy, implying use of the system for pinpoint paradropping) in a chin fairing and the Groza weather radar (Thunderstorm, pronounced *grozah*) ahead of the navigator's station. Consequently the nose was made more elongated to incorporate the weather radar. The Koopol radar was a product of LNPO[2] Leninets (Leninist) based in Leningrad, one of the Soviet Union's major avionics designers (aka the Ministry of Electronics Industry's NII-131[3]).

The rear fuselage became even fatter, making the fin look disproportionately small. The upswept rear fuselage could easily have earned the IL-76 the nickname 'flying banana', had it flown in this guise. The aircraft had one port side crew entry door near the nose gear and two doors for paradropping aft of the main gear fairings *à la* C-130.

The wings were swept back 25° at quarter-chord, with 4° incidence, an aspect ratio of 8, a taper of 3 and an area of 240m² (2,582ft²). Thickness-to-chord ratio was 13% at root and 10% at the tips. Structurally the wings were made up of five sections, the centre section being integral with the fuselage and located outside the circular-section pressure cabin so as not to infringe on cargo bay height. The wings had a straight leading edge and a sharply kinked trailing edge where the inner and outer wing panels were joined.

The inboard engine pylons were attached to the inner wings and the outboard pylons to the outer wings with sharply raked detachable tip fairings. The integral wing tanks held 86,360 litres (18,999 Imperial gallons) or 66.95 tons (147,597 lb) of fuel.

The IL-76 featured two-section triple-slotted flaps (for the first time on a transport aircraft; the C-141 has double-slotted flaps) and five-section leading-edge slats to ensure good field performance. The flaps were set at 20° for take-off and 40° for landing; the slats were deflected 20° and terminated some way short of the fuselage. The flap and slat drive motors were housed in the large wing/fuselage fairing, along with air conditioning heat exchangers and a rescue dinghy. Roll control was by means of large ailerons occupying the outer third of the trailing edge and four-section spoilers/lift dumpers.

The main gear was thoroughly redesigned, featuring two independent twin-wheel levered-suspension units in tandem each side. These were spaced so as to increase the landing gear footprint, reducing ground pressure, and enable the aircraft to land on three main units without taking damage if one failed to extend. Tyre size was 1,450 x 580mm (57 x 22.8in) on the mainwheels and 1,140 x 350mm (44.8 x 13.7in) on the nosewheels.

The freight hold measured 24.0 x 3.4 x 3.45m (78ft 9in x 11ft 2in x 11ft 4in),[4] with a volume of 330m³ (11,654ft³) and a floor area of 67m² (720ft²). The dimensions were selected so as to

Designed in the early '60s, the massive An-22 could lug almost every kind of equipment the Soviet armed forces had. However, this capable transport was built in even smaller numbers and could not fill the Air Force's needs. The type still soldiers on with the Russian air arm; RA-09306 (c/n 9340206) was photographed in Akhtoobinsk, seat of the Russian Air Force Research Institute, in the mid-90s. Yefim Gordon

permit carriage of a standard Soviet Model 02-T boxcar. The hold was equipped with a gantry crane which ran on rails running the full length of the roof and beyond the pressure bulkhead; this enabled it to lift loads right off a truck or trailer standing near the cargo ramp. In fully lowered position the ramp was inclined 14°, allowing wheeled and tracked vehicles to be loaded under their own power; there were two winches for loading trailers and the like. The freight hold floor was 2m (6ft 7in) above ground level.

The flight deck located on the 'second floor' was accessed by a ladder from freight hold floor level while the navigator entered his compartment via a door to the right of this ladder; a toilet was located symmetrically to port. A compartment for eight passengers was envisaged aft of the flight deck. The stillborn double-deck airliner project of 1967 inspired the engineers to provide a removable top deck in the freight hold for carrying troops. In an emergency the crew and troopers evacuated via three dorsal emergency exits (two ahead of the wings and one aft). The crew consisted of two pilots, a navigator, a flight engineer, a radio operator, two equipment operators and two technicians.

The port main gear sponson housed a TA-6A auxiliary power unit (TA = *toorboagregaht* – lit. 'turbo unit') for self-contained engine starting, equipment operation and air conditioning; it had a lateral air intake and a dorsal exhaust. This APU had originally been developed for the IL-62 by the Stoopino Machinery Design Bureau[5] near Moscow. DC batteries and a reconnaissance camera (primarily for checking paradropping accuracy) were located symmetrically in the starboard sponson. Unusually, four 500kg (1,102 lb) bombs could be carried in closed bays at the rear of the main gear sponsons; this was a requirement of the VVS which insisted that a transport aircraft *absolutely* had to be capable of dropping bombs. There was as yet no defensive armament.

As of February 1967 the IL-76 had an overall length of 46.85m (153ft 8½in), a fuselage length of 42.5m (139ft 5in), a fuselage diameter of 4.8m (15ft 9in), a wingspan of 43.8m (143ft 8½in) and a height of 13.7m (44ft 11in).

More major changes came by 1969, however. The fuselage nose ahead of the flight deck glazing was shortened and recontoured to reduce the blind spot during taxying. Both radomes were reshaped and optically flat glass panels were introduced in the navigator's glazing to improve visibility. The radome of the ground mapping radar protruded below the lower fuselage contour to give the radar 360° coverage, so a special towbar with a characteristic kink in the middle had to be designed for the IL-76 to avoid damaging the radome.

The aircraft looked as if it had gone on a diet: the aft fuselage was much slimmer with virtually no adverse effect on freight hold space, which was 321m³ (11,336ft³). The paratroop doors aft of the wings were deleted, but a second entry door was added symmetrically to starboard; the doors could be opened hydraulically 90° in flight for paradropping. The dorsal escape hatches in the freight hold were replaced by four emergency exits – two at main deck level ahead of the wings and two at upper deck level aft of the wings; the flight deck roof hatch was retained for quick access to the dinghy in the event of ditching. A flight deck escape hatch with hydraulically-powered door doubling as slipstream deflector was added on the port side of the nose just aft of the navigator's station.

The wings underwent a major redesign. Flap settings were now 15° or 30° for take-off and 43° for landing; the slats were deployed 14° (at 15° flap) or 25°. There were four-section airbrakes inboard and four-section spoilers/lift dumpers outboard, and the ailerons were now divided into two sections. Trailing-edge sweep was increased slightly on the inner wings, making the kink less pronounced, and the wingtips were reshaped, being parallel to the fuselage axis. All four engine pylons were now attached to the inner wings and more sharply swept; full-span slats were provided (with cutouts in the two inboard sections to stop them from striking the pylons when fully deployed), and the air conditioning intakes were moved to the wing/fuselage fairing.

The vertical tail was reshaped, closely resembling that of the IL-62, with a much smaller root fillet and a smooth transition from fin to

fuselage. The rudder now stopped short of the rear fuselage, thus allowing a tail gunner's station to be incorporated – the aircraft was designed primarily as a military transport, after all. Unlike the IL-62, however, the IL-76 featured a one-piece rudder (not split into upper and lower halves) and the stabiliser tip fairings were rounded, not angular.

The landing gear was totally reworked once again, as the engineers decided to improve soft-field performance while 'cleaning up' the bulky main gear sponsons. The answer to the first problem was to increase the gear's footprint once again. The result was an unconventional arrangement with five independent units, each having four wheels on a single axle (ie, two pairs each side of the oleo). The nose unit retracted forwards and the four main units inwards to lie in two shallow ventral fairings. During retraction the mainwheel axles rotated around the oleos by means of simple mechanical links so that the wheels stowed vertically with the axles parallel to the fuselage axis; a similar arrangement had been used earlier on the Hawker Siddeley HS.121 Trident airliner. Tyre size was 1,300 x 480mm (51.2 x 18.9in) on the mainwheels and 1,100 x 330mm (43.3 x 13in) on the nosewheels. Tyre pressure could be adjusted in flight between 2.5 to 5 bars (36 to 73psi) to suit different types of runways (paved or unpaved).

The gear attachment points and actuators were enclosed by separate lateral fairings of quasi-triangular section which also housed the APU and single-point pressure refuelling panel (port) and DC batteries (starboard). The APU

intake now featured an inward-opening door to prevent windmilling during cruise and the exhaust was located laterally.

Besides being much cleaner aerodynamically, the new arrangement gave a much wider gear track (and hence footprint). It also allowed the main gear doors to close when the gear was down, preventing mud, water and slush from entering the wheel wells, which was important when operating from unprepared runways. Previously the mainwheels had been semi-recessed in the sponsons *à la* An-22 when the gear was down, rendering this impossible.

Changes were made to the cargo handling equipment. The overhead gantry crane was replaced initially by two and then by four separate cargo hoists capable of lifting 2,500kg (5,511 lb) each. These could move 5.65m (18ft 6½in) beyond the cargo ramp for straight-in loading from a truck bed, since the cargo door centre segment fitted nicely between the tracks on which they moved. The titanium floor incorporated fold-away roller conveyors for container handling and recessed cargo tiedown points, with removable roller conveyors on the cargo ramp; palletised or containerised cargo could be easily secured by chains and quick-release shackles. Importantly, the cargo tiedown lugs were installed permanently, unlike the An-12 where they were normally stowed in the hold and had to be screwed into place as required – with all the resulting inconveniences (the need to cart a set of spanners around, the time needed to install and remove the lugs, the risk of losing them etc).

A model of the IL-76 in the TsAGI wind tunnel.
Yefim Gordon archive

The cargo ramp incorporated a U-shaped tail bumper and four manually-retractable vehicle loading ramps. It could be used to lift loads weighing up to 2.5 tons (5,511 lb), though some sources quoted an exorbitant figure of 30 tons (66,137 lb); this was a useful feature when loading vehicles which have difficulty negotiating the angle between the ramp and freight hold floor (especially tracked vehicles). In this case a hydraulically-powered support stowed in the cargo ramp would be extended to stop the aircraft from falling over on its tail.

The external dimensions and proportions were also rather different. The aircraft was 46.5m (152ft 7in) long, 14.7m (48ft 3in) high, had a 50.5m (165ft 8in) wingspan and a 300m² (3,228ft²) wing area. The well-knit aircraft had an air of rugged dependability about it – a real transporter which will get your cargo there no matter what.

Empty weight was 86 tons (189,594 lb) and MTOW 157 tons (346,120 lb). On paved runways the IL-76 had a payload of 40 tons (88,183 lb) decreasing to 33 tons (72,751 lb) on grass, dirt or snow strips. The aircraft was designed for a service life of 30,000 hours, 10,000 cycles and 20 years.

Ilyushin engineers had gone to great lengths to increase reliability. For instance, the control runs, electric wiring and hydraulic lines were routed along both sides of the fuselage to prevent them from being totally disabled by a single hit. Also, much attention had been paid to flight deck and navigator's station design to make the aircraft 'user-friendly'. Completely new flight instrumentation, navigation and targeting systems were developed to make sure the aircraft would fulfil its mission anytime.

The advanced development project was reviewed by a so-called mockup review commission during 12th-31st May 1969 and received the go-ahead. Construction of a full-scale wooden mockup commenced in December at the OKB's experimental plant, MMZ No 240 'Strela' (Arrow, pronounced *strelah*),[6] at Moscow's Central airfield named after Mikhail V Frunze – better known as the Khodynka airfield. To save space the mockup featured only the complete fuselage and vertical tail, part of the horizontal tail and part of an inner wing with the inboard engine. Yet the cargo doors and ramp were fully operational and the freight hold floor was stressed so that real vehicles could be driven inside to demonstrate the freighter's capacity without falling through. The mockup review commission chaired by Lt Gen Gheorgiy N Pakilev was quite satisfied with the aircraft, pointing out only minor deficiencies. It was green light for the IL-76.

To be perfectly honest, Pakilev was unimpressed at first, as the grey-painted mockup occupying the better part of the dimly lit hangar did not look particularly appealing. He voiced his doubts to Ilyushin who attended the 'presentation'. 'You will see the aircraft's merits and capabilities for yourself later', Ilyushin replied. And he was right.

The original IL-76 preliminary development project evolved into this 250-seat 'airbus' *(sic)* in January 1967. The drawing illustrates the double-deck layout (which later inspired the removable upper deck for carrying troops), the integral airstairs and the An-12-style nose profile. Sergey and Dmitriy Komissarov collection

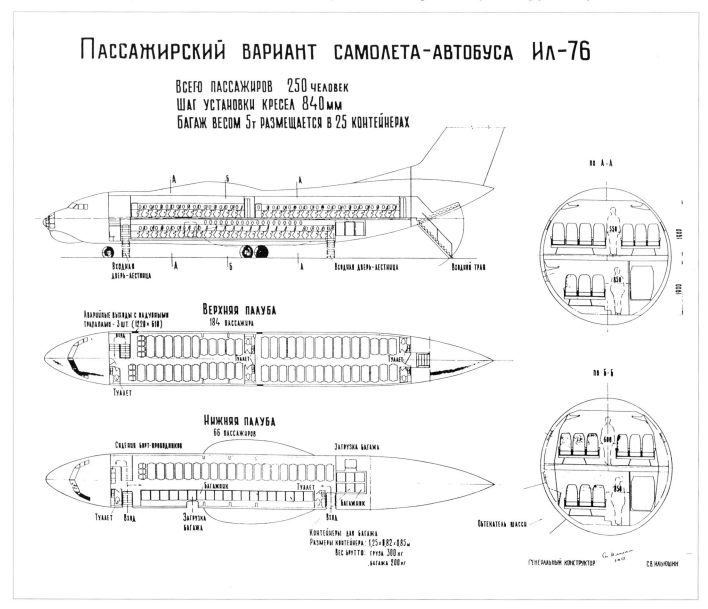

Chapter Two

A First Flight from Downtown

After some minor changes based on the commission's findings the design was frozen in December (no pun intended) and MMZ No 240 began construction of the first prototype registered CCCP-86712[1] (construction number 01-01, ie, Batch 1, first aircraft in batch). Work on the aircraft's systems proceeded in parallel; an 'iron bird' for control system testing was built at plant No 240 along with hydraulics, electrics and landing gear test rigs. The IL-76 had a duplex control system with irreversible hydraulic boosters and a backup manual mode – an unusual feature for an aircraft of this size.

Being virtually hand-crafted, as it were, the first prototype of any aircraft takes time to build; given the size of the IL-76, the job took more than a year to accomplish. CCCP-86712 was rolled out in early March 1971. The familiar Aeroflot standard colour scheme was not introduced until 1973, so until the mid-70s every type operated by the airline had a colour scheme of its own. CCCP-86712 had a white upper fuselage and fin, light grey undersurfaces, wings, stabilisers and engine nacelles, a blue rudder and a blue/white/blue cheat line fanning out towards the front. The extensive glazing of the navigator's station wrapped around the underside of the nose made the IL-76 look as if it was grinning from ear to ear when seen head-on, and the prototype's paint job added to this impression.

Ground systems tests went well and the OKB was eager to begin flight tests. These would be held at the then top-secret flight test centre in Zhukovskiy[2] south-west of Moscow operated by LII (**Lyot**no-is**sled**ovatel'skiy insti**toot** – Flight Research Institute named after test pilot Mikhail M Gromov). Usually prototypes built by the experimental shops of various bureaux were trucked to LII from Moscow in dismantled condition. However, plant No 240 had the advantage of being located at Khodynka with its 1,700m (5,577ft) runway, so the OKB lead-

ers decided the aircraft should be *flown* to Zhukovskiy.

The opening lines of a feature in the *Pravda* (Truth) daily newspaper on 19th May 1971 describing the type's first flight read as follows: '*It was March. The country was getting ready for the Congress of the Communist Party.*' Sure enough, timing major achievements to coincide with CPSU congresses was the order of the day in the Cold War-era Soviet Union. But there was an even more important reason for rushing the first flight: the 29th Paris Aerospace Salon at Le Bourget was due to take place from 25th May to 6th June 1971 and the Ilyushin

OKB wanted to unveil the aircraft there. This was a matter of national prestige, and the Soviet Union created sensations at Le Bourget at more or less regular intervals.

An MAP council convened to decide whether the aircraft was ready to fly (this was standard operational procedure in the Soviet Union). The situation was undoubtedly complicated; an aircraft grossing more than a hundred tons (220,458 lb) was due to take off in a heavily populated area some 6km (3.72 miles) from the Kremlin! Besides, the Igor' V Kurchatov Nuclear Physics Research Institute with its reactors was directly in the flight path; the con-

The first prototype, CCCP-86712, on the apron at Moscow/Vnukovo-2 airport. Note open APU air intake, and the spike on the No1 engine intake bullet fairing, probably associated with test equipment. Yefim Gordon archive

With the IL-62M prototype (CCCP-86673) in the background, the first prototype IL-76 is pushed back by a KrAZ-214B lorry. This view illustrates the varied colour schemes worn by Aeroflot aircraft in those days.
Sergey & Dmitriy Komissarov collection

sequences of the aircraft crashing there could be disastrous.

On the other hand, MMZ No 30 'Znamya Truda' (Banner of Labour; pronounced **znah-mya troodah**),[3] a production plant located right across the apron from Ilyushin's experimental shop, had built IL-14 and IL-18 airliners for years and all of them had flown out of Khodynka without mishap. Eventually the council gave the go-ahead.

On 25th March 1971, with nearly every Ilyushin employee watching anxiously, the IL-76 prototype became airborne after a take-off run of only 685m (2,247ft) and made for Zhukovskiy. The aircraft was captained by Eduard I Kuznetsov, Hero of the Soviet Union (HSU); the crew also included first officer G N Volokhov, navigator V I Milyootin, flight engineer Igor' N Yakimets and radio operator I S Kondaoorov.

The first flight lasted little more than an hour. Immediately upon arrival CCCP-86712 commenced the preliminary performance and handling test programme aimed at obtaining clearance to display the aircraft in Paris. Kuznetsov said the aircraft behaved almost flawlessly from the start; hence Stage 1 of the manufacturer's flight tests was rather brief and on 17th May the prototype was demonstrated to Soviet government and Communist Party leaders at Moscow's Vnukovo-2 airport (the government VIP terminal) – which came as a total surprise for the Western world.

A week later, on 25th May, the IL-76 arrived at Le Bourget wearing the exhibit code 829 – and stole the show. Western observers named it the most notable debutante of the show. Until 1988, when the MiG-29 *Fulcrum-A* fighter and MiG-29UB *Fulcrum-B* conversion trainer appeared at Farnborough International, Soviet participation in airshows had been strictly civilian, displaying the Soviet Union's peaceful intentions for the world to see. Yet this time the message was patently clear: the Soviets were rapidly catching up with the West in strategic airlift capability.

When questioned about possible military uses of the jet, Ilyushin OKB representatives at the show steadfastly maintained that the IL-76 was 'a purely commercial aircraft'. This elicited ironic smiles from Western journalists; the unspoken comment was 'who are you trying to fool?'. Indeed, a 'purely commercial aircraft' following predetermined air routes has no real use for a ground mapping radar. Also, the high-flotation landing gear clearly indicated that the aircraft was designed with semi-prepared tactical airstrips in mind, not commercial airports.

Western specialists were not allowed inside the aircraft at Le Bourget '71 and OKB reps were pretty close-mouthed about technical details even by pre-*glasnost* standards. This led the West to conclude the IL-76 had few novel features, even if it doubtlessly represented a major advance in Soviet aircraft technology and a colossal boost to the Soviet Air Force's logistical support capability. (As for novel features, the sceptics were wrong; the aircraft incorporated more than 180 inventions of varying degrees of importance for which more than 30 international patents were issued.) Acid-tongued critics started questioning the 'coincidence' in layout with the C-141. Observers *did* note that the freight hold was somewhat roomier than the C-141's and that rather more power was needed to achieve the specified performance (the Starlifter's Pratt & Whitney TF33-P-7s are rated at 9,525kgp/ 21,000lbst).

After its Paris debut the IL-76 was allocated the NATO code name *Candid*. At the same time the first (and inaccurate) three-view by Dennis Punnett appeared in the Western press and started circulating from publication to publication. Apparently the author of the drawings had no opportunity to get a top view of aircraft and the result was a Boeing 707-style pointed nose, which is incorrect. The aft portion of the wing/fuselage fairing was also depicted incorrectly. (That's not the worst, however; some artists depicted the IL-76 with an *aft-retracting nose gear!*)

After coming back from Le Bourget CCCP-86712 resumed flight tests, with black and white phototheodolite calibration markings applied to the fuselage in several places. For low-speed/high-alpha handling trials the tailcone was modified to house a large anti-spin parachute canister with a downward-hinging hemispherical cover. The first prototype was also used for electromagnetic compatibility tests.

Initial trials for the military transport role which commenced on 3rd February 1972 when parachutists were dropped for the first time; the aircraft was flown by Eduard I Kuznetsov. The parachutists jumped through the cargo door, entry doors (which opened hydraulically 90° for protection against the slipstream) and the flight deck escape hatch. To use the latter, one had to kneel and then dive head first down a 2m (6.5ft) sloping chute. (This arrangement was

never used operationally, as crews seemed to prefer crashing with the aircraft; besides, it was unusable in the event of hydraulics failure. Instead, the chute was often used for keeping various odds and ends – including stolen goods.)

On 19th February the aircraft successfully performed the first drop of a 5-ton (11-023 lb) load. The first jumps went well and on 3rd April CCCP-86712 was used for a full-scale paradrop test, disgorging a full load of 115 paratroopers not far from Zhukovskiy. MAP and Parachute Design Institute personnel and cadets from the Ryazan' Airborne Troops Command Academy took part in these trials. Again, Kuznetsov flew the aircraft on both occasions. After this, MAP and the Air Force requested that a detachable upper deck be designed for the IL-76 to permit carriage of an additional 100 soldiers in troop transport configuration. The aircraft was also evaluated in the casualty evacuation (CASEVAC) role.

On 17th August 1972 Eduard I Kuznetsov was promoted to Distinguished Test Pilot (an official grade reflecting pilot expertise and experience) in recognition of his service – including the IL-76 test programme.

Meanwhile, a static test airframe (c/n 01-02) was built at MMZ No 240, followed by the second prototype, CCCP-86711 (c/n 01-03). This made its maiden flight from Khodynka on 25th February 1973 – again captained by Kuznetsov, with P M Fomin as engineer in charge.

The aircraft featured some minor improvements which found their way into production. For instance, the landing lights were moved forward and down to a position immediately aft of the navigator's glazing. The upper anti-collision light, which was mounted atop the fin *à la* IL-62 on CCCP-86712, was relocated to the wing centre section, and the identification friend-or-foe (IFF) aerials ahead of the flight deck glazing and under the tailcone were enclosed by fairings.

Unlike the first prototype, CCCP-86711 had an electro-pulse de-icing system on the wings (used later on the IL-86 *Camber* widebody airliner). However, the traditional hot air de-icing system was found to be adequate and fitted to all subsequent *Candids*. The tail unit was electrically de-iced.

The second prototype was used primarily for powerplant, avionics and cargo handling equipment testing. Later it was loaned to NII VVS (*Naoochno-issledovatel'skiy institoot voyenno-vozdooshnykh sil* – the [Soviet] Air Force Research Institute named after test pilot Valeriy P Chkalov), operating from Chkalovskaya airbase east of Moscow where the institute's transport aircraft section is located. While on loan to NII VVS the aircraft paid a visit to Kubinka airbase some 65km (40 miles) west of Moscow. CCCP-86711 was also used in 'Operation Cold Soak' in Yakutsk and Petropavlovsk-Kamchatskiy to evaluate the type's suitability for operation in harsh climates.

A rare air-to-air shot of CCCP-86712.
Yefim Gordon archive

Soon after the beginning of the flight test programme the first prototype was equipped with an anti-spin parachute for low-speed/high/alpha trials. It is seen here during service trials with Aeroflot in 1975, disgorging an Ikarus 250 coach. Sergey & Dmitriy Komissarov collection

Wearing the exhibit code 455, the second prototype was displayed at the 30th Paris Aerospace Salon from 26th May to 3rd June 1973. This time Western observers were allowed to examine the interior. Once again OKB representatives stuck rigidly to the official 'purely commercial freighter' story; General Designer Genrikh V Novozhilov stated to *Air International* that the principal purpose of the IL-76 was supply of remote regions of the Soviet Union having no railway facilities. Other Soviet delegates at Le Bourget, however, tacitly admitted that the *Candid* had military uses as well.

The career of CCCP-86711 ended when the aircraft struck an airport building while taxiing and was damaged beyond repair. It became a ground instructional airframe at RIIGA (*Rizhskiy institoot inzhenerov grazhdahnskoy aviahtsii* – Riga Institute of Civil Aviation Engineers) and sat at Riga's Spilve airport. Sadly, this aircraft was broken up in mid-1997

along with the other aircraft preserved there (IL-18A CCCP-75645, the prototype IL-62M CCCP-86673, Tu-134 CCCP-65645 and Tu-134A CCCP-65654), and it is more than likely that political motives were involved. As a point of interest, the registrations CCCP-86711 and -86712 were later reused by two VIP-configured IL-62Ms (c/ns 4648414 and 4648339) operated by Flight Detachment 235, the Soviet Union's government flight.[4]

Meanwhile, MAP aircraft factory No 84[5] in the Uzbek capital of Tashkent was gearing up for full-scale production of the IL-76. The factory had been established in Khimki, a suburb of Moscow, evacuating to Tashkent in 1941 when German troops came dangerously close to the city. Over the years, factory No 84 had built the PS-84/Lisunov Li-2 *Cab* (licence-built DC-3), IL-14, An-8, An-12 and An-22. The transition to a new aircraft was difficult but Tashkent had had some experience with Ilyushin aircraft and this surely helped.

The first production IL-76 built in Tashkent, CCCP-76500 (c/n 033401016, f/n 0104) took off on 8th May 1973. Like the two prototypes, it was built in unarmed commercial configuration and was the first *Candid* to wear full 1973-standard Aeroflot colours. It differed from the prototypes in having a shorter rear portion of the wing/fuselage fairing – a feature introduced on all subsequent aircraft. The aircraft was flown by captain Aleksandr M Tyuryumin (an OKB test pilot who received the HSU title in 1976 for the IL-76's trials programme) and first officer K G Koodinov; V S Krooglyakov was the engineer in charge.

The second prototype, CCCP-86711, in flight.
Sergey & Dmitriy Komissarov collection

CCCP-76500 photographed during trials.
Note the small air intake under the Aeroflot logo
which was deleted on later aircraft. ITAR-TASS

(A note must be made here on **construction numbers (manufacturer's serial numbers)**. Production aircraft built in Tashkent have nine- or ten-digit c/ns. The first two or three digits respectively denote the year of certification: 03 = 1973 etc, 000 = 1980, 001 = 1981 etc, 100 = 1990, 101 = 1991 etc. The next two digits are always 34; this is a code for factory No 84 introduced after the evacuation to Tashkent because the factory took up residence at the site of the unfinished aircraft factory No 34 (which, as such, never built a single aircraft). The remaining five digits do not signify *anything at all*; the idea is to confuse would-be spies so that the c/n would not reveal how many aircraft have been built. The first two of these 'famous last five', as they are often called, accrue smoothly from 01 through 99 and then start all over again, while the final three accrue in steps from 001 through 999 by adding a random number from 1 to 7 and start all over again. (See Appendix One). A given five-digit combination is never repeated.

Additionally, IL-76s have **fuselage numbers** (f/ns); security is all very well but the manufacturer has to keep track of production, after all. Typically of Soviet aircraft, the f/n is not just a sequential line number (as in the case of Boeing and Douglas aircraft) but consists of a batch number and the number of the aircraft in the batch; in the case of the IL-76, normally there are ten aircraft to a batch.[6] For instance, IL-76T CCCP-76519 manufactured on 31st October 1979 (c/n 093420599) is f/n 1510 – ie, the 150th aircraft built, the 149th flying example and the 147th production example of the *Candid* family.

The c/n is stencilled in large digits on the rear pressure bulkhead and thus visible only from inside or when the cargo doors are open. It is also embossed on tiny metal plates found on the inner faces of the nose gear doors and on one side of the vehicle loading ramps which are normally stowed in the cargo ramp. Aircraft built from approximately 1989 onwards have the 'famous last five' and date of manufacture

embossed on small metal plates attached to the lower edges of both entry doors, but these are not easy to find, as they are often over-painted. Conversely, the f/n is usually found only in 'ship's papers', but Soviet/CIS Air Force examples often have it stencilled or hand-painted on intake and exhaust covers, wheel chocks etc, to prevent these from being stolen and used on another aircraft.)

CCCP-76500 was also flown to Ilyushin's flight test facility at LII and used for cargo handling equipment tests and stability trials during personnel and cargo drops. The aircraft was subsequently retained by the OKB which used it for various test and development work.

During 24-29th August 1973 the second prototype completed a special test programme to check the type's suitability for operation from unpaved strips. The aircraft was captained by G N Volokhov and P M Fomin was the engineer in charge of the tests. The take-off and landing proper caused no problems; the 20-wheel landing gear did an excellent job – the C-141 would be no match for this 'centipede'. However, as the IL-76 took off it kicked up a terrific dust cloud which obscured the strip completely; the pilots had to circle for some 20 minutes, waiting for the dust to settle before a landing could be attempted.

From 10-16th September 1973 the CCCP-86711 was displayed at an airshow in Iruma, Japan. Again the aircraft was captained by G N Volokhov, with P M Fomin as engineer in charge.

Chapter Three

Versatility

The IL-76 turned out to be an extremely versatile aircraft, with numerous more-or-less specialised versions appearing as the Ilyushin OKB strove to improve the design. Known versions of the aircraft are detailed below.

IL-76 (military) *Candid-B*

Rolled out in October 1973, the second production aircraft, CCCP-76501 (c/n 033401019, f/n 0105), was the prototype of the armed military transport version. Curiously, this initially had no separate designation to distinguish it from the commercial version, both variants being known simply as 'IL-76'. Later, when new versions designated by suffix letters appeared, the initial production versions became known unofficially as *il-sem'desyat-shest' 'bez bookvy'* – 'IL-76 with no [suffix] letter', or *sans suffixe*, as we will call them hereinafter. When the West became aware of its existence, the military version was code-named *Candid-B*, the original civil version becoming the *Candid-A*.

The most obvious recognition feature of the *Candid-B* is, of course, the tail gunner's station and UKU-9K-502-1 powered turret[1] with two Gryazev/Shipoonov GSh-23 double-barrelled 23mm (.90 calibre) cannons. A PRS-4 Krypton gun ranging radar, aka *izdeliye* 4DK,[2] is fitted at the base of the rudder above the gunner's glazing; its boxy radome gave rise to the the NATO code name *Box Tail*. (It has to be said that the efficacy of the armament is questionable, to say the least, as a modern fighter would more than likely fire an air-to-air missile without coming within range of the cannons!)

The gunner's station, which technologically is the rearmost section of the fuselage, is a separate pressurized compartment accessed from the freight hold via a door in the rear pressure bulkhead. The gunner walks up the centre cargo door segment and enters his compartment via a door in the forward wall. An escape door is provided on the starboard side, opening hydraulically to protect the gunner against the slipstream in the event of bailing out.

IL-76 CCCP-86726 sits at an airbase somewhere in the Far East, with rugged mountains as a backdrop; the concrete structure in the background is a jet blast deflector. This particular aircraft was later sold to the Russian airline Transaero. Yefim Gordon archive

Paratroopers getting ready to board a *Candid-B*. This view gives details of the UKU-9K-502-1 tail turret and cargo door/ramp design.
Yefim Gordon archive

Besides shooting down unwary fighters, the cannons could be used against ground targets (!) and for passive electronic countermeasures (ECM) and infra-red countermeasures (IRCM). Quite simply, they could fire PRLS rounds filled with metal-coated fibreglass strips (*protivorahdiolokatseeonnyy snaryad* – lit. 'anti-radar round') and PIKS rounds filled with a termite mixture (*protivo-infrakrahsnyy snaryad* – 'IR protection round') along with ordinary ammunition. Exploding behind the aircraft, these special rounds would decoy radar-guided and IR-homing missiles respectively.

The other major difference from the *Candid-A* is the provision of paradropping equipment; hence the crew includes a paradrop equipment operator. The freight hold is equipped with 'traffic lights', an illuminated '*GOTOV – POSHOL!*' ('READY – GO!') sign and a siren to tell the paratroopers it was time to hit the silk. As one IL-76 crewman put it, '*the siren is enough to make you jump out, too: it is absolutely unbearable, and I'd rather not be the enemy when troopers infuriated by that infernal sound come tumbling down!*'

A double row of quickly removable seats, back to back, can be installed down the centre of the freight hold to complement the standard collapsible seats along the walls. An upper deck can be suspended from the ceiling if troops are to be airlifted; the aircraft can carry 140 fully-equipped troops or 125 paratroopers.

Oxygen and rescue equipment is provided for the troops. The freight hold can be decompressed for paradropping, leaving the flight deck pressurized.

The starboard main gear fairing houses an inert gas generator burning jet fuel to pressurize the fuel tanks and reduce the hazard of explosion if hit by enemy fire. This can be identified by a small circular air intake at the front.

CCCP-76501 underwent armament trials at the NII VVS test facility in Akhtoobinsk in southern Russia (near Saratov on the Volga river); the possibility of dropping bombs via the cargo ramp was investigated among other things. After retirement the aircraft became a ground instructional airframe at the Kirovograd Civil Aviation Flying School (KVLUGA – *Kirovograhdskoye vyssheye lyotnoye oochilischche grazhdahnskoy aviahtsii*) in the Ukraine.[3]

The first 'real production' *Candid-B*, CCCP-86600 (c/n 033401022, f/n 0106), was delivered to the Soviet Air Force in late 1973. The first fifty or so production aircraft were all military examples; it was not until December 1976 that commercial IL-76s *sans suffixe* started rolling off the line! Production aircraft had an active ECM system with six teardrop antenna fairings (four on the forward fuselage sides and two on the aft fuselage) to give 360° coverage and two small rounded fairings on the navigator's glazing. However, the system was removed from many Soviet AF *Candid-Bs* in service.

One of the port side forward ECM fairings incorporated a wing/air intake inspection light. This had been tested on CCCP-86712, appearing on civil and military IL-76s alike in late 1977, and was subsequently retrofitted to all previously built aircraft.

Export *Candid-Bs* (IL-76s *sans suffixe*, IL-76Ms and IL-76MDs) are unusual in lacking the inert gas generator in the starboard main gear fairing; also, no ECM gear is fitted as standard.

IL-76MGA *Candid-A* commercial transport

This designation has been quoted for the civil IL-76 *sans suffixe;* MGA stands for *Ministerstvo grazhdahnskoy aviahtsii* – Ministry of Civil Aviation. However, the source says only two were built, which cannot be true – twelve civil examples *sans suffixe* are known, including the prototypes.

IL-76M *Candid-B* military transport

In 1978 the military version received an upgrade. The wing torsion box was reinforced and an additional integral tank was provided in the wing centre section, increasing the fuel load to 80 tons (176,388 lb)[4] and fuel capacity to 104,171 litres (22,917 Imperial gallons). Maximum payload when operating from paved runways was increased to 48 tons (105,820 lb) and MTOW to 170 tons (374,779 lb). The upgraded airlifter was designated IL-76M (*modifitseerovannyy* – modified).

The only external recognition features were appropriate nose titles and dark blue panels on the engine pylon trailing edges, wing undersurface (near the outer engines) and the port main gear fairing aft of the APU exhaust. These blue areas were introduced for cosmetic reasons. The D-30KP is a rather smoky engine; when reverse thrust was repeatedly applied on landing the wings and pylons soon became black with soot, making the aircraft look rather untidy. Washing it every now and again would be too troublesome, so neat dark panels were introduced to make the dirt less conspicuous. Previously built aircraft were soon painted up in this fashion. (On civil *Candids* the 'anti-soot panels' may be black, dark red or green to match the aircraft's basic colours.)

(Speaking of which, the An-32 *Cline* tactical transport has an all-black horizontal tail for much the same reason, as its Ivchenko AI-20 turboprops leave a conspicuous smoke trail. Likewise, the Tu-154M medium-range airliner powered by D-30KU-154-IIs has a perpetually dirty rear end, which probably led Aeroflot Russian International Airlines to introduce blue rear fuselage/fin flashes on its Ms.)

The prototype IL-76M, CCCP-86728 (c/n 073410322, f/n 0901) made its first flight at Tashkent-Vostochnyy airfield on 24th March 1978 with captain Stanislav G Bliznyuk and first officer V I Sviridov at the controls. Deliveries to the Soviet Air Force and foreign customers began same year.

IL-76T *Candid-A* commercial transport

Predictably, the improvements introduced on the IL-76M (more fuel and higher payload/gross weight) were soon incorporated in the civil version. The resulting aircraft was designated IL-76T (*trahnsportnyy* – [civil] transport, used attributively) and superseded the commercial IL-76 *sans suffixe*, of which only twelve were built, including the two prototypes. IL-76T project review by an MAP and Ministry of Civil Aviation commission was completed on 6th June 1973.

CCCP-86871, the prototype IL-76MD, during manufacturer's flight tests; note the underwing external stores pylons and the strake aerials on the aft fuselage characteristic of military *Candids*. Ilyushin OKB

The same aircraft as it banks away from the camera, showing the black 'anti-soot' areas under the wings. Ilyushin OKB

Captained by V I Sviridov, the IL-76T prototype (CCCP-76511, c/n 083414444, f/n 1201)[5] made its maiden flight in Tashkent on 4th November 1978. On 8th February 1979 it was unveiled at a civil aircraft display at Moscow-Sheremet'yevo airport, courtesy of GosNII GA (*Gosoodahrstvennyy naoochno-issledovatel'skiy institoot grazhdahnskoy aviahtsii* – State Civil Aviation Research Institute). After retirement the aircraft was relegated to KIIGA (*Kiyevskiy institoot inzhenerov grazhdahnskoy aviahtsii* – the Kiev Institute of Civil Aviation Engineers) as a ground instructional airframe at Kiev-Zhulyany airport.

IL-76MD *Candid-B* military transport

The IL-76M evolved into a high gross weight/extended-range version designated IL-76MD (*modifitseerovannyy, dahl'niy* – modified, long-range). It features D-30KP Srs 2 turbofans uprated to 12,500kgp (27,557 lbst) and maintaining full power up to ISA +23°C (73°F)[6] instead of ISA +15°C (59°F). These are interchangeable with the D-30KP Srs 1; pairs of Srs 1 engines can be replaced by Srs 2 or vice versa during repairs, providing they are installed symmetrically (Nos 1 and 4 or Nos 2 and 3).

Internal fuel capacity is increased to 90 tons (198,412 lb) or 117,192 litres (25,782 Imperial gallons) by enlarging the wing tanks; this extends range by 400km (216nm) when operating from paved runways or by 300km (162nm) when operating from dirt strips. MTOW is 190 tons (418,871 lb) on paved runways or 157.5 tons (347,222 lb) on dirt strips. Maximum payload is increased to 50 tons (110,229 lb). The wings and landing gear are beefed up to absorb the higher gross weight. Outwardly the IL-76MD is almost identical to the M except for the nose titles; also, the outer landing lights originally built into flap track fairings at approximately mid-span are moved outboard, being located under the wingtips.

As with the IL-76M, not all MDs have ECM gear. Late-production aircraft built from approximately 1987 onwards have the SRO-2M Khrom (Chromium; NATO *Odd Rods*) IFF transponder[7] with its trademark triple aerials of unequal length replaced by an SRO-1P Parol' (Password) transponder, aka *izdeliye* 62-01, with equally characteristic triangular blade aerials.

Two small pylons can be fitted under each outer wing for carrying bombs up to 500kg

(1,102 lb). (The requirement about bombs mentioned in Chapter 1 was still there, but on the real aircraft the main gear fairings had no room for bombs.) The pylons were rarely used; as one IL-76 crewman put it, *'they could be fitted quickly but the process was accompanied by a lot of four-letter words – the pylons are heavy and have to be fitted while standing on a high stepladder. Periodically IL-76 crews would practice dropping bombs – mostly AgitAB-250 or -500 psy-war bombs[8] containing age-old Pravda newspapers with historic Communist Party edicts. The locals would go nuts, finding the nearby forest littered with these papers; some people thought the Communists were running the country again!'*

There are some minor changes to the equipment, including the electric system and the cargo door controls. On the IL-76MD the outer door segments open first and close last; on the IL-76M it is the centre door segment which opens first and closes last.

The prototype IL-76MD, with the out-of-sequence registration CCCP-86871 (c/n 0013434002, f/n 2601) made its maiden flight from Tashkent on 6th March 1981 with a crew captained by Vyacheslav S Belousov. This aircraft was retained by the Ilyushin OKB and used a lot for various development work. The MD replaced the earlier model on the production line starting from Batch 26.

An important feature introduced on the IL-76MD in late 1984 is provision for IRCM equipment for protection against heat-seeking missiles – an improvement based on Afghan war experience (see next chapter). Initially, 96-round APP-50 chaff/flare dispensers[9] firing 50mm (1.96in) magnesium IRCM flares were faired into the aft portions of the ventral main-wheel fairings; these protruded slightly and were canted outwards to cover a wider area. Tests continued from 28th December 1984 to 26th March 1985; the development aircraft was flown by crews captained by Yuriy P Klishin (who went on to become Lieutenant-General and Russian Air Force Deputy C-in-C [Armament]) and V Kotov; M S Gol'dman and M A Alekseyev were the engineers in charge of the test programme.

In 1987 the built-in version was supplanted/supplemented by podded 96- or 192-round dispensers strapped on to the rear fuselage sides just aft of the main gear fairings; this arrangement was tested on IL-76MD CCCP-76650 (c/n 0053462865, f/n 4707). The strap-on dispensers create more drag than the built-in version, of course, but can be fitted and removed as required; the electrical connectors for the APP-50s are protected by small elongated covers when the dispensers are not fitted. Not all IL-76MDs received these updates. After the Afghan War the built-in flare packs were removed on many aircraft as unnecessary and their locations faired over with sheet metal.

Believe it or not, the IL-76 also has a VIP/staff transport role. The Tashkent plant's own design bureau developed the KShM-76 module (ko*mahnd*no-shtab*noy* mo*dool'* – command and headquarters module) from the UAK-20 cargo container (oo*niversahl'*nyy aviat-

seeonnyy konteyner – multi-purpose, ie, air/sea/land container), up to three of which can be carried by the IL-76. The KShM-76 incorporates air conditioning and power systems, oxygen and communications equipment and affords comfortable working conditions for up to eight VIPs. The module measures 6.098 x 3.2 x 2.758m (20ft 0in x 10ft 6in x 9ft ½in) and weighs 4,000kg (8,818 lb) fully equipped. The KShM-76 module was unveiled at the MAKS-95 airshow in Zhukovskiy.

IL-76TD *Candid-A* commercial transport

This is the civil equivalent of the IL-76MD incorporating the same improvements (TD = ***trahnsportnyy, dahl'niy*** – [civil] transport, long-range). The prototype, CCCP-76464 (c/n 0023437090, f/n 2803), took to the air on 5th May 1982; it was delivered to Aeroflot in 1985 after comprehensive testing. All commercial *Candids* built from 1982 onwards were IL-76TDs. One aircraft, CCCP-76481 (c/n 0053460795, f/n 4509), was used for prolonged tests and development work by GosNII GA.

Apart from cargo, the IL-76 can carry three passenger modules, likewise based on the UAK-20 container. Each module accommodates up to 32 passengers four-abreast and is equipped with a galley and a toilet.

IL-76T 'Falsie', IL-76TD 'Falsie'

Curiously, some *Candid-Bs* obviously built as military aircraft with a tail gunner's station wear misleading inscriptions – 'IL-76T' or 'IL-76TD'. The author chooses to refer to such pretenders

IL-76MD CCCP-86871 takes off on a demo flight at MosAeroShow'92. The black markings on the tail (on the port side only) are test equipment sensors and wiring for same protected by a sealing compound. Dmitriy Komissarov

Close-up of the test equipment sensors and wiring on the port side of CCCP-86871. Dmitriy Komissarov

The KShM-76 passenger/HQ module designed to be carried by the IL-76. Arrow marks direction of flight and the stencil on the entry door says 'Cut here' [in emergency]. Dmitriy Komissarov

as IL-76T 'Falsie' and IL-76TD 'Falsie' respectively (by analogy with the so-called Boeing C-135A 'Falsie', which was really a KC-135A tanker with the 'flying boom' removed).

Moreover, many IL-76T/TD 'Falsies' have been demilitarised – ie, the tail turret and gun ranging radar are removed and faired over (and sometimes even the gunner's station windows are overpainted) so as to dispel any doubts about their civilian status; a practice also followed by ex-Air Force An-8s and An-12s. Two slightly different styles of the dished fairing replacing the tail turret have been noted; this is probably because demilitarization work was performed by several aircraft overhaul plants.

Until the mid-1990s, such aircraft were all ex-Iraqi IL-76M/MDs (mostly operated by MAP). Thus a possible explanation is that, since Iraqi *Candids* were operated by the Iraqi Air Force, they were considered military equipment for legal purposes. Since Russian trade legislation prohibits purchase of military equipment by civilian organizations, the aircraft had to be redesignated to pass them off as the commercial version. Lately, however, a number of IL-76MDs (notably those operated by the Belorussian airline TransAVIAexport, a subsidiary of the Belorussian Air Force) have been demilitarised and partially repainted, wearing 'IL-76TD' titles. While these are *not* ex-Iraqi aircraft, they were 'renamed' for much the same reason, since they operate on civil cargo flights and a 'military' designation would be somewhat inappropriate.

Known IL-76T 'Falsies' are CCCP-06188* (ex-YI-AKQ), RA-76372 (ex-CCCP-86723), RA-76430 (ex-CCCP-86729), CCCP-76490* (ex-YI-AKO), CCCP-76491 (ex-YI-AKP), RA-76492* (ex-YI-AKT),[10] CCCP-76495* (ex-YI-AIK), CCCP-76497* (ex-YI-AIM?), CCCP-76528* (ex-YI-AIL), CCCP-76754* (ex-YI-AKU), CCCP-76755 (ex-YI-ALL), CCCP-76756 (ex-YI-AKW), CCCP-76757* (ex-YI-AKX), CCCP-76759* (ex-YI-AKS), CCCP-76788* (ex-YI-ALO), CCCP-76789 (ex-YI-ALP), CCCP-78731* (ex-YI-AKV), RA-86604, RA-86715*, RA-86720 and RA-86846*.

IL-76TD 'Falsies' reported to date are RA-76382 (ex-UR-86903), RA-76383 (ex-UR-86909), UR-76412 (ex-IL-78 CCCP-78773), UR-76413 (ex-CCCP-78853), UR-76438 (ex-CCCP-78751), UR-76628, UR-76636, RA-76659, RA-76672, UR-76688, UR-76727, EW-76737, RA-76758, UR-76777, RA76790*, CCCP-76821 (ex-YI-ALR), RA-76823* (ex-YI-ALQ), UR-78734, UR-78736, CCCP-78738* (ex-YI-ALS), EW-78779*, EW-78808*, EW-

78819*, EW-78826*, EW-78827*, EW-78843*, EW-78848 and CCCP-86896*. Aircraft marked with an asterisk have been demilitarised.

IL-76M 'Falsie', IL-76MD 'Falsie'

Conversely, some aircraft in apparently commercial configuration with pointed tailcone are marked 'IL-76M' or 'IL-76MD'! These are *not* conversions of 'true' *Candid-Bs*; they were actually *built* with no tail gunner's station and nobody seems to know the reason why. Another peculiarity of such aircraft is that the inert gas generator air intake in the starboard main gear fairing is usually faired over with a neat elliptical plate but still visible upon close inspection.

Only two IL-76M 'Falsies' are known (CCCP-86879 and CCCP-86891). On the other hand, IL-76MD 'Falsies' are plentiful. Known aircraft are CCCP-76445 (?), CCCP-76446 (?), CCCP-76492, CCCP-76493 (?), CCCP-76753, CCCP-76803, CCCP-76822, CCCP-76825 (?), CCCP-76826, CCCP-76828 (?), RA-76845, CCCP-78850 through CCCP-78852, 7T-WIC, B-4030 through B-4043 (and B-4044 through B-4049?), CU-T1258, CU-T1271, YI-ANA through YI-ANO and P-912 through P-914.

Some *Candids* known to be IL-76MD 'Falsies' have now been repainted as IL-76TDs! Known aircraft are RA-76388 (ex-CCCP-78851), RA-76389 (ex-CCCP-78852), RA-76822 and RA-76845. The latter aircraft is the only known IL-76MD 'Falsie' to have an inert gas generator air intake.

IL-76MD to IL-76TD (IL-76M to IL-76T) conversions

Obviously someone decided that simply demilitarising an ex-Air Force *Candid-B* is not enough. In early 1998 the Russian Air Force's aircraft overhaul plant No123 in Staraya Roossa began converting IL-76MDs to IL-76TD standard, mostly for civil operators. This involves cutting away the gunner's pressurized compartment (section F4) at fuselage frame 90 (see Chapter 7) and riveting on a 'scratchbuilt' *Candid-A* tailcone. Strictly speaking, this 'plastic surgery' makes sense, as it cuts empty weight by some 1,000kg (2,200 lb) .

Known aircraft converted in this fashion are RA-76591, RA-76666, EW-76710 through EW-76712, EW-76734, EW-76735, EW-76737, CCCP-76781, RA-76790, RA-76823, RA-78792, EW-78799, EW-78801 and EW-78828. A curious feature of these aircraft is the inert gas generator air intake crudely faired over by a protruding plate with three prominent stiffening ribs. This is the giveaway that the aircraft is a converted 'true' IL-76MD, not an IL-76MD 'Falsie' renamed to match the exterior. Sometimes the conversion is even more obvious because nobody took the trouble to repaint the whole aircraft; as a result, the freshly-painted tailcone and freshly-applied 'IL-76TD' titles make a sharp contrast with the weathered finish on the rest of the airframe! Moreover, quasi-civilian IL-76TD CCCP-76781 (ex-IL-76MD CCCP-86927, c/n 0023439133, f/n 2904) oper-

Top left and top right: **These photos illustrate the two different styles of rear fairing on demilitarised IL-76T/TD 'Falsies': one-piece dome with vertically cut-off superstructure on IL-76T 'Falsie' RA-76757 and two-piece dome with sloping superstructure on IL-76TD 'Falsie' EW-78819. Note also that the gunner's station glazing has been overpainted differently and the PRS-4 radome has been removed on RA-76757.** Dmitriy Komissarov

Left: **IL-76MD 'Falsie' CCCP-76822 operated by the Ilyushin Design Bureau.** Ilyushin OKB

Centre: **Ilyushin Design Bureau IL-76MD 'Falsie' CCCP-76822 at Prague-Ruzyne in December 1991 during lease by Air Moravia Czech Charter Airline Ltd.** Milan Cvrkal

Bottom: **Starting in 1998, several 'true' IL-76MDs, like EW-76734 here (operated by Ilavia but owned by TransAVIAexport, hence the Belorussian prefix), have been 'surgically' converted to IL-76TDs. The white nacelle of the No 2 engine suggests this has been fitted as a replacement.** Dmitriy Komissarov

Below: **A curious feature of IL-76MDs converted to IL-76TDs is that the inert gas generator intake is crudely faired over. Here, on EW-76710, they didn't even take the trouble to paint the patch!** Dmitriy Komissarov

ated by the Federal Border Guards retains the built-in APP-50 chaff/flare dispensers (!), which reveals it has seen action in Afghanistan.

Quasi-civilian IL-76T CCCP-76457 (c/n 093421621, f/n 1606), another FBG aircraft, is a converted and reregistered IL-76M (ex-CCCP-86925 No1) – the only known conversion among Ms. Like many Aeroflot and quasi-Aeroflot aircraft, IL-76s had two registration styles (in a rounded or an angular typeface), and CCCP-76457 showed obvious signs of being reregistered: the CCCP- prefix was in rounded type characteristic of early *Candid-Bs* while the digits were in the later angular type! This aircraft is unique among IL-76Ts in having built-in APP-50 chaff/flare dispensers – a left-over from its days as an IL-76M and an Afghan War veteran. IL-76T CCCP-86926 (later CCCP-76780; c/n 0013430901, f/n 2306) may be a similar conversion.

IL-76MD Skal'pel'-MT (*izdeliye* 576) mobile hospital

From the outset the *Candid-B* could be used for CASEVAC duties. To this end several tiers of stretchers were fixed to uprights in the freight hold; the medevac kit could be installed or removed in about two hours. In reality, however, it was rarely used and many IL-76 crews have never even seen it.

Yet what the army needed was not just a 'stretcha fetcha' but a real flying hospital where surgery could be performed en route – this could make the difference between life and death or a whole man and a cripple. Thus on 6th January 1976 MAP issued a directive ordering the development of a 'flying operating room' based on the IL-76; this received the appropriate code name Skal'pel'.[11]

The CASEVAC issue suddenly became very acute when the Soviet Union became involved in the Afghan war; getting critically wounded personnel to 'Unionside' hospitals quickly was a real problem. Still, development was rather slow. The prototype of the IL-76MD Skal'pel'-MT flying hospital, CCCP-86906 (c/n 0023436064, f/n 2706), did not make its first flight until 23rd July 1983; the test crew was captained by Vyacheslav S Belousov. Two *Candids* have been equipped to this standard; the other aircraft is reportedly c/n 1023412408 (f/n 8602, identity unknown).

By mid-1988 CCCP-86906 received special markings in accordance with its role – a large red cross on the tail instead of the Soviet flag and smaller red crosses on the wing undersurface. The aircraft is equipped with four APP-50 chaff/flare dispensers.

The freight hold of the Skal'pel'-MT houses three modified UAK-20 cargo containers. One of them is an operating room, another is equipped as an intensive care unit and the third is the 'ready room' accommodating stretchers with patients. The containers can be unloaded and function as a stationary hospital in case of need; to this end a petrol-driven generator is provided to power the equipment.

Besides the Afghan war, the IL-76MD Skal'pel'-MT prototype was called upon to treat victims of the Armenian earthquake in December 1988 and the major train crash near the Bashkirian capital of Ufa in 1990. Duly reregistered RA-86906, it was later used operationally in the First Chechen War of 1994-96, making daily flights to Mozdok and Beslan to pick up casualties.

There have been less bloody tasks, however; for instance, the aircraft airlifted the Russian Army hospital at Beelitz to Russia as Russian troops pulled out of Germany. In February 1996 RA-86906 participated in the SAREX'96 army rescue service exercise staged in Canada by the US, Canadian and Russian armed forces. The aircraft operates from Chkalovskaya air-base.

IL-76TD-S mobile hospital
Building on operational experience with the IL-76MD Skal'pel'-MT, the Ilyushin OKB developed a similar mobile hospital for civilian needs in 1991. This is known as the IL-76TD-S (*sani-tahrnyy* – medical), aka the Aibolit airliftable medical complex.[12]

Additionally, the IL-76 can deliver the Ganimed paradroppable containerised medical unit developed by the Aviaspetstrans consortium (or, to be precise, the Myasishchev OKB which was part of it) and the Parachute Systems Design Institute (*Naoochno-issle-dovatel'skiy instituot parashootostroyeniya*). The Ganimed container, also called *izdeliye* 27, was dropped by the first production *Candid-A* (CCCP-76500) and an unidentified IL-76MD during trials.

IL-76PS (IL-76MDPS) maritime SAR aircraft
Development of a maritime search and rescue version of the *Candid* was initiated by a ruling of the Soviet Council of Ministers' Defence Industry Commission on 28th June 1972. Designated IL-76PS (*poiskovo-spasahtel'nyy* – SAR, used attributively), the aircraft was to supplant the An-12PS and Tu-16 Fregat (Frigate)[13] *Badger-A* operated by the Soviet Naval Air Arm (AVMF – *Aviahtshiya voyenno-morskovo flota*). Some sources claim that, apart from rescuing the occupants of ships in distress or downed aircraft, the SAR version was also to support the Soviet manned space programme, rescuing space crews in the unlikely event of a splash-down somewhere in the world ocean.

The IL-76PS carried a 7.4 ton (16,314 lb) Gagara (Loon) lifeboat which could be paradropped with a crew of three on sighting people in distress. The Gagara had a 500km (270nm) range and a top speed of 7kts. Maximum seating capacity was 20 rescuees; additionally, the lifeboat could tow a PSN-25/30 inflatable rescue raft (*plot spasahtel'nyy nadoovnoy*) with another 25 or 30 persons.

The lifeboat was loaded on a purpose-built P-211 pallet and equipped with an MKS-350-10 parachute system comprising ten 350m² (3,763ft²) parachutes.[14] Paradropping was pos-

sible at 600 to 1,500m (1,968 to 4,921ft) and 350 to 370km/h (189 to 200kts) in conditions up to sea state five (ie, waves up to 2.9m/9½ft high) and winds up to 20m/sec (40kts). After being extracted by an 8m² (86ft²) VPS-8 drogue parachute[15] the pallet fell away and a 100m (328ft) guiderope was deployed to orientate the lifeboat downwind before splashdown. After that, the lifeboat would be guided by UHF remote control or by making a pass over it in the direction of the target. The Gagara was a product of the Leningrad-based Redan (Planing step; pronounced re*dahn*) SKB,[16] while the parachute system was developed by the Parachute Systems Design Institute.

Apart from the lifeboat, it was possible to drop KAS-150 rescue capsules (*konteyner ava-reeyno-spasahtel'nyy*) and teams of up to 40 rescue workers. The navigation system was upgraded, permitting the aircraft to reach the designated target area with an error margin of 2% of the distance covered; the system could use emergency radio transmitters or beacons to home in on the stricken ship or aircraft.

Development began in 1981. With the advent of the longer-range IL-76MD this was selected as the carrier aircraft and the SAR version was redesignated IL-76MDPS. Captained by Yuriy V Mazonov, the prototype, IL-76MD 'Falsie' CCCP-76621 (c/n 0043456695, f/n 4304), took off at Tashkent on 12th December 1984 (some sources say 18th December). At least two more *Candids* – IL-76TD CCCP-76471 (c/n 0033446345, f/n 3407) and an unidentified IL-76MD – participated in the trials programme, performing test drops of the lifeboat.

Trials continued until 1987 at three locations – Pskov Lake, the Minghechauri Reservoir (Azerjaijan) and the Black Sea (near Feodosiya on the Crimea Peninsula), with A M Tyuryumin (HSU) as project test pilot. 17 test drops of the Gagara were made, including two with people on board. The results were good and the IL-76MDPS was recommended for production. The aircraft had a maximum operating radius of 4,700km (2,540nm). An IL-76MDPS standing on ready alert could be prepared for a sortie in just 35 minutes.

Sadly, the programme was terminated on 7th April 1989 – incidentally, the very day when the nuclear submarine SNS[17] *Komsomolets* (K-278) sank in the Barents Sea with the tragic loss of nearly all hands. The reason was the Air Force's wish to keep the An-12PS and Tu-16 Fregat, both of which were developed 'in-house', and eliminate competition. IL-76MDPS CCCP-76621 was relegated to the Kirovograd flying school as a ground instructional airframe with a mere 300 hours total time on it.

IL-76P (IL-76TP, IL-76TDP, IL-76MDP) firebomber
Nikolay Dmitriyevich Talikov, who succeeded Radiy P Papkovskiy as IL-76 project chief, led the development of a waterbomber version of the *Candid* for fighting forest fires. This was an important task, considering the vast expanse of

The still unpainted new 'commercial' tailcone and the built-in chaff/flare packs in the main gear fairings (almost invisible in this view) on IL-76T CCCP-76457 reveal this is in fact a converted IL-76M. Note that the registration digits are written in a different typeface from the CCCP- prefix, showing that the aircraft has been reregistered (ex CCCP-86925 No1).
Yefim Gordon archive

CCCP-86906, the IL-76MD Skal'pel'-MT flying hospital with appropriate red cross markings. This aircraft has seen action in Afghanistan and elsewhere; note the strap-on chaff/flare packs.
Sergey & Dmitriy Komissarov collection

The Ganimed paradroppable medical container developed by the Aviaspetstrans consortium, designed to be delivered by the IL-76.
Sergey & Dmitriy Komissarov collection

taiga in the eastern regions of the country. Until then, however, the capabilities of Soviet firefighting aircraft had been rather modest. The An-2PP (*protivopozhahrnyy* – firefighting), a modified An-2V floatplane (CCCP-01262), did not progress beyond the prototype stage; nor did a landplane waterbomber version of the *Colt*. The most common solutions were helicopters with externally slung tanks (the Mil' Mi-6PZh and Mi-6PZh-2 *Hook* with internal tanks was an exception) or simply paradropping firefighters into the area.

The Antonov OKB continued working in this direction, developing the An-24LP (*lesopozhahrnyy* = for fighting forest fires), a simple adaptation of the An-24RV *Coke* twin-turboprop airliner which seeded cumulus clouds with chemicals to cause rain. This was followed by the An-26P *Curl* and An-32P Firekiller, both of which had large water tanks scabbed on to the fuselage sides. The Beriyev OKB in Taganrog on the Black Sea joined the race in the late 1980s, modifying the Be-12 Chaika (*Mail*) ASW

amphibian into the Be-12P firebomber; four ex-Russian Navy aircraft registered RA-00041, RA-00046, RA-00049 and RA-00073 (c/n 2602505) have been converted to date.

Talikov's idea, however, was that any IL-76 should be quickly adaptable for firefighting duties without modifications (unlike the Antonov and Beriyev competitors) and revert to standard configuration just as easily. The obvious solution was a modular system with tanks in the freight hold so that the water was emptied over the cargo ramp.[18] The waterbomber was designated IL-76P (*pozhahrnyy* – firefighting); since any *Candid* can be configured for the firefighting role, the designations IL-76TP, IL-76TDP and IL-76MDP are also used occasionally.

The firefighting system was developed in late 1988 and a prototype was built early in the following year. The module consisted of two tubular tanks running almost the full length of the freight hold. The tanks were mounted on a frame sloping gently towards the rear to facilitate emptying; wheels and a towbar could be attached to this frame for ground handling. Each tank had a hinged door at the rear, with two counterweights sticking up like horns, and a trough to guide the water over the cargo ramp; the door lock was controlled by a system of linkages. The front end featured standard fire hose connectors for filling up and overflow hoses; supply and overflow hoses went through the entry doors, so that any excess water ended up outside the aircraft.

On the original VAP-1 experimental firefighting module, sections of ordinary steel pipes (the kind used in gas pipelines) were utilised to save time. Thus the tanks were 1.22m (4ft) in diameter and 14m (45ft 11in) long, with walls 14mm (½in) thick. Their total capacity was 32m³ (1,130ft³) or 32,000 litres (7,040 Imperial gallons) of water, which equals 32 tons (70,546 lb).

Ironically, during the Second World War the acronym VAP (*vylivnoy aviatseeonnyy preebor* – aviation device for pouring liquids) was a designation for incendiary tanks used for pouring liquid phosphorus on the enemy; such tanks were fitted, for instance, to the IL-2 attack aircraft and the Tupolev SB fast medium bomber. Thus the 'new VAP' became the reverse of its original purpose.

Water drops are made at an altitude of 80 to 200m (262 to 626ft), depending on the terrain and visibility conditions; the tank doors are opened by two equipment operators as commanded by the navigator over the intercom. The two tanks can be emptied simultaneously to extinguish a small fire or consecutively to keep a major fire from spreading; in the latter case a special OS-5 fire retardant (*ognegasyaschchaya smes'* – fire extinguishing mixture) may be used instead of water. In a simultaneous dump at 80m and 280km/h (151.35kts) the IL-76P can drop a full load of water in four or five seconds, dousing an area measuring 400 x 100m (1,312 x 328ft) with up to 5 litres/m²; in a consecutive drop at the same speed and altitude the area covered is 600 x 80m (1,968 x 262ft).

Special piloting techniques are used for firefighting sorties. For example, in hilly or mountainous terrain the aircraft approaches the fire from the higher ground so as not to collide with the mountains after entering the smoke pall. Immediately after dropping the water the aircraft climbs away sharply. If there is a really big fire, several aircraft can work consecutively.

On 22nd September 1989 IL-76MD CCCP-76623 (c/n 0053457705, f/n 4307) operated by the Ilyushin OKB made the first flight with the

VAP-1 module, thus becoming the prototype IL-76P; the aircraft was captained by Igor' R Zakirov. The 'company-owned' IL-76MD prototype, CCCP-86871, joined the programme later when a second module was built. The two aircraft were tested operationally, successfully fighting forest fires in the Krasnoyarsk Region.

Originally the cargo doors were fully opened for water drops. However, it was quickly established that vortices around the doors would cause water to enter the aft fuselage and soak the equipment located there, causing short circuits. Ilyushin engineers tried covering the equipment with tarpaulins but these were torn to shreds by the turbulent airstream as soon as the cargo doors were opened. The problem was cured by simply lowering the cargo ramp, leaving the doors closed.

The IL-76P was publicly unveiled on 2nd August 1990 when CCCP-76623 performed 'live' at Moscow's Tushino airfield, taking part in a show on occasion of the semi-official Airborne Forces Day. Unfortunately, few were able to witness this because the show took place on a business day; it would have been a better idea to stage it during the nearest weekend.

More action came during the spring of 1992. On 9th April fire broke out at an ammunition dump near Yerevan, causing violent explosions. Splinters and unexploded ammunition rained down on the nearby village of Balaovit, forcing an urgent evacuation. The Armenian authorities immediately contacted the Ilyushin OKB, and shortly after 1100 the company-owned IL-76MD 'Falsie' CCCP-76822 (c/n 0093499982, f/n 7506) equipped with a full VAP-1 module took off for Yerevan. The crew was captained by Igor' R Zakirov. Meanwhile, pumps and an adequate supply of water were set up at Yerevan-Zvartnots airport.

Before the day was out the aircraft had made three sorties, extinguishing the fire almost completely; after that, ground forces could move in. During the next day Zakirov flew two more sorties for good measure to make sure the dump would not flare up again.

A month later, on 15th May another ammunition dump blew up near Vladivostok in the Far East. This time IL-76MDP CCCP-76623 cap-

tained by Ilyushin's CTP, Distinguished test pilot Stanislav G Bliznyuk (HSU) was dispatched to take care of the fire. The mission was far more complicated. The dump was surrounded by mountains up to 400m (1,312ft) high, which meant it could only be approached from one direction, with a power station chimney straight ahead. The IL-76MDP flew seven sorties in all; several times violent explosions forced a go-around because there was imminent danger of being hit by fragments and 'shot down'. Nikolay D Talikov commanded the mission on both occasions.

The OKB had been trying to win government support for the IL-76P for a long time, and it was these successful firefighting operations that tipped the scales. In July 1992 the Russian government allocated 31 billion roubles to the State Committee for Emergency Control (EMERCOM; since transformed to Ministry of Emergency Control) for the outfitting of five *Candids* as firebombers. Reinforcing the point, peat fires broke out around Moscow in August, and IL-76Ps were enlisted to fight fires near Noginsk and Shatoora in the Moscow Region.

On 28th January 1993 CCCP-76623 commenced a new round of trials with the new VAP-2 firefighting module. This was larger than the original model, holding 42,000 litres (9,240 Imperial gallons) or 42 tons (92,592 lb) of water. Tank diameter was increased to 2.2m (7ft 2⅖in), but the tanks were made of aluminium alloy and the walls were just 5mm (0.19in) thick. The module could be loaded and secured by four men in 1½ to 2 hours, using the aicraft's cargo handling equipment, and then filled up from a hydrant or a fire engine in just 15 minutes.

Once again Igor' R Zakirov flew the aircraft and M N Weinshtein was in charge of the test programme. VAP-2 completed trials successfully and a batch of five units was built for EMERCOM. Meanwhile, the Ilyushin OKB is contemplating an even bigger firefighting module holding 60,000 litres (13,200 Imperial gallons)!

The IL-76P had its share of airshow performances. On 18th August 1991 – one day before the failed hard-line Communist coup d'état which brought an end to the Soviet Union's existence – CCCP-76623 was to demonstrate

firefighting at the Aviation Day flypast in Zhukovskiy (the LII airfield was then still off limits to the general public). Unfortunately, the demonstration fizzled when the tower did not authorise the crew to dump the water; when the go-ahead was finally given 20 minutes later the spectators had given up and gone home.

On 15th August next year, however, the same aircraft performed excellently at Mos-AeroShow '92 in Zhukovskiy, Russia's first major airshow (11-16th August), extinguishing a very smoky pile of burning car tyres. Some all-too-eager photographers who were standing a bit too close (way outside the public area) got drenched! They had it coming.

On 19th May 1993 two IL-76TPs took part in a civil defence exercise near Noginsk in the Moscow region which was part of the Central, East and South-East European Conference on Civil Defence and Disaster Control. In July 1993 company demonstrator, IL-76TDP RA-76835 (c/n 1013408244, f/n 8201), was displayed at the Paris airshow with the exhibit code 306 and an 'Ilyushin Aviation Complex' badge on the nose. This aircraft remained firmly in the static park at the MAKS-93 airshow in Zhukovskiy (31st August to 5th September 1993), with nothing to identify it as a firebomber, leaving the visitors guessing why it was there. Yet the visitors were treated to a display of firefighting technique on 2nd September when Veteran Airlines IL-76MDP UR-76698 (c/n 0063471123, f/n 5401) made a demonstration flight. This time there were no more burning tyres – the organizers of the show were clearly becoming more environmentally conscious!

From 19th to 22nd October 1993 IL-76MDP UR-76727 (c/n 0073475268, f/n 5707) loaned from Veteran Airlines and captained by Stanislav G Bliznyuk helped extinguish a forest fire near Yalta, the famous Black Sea resort. At the same time (20th-22nd October) the Ilyushin OKB's IL-76MD 'Falsie' RA-76822 captained by I I Goodkov fulfilled an identical mission near Kislovodsk, a Caucasian resort.

More show performances came in 1994 when IL-76TDP RA-76389 (c/n 1013407212, f/n 8103) with 'Water Bomber' titles took part in Farnborough International '94. This aircraft

The IL-76MDPS paradropping the Gagara lifeboat. Sergey & Dmitriy Komissarov collection

The Gagara at the moment of splashdown. Sergey & Dmitriy Komissarov collection

The open cargo doors of Veteran Airlines' IL-76MD UR-76729 reveal the business end of the VAP-2 firefighting module. Yefim Gordon

belonged to the *Russian* Veteran Airline, a sister company of the Ukrainian carrier of the same name. On 8-9th September same year Veteran Airline IL-76T 'Falsie' RA-86846[19] (c/n 0003426765, f/n 2002) equipped with a VAP-2 module and flown by Igor' R Zakirov was demonstrated to US Forestry Department officials at the Larkhill artillery range near RAF Boscombe Down. On 21st-26th March 1995 the same aircraft participated in Airshow Down Under'95 in Melbourne. Finally, EMERCOM IL-76TDP RA-76845 (c/n 1043420696, f/n 9304) took part in the flying display at the MAKS-97 airshow (19-24th August 1997).

IL-76K zero-G trainer

Zero-gravity training is an important part of an astronaut's training programme. Part of it is done in a special water tank with a submerged spacecraft mockup. However, nothing beats real weightlessness, so space centres the world over use specially-modified aircraft for astronaut training. Such aircraft follow a parabolic trajectory, and on the way down zero gravity is experienced for 20 to 30 seconds.

The Soviet cosmonaut group in Zvyozdnyy Gorodok (Star Town) near Chkalovskaya AB used different aircraft for these purposes. First, it was three Tu-104AKs (specially-modified ex-Aeroflot Tu-104A *Camel* airliners) coded 46

Red (ex-CCCP-42390, c/n 8350705), 47 Red (ex-CCCP-42389, c/n 8350704) and 48 Red (c/n 86601302).[20] These were superseded in 1980-81 by two custom-built Tu-134LKs (a derivative of the Tu-134AK VIP aircraft)[21] – 02 Red (c/n 62732, f/n 5503) and 03 Red (c/n 63620, f/n 6105).

However, all of these are/were narrowbody aircraft and offer(ed) rather limited room for floating around or staging experiments in zero-G conditions. Therefore, as early as 24th July 1972 the Council of Ministers' Defence Industry Commission ruled that the Ilyushin OKB should develop a zero-G trainer version of the *Candid*. This was designated IL-76K (once again, K means [*dlya podgotovki*] *kosmonahvtov* – for cosmonaut training).

The prototype, CCCP-86638 (c/n 073409232, f/n 0608), was converted from a standard military IL-76 *sans suffixe* at the Tashkent aircraft factory and made its first flight on 2nd August 1981 at the hands of Ilyushin CTP Stanislav G Bliznyuk. Outwardly the IL-76K was identical to the very first *Candid* (CCCP-86712) at a late stage of the manufacturer's flight tests: the gunner's station had been eliminated and replaced by a rounded 'solid' tailcone housing an anti-spin parachute. The airframe was suitably reinforced, however, to cope with the augmented loads which are equivalent to several normal flights.

The freight hold had handrails running along the walls at three levels and additional lighting. The capacious interior of the *Candid* (235m³/8,299ft³) certainly gave the cosmonauts plenty of room to bounce. Besides, it could accommodate mockups of spacecraft modules and test rigs weighing up to 6 tons (13,227 lb) for verifying the operation of the spacecraft's systems in zero-G conditions; these were easily loaded through the standard cargo doors. Test equipment was installed at the front of the hold to monitor and record the results of the experiment and the cosmonauts' vital signs.

The parabolic trajectory flown by the IL-76K was developed by leading engineer V V Smirnov. This trajectory was normally repeated 10 to 25 times during a sortie. The techniques used on the IL-76K included the use of 'free-floating' test rigs which were disengaged from the aircraft's structure once weightlessness began to make the experiment more realistic.

Two more military IL-76s *sans suffixe,* CCCP-86723 (c/n 073410279, f/n 0710) and CCCP-86729 (c/n 073410300, f/n 0805), were converted to IL-76K standard. Interestingly, both were sold in 1996-97 (to Express Joint-Stock Company and IDF Iron Dragonfly respectively) becoming RA-76372 and RA-76430 respectively, and are now listed as IL-76Ts (!). The prototype (CCCP-86638) ended its days as a ground instructional airframe.

IL-76MDK, IL-76MDK-II zero-G trainers

In 1987 a follow-on version designated IL-76MDK was derived from the IL-76MD. Outwardly it differs from the IL-76K only in having 'IL-76MDK' nose titles; the gunner's station is again deleted and replaced with an anti-spin 'chute canister.

Captained by V I Sviridov, the IL-76MDK prototype registered CCCP-76766 (c/n 0073481431, f/n 6108) made its first flight in Tashkent on 6th August 1988. This was followed by a second example, CCCP-78770 (c/n 0083487617, f/n 6605). Once again these aircraft are probably conversions of standard *Candid-Bs* (or IL-76MD 'Falsies'?). The State acceptance trials were led by Col Anatoliy Andronov, chief of the Soviet Air Force's flight test department.[22]

The next zero-G trainer, CCCP-78825 (c/n 1013495871, f/n 7208), was designated IL-76MDK-II (also referred to as IL-76MDK-2). The difference between this version and the IL-76MDK is not known; anyway, CCCP-78825 is outwardly identical to the two preceding aircraft. The IL-76MDK-II entered flight test on 25th April 1990 and completed the trials programme on 7th August same year. Reregistered RA-78825, it was displayed statically at the ILA-94 airshow at Berlin-Schönefeld with the exhibit code 164.

IL-76PP ECM aircraft (*izdeliye* 176)

In the mid-1980s the IL-76MD evolved into a specialised ECM version developed jointly with the Beriyev OKB and designated IL-76PP (*postanovschchik pomekh* – ECM aircraft); some sources refer to it as *izdeliye* 176. It featured the Landysh (Lily of the valley) ECM suite. The appearance of this aircraft was anything but conventional. Large teardrop antenna fairings were ideally positioned on the forward and rear fuselage sides to give 360° coverage. They were identical to those of the Ilyushin/Beriyev A-50 *Mainstay* airborne warning and control system (AWACS) aircraft described later in this chapter. Smaller antenna blisters and numerous blade aerials were located on the main gear fairings. More equipment was housed in large cylindrical pods at the wingtips with dielectric front and rear portions.

The ECM suite demanded a lot of power which the engine-driven generators were unable to provide. Hence two mighty gas turbine power units were installed in huge fairings on the forward fuselage sides which blended into the main gear fairings, making the aircraft look like a chipmunk. Each unit was a 2,820ehp (2,103kW) Ivchenko AI-24VT turboprop engine (the type used on the An-24 airliner, An-26 transport and An-30 *Clank* photo survey aircraft) driving four 90-kilowatt GT-90PCh6A three-phase AC generators. The fairings had large circular air intakes at the front and downward-angled jetpipes at the rear.

The ECM suite necessitated some airframe changes. The power unit fairings overlapped the entry doors which had to be modified (a small part of each fairing swung open together with the door and the handle was relocated). The mission equipment obstructed the forward emergency exits, so these were deleted and the windows moved up. The TA-6A APU was moved to the rear portion of the port main gear fairing, receiving a dorsal 'elephant's ear' intake and a downward-angled exhaust in the style of the A-50.

The aircraft sported large cylindrical antenna pods on the wingtips which carried the navigation lights; their front and rear portions were dielectric, with prominent ventral 'outgrowths'. Additional antenna blisters were located on the power unit fairings, between the main gear struts and under the wingtip pods. Four blade aerials were mounted each side near the main gear units; the forward pair was raked aft and the aft pair forward. The front ends of the main-wheel fairings incorporated non-standard cooling air intakes. Apparently someone decided that active jamming was not enough, so chaff outlets were provided in the cargo ramp.

Four IL-76MDs, including CCCP-86889 (c/n 0013434009, f/n 2603), were reportedly converted at the Beriyev facility in Taganrog and delivered to NII VVS for trials. The IL-76PP was tested at the Chornaya Rechka (Black River) test range near Tashkent but its performance was disappointing. The ECM suite proved to be rather unreliable, used too much power and had poor electromagnetic compatibility. The aircraft was evaluated by the Air Force, reputedly even deploying to Cuba, but did not enter service. CCCP-86889 now resides at the Irkutsk Military Technical School (IVATU – *Irkootskoye voyennoye aviatseeonnotekhneecheskoye oochilischsche*) as a ground instructional airframe.

IL-76MD CCCP-76655 (c/n 0053463885, f/n 4802) was also reported as an IL-76PP. However, this aircraft was rather different. Apart from the wingtip pods and large ECM blisters on the forward fuselage sides, it was a perfectly ordinary *Candid-B*. There were no monstrous cheek fairings, no rear ECM antennas, and the main gear fairings, APU placement and emergency exits were unchanged. It seems highly unlikely that the aircraft had the gas turbine power units and all associated changes and was later reconverted to standard – the modification is simply too extensive.

Top: **IL-76MD CCCP-76623 owned by the Ilyushin OKB served as the prototype for the IL-76MDP firebomber version. In this test drop the cargo doors are fully open.** Yefim Gordon

Above: **IL-76TDP RA-76835 participated in the 1993 Paris airshow. Here, it is seen at MAKS-93.** Dmitriy Komissarov

Above left: **The Ilyushin Aircraft Complex badge on IL-76TDP RA-76835.** Dmitriy Komissarov

Above right: **Cosmonaut trainees floating around in the freight hold of an IL-76K zero-G trainer.** Yefim Gordon archive

Bottom: **RA-76766, the IL-76MDK prototype, parked at Chkalovskaya AB on 15th August 1999.** Dmitriy Komissarov

Left: **Redolent with Cold War intrigue, these shots of IL-76PP CCCP-86889 illustrate the ECM version's monstrous cheek fairings, wingtip pods and lateral antenna blisters.**
Victor Drushlyakov

Centre two pictures: **IL-76PP CCCP-86889 in its latter days as a ground instructional airframe in Irkutsk; the gas turbine power unit air intakes have been blanked off for some reason. Note how portions of the power unit fairing swing open with the entry doors. The significance of the brown markings on the nose is unknown.**

Bottom: **The starboard power unit/main gear fairing mounting an array of ECM aerials. The aircraft shows signs of considerable wear and tear; note the tell-tale exhaust stain on the outboard pylon caused by reverse thrust.**
All Yefim Gordon

The wingtip pods, too, were different from those of CCCP-86889, being somewhat smaller in diameter and lacking the ventral bulges; their dielectric portions and the ECM blisters were painted white. Also, unlike CCCP-86889, this aircraft featured built-in APP-50 chaff/flare dispensers.

Whatever mission equipment had been installed in the freight hold was removed by 1991, since CCCP-76655 was used on regular transport flights, carrying personnel to and from Germany during troop rotation in the Western Group of Forces. Based at Melitopol'-2 AB, the aircraft was later included into the Ukrainian Air Force inventory as UR-76655.

IL-76 – Tu-160 tailplane transporter
Shortly after the Tu-160 *Blackjack* strategic bomber attained initial operational capability with the 184th GvTBAP (*Gvardeyskiy tyazhelobombardeerovochnyy aviapolk* – Guards heavy bomber regiment) at Prilooki AB in the Ukraine, the VVS began experiencing structural strength problems with the bomber's slab stabilizers. Fatigue cracks appeared and on several occasions fragments of the horizontal tail broke away in flight, forcing the Tupolev OKB to ground the bombers and undertake an urgent redesign.

Eventually all Tu-160s built in 1990-91 had to have their stabilizers replaced with reinforced units, and an immediate problem arose: the new stabilizers were too large to be carried internally by any freighter in VVS service. The solution was to carry them externally, as had been the case with wings for the An-124 Ruslan (*Condor*) widebody freighter. These were manufactured in Tashkent and carried to Kiev and Ul'yanovsk by two specially modified An-22 prototypes, CCCP-64459 and CCCP-64460, designated An-22PZ (for *perevozchik* – carrier).

Thus military IL-76 *sans suffixe* CCCP-76496 (ex-YI-AIN?, c/n 073410301, f/n 0806) owned by the Kazan' aircraft factory No.22 was modified to carry complete Tu-160 horizontal tail assemblies from Kazan' to Prilooki AB where the old stabilizers were replaced *in situ*. The stabilizers were mounted atop the fuselage

immediately aft of the wings on special struts; hence the aircraft was popularly known as the *triplahn* (triplane). The first flight in this configuration took place on 30th October 1986; when the Tu-160 stabilizer problem was solved, CCCP-76496 reverted to standard configuration.

IL-76MF military transport

From the start the IL-76 had obvious growth potential. The general development trend for transport aircraft in this class has been towards a roomier freight hold rather than bigger payload. Quite often a load that weighed far less than the IL-76 could carry could not be transported because it was too long to fit into the hold. Thus, the aircraft's capabilities could be greatly enhanced by stretching the fuselage and fitting more powerful, fuel-efficient engines.

Development of the US counterpart, the Starlifter, showed this to be the right approach. In January 1977 the C-141A evolved into the C-141B with a 7.11m (23ft 4in) fuselage stretch and flight refuelling capability. All but two Starlifters were eventually converted to C-141B standard.

Preliminary development of the 'Candid Plus' began almost simultaneously with the C-141B; it was initiated by an MAP directive issued on 1st January 1976. Putting the idea into practice, however, took nearly twenty years. While the fuselage stretch was the easy part, the choice of powerplant proved to be a problem. The D-30KP had no reserves for further uprating. Originally the aircraft was to be powered by 14,000kgp (30,864 lbst) turbofans developed by RKBM (*Rybinskoye konstrooktorskoye byuro motorostroyeniya* – the Rybinsk Engine Design Bureau) but this engine never materialised. As a stopgap measure, Ilyushin contemplated the 13,000kgp (28,659 lbst) Kuznetsov NK-86 turbofan which was used to power the IL-86. However, like the D-30KP, this engine had no growth potential, being in fact a spinoff of the good old NK-8 which powers the IL-62 *sans suffixe* and early versions of the

Tu-154. The thrust increase was just too small and the idea was dropped.

However, in the early 1980s the Solov'yov OKB started work on a new turbofan, the D-90 intended for the Tu-204 medium-haul airliner (the engine was renamed PS-90 in 1987). Initially delivering 12,500kgp (27,557 lbst), it was uprated to 15,000kgp (33,068 lbst) and then to 16,000kgp (35,273 lbst) in due course; this brought about a change in the Tu-204's configuration from a 'Lockheed TriStar gone on a diet' lookalike to the current twinjet. The PS-90 incorporated all the latest features, including full authority digital engine control (FADEC).

Hence the IL-76 stretch project was revived in the late 1980s as the IL-76MF; the F is an allusion to the stretched fuselage. Two 3.3m (10ft 10in) plugs are inserted ahead of and aft of the wings, increasing freight hold volume 1.5 times to 400m³ (14,125ft³). This allows such loads as four 20' containers to be transported and, of course, substantially increases capacity in troopship configuration, reportedly allowing the aircraft to carry up to 500 servicemen (?!). This, in turn, required the addition of two pairs of emergency exits (one ahead and one aft of the wings). The wing/air intake inspection light fairing ahead of the port entry door is deleted; this light is now buried in the fuselage about halfway between the door and the foremost emergency exit. A pair of taxi lights (runway turnoff lights) is installed symmetrically at the same location.

The aircraft has a *Candid-A*-style pointed tailcone – the gunner's station is eliminated to save weight. Besides, as noted earlier, defensive avionics are of more use than defensive armament to a modern military transport. Speaking of which, the ECM antennas are relocated from the forward/aft fuselage sides to the wingtips on the IL-76MF in order to reduce drag.

The IL-76MF is powered by PS-90A-76 turbofans. The new engine has a much larger casing diameter and a cascade-type thrust reverser with translating cowl. Hence the engine pylons and nacelles had to be designed from scratch (the leading edge of the pylon is curved where it joins the nacelle; also, the leading and trailing edges are no longer parallel). The production-standard PS-90A has a 15% lower specific fuel consumption (SFC) than the

D-30KP and much lower noise and emission levels – important, considering all those ICAO annexes regarding noise and pollution.

The aircraft's systems and equipment are thoroughly updated. The Koopol ground mapping radar is replaced by an upgraded Koopol-3 model; a 'glass cockpit' with multi-function colour LCDs is introduced, along with new communications equipment, allowing the radio operator to be automated away. The TA-6A APU is replaced by a TA-12-60 unit; this is also a Stoopino Machinery Design Bureau product and is used on some other aircraft powered by the PS-90 (the Tu-204 and the projected Tu-330). Originally, the Omsk Engine Design Bureau VGTD-43 (*vspomogahtel'nyy gahzotoorbinnyy dveegatel'* – auxiliary gas turbine engine) was envisaged, but development of this APU is taking rather longer than expected.

MTOW is increased to 210 tons (462,962 lb) and payload to 52 tons (114,638 lb). Nevertheless, the fuel-efficient engines afford a 15 to 20% increase in range. The wing structure had to be reinforced, of course, to cater for the higher gross weight.

The IL-76MF was unveiled in model form at MosAeroShow '92 in August 1992. Curiously, the model showed only two emergency exits on each side.

Construction of the first prototype (c/n 1053417563, f/n 9001) began in Tashkent in February 1994. The OKB chose to build the aircraft from scratch rather than cut up an existing airframe and insert plugs, as had been the case with the IL-96M prototype,[23] RA-96000, which was converted from the first prototype IL-96-300. The rollout was planned for the end of the year but funding shortfalls caused construction to drag on until early 1995.[24]

By then Ilyushin had some operational experience with the PS-90A, and unfortunately this was not all positive. Reliability was rather poor at first (Aeroflot's IL-96-300s had 32 unscheduled engine changes in the first two years of service), and some writers even deciphered PS mockingly as *pozor sotsializmu* – 'shame on socialism'! Hence the engine was temporarily derated to 14,500kgp (31,966 lbst) by making changes to the FADEC software and it was this derated version that powered the prototype. The aircraft was unarmed, but the inert gas

CCCP-86889

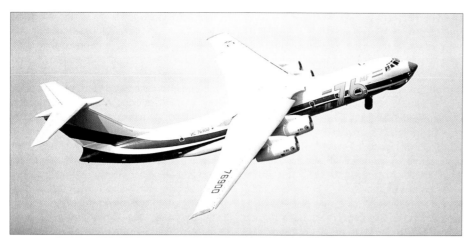

Left: **The first prototype IL-76MF, IS 76900, banks during a demo flight. The aircraft demonstrated surprising agility at MAKS-95.** Yefim Gordon

Below left: **The IL-76MF has characteristically restyled wingtips incorporating ECM antennas.** Dmitriy Komissarov

Below right: **The new engine nacelles and pylons of the IL-76MF's PS-90A engines. The winged bear logo on the cowlings is that of the Perm' (Solovyov) Engine Design Bureau.** Dmitriy Komissarov

Above: **A crewman flies the Russian and Uzbek flags from the dorsal flight deck escape hatch as the IL-76MF completes its landing run at MAKS-95.** Yefim Gordon

Left: **Still engineless and in primer, the second prototype IL-76MF basks in the sun at the Tashkent aircraft factory in November 1999. The engine in the foreground is not intended for this aircraft, being a D-30KP.** Victor Drushlyakov

Photograph on the opposite page:

The second IL-76MF is fitted with external stores pylons. Concrete cubes are suspended on the engine pylons for CG reasons. Victor Drushlyakov

generator intake in the starboard main gear fairing, the characteristically reprofiled wingtips incorporating ECM antennas and the 'READY – GO!' sign in the freight hold left no doubts that this was indeed an IL-76MF, not a civil IL-76TF (see below).

Originally the first flight date was set for May 1995, then for late July, but kept slipping for various reasons. Finally, at 1024 Moscow time on 1st August the IL-76MF took to the air at long last. The mixed Russian-Uzbek crew was captained by Ilyushin test pilot (1st Class) Anatoliy N Knyshov and included first officer V I Sviridov, navigator B A Tver'ye, flight engineer S N Goryunov, radio operator Ye E Bokoonovich (yes, there was a radio operator that time) and electrics engineer Yuriy G Bliznyuk. Yuriy M Arandt was the engineer in charge of the tests. The 35-minute flight went smoothly.

For the maiden flight the aircraft was registered 17563 without any country prefix; this was the 'famous last five' of the c/n, which is common practice at the Tashkent plant during checkout flights. On 7th August, however, it was reregistered IS 76900 (ИС 76900). The unusual prefix in Cyrillic characters – which was unheard-of in post-Soviet times, – denoted *ispytahniya* (tests or trials). This avoided the touchy issue of whether the prototype belonged to the OKB in Russia or the plant in Uzbekistan (and thus whether it should be registered RA-76900 or UK-76900). For the same reason the prototype carried both Russian and Uzbek flags on the fuselage.

Next day the aircraft arrived in Zhukovskiy to continue its flight test programme. The IL-76MF was one of the stars of the MAKS-95 airshow (22nd-27th August), making its tenth flight by closing day. The public was allowed inside the freight hold which was lined with racks of test equipment, but, understandably enough, the flight deck was off limits.

From 5-10th November, 1996 the aircraft had its international debut at Airshow China '96 in Zhuhai (Sanzao airport); the crew was captained by Stanislav G Bliznyuk. Now using the unofficial IS- prefix was no longer possible and the prototype had to be reregistered RA-76900 for the occasion.

On 11th April 1997 the IL-76MF was certificated according to ICAO Annex 16 Chapter 3 and FAR Pt 36 noise regulations. During the same year RA-76900 took part in the 42nd Paris Aerospace Salon at Le Bourget (15th-22nd June) with the exhibit code 338 and in the MAKS-97 airshow (19-24th August). It was also on display at ILA'98 with the exhibit code 236 and at MAKS-99 (17th-22nd August 1999).

By November 1999 the second IL-76MF (c/n 1063421724, f/n 9401) had been rolled out in Tashkent. The still engineless and unpainted aircraft differed from the first prototype in having four external stores pylons under the outer wings à la IL-76MD. Eight more examples and the commercial IL-76TF prototype were reportedly in various stages of completion. The Russian Air Force, which had announced its

intention to purchase the type, was due to loan RA-76900 for evaluation in late 1997. On 15th March 1996 the Commander of the VTA stated the IL-76MF would be one of the three types operated by the Russian Air Force's transport element in the 21st century (alongside the An-70 and Tu-330VT, that is).

In the last days of June 2000 the first prototype demonstrated its paradropping capabilities to Russian Air Force and Airborne Forces top brass (including VDV C-in-C Col Gen Gheorgiy Shpak) at Dyaghilevo AB near Ryazan'. In so doing it achieved a 'world first' by dropping six cargo pallets – two with BMD-2 IFVs and four with ammunition crates, followed by a load of paratroopers.

In due course the IL-76MF's maximum payload increased to 60 tons (132,275 lb). This was demonstrated in May 2000 when RA-76900 delivered 60 tons of cargo to Pevek on the Chukotka Peninsula. By October 2000 Ilyushin had invested US$ 20 million into IL-76MF development; with no state funding, the company flies commercial cargoes on the prototype to finance the completion of the trials programme!

Ilyushin is also targeting the export market with the IL-76MF; an export price of US$ 30 to 35 million was quoted in late 1995 for the Russian-engined version. Export aircraft could be powered by Western engines – 14,152kgp (31,200 lbst) CFM International CFM56-5C2 or 17,327kgp (38,200 lbst) Pratt & Whitney PW2337 turbofans – and equipped with Western avionics at customer request.

IL-76TF commercial transport
This is the civil equivalent of the IL-76MF (the commercial version has also been referred to as IL-76MT by some sources). It differs from the military version in lacking paradropping equipment, the inert gas generator and ECM equipment (and hence having ordinary wingtip fairings); the communications suite is probably slightly different, too.

The stretched fuselage enables the aircraft to carry four 20' air/sea/land containers instead of three, nine UAK-5 cargo containers instead

of six or two coaches instead of one. Additionally, special double-deck modules can be installed for carrying up to 24 passenger cars.

IL-78 (IL-78T) *Midas*
refuelling tanker/transport
Aerial refuelling had been a sore spot for the VVS for years. Tactical aviation had to do without, and only a few bombers had flight refuelling capability. These were Tu-4s and Tu-16s equipped with the Soviet wingtip-to-wingtip system developed by Igor' Shelest and Viktor Vasyanin. The tanker deployed a hose stabilised by a drogue parachute from the starboard wingtip and the receiver aircraft placed its port wingtip over the hose. Then the hose was rewound until the fitting at the end engaged a receptacle under the receiver aircraft's wing. The receiver increased speed so that the hose formed a loop and rotated the receptacle, opening a valve, whereupon fuel transfer could begin.

This technique was complicated; worse, a Tu-16Z *Badger-A* (Z = *zaprahvschchik* – tanker) could only refuel other Tu-16s. Hence the VVS soon switched to the hose-and-drogue system. This offered greater versatility, since Tu-16N *Badger-A* and Myasischchev M-4-2 *Bison-A*, 3MS2 and 3MN2 *Bison-B* tankers could work with any aircraft fitted with the standard refuelling probe. Yet again the Tu-16N and M-4-2 *et seq* were single-point tankers, with the hose drum unit (HDU) installed in the bomb bay. Meanwhile, by the late 1970s the Western air forces had introduced three-point tankers; the VVS had a requirement for a similar aircraft.

Development of the IL-78, as the tanker/transport derivative of the *Candid* was designated, began pursuant to an MAP and VVS order issued on 14th March 1968 – three years before the IL-76 flew! However, calculations showed that the IL-76 *sans suffixe* adapted to the tanker role could transfer only 10 tons (22,045 lb) of fuel; this was insufficient and the project was shelved.

Interest in the idea revived when the high gross weight IL-76MD with increased fuel

the former gunner's station is occupied by the refuelling systems operator. Hence the tail turret is replaced by a characteristic dished fairing and the gun ranging radar is deleted, with a flat cover supplanting the radome. Another difference from the IL-76 is that the IL-78 has a fuel jettison system; the fuel jettison pipes are located at the wingtips.

With a 1,000km (540nm) combat radius the IL-78 can transfer up to 65 tons (143,300 lb)/ 84,639 litres (18,620 Imperial gallons) of fuel. Maximum combat radius with 32 to 36 tons (70,545 to 79,365 lb) of transferable fuel (equalling 41,668 to 46,877 litres/9,167 to 10,313 Imperial gallons) is 2,500km (1,350nm). It is possible to refuel one heavy bomber, using the centre pod, or two tactical aircraft, using the underwing pods.

Refuelling is done at 2,000 to 9,000m (6,561 to 29,525ft) and 430 to 590km/h (232 to 318kts) or Mach 0.72.[26] The minimum safe distance between the tanker and receiver aircraft is 13m (42ft). Refuelling is allowed in direct visibility conditions only. Two lights in characteristic fairings under the refuelling systems operator's station illuminate the lower rear fuselage during night refuelling; this gives the pilot of the receiver aircraft a visual reference, minimising the danger of collision. To ensure rendezvous with the receiver aircraft the IL-78 is equipped with an additional RSBN-7S Vstrecha (Rendezvous) SHORAN system,[27] with three antennas built into the fin each side instead of one on the IL-76; these provide mutual detection and approach at up to 300km (160nm). Also, the usual stabilizer inspection light buried in the rear portion of the port main gear fairing is augmented by three more lights (two to port, one to starboard) for checking refuelling pods in icing conditions.

Wearing the out-of-sequence registration CCCP-76556 (c/n 0033445294, f/n 3304), the IL-78 prototype made its first flight in Tashkent on 26th June 1983 with OKB test pilot Vyacheslav S Belousov at the controls. Ilyushin CTP Stanislav G Bliznyuk flew the aircraft at a later stage when refuelling techniques were practiced. Manufacturer's flight tests took place during September to December 1983; these were followed by State acceptance trials which began in March 1984 and were completed on 30th June. CCCP-76556 was retained by the OKB and used for test and development work together with the Mikoyan and Sukhoi bureaux, LII etc.

Deliveries to the VVS began in 1984 (initially to the VTA training centre at Ivanovo-Severnyy

capacity came on the scene. On 10th March 1982 the Council of Ministers and the Central Committee of the Communist Party issued a directive ordering the development of the IL-78, and the design effort was completed next year. Development was led by project chief Radiy P Papkovskiy assisted by G K Nokhratyan-Torosyan, A V Leschchiner and Dmitriy V Leschchiner, A L Dobroskov, G V Mashkov and N F Makokin.

The aircraft is equipped with three UPAZ-1A Sakhalin refuelling pods[25] developed by the Zvezda (Star; pronounced zvezdah) design bureau (formerly OKB-918) under Guy Il'yich Severin – the same house that is responsible for the famous K-36 ejection seat. Two pods are conventionally mounted on pylons under the outer wings. The third pod is suspended from a short horizontal pylon on the port side of the aft fuselage; this is a unique arrangement not used by any other tanker.

The UPAZ-1A has a 26m (85ft 4in) hose and a flexible 'basket' drogue. The hose drum is powered by a ram air turbine (RAT) with an opening intake scoop on the port side at the rear. A second air intake at the front closed by a movable cone is for the RAT driving a generator for the electric transfer pump. Normal delivery rate is 1,000 litres/min (220 Imperial

gallons/min) but this can be increased to 2,200 litres/min (484 Imperial gallons/min) in case of need. 'Traffic lights' are installed at the rear end of the pod to indicate fuel transfer status to the pilot of the receiver aircraft.

Most of the fuel is carried in the standard wing tanks. Additionally, two cylindrical metal tanks connected to the aircraft's fuel system are installed in the freight hold. These can be easily removed if required, allowing the aircraft to be used for transport or paradropping duties, since the cargo doors and cargo handling equipment are retained. Hence the initial tanker version is also referred to as IL-78T (**trahn**sportnyy). The IL-78 can also refuel other aircraft on the ground (up to four at a time), using conventional hoses.

The wing tanks hold 90 tons (198,412 lb) of fuel; the extra tanks in the fuselage increase this to 118 tons (260,141 lb) or 153,652 litres (33,803 Imperial gallons). Maximum transferable fuel with or without fuselage tanks is 85.72 or 57.72 tons (188,977 or 127,248 lb) respectively, which amounts to 111,620 or 75,160 litres (24,556 or 16,535 Imperial gallons) respectively. Takeoff weight is 190 tons (418,871 lb) on paved runways and 157.5 tons (347,222 lb) on semi-prepared runways.

Unlike the Candid-B, the tanker is unarmed;

AB), but it was not until 1st June 1987 that the tanker was officially included into the Soviet Air Force inventory. The 409th SAP (*smeshannyy aviapolk* – composite air regiment) at Uzin AB near Kiev was the main operator of the IL-78.

The West had been speculating on a possible tanker version of the IL-76 since 1980; by 1986 the aircraft had been assigned the reporting name *Midas*. On 2nd August 1988 US Secretary of Defense Frank C Carlucci and his senior aide Maj Gen Gordon E Fornell visited Kubinka airbase, examining the latest Soviet military aircraft, including the IL-78, and the true designation was revealed.

The tanker at Kubinka had an Aeroflot-style paint job and VVS insignia (but no tactical code). This was highly unusual because, despite their obvious military role, the IL-78s usually wore Aeroflot colours and civil registrations. Known examples are CCCP-76556*, -76607*, -76609*, -76610, -76616, -76632, -76646, -76653, -76662, -76670, -76675, -76682,-76685, -76689, -76690, -76715*, -76721, -76730, -76736, -76742, -76744, -76760, -76774, -76775*, -78759, -78767, -78773, -78782, -78798, -78806, -78812 and -78814. Aircraft marked with * have out-of-sequence registrations. Six more aircraft (CCCP-76636, -76639, -76651, -76660, -76663 and -76724) are reported as IL-78s by some sources, but as IL-76MDs by others.

Some aircraft were seen carrying only the underwing UPAZ-1A pods or the fuselage pod. Late production IL-78s had the fuselage pod mounted on an L-shaped pylon identical to that of the IL-78M (see below). Accompanied by a Tu-95MS-6 *Bear-H* bomber and four escorting MiG-29s, one such aircraft painted in a grey/white Air Force colour scheme and coded 34 Blue (c/n 1013404138, f/n 7905) took part in the demonstration flights at the Kubinka-92 air fest on 11th April 1992, in what was probably the type's public debut. 34 Blue is one of only two IL-78s *sans suffixe* to wear overt military markings, the other one being 616 Black (ex-CCCP-76616, c/n 0053455676, f/n 4209). Incidentally, the Tu-95/Tu-142 is said to have trouble refuelling from the IL-78 because of exhaust gas ingestion.

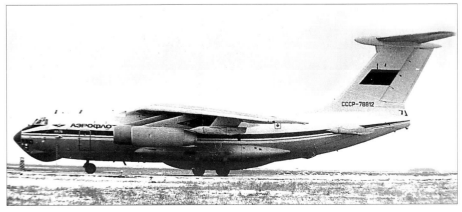

CCCP-76556 topping up the MiG-25RBVDZ refuelling systems testbed (68 Blue) and a standard Su-24M (29 Blue). Yefim Gordon archive

A Tu-22M3 armed with two Kh-22M anti-shipping missiles formates with an IL-78 for a so-called 'tactical refuelling'. The *Backfire-C* could not refuel from the *Midas*, since the refuelling probe was removed in compliance with the SALT-2 treaty. Yefim Gordon archive

An IL-78 on takeoff. Ilyushin OKB

***Midas* CCCP-78812 poses for an 'official photograph' for a NATO information exchange album. Note striped rod positioned near the ground mapping radar to provide scale.** Yefim Gordon archive

IL-78 CCCP-76744 (note last three digits stencilled on the air intake covers) was demonstrated to CIS leaders at Machoolischchi airbase on 13th February 1992, hastily 'disguised' with VVS markings. The star on the fin is much smaller that usually applied to the type. Yefim Gordon

The same aircraft all set for demonstration. Note hose and drogue basket drooping from No1 UPAZ-1A pod for ease of inspection and black cloth draped over data table. Yefim Gordon

Airbrakes and spoilers deployed, IL-78M prototype CCCP-76701 completes a demo flight at MosAeroShow-92. Yefim Gordon

IL-78M prototype CCCP-76701 on takeoff at LII. Yefim Gordon

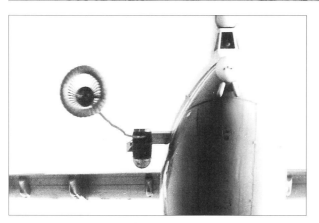

A receiver's eye view of an IL-78 *sans suffixe*; the cargo doors and faired fuselage illumination lights are plainly visible. Note the open air intake on the UPAZ-1A pod. Yefim Gordon archive

On 13th February 1992 IL-78 CCCP-76744 (c/n 0073478359, f/n 5910) was demonstrated to top-ranking military officials and the leaders of the CIS states at Machoolischchi AB near Minsk. Once again the aircraft had the civil markings painted out and VVS markings (but no tactical code) hastily applied for the occasion because the organizers felt it would be 'improper' to display a civil-registered aircraft. Curiously, the data plates for the exhibits were carefully draped with black cloth to hide the 'top secret' figures from prying journalists (who arrived in force) and unveiled only for the visiting VIPs. Obviously *glasnost'* still had a *long* way to go in 1992!

Twenty aircraft in strength with the 409th SAP at Uzin AB were retained by the Ukrainian Air Force after the collapse of the Soviet Union. Since the Ukraine did not need tankers (the UAF's Tu-22M3 *Backfire-C* bombers were deprived of flight refuelling capability under the SALT-2 treaty), nearly all Ukrainian IL-78s have been converted into pure transports by removing all refuelling equipment, including the pylons. Some even have 'IL-76MD' nose titles, but the triple SHORAN antennas in the fin and the fuselage illumination lights under the refuelling systems operator's station reveal their true identity. Aircraft thus converted are UR-76412 (IL-76TD 'Falsie', ex-CCCP-78773/ to UR-UCF), UR-76414 (ex-CCCP-76774/ to UR-UCG), UR-76415 (ex-76775/to UR-UCI), UR-76609, UR-76610, UR-76651?, UR-76670, UR-76682, UR-76689, UR-76690, UR-76715 (to UR-UCA), UR-76721, UR-76724?, UR-76730, UR-76742, UR-76744, UR-76759 (a mispaint for UR-78759), UR-76760 and UR-76767 (a mispaint for UR-78767).

IL-78E *Midas* refuelling tanker

Unlike the *Candid,* the IL-78 has not been widely exported. Libya is the sole foreign customer; in 1989 the Libyan Arab Air Force took delivery of a single aircraft registered 5A-DLL (c/n 0093493799, f/n 7010). The export version is designated IL-78E (*eksportnyy*). (To be precise, India is also reported to operate IL-78s but these are merely on loan from the Russian Air Force. Algeria also reportedly has a number of ex-Russian Air Force IL-78s but no details are known).

IL-78M *Midas* refuelling tanker

On 20th December 1984, soon after the basic *Midas* completed its flight tests, the Council of Ministers and the Central Committee of the Communist Party issued a directive ordering the development of an upgraded tanker designated IL-78M. Unlike the IL-78 *sans suffixe*, this is a dedicated (non-convertible) tanker version. It features a third fuselage fuel tank increasing total fuel to 138 tons (304,233 lb) or 179,965 litres (39,533 Imperial gallons); transferable fuel is thus increased to 105,720kg (233,068 lb) or 137,662 litres (30,285 Imperial gallons). All cargo handling equipment is deleted to reduce structural weight. MTOW on paved runways is increased to 210 tons (462,962 lb). Furthermore, the IL-78M is equipped with improved UPAZ-1M pods having a higher delivery rate (2,340 litres/min or 514.8 Imperial gallons/min).

The main external recognition features are the absence of the port entry door and the redesigned L-shaped pylon of the fuselage pod; the latter is caused by the need to move the drogue away from the turbulence generated by the fuselage. The cargo doors are deleted (this can be clearly seen from the transverse skin joint lines under the aft fuselage and the absence of outer door hinge fairings) and the cargo ramp is non-functional. Finally, the wing/air intake inspection light is relocated to starboard, since there is no longer a window on the port side.

The prototype IL-78M, CCCP-76701 (c/n 0063471139, f/n 5405), entered flight test on 7th March 1987; again it was Vyacheslav S Belousov who captained the aircraft on its maiden flight. Like the original IL-78 prototype, this aircraft was retained by Ilyushin and used for trials of tactical aircraft – eg, the ninth prototype Su-27M (Su-35), 709 Blue[28] (c/n 79871011001). Interestingly, the ASCC did not react in any way to the appearance of a new tanker version; it would be logical to codename it *Midas-B*!

CCCP-76701 participated in the flying display at MosAeroShow '92, formating with two Sukhoi Su-30 multi-role fighters operated by LII's Ispytahteli (Test Pilots) display team – 596 White and 597 White (c/ns 79371010101 and 79371010102) – and the experimental Su-27IB fighter-bomber (42 Blue), the precursor of the Su-34/Su-32FN. Unlike earlier demonstrations of a similar kind, all three receiver aircraft actually 'hit the tanker' in a simulated refuelling. By August 1997 the prototype (by then reregistered RA-76701) was withdrawn from use in Zhukovskiy.

Unlike the basic IL-78 tanker/transport, production IL-78Ms usually have overt military markings and a grey/white Air Force colour scheme. Known aircraft are coded 30 Blue through 33 Blue, 35 Blue, 36 Blue and 50 Blue through 53 Blue. Only the first four production IL-78Ms, CCCP-78800 and CCCP-78822 through CCCP-78824, are quasi-civilian. The type is operated by the 230th APSZ (*aviapolk samolyotov-zaprahvschchikov* = aerial refuelling regiment) in Engels in southern Russia which had 12 aircraft on strength in early 1992. Some sources claim that 45 *Midases* of both versions had been built by 1991; however, even without the six doubtful aircraft mentioned earlier, a 'nose-count' gives 49 examples. Curiously, production IL-78s were often the seventh and tenth aircraft in the batch.

The IL-78M was also a regular participant at various airshows. For example, 30 Blue was displayed at Kubinka in March 1992 during a show marking the 50th anniversary of the Russian Air Force's strategic bomber arm (DA, *dahl'nyaya aviahtsiya* – long-range aviation). 50 Blue participated in the Tushino flypast on 9th May 1993 in a simulated refuelling of a Tu-95MS-6, and the formation certainly looked and sounded impressive.

The flying display at the 1994 Kubinka open doors day (14th May 1994) featured two IL-78Ms. First, 35 Blue formated with a Tu-95MS-6 escorted by two MiG-29s of the Strizhi (Swifts) display team and two Su-27 of the Roosskiye Vityazi (Russian Knights) team. Next came 30 Blue in formation with two Su-24M *Fencer-D* tactical bombers (91 Blue and 93 Blue), one of which was flown by Russian AF C-in-C Col Gen Pyotr S Deynekin.

30 Blue and 36 Blue took part in the grand military parade in Moscow on 9th May 1995 on occasion of the 50th anniversary of VE-Day. Finally, IL-78M '36 Blue' participated in the flying display at MAKS-99, demonstrating a simulated refuelling of Su-30s '302 Blue' and '597 White'.

Forward fuselage of the IL-78M, showing the lack of the port entry door characteristic of the IL-78M. Yefim Gordon

The port and centre UPAZ-1M pods. This view shows clearly the IL-78M's L-shaped fuselage pylon. The number 3489370 on the port pod is its own construction number, not the last digits of the aircraft's c/n; the centre pod is c/n 3489371. Yefim Gordon

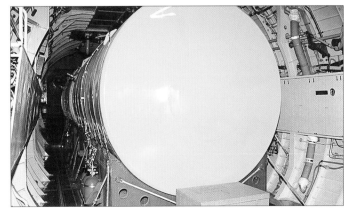

The internal fuel tanks of IL-78M '36 Blue'. The vertical pipes connecting these to the aircraft's wing tanks are just visible in the background. Note the triple fire extinguisher bottles near each tank. Yefim Gordon

Flying over a barge chugging along the Moskva River near Zhukovskiy, CCCP-76701 is seen here practicing for MosAeroShow-92 in a rare formation with three fighters. The Su-27IB fighter-bomber prototype (42 Blue) using the central station is flanked by two colourful Su-30s (596 White and 597 White) of LII's own display team, *Istrebiteli* (Fighters). Yefim Gordon

Another view of the same quartet. This view shows that the four aircraft have to fly in very close formation during refuelling. Yefim Gordon

CCCP-78822, one of the few quasi-civilian production IL-78Ms, in service with the 230th APSZ at Engels. The red object in front of the aircraft is a fire extinguisher. Yefim Gordon

IL-82 ABCP/communications relay aircraft (IL-76VKP, 'version 65C')

Two IL-76MD 'Falsies' built in late 1985, CCCP-76450 (c/n 0053463900, f/n 4805) and CCCP-76451 (c/n 0053464938, f/n 4905), were extensively converted at the Tashkent factory for the communications relay role. In the event of war these aircraft would ensure communication between the strategic nuclear forces and command, control and communications (C^3) centres – or IL-86VPU[29] (IL-80) *Maxdome* national emergency airborne command posts (NEACPs) in case ground C^3 centres were knocked out. The manufacturer's designation of the comms relay *Candid*, the Soviet equivalent of the US Navy's Boeing E-6A Hermes, is IL-82; it was previously used for a projected 120 to 138-seat short-haul airliner powered by two Solov'yov D-30M-1 turbofans which was abandoned in favour of the Tu-134A. Some sources refer to the aircraft as 'version 65C'.

The aircraft has some equipment commonality (and hence common exterior features) with both the IL-80 and the A-50 AWACS. Recent publications say it also has an airborne command post role, hence the alternative designation IL-76VKP (voz**doosh**nyy ko**mahn**dnyy poonkt – ABCP).

The IL-82 is immediately recognizable by the large boxy dorsal canoe fairing (similar to that of the *Maxdome*) which runs the full length of the forward fuselage from flight deck to wing leading edge. This houses satellite communications and navigation equipment. The navigator's glazing, cockpit eyebrow windows and the two rearmost flight deck windows on each side are deleted. So is the port entry door but, illogically, the engine/wing inspection light remains on the port side where there is no window through which to inspect the intakes!

The main gear fairings are borrowed from the A-50, with much thicker and blunter forward portions, though the starboard fairing has one circular intake instead of two. The APU is housed in the aft portion of the port fairing, with an 'elephant's ear' intake. A second APU is located symmetrically to starboard; this is because the APUs are used to power the mission equipment in flight. The starboard fairing also has prominent bulges over equipment at the rear. A long shallow fairing with small blade aerials runs along the lower port side of the fuselage from the nose gear to the port main-wheel fairing; two small canoe fairings with blade aerials are located in tandem symmetrically to starboard.

Two small streamlined pods with forward-pointing HF probe aerials are carried on short strut-braced pylons under the outer wings. Additionally, CCCP-76450 had small hemispherical fairings under the wingtips. Two small blade aerials are located side by side just aft of the wing leading edge, with three more in a triangle (facing the tail) at the trailing edge. The dorsal fin is flanked by two elongated semicylindrical antenna fairings à la IL-80.

The outer cargo doors are modified; their

rearmost portions are fixed and carry huge outward-canted blade aerials. A very low frequency (VLF) trailing wire aerial with a stabilising drogue is faired into the centre door segment; this is used for communication with submerged nuclear submarines. After deploying the 5km (3.1 mile) TWA the IL-82 starts circling and the drogue stalls so that the wire droops almost vertically; this is the only way for the radio signals to penetrate deep water. A similar aerial with a float is deployed by the sub.

Conversion and outfitting took more than a year, though this could be partly accounted for by delays in equipment delivery. CCCP-76450 made its first flight on 29th April 1987, captained by Yuriy V Mazonov. Both aircraft were ferried to LII, and the existence of the new version came to light on 16th August 1988 during the Aviation Day flypast in Zhukovskiy. Curiously, this highly specialised version never received a separate NATO code name.

After completing their trials successfully the two IL-82s were delivered to the 8th ADON (*aviadiveeziya osobovo naznacheniya*) – Special Mission Air Division (air wing) at Chkalovskaya AB. Needless to say they spend most of their time in storage.

Ilyushin/Beriyev A-50 *Mainstay-A* AWACS (IL-76A)

Chronologically this was probably the second military version of the *Candid* to have a separate designation. It owed its existence to the need to replace the Tu-126 *Moss* airborne warning and control system (AWACS) aircraft. Derived from the Tu-114 *Cleat* four-turboprop long-range airliner, the Tu-126 had been in service with the Soviet Air Defence Force (PVO – *protivovozdooshnaya oborona*) since 1961 and had become obsolescent by the early 1980s.

Actually work on a successor to the Tu-126 had begun as early as 1965 when the Beriyev OKB experimentally fitted an An-12BP with a surveillance radar in a conventional rotodome. Performance was poor (to say nothing of the fact that the *Cub* is unpressurized) and the project was abandoned. However, a logical explanation is that the aircraft was nothing but an avionics testbed.

On 7th August 1969 the Council of Ministers' Defence Industry Commission tasked the Ilyushin OKB with preliminary development of the IL-70 AWACS, a derivative of the as-yet unflown IL-76.[30] With its high speed, payload and range the *Candid* was an excellent AWACS platform.

Thus in the late 1970s the IL-76M evolved into the A-50. The 'non-Ilyushin' designation is due to the fact that the aircraft is a joint effort with the Beriyev OKB and the Taganrog machinery plant No 86 named after Gheorgiy

Dimitrov (TMZD – *Taganrogskiy mashinostroitel'nyy zavod imeni Gheorgiya Dimitrova*) which integrated the mission avionics suite. (Cf. A-40, the manufacturer's designation of the Beriyev Be-42 Albatross (*Mermaid*) ASW amphibian.) Had Ilyushin alone been responsible for the job, the designation would have been something like IL-76RLD (*rahdiolokatseeonnyy dozor* – radar picket) – or IL-70. At the Tashkent Aircraft production Corporation which manufactures the airframe, however, the A-50 is referred to as IL-76A.

The A-50 is equipped with the Shmel' (Bumblebee) mission avionics suite built around a coherent pulse-Doppler 360° surveillance radar of the same name. The radar can track up to 50 targets at a time with a maximum range of 230km (124nm); large targets like surface ships can be detected and tracked at up to 400km (216nm). The suite also includes an IFF system, a data processing and presentation system, data storage equipment and secure digital communications/data link equipment for communicating with ground and shipboard command, control, communications and intelligence (C³I) centres, and friendly fighters. The radar was developed by the Moscow Research Institute of Instrument Engineering (MNIIP – *Moskovskiy naoochno-issledovatel'skiy institoot preeborostroyeniya*), aka NPO Vega-M, under General Designer V P Ivanov. The same house was responsible for the Tu-126's Liana (Creeper; NATO *Flat Jack*) radar. A K Konstantinov supervised the integration and debugging effort at the Beriyev OKB.

The A-50's main recognition feature is, of course, the conventionally located 'saucer' rotodome of the Shmel' radar mounted on two pylons immediately aft of the wings. It has a 9m (29ft 6in) diameter and is some 2m (6ft 7in) deep. The rotodome is mounted more than one diameter ahead of and well below the stabiliz-

Most IL-78Ms sport this grey/white colour scheme. Yefim Gordon

This view of 36 Blue at Engels shows clearly the missing cargo doors of the IL-78M. Yefim Gordon

ers. There have been speculations that lift generated by the rotodome increases downwash on the stabilizers, reducing their efficiency, but the rotodome itself contributes a stabilising influence. Also, wake turbulence from the rotodome reduces the efficiency of the vertical tail but the rotodome pylons make up for this – albeit at the expense of reduced lateral stability because of the additional sideforce above the centre of gravity. Anyway, the fact that the A-50 has entered quantity production implies that the arrangement works satisfactorily.

The extensive navigator's glazing has been replaced by a large curved dielectric panel, leaving only a single small window on each side; the A-50 is obviously not the best aircraft for a navigator prone to claustrophobia! These windows and the two rearmost flight deck windows on each side have gold plating to protect the crew from radiation. The said dielectric panel features four tooth-like projections at the bottom, making the aircraft look like a pleased rodent. The weather radar's radome is slightly smaller and has a reshaped joint line with the fuselage, with two small dielectric panels on either side aft of it.

IL-78M '36 Blue' takes off for a demo flight at the MAKS'99 airshow in Zhukovskiy. Yefim Gordon

36 Blue performs a simulated refuelling of an unpainted Su-30 with a new avionics fit (302 Blue, c/n 79371010302) and Su-30 '597 White'. Yefim Gordon

The port entry door is deleted; so is the gunner's station, which is replaced by an avionics bay with two aft-facing antennas covered by large fairings where the tail turret and the glazing used to be. A large cooling air intake is provided at the base of the fin. The cargo ramp is retained but is non-functional, and the cargo doors are deleted. The main gear fairings have constant cross-section almost throughout; the blunt forward portions incorporate two circular air intakes of unequal size. The APU is relocated to the rear portion of the port fairing, with an 'elephant's ear' intake and a downward-angled exhaust (the arrangement was borrowed for the IL-76PP and IL-80).

The A-50 bristles with various antennas. Four ECM antennas in large teardrop fairings are located on the forward and aft fuselage sides; a large dielectric fairing ahead of the wing torsion box covers satellite communications (SATCOM) and navigation antennas. Numerous blade aerials are located dorsally and ventrally on the forward fuselage and ahead of the cargo ramp, and two large strake aerials are fitted aft of the nose gear. Chaff/flare dispensers are incorporated into the rear fuselage flush with the skin.

Like its predecessor (the Tu-126), the A-50 has flight refuelling capability – in theory at least. A telescopic refuelling probe is located ahead of the flight deck glazing, with an external fuel conduit running along the starboard side above the entry door to the wings. For night refuelling the probe is illuminated by retractable lights, a standard feature on Soviet heavy aircraft using the probe-and-drogue system.

Western intelligence got wind of the A-50's development in 1983 and the aircraft was allocated the unusually laudatory reporting name *Mainstay*. At first, however, the West had a rather vague idea of what the aircraft looked like; artist's impressions showed a conventional glazed nose and tail gunner's station, and there have been claims that the fuselage was stretched ahead of the wings (which is clearly not the case). An early drawing even showed the rotodome mounted on a single short pylon, Tu-126 style.

Several A-50 prototypes converted from *Candid-Bs*, including 10 Red (ex-IL-76 *sans suffixe* CCCP-76641, c/n 073409243, f/n 0701) and 20 Red (c/n 0013430875, f/n 2209A),[31] were involved in the test programme. These had minor detail differences; for instance, 10 Red and 15 Red (possibly c/n 073410311, f/n 0808) had standard *Candid*-style tapered aft portions of the main gear fairings. A further uncoded aircraft lacked the 'teeth' and ECM blisters but had the definitive gear fairings. To improve longitudinal stability two large strakes of quasi-triangular planform were added to the aft portions of the main gear fairings on later prototypes and production *Mainstays*. The rearmost portions of the strakes are attached to the cargo ramp and the APU nozzle is located beneath the port strake.

Test flights showed that aerial refuelling was all but impossible because the rotodome would hit wake turbulence from the tanker, causing severe buffeting. On internal fuel the A-50 has an endurance of four hours at 1,000km

(540nm) from base; MTOW is 190 tons (418,875 lb).

Production apparently began in 1981, with deliveries to the PVO commencing in 1984. Initially the type was operated from a base near Siauliai in Lithuania which had earlier been home to the Tu-126. However, this soon had to be vacated for political reasons and the *Mainstays* moved north to Beryozovka AB near Pechora on the Kola peninsula, to the displeasure of the crews. The first three years of service were more of an evaluation period and flights were confined to Soviet territory. In fact, the first actual sighting by a Western combat aircraft over international waters did not take place until 4th December 1987 when a Royal Norwegian Air Force (333 Sqn) P-3B Orion from Bodø airbase photographed an uncoded A-50 over the Barents Sea.

A-50s were also detached to the Far East Defence District and to the Crimea peninsula, operating from Black Sea Fleet airbases and checking on the Soviet Union's southern borders in practice missions. During Operation *Desert Storm* in 1990 two *Mainstays* continuously monitored the operations of Iraqi and Allied forces, keeping a watch for stray US cruise missiles which might be heading towards CIS territory. Several aircraft were based at Ukurey, an IL-76 base; in 1999, however, all operational *Mainstays* were concentrated at Ivanovo-Severnyy AB.

Production proceeded at a rate of one to five aircraft a year until 1991. For some obscure reason all production A-50s except one were the fifth aircraft in their respective batches. Twenty-eight aircraft have been identified by the c/ns and about 25 were believed to be oper-

CCCP-76450, the first IL-82, in landing configuration. These views show the characteristic dorsal canoe fairing over satcom gear, the rear blade aerials, the underwing antenna pods and absence of port entry door.
Victor Drushlyakov

ational in 1992 (this figure includes the later A-50M described below). Confirmed A-50s *sans suffixe* are 10 Red, 15 Red, 20 Red (all based at Taganrog), 30 Red, 33 Red, 38 Red, 40 Red through 43 Red and 45 Red through 47 Red; aircraft coded 31 Red, 32 Red, 34 through 37 Red, 39 Red, 48 Red and 49 Red probably belong to the same version.

In a typical mission the A-50 loiters at about 10,000m (32,808ft) on a figure-eight course with 100km (54nm) between the centres of the two orbits. The surveillance radar can track targets over land and water and detect surface ships as well as aerial targets. V P Ivanov claimed the Shmel' has shorter detection range but better resistance to ground clutter than the Westinghouse AN/APY-1 fitted to the Boeing E-3A AWACS.

The colour CRT radar displays show targets marked as 'friendly', 'identity unknown' or 'hostile'; 'friendly' aircraft blips are accompanied by the aircraft's tactical code or callsign and information on speed, altitude, heading and fuel status. The *Mainstay* has a crew of fifteen: two pilots, flight engineer, navigator, radio operator and ten mission equipment operators – radar intercept officers (RIOs), ECM operators and comms officers.

The A-50 usually works with MiG-31 *Foxhound* interceptors, though the MiG-31's powerful Phazotron SBI-16 Zaslon (Shield) phased-array pulse-Doppler radar enables it to act as a 'mini-AWACS' in its own right. Target data are transmitted to the interceptors automatically via data link or by secure voice link. Transmission range to ground C³I centres is 350km (189nm) in the metre and decimetre wavebands and 2,000km (1,081nm) in the UHF range; SATCOM equipment is used over longer distances.

Pilots are quick to give nicknames to aircraft – affectionate or otherwise. The A-50 was dubbed *shestikrylyy serafim* (six-winged seraph),[32] alluding both to the numerous aerodynamic surfaces and the 'eye in the sky' role. Yet the *Mainstay* could easily have earned some disparaging nickname, and with good reason.

recognition features are the lack of the navigator's station port side window, an additional small blister fairing on each side of the lower aft fuselage near the cargo ramp and additional strap-on 96-round chaff/flare dispensers. These are of a different type than used hitherto on the IL-76MD, being much narrower.

The A-50M prototype was apparently coded 44 Red (c/n 0093486579, f/n 6505). Other confirmed examples are 50 Red and 51 Red, though 52 Red and 53 Red are probably 'Ms as well. 51 Red was in the static park at MosAeroShow '92, making the *Mainstay's* public début, and at MAKS'93. Escorted by four Su-27 *Flanker-B* fighters from the PVO combat and conversion training centre at Savostleyka AB near Nizhniy Novgorod, the same aircraft took part in the military parade in Moscow on 9th May 1995. The A-50M was code-named Mainstay-B, the original A-50 becoming the *Mainstay-A*.

As a point of interest, in July 1987 *Air International* published a drawing of the A-50 with triple vertical tails (!), wingtip ECM pods and a conventional glazed nose. However, there is no evidence that such a version ever existed. Indeed, Western magazines sometimes published total science fiction about Soviet aircraft, such as the feature in the October 1978 issue of *International Defence Review* with 'artist's impressions' of AWACS and tanker versions of the IL-86 obtained by retouching photos of the prototype (CCCP-86000).

For one thing, the mission avionics were rather troublesome at first. As a result, the equipment often had to be switched from automatic to manual mode a dozen times in a mission. Interviewed by the *Nedelya* (Week) newspaper, Maj Sergey Kholin, an A-50 RIO, said something like *'those who designed the avionics for us should have their asses kicked from here to craptown'*. Besides, getting the equipment in was a bit of a squeeze and there was no room left for a toilet and a galley (no small thing on a four-hour mission), to say nothing of room to walk around and stretch one's legs.

Ilyushin/Beriyev A-50M (A-50U?) *Mainstay-B* AWACS

Ilyushin, Beriyev and NPO Vega-M kept working on improving the *Mainstay* – primarily improving reliability and reducing avionics weight. (Soviet avionics weigh about half as much again as their Western counterparts, hence the old joke about Soviet microchips being the largest microchips in the world.) The A-50M equipped with the Shmel'-2 avionics suite was brought out in 1989; this version has also been referred to as A-50U (*oosovershenstvovannyy* – improved or upgraded). External

Top left: **The A-50's rotodome undergoing static testing at Beriyev's Taganrog facility. Note the prototype A-40 *Mermaid* ASW amphibian nearing completion in the background.** Yefim Gordon

Top right: **The *Mainstay*'s rotodome is deep enough to stand inside it even when wearing a top hat!** Sergey & Dmitriy Komissarov collection

Above left: **Close-up of the rotodome on A-50M '50 Red'. Note the excellent rotodome finish on this example.** Yefim Gordon

Above right: **Close-up of the *Mainstay*'s extensively modified nose. The bronze colour of the glazing is due to gold plating to protect the crew against radiation.** Yefim Gordon

Above: **Close-up of the A-50's tail radome and rear lateral ECM blisters.** Dmitriy Komissarov

Right: **A-50s *sans suffixe* have navigator's station windows on both sides, as illustrated by this aircraft coded 10 Red in Taganrog. Note the ladder propped against the rotodome for maintenance.** Yefim Gordon

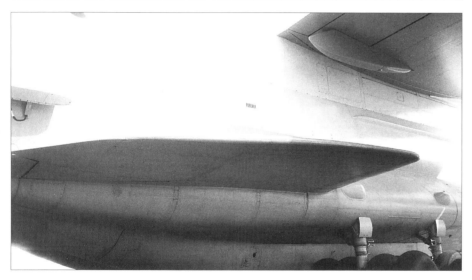

Ilyushin/Beriyev/Israel Aircraft Industries A-50I ('aircraft AI') AWACS

In 1994 the Chinese People's Liberation Army Air Force (PLAAF) started negotiations with Russia and Western avionics manufacturers on the conversion of the *Candid* into an AWACS platform. GEC-Marconi (UK) offered the Argus 2000 mechanically-scanned AEW radar system fitted earlier to the unsuccessful British Aerospace Nimrod AEW Mk.1, but lost out to Elta Electronics, a division of Israel Aircraft Industries (IAI) which offered a more sophisticated mission avionics suite built around the EL2075 Phalcon phased-array radar. Interestingly, China was adamant that it would only buy the Phalcon system if it was installed on the IL-76.

Originally the radar arrays were to be housed in the nose, the tailcone and on the forward fuselage sides in similar fashion to IAI's Boeing 707-320 AWACS equipped with the Phalcon radar (as delivered to the Chilean Air Force). However, this was soon abandoned in favour of a conventionally mounted rotodome. The resulting combination is known as A-501 or *samolyot AI* (aircraft AI), the I standing for *izrail'skoye [oboroodovaniye]* – Israeli equipment.

It took a lot of persuasion before the Russian government gave the go-ahead for the A-50 to be exported. Some sources suggest the Russian government was reluctant to allow a *Mainstay* to be sold to IAI for conversion because it had hoped to sell the A-50 to China in an 'as was' condition.

Outwardly the A-50I differs from the basic *Mainstay* it a number of respects. The rotodome is slightly larger in diameter and the pylons are of constant chord (ie, do not taper towards the top). Also, the rotodome has a much wider metal centre portion and **three** dielectric portions instead of two; this suggests that the 'rotodome' is in fact **fixed** and the radar beam is scanned electronically. An official Beriyev display model unveiled in January 2000 shows that the metal centre portion is an equilateral triangle with cropped apexes (ie, there are three antenna arrays, each covering a 120° sector). The model also shows non-standard extended and rounded wingtips probably housing ESM antennas.

A-50 '41 Red' paid a surprise visit to Kubinka on 22nd March 1998 and is shown here landing past a line of tired old An-12BP *Cubs* resident at the base. Yefim Gordon

Ground crews watch as 47 Red is pushed into position by a KrAZ-255B 6x6 truck. A TZ-22 fuel bowser (KrAZ-258 tractor and semitrailer) stands ready to top up the aircraft for the next mission. Yefim Gordon

The horizontal strakes offsetting the destabilising effect of the rotodome are another trademark feature of the A-50. Dmitriy Komissarov

A-50 '42 Red' cruises over thick overcast. Sergey Skrynnikov

44 Red displays the main recognition features of the A-50M – the additional antenna blisters and strap-on chaff/flare dispensers on the aft fuselage. Yefim Gordon

A-50M '50 Red' languishes in Taganrog with the rotodome removed in company with an A-40 Albatross and a Tu-142MZ *Bear-F Mod*. This view illustrates the sheer size of the *Mainstay*'s 'saucer'. Yefim Gordon

The triangular horizontal strakes characteristic of the standard A-50 have been deleted. Instead, the A-50I has twin splayed trapezoidal ventral fins in the manner of the Iraqi Adnan-1 and -2 conversions (see below); however, these are rather shorter and deeper and have rounded corners. The large cooling air intake at the base of the fin, another trademark feature of the standard *Mainstay*, is also omitted, as are the dielectric panel immediately below the rudder and the large ECM blisters on the forward and aft fuselage sides. On the other hand, the A-50I has an unswept blade aerial atop the fin about level with the stabilizer leading edge (which Russian Air Force aircraft do not have) and a single unswept blade aerial immediately ahead of the dorsal SATCOM fairing has been replaced with two small swept aerials.

The basic A-50's refuelling probe has been retained. The PLAAF has converted a small number of H-6 (licence-built Tu-16 *Badger-A*) bombers to single-point hose-and-drogue tankers, the local equivalent of the Tu-16N, and these were to be used to support the operations of the A-50I.

Wearing a standard *Mainstay* grey/white colour scheme and the test and delivery registration RA-78740 (!), the A-50I prototype (ex-Russian Air Force '44 Red', c/n 0093486579, f/n 6505) was delivered to Tel Aviv (Ben Gurion airport) for conversion on 25th October 1999 after several months of delays. The cost of outfitting a single aircraft to A-50I standard (not counting the aircraft itself) was estimated at US$ 250 million. In July 2000, however, the programme was cancelled because the US government pressured Israel into doing so, threatening to withdraw US$ 20 billion worth of military aid. This was because the USA regarded A-50I as a threat to their ally, Taiwan, which Beijing purportedly still aims to recapture by force.

Ilyushin/Beriyev A-50E *Mainstay* AWACS
This is the export version of the A-50 (E = *eksportnyy*) probably differing from the standard *Mainstay* in avionics fit. China is the 'launch customer' following the demise of the A-50I programme.

'Aircraft 676', 'Aircraft 776' development aircraft; 'Aircraft 976' (SKIP, IL-76SK) *Mainstay-C* radar picket aircraft
Monitoring and recording systems operation during test launches of ballistic and cruise missiles is something of a problem, since conventional data recorders are highly unlikely to be

The aft fuselage of A-50M '51 Red' (c/n 1003488634) displayed at MosAeroShow'92, showing the cooling air intake at the base of the fin and the chaff/flare dispensers. Dmitriy Komissarov

The A-50M can be identified, among other things, by the lack of the port side navigator's station window. Yefim Gordon

'Aircraft 676' CCCP-86721 in early configuration with pitot booms on nose, white tail radome, lateral ECM blisters and standard navigator's glazing. The radome of the ground mapping radar is removed for maintenance; note pylons under wings. Just visible beyond is 'aircraft 776' CCCP-86024; note single aerials immediately below flag on fin on both aircraft. Yefim Gordon archive

The almost identical 'aircraft 776', CCCP-86024, comes in to land at LII. The different designation suggests the two aircraft differed considerably in equipment fit. Victor Drushlyakov

CCCP-76453, the second 'aircraft 976', at a display for aviation experts dedicated to LII's 50th anniversary in March 1991. Yefim Gordon

were converted into almost identical telemetry pickup aircraft known as 'aircraft 676' and 'aircraft 776' respectively. These shared some of the equipment with the IL-18SIP and IL-20RT, including the rear antenna in a characteristic thimble radome (supplanting the tail turret on the *Candids*). An L-shaped aerial was mounted on each side of the fin; this caused the Soviet flag to be painted unusually high on the fin. Four long probes were fitted around the navigator's station, and two large strake aerials were mounted aft of the nose gear *à la* A-50. The ECM suite was originally retained. Later CCCP-86721 had the probes removed and the navigator's glazing partly faired over; also, the tail radome, originally white on both aircraft, later became dark grey on 'aircraft 676'.[33]

Operational experience with 'aircraft 676' and 'aircraft 776' led to the development of a specialised radar picket version of the IL-76MD designated 'aircraft 976' or SKIP (*samolyotnyy komahndno-izmereetel'nyy poonkt* – airborne measuring and control station, AMCS). Development was completed in the mid-80s; the aircraft was developed jointly with the Beriyev OKB and hence has been erroneously referred to in the West as 'Be-976' (some sources call it Myasischchev-976'). The unusual designation is probably derived from the aircraft's product code which could be *izdeliye* 976.

'Aircraft 976' is superficially similar to the A-50 AWACS, featuring an identical rotodome – which, incidentally, has earned it the nickname *Pogahnka* (Toadstool) at LII. Like the A-50, it has satellite communications and data link antennas in a large dielectric fairing ahead of the wings and two strake aerials aft of the nose gear.

But here the similarity ends. The AMCS retains the standard navigator's glazing, the tail gunner's station (used as an equipment operator's station), the cargo doors and both entry doors. The main gear fairings and APU location are likewise unchanged from the IL-76MD, and the A-50's characteristic horizontal strakes have been omitted. This is probably because the equipment installed in the freight hold and rotodome is different; hence the weight distribution is also different and the rotodome does not have such a drastic effect on longitudinal stability.

retrieved intact when the missile drops – or blows up in mid-air. As one Russian author put it, the wreckage can then tell no more about the cause of the accident than the ashes of a burnt book can tell about its contents. The only reliable method is to transmit systems data by means of telemetry which is picked up by ground measuring stations or specially equipped aircraft.

For years LII had used the IL-18SIP (*samolyotnyy izmereetel'nyy poonkt* – airborne measuring station) with the non-standard registration CCCP-27220. This aircraft, a converted IL-18A (ex-CCCP-75647, c/n 188000401) with its characteristic huge dorsal canoe fairing and 'thimble' tail radome over data link antennas, was the prototype of the IL-20RT space tracker/telemetry and communications relay aircraft, four of which (CCCP-75480 through CCCP-75483) were used in the Soviet space programme. However, in due course the IL-18SIP had to be retired, forcing LII to find a replacement.

First, two *Candid-Bs* – IL-76 *sans suffixe* CCCP-86721 (c/n 073410271, f/n 0708) and IL-76M CCCP-86024 (c/n 083414425, f/n 1107) –

The tail turret is replaced by a hemispherical radome which is more bulbous than the rear fairing of demilitarised *Candid-Bs*, and the gun ranging radar is deleted. Two massive cylindrical equipment pods similar to those of the IL-76PP are carried on the wingtips. Their front and rear portions are dielectric, enclosing flat-plate antennas.

As on 'aircraft 676' and 'aircraft 776', four long probes are located around the navigator's station. The fin has three L-shaped aerials on each side instead of one. Four L-shaped aerials of a different type are mounted ahead of the flight deck glazing, the inner ones facing forward and the outer ones aft; several blade aerials are fitted under the main gear fairings. The freight hold is crammed with data processing and storage equipment which appears to be modular, allowing the aircraft to be reconfigured for specific missions (part of it is mounted on the cargo ramp on some aircraft).

Five new IL-76MDs built in 1986-87 were converted to 'aircraft 976' standard. Despite their near-military role they wore Aeroflot colours and were registered CCCP-76452 (c/n 0063465965, f/n 5002), CCCP-76453 (c/n 0063466995, f/n 5009), CCCP-76454 (c/n 0063469074, f/n 5209), CCCP-76455 (c/n 0063471125, f/n 5402) and CCCP-76456 (c/n 0073474208, f/n 5602); three out of five aircraft still have the old Soviet prefix and flag as of this writing. The only deviation from the standard Aeroflot colour scheme is that the nose titles read '976' instead of 'IL-76MD' and the flag is carried higher on the tail than usual.

The aircraft differ in detail. For example, at least two aircraft (CCCP-76452 and -76453) have an orange-painted cylindrical fairing of unknown purpose (looking like something unprintable) protruding downwards immediately ahead of the cargo ramp. CCCP-76452 also has L-shaped aerials mounted above and below the wingtip pods.

The AMCS is used to monitor the trajectories and systems status of manned and unmanned aerial and space vehicles in real time. UAVs can be remote-controlled; a self-destruct command can be transmitted if an experimental missile goes haywire and heads where it should not. Telemetry data is processed, taped and transmitted in real time to build ground control and telemetry processing centres by radio or satellite link, thus obviating the need to build additional facilities in remote areas. Tracking range is 1,000km (540nm) and trajectories are measured with an accuracy of 30m (98ft). The six telemetry channels have a data transfer rate of 2 million baud (2 Mb per second). Endurance is 8 hours.

The existence of 'aircraft 976' was revealed on 16th August 1988 during the Aviation Day flypast in Zhukovskiy. Spectators sitting on vantage points near LII's perimeter fence could see all five aircraft parked in a neat row at the end of the old runway where it joined the active 5,000m (16,404ft) runway. The A-50, as already mentioned, had been sighted in late 1987, and of course Western journalists believed the 'toadstools' to be prototypes of the A-50 (what else could they think?); it was some time before the matter was clarified. Nevertheless, 'aircraft 976' now has the reporting name *Mainstay-C*!

Of course the Powers That Be were aware that there was no point in concealing the existence of the AMCS any longer. Hence LII's display stand at the Moscow Aerospace '90 trade fair held at the VDNKh exhibition centre in October 1990 featured a photo of 'aircraft 976'. On 23rd May 1991 the *Soviet Weekly* gazette ran a story about LII titled *Secret Centre of Excellence* and featuring, among other things, a photo of CCCP-76453. The caption read *The Ilyushin-76 flying laboratory, used to study the chemical composition of the atmosphere*. This was nonsense, of course, as the rotodome obviously had nothing to do with 'studying the chemical composition of the atmosphere'!

A year later the same aircraft was in the static display at MosAeroShow '92 – this time with a tablet truthfully saying 'airborne measuring and control station' but containing no data whatever. CCCP-76456 was displayed next year at MAKS-93 and for the first time visitors were allowed inside the thing but, understandably enough, photography was out of the question. RA-76453 was present again at MAKS-95 (so far it is the only 'aircraft 976' to have the Russian prefix and the LII logo), and CCCP-76452 was on display at MAKS-97.

The MAKS-99 airshow featured *two* examples: 76455 was in the static park (the aircraft sported the Russian flag but no prefix), while RA-76453 served as a backdrop for a rock concert held on an improvised stage. This sheer lunacy was prompted by the organizers' burning desire to make more money (can you imagine a rock concert at Farnborough or Le Bourget?). As a result, some gentlemen – strong in the arm but weak in the head – badly bent two of the four nose probes (after having had too many beers, no doubt). The cost of repairing the aircraft probably wiped out the profit from that concert!

Curiously, a model of RA-76453 displayed at MAKS-95 showed 'IL-76SK' (*spetseeahl'nyy komahndnyy* [*samolyot*] – special command aircraft) nose titles. This is a proposed development of 'aircraft 976' to be used for monitoring launches of the Burlak suborbital launcher carried by the the Tu-160SK; there are reasons to believe the IL-76SK differs in equipment fit from the other 'toadstools'. The same model was also displayed at Farnborough International '96.

'Aircraft 976' are known to have been used in the Tu-160's trials programme, monitoring test launches of RKV-500 (Kh-55M)/AS-15 *Kent* cruise missiles. LII claims the AMCS may also be used for ecological monitoring 'and other purposes' (*sic*).

Izdeliye 1076

There have been reports of an unidentified special mission version of the IL-76 designated *izdeliye* 1076. No information is available except that the prototype is c/n 1033410351 (f/n 8408).

The IL-76 has been extensively used for testing new equipment, civil as well as military. Of course it cannot beat such testbed workhorses as the IL-18 or An-12 in terms of numbers. Still, the the *Candid*'s high performance and spacious freight hold which can accommodate lots of bulky and heavy test equipment (and is pressurized – a major advantage over the An-12!) make it eminently suitable for the testbed role.

CCCP-76453 on final approach to Zhukovskiy.
Victor Drushlyakov

IL-76LL engine testbed

The IL-76LL engine testbed is perhaps the best-known of the R&D *Candids* – probably because it was used to test mainly 'civilian' engines and thus could be demonstrated publicly without causing a security breach. The suffix means *letayuschchaya laboratoriya* – lit. 'flying laboratory'. This Russian term is used indiscriminately and can denote any kind of testbed (avionics, engine, equipment, weapons etc), an aerodynamics research aircraft or control configured vehicle (CCV), a weather research aircraft, a geophysical survey aircraft etc. In the case of the IL-76, however, the LL suffix applies only to the engine testbed.

Development of the IL-76LL began in the late 1970s when LII was faced with the need to test new powerful jet and turboprop engines. Previously converted bombers (eg, Tu-4LL, Tu-16LL and Tu-142LL)[34] had filled this role, but they had a major deficiency, namely limited space for test equipment. By then real-time on-board processing of test data had become a priority task. This meant the aircraft had to carry a crew of test engineers which could decide if a particular test mode needed to be repeated, and there was simply no room for them in a bomber.

The experimental engine is fitted on a special pylon instead of the No 2 (port inboard) D-30KP. The pylon has special fittings enabling different engines to be installed quickly; hence the aircraft has also been referred to as ULL-76 or ULL-76-02 (*ooniversahl'naya letayuschchaya laboratoriya* – multi-purpose testbed). The main shortcoming of this installation is that the experimental engine can create a thrust asymmetry which has to be countered by differential thrust of the other engines and/or control input.

The IL-76LL can be used to test engines rated at up to 25,000kgp (55,114 lbst) and having a nacelle diameter up to 3.56m (11ft 8in). Since the experimental engine can be both heavier and more powerful than the D-30KP, the wing centre section and No 2 pylon attachment points have been reinforced.

The freight hold houses five test engineer workstations and two equipment modules for recording and monitoring engine parameters. The modules can be changed to suit the mission; part of the equipment (eg, video recorders) is of Western origin. Test equipment heat exchangers, a characteristic feature of the IL-76LL, are installed on the fuselage sides immediately aft of the wings; their quantity differs on different examples. The electric system has been modified to supply 208 V/115 V/36 V (400 Hz) AC, 220 V/127 V (50 Hz) AC and 27 V/6 V DC for the test equipment.

Five *Candids* were converted to IL-76LLs.[35] The first of these was the first prototype, CCCP-86712 (c/n 0101), which ended its days as a testbed for the Kuznetsov NK-86 turbofan – curiously, minus thrust reverser. Tests began in 1975. By then CCCP-86712 had reached the limit of its useful life and the aircraft was scrapped once the trials programme had been completed in the late 1970s.

The second aircraft, IL-76M 'Falsie' CCCP-86891 (c/n 093421628, f/n 1607A),[36] was used to test the 23,400kgp (51,587 lbst) Lotarev (ZMKB)[37] D-18T high-bypass turbofan. This engine developed for the An-124 heavy trans-port had nearly twice the diameter of the D-30KP. One test equipment heat exchanger was fitted to port and two to starboard. A small cigar-shaped fairing of unknown purpose was mounted on a short pylon above the flight deck.

Tests began in 1982 and the engine logged 1,285 hours in 418 test flights. Black and white stripes were applied to the intake de-icer for icing visualization and a video camera was fitted in place of the wing/air intake inspection light at a late stage of the trials. Reregistered RA-86891, the aircraft was in the static park at the MAKS-95 airshow.

The Kuznetsov NK-93 contra-rotating integrated shrouded propfan (CRISP) rated at 18,000kgp (39,682 lbst) was the next candidate for testing aboard CCCP-86891. The engine, which had eight scimitar-shaped blades on the front row and ten on the rear row, was envisaged for several projects, all of which remain 'paper airplanes' – the IL-90-200 long-haul widebody airliner (a twin-engined spinoff of the

The forward fuselage of 'aircraft 976'. This view shows well the characteristic probes on the forward fuselage. Dmitriy Komissarov

The wingtip antenna pods of 'aircraft 976' differ considerably from those of the IL-76PP. Dmitriy Komissarov

The tail radome of 'aircraft 976' is shorter than that of the '676' and '776' testbeds. Note the unequally spaced fin aerials. Dmitriy Komissarov

The purpose of this, er, *curious-looking* fairing on 'aircraft 976' is unknown. Dmitriy Komissarov

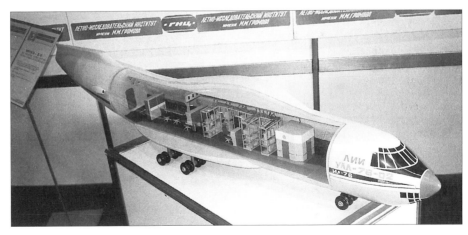

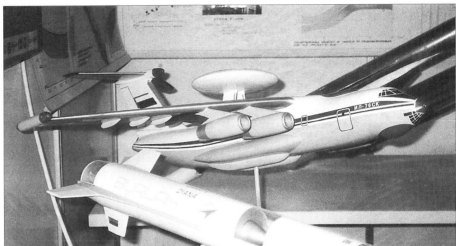

IL-96-300), the IL-106 heavy transport, the Myasischchev MGS-6[38] Gherakl (Hercules) *horrendously* heavy transport and the Tu-214 (the first aircraft to have this designation).[39]

Five prototype engines had been completed by 1995 but the trials were postponed indefinitely because the Kuznetsov OKB[40] could not afford to pay for them. Meanwhile, RA-86891 was retired and was being broken up at LII in August 1999.

As for the D-18T, ZMKB has developed growth versions intended for the An-218 wide-body airliner – the 25,000kgp D-18TM and the 27,500kgp (60,626 lbst) D-18TP/TR. However, these are too large for the IL-76LL and will have to be tested on a suitably modified An-124.

The third IL-76LL (sometimes called IL-76LL3) is an IL-76MD 'Falsie' registered CCCP-76492 (c/n 0043452549, f/n 3908) – the first aircraft to have this registration.[41] It was used to test the Solov'yov D-90 (PS-90A) turbofan and has two heat exchangers on each side (a late addition). Testing began on 26th December 1986 and the prototype engine logged about 400 hours in 188 flights. It transpired that cruise SFC was better than anticipated but the engine was delivering less power than it should. This was proved by the Tu-204's poor single-engine performance and led the Solov'yov OKB to uprate the PS-90A, whereupon reliability problems began.

Other versions of the PS-90 family were developed in the early 1990s, including the PS-90P (a joint effort with Pratt & Whitney, MTU and MAN) and the derated 12,000kgp (26,455 lbst) PS-90A-12 for the Yakovlev Yak-242 airliner project. These would probably have been tested on the same IL-76LL but the collapse of the Soviet Union and ensuing economic problems meant trials had to be put on hold. CCCP-76492 was on display at MosAeroShow '92 and visitors were even allowed inside the aircraft. Currently CCCP-76492 is withdrawn from use at LII.

The fourth and perhaps best-known example (IL-76LL4) is a demilitarised IL-76 *sans suffixe*, CCCP-76529 (ex-YI-AIP, c/n 073410308, f/n 0807). Initially this aircraft was fitted with the first Soviet propfan engine – the 10,900eshp (8,128kW) Lotarev D-236T driving SV-36 contraprops developed by the Stoopino Machinery Design Bureau. The engine was a derivative of the D-136 turboshaft powering the Mi-26 *Halo*

Close-up of the heat exchanger pods on IL-76LL CCCP-76492; the heat exchangers proper have been removed as the aircraft is non-operational. Yefim Gordon

The very first *Candid*, CCCP-86712, following conversion as the first IL-76LL engine testbed with the NK-86 turbofan. Note scuffed black markings on wing and tailplane leading edges for de-icing system tests, relocated landing lights and calibration markings on aft fuselage. Yefim Gordon archive

IL-76M 'Falsie' CCCP-86891, the second IL-76LL, on short finals to Zhukovskiy. Yefim Gordon archive

This view of CCCP-86891 emphasises how much bigger the experimental D-18T turbofan is than the standard D-30KPs. Victor Drushlyakov

IL-76LL RA-86891 (note Russian flag on tail) sits on a rain-lashed hardstand, which is really LII's old runway, prior to the opening of the MAKS-95 airshow. Yefim Gordon

heavy transport helicopter. This in turn was based on the core of the 6,500kgp (14,330 lbst) D-36 turbofan powering the An-72/An-74 *Coaler* STOL transport and Yak-42 *Clobber* short/medium-haul airliner.

Propfan airliner projects, which were plenty in the late 1980s, invariably had the engines in pusher configuration. The D-236T, however, had tractor propellers, being intended for the An-70 transport developed since the early 1980s as an An-12 replacement, and thus could be readily installed on the IL-76LL. The SV-36 had glassfibre blades with a hollow composite spar and integrated electric de-icing threads. The front and rear rows had eight and six blades respectively, running at 1,100 and 1,000rpm respectively; the 100rpm difference was intended to reduce noise and vibration.

Tests began in 1987. A model of the IL-76LL with the D-236T propfan and the non-existent registration CCCP-86786 (?!) was displayed at the Le Bourget airshow in June 1989. In August of the following year the real aircraft showed up at the ILA'90 airshow in Hannover, creating a veritable sensation. It was immediately apparent that the abovementioned model had been inaccurate: the SV-36 had straight blades with slightly raked tips, not scimitar-shaped blades. CCCP-76529 took part in the flying display and the engine demonstrated remarkably low noise levels, both on the ground and in flight, thanks to the low propeller speed.

As originally flown the propeller blades were grey with red and yellow calibration markings on the front row, and a vibration sensor cable was stretched between the propeller hub and the fuselage. By the time of the aircraft's Hannover appearance the cable had been removed and two test equipment heat exchanges installed on each side of the fuselage. The propeller blades were painted bright blue with yellow tips; black stripes were applied to the engine pylon and wing leading edge for icing visualization, and large orange Cyrillic 'LII' titles added to the forward fuselage.

Because of the straight blades, the fairly large propeller diameter (4.2 m/13ft 9in) and

tractor configuration Western observers were wont to regard the D-236T as an 'advanced turboprop' rather than a pure propfan. In contrast, experimental US propfan engines (General Electric GE36 and Allison Model 378-DX) had pusher propellers of 3 to 3.5m (9ft 10in to 11ft 6in) diameter with sharply curved blades.

This was probably because Western propfan airliner projects (Boeing 7J7 etc) had a T-tail, rear-engine layout with the engines mounted as close to the fuselage as possible to reduce thrust asymmetry in the event of an engine failure. This inevitably resulted in small-diameter props which had to turn at high speed to generate adequate thrust. At 1,300rpm the blade tips reached almost supersonic speeds, producing a deafening noise, which of course was totally unacceptable; hence scimitar-shaped blades were used to cure the problem.

(Incidentally, the model had misled Western observers in more ways than one. Several reference books, including *JP Airline-Fleets International*, list the non-existent IL-76LL CCCP-86786 with an Izotov TV7-117 turboprop!)

The D-236T logged 70 hours in 36 flights on the IL-76LL. Further trials were made on the Yak-42LL[42] CCCP-42525 (c/n 11030703) which had the propfan installed on a long pylon in place of the No 3 engine – again in tractor configuration. Meanwhile, however, the An-70's MTOW had increased from 93,100kg (205,247 lb) to 112,000kg (246,800 lb). The Antonov OKB apparently considered the D-236T too small and by 1990 the project was altered to feature 14,000eshp (10,290kW) Muravchenko (ZMKB) D-27 propfans driving Stoopino SV-27 contraprops of 4.49m (14ft 9in) diameter.

In late 1990 a prototype D-27 engine was fitted to IL-76LL CCCP-76529. Outwardly the engine installation was very similar to the D-236T, except that the blades were scimitar-shaped. The engine nacelle was somewhat more streamlined and the oil cooler was recontoured (the result was vaguely reminiscent of the 'Andy Gump' nacelles of the Boeing B-50). Again a vibration sensor cable was fitted to the propeller hub, and a video camera was added aft of the port side heat exchangers to monitor engine operation.

In this guise CCCP-76529 was displayed statically at the MAKS-93 airshow. During the next year it participated in the FI'94 and ILA'94 shows, appropriately reregistered as RA-76529; the sensor cable was removed and a normal spinner installed for the occasion. Meanwhile, the first prototype An-70 was rolled out at Kiev-Svyatoshino on 20th January 1994 and entered flight test on 16th December of the same year, becoming the world's first aircraft to fly solely on propfan power. RA-76529 was on show again at MAKS-97.

Finally, the fifth aircraft (IL-76LL5) is a demilitarised IL-76T 'Falsie' with the non-standard registration CCCP-06188 (ex-IL-76M YI-AKQ, c/n 093421635, f/n 1609). This aircraft was

The D-18T during installation in LII's hangar. Yefim Gordon archive

The streamlined antenna pod atop the forward fuselage of RA-86891. Dmitriy Komissarov

Test equipment in the freight hold of IL-76LL RA-86891. Dmitriy Komissarov

The third IL-76LL (IL-76MD 'Falsie' CCCP-76492) with a PS-90A turbofan at MosAeroShow'92. Dmitriy Komissarov

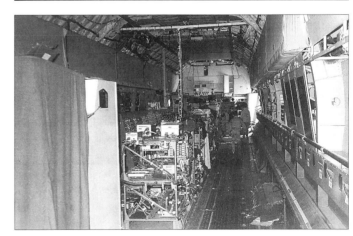

Left: **The D-27/SV-27 propfan installation on IL-76LL RA-76529 at MAKS-97. Note vibration sensor cable and video camera aft of the twin heat exchangers.**
Dmitriy Komissarov

Top: **CCCP-76529, the fourth IL-76LL, in its second configuration with Lotarev D-27 propfan. The SV-27 contraprops appear to be feathered.**
Victor Drushlyakov

Above: **IL-76LL RA-76529 caught on landing. The D-27 propfan has a conventional pointed spinner and the vibration sensor cable has been removed.** Yefim Gordon

used to test the Izotov (Klimov) TV7-117A turboprop driving an SV-34 six-bladed propeller. The engine was developed for the IL-114 feederliner and originally rated at 2,350eshp (1,760kW).[43] It was also selected for a number of transport aircraft projects, including the IL-112, Mikoyan MiG-101M, MiG-110, MiG SVB and the Sukhoi S-80.[44] The original plan was to test the TV7-117A on a modified IL-18, but this was rejected in favour of the *Candid*.

The aircraft has two heat exchangers to port and one to starboard. Unlike all other IL-76LLs, CCCP-06188 retains the standard No 2 engine pylon (the development engine is attached by means of an adapter). The nacelle of the turboprop has an unusual banana-like shape and numerous small cooling air intakes, most of which have been omitted on the IL-114. Once again the propeller was rigged with a vibration sensor cable and had red and yellow calibration markings on the blades.

CCCP-06188 was the first IL-76LL to be demonstrated publicly, taking part in the Aviation Day flypast in Zhukovskiy on 16th August 1990. It also made a single demonstration flight at MosAeroShow '92 (on 12th August, one of the press days).

The basic idea behind many-bladed props is that lower propeller speed is needed to produce the required thrust, thereby reducing noise. Sure enough, the IL-114 is an extremely quiet aircraft – in flight. Contrary to all logic, however, the TV7-117A produced an almighty roar at ground idling rpm, earning the IL-114 the disparaging nickname of *lesopilka* (sawmill). When IL-76LL CCCP-06188 lined up for take-off at MosAeroShow '92 the unmistakable turboprop sound could be heard even through the whine of the three D-30KP turbofans.

Obviously the engineers were unhappy about it, and apparently changes were made to the propellers or to the engine control software (the IL-114 has FADEC). Anyway, production IL-114s are somewhat quieter on the ground than the three prototypes (CCCP-54000, CCCP-54001 and RA-54002). Still, the Ilyushin engineers are not satisfied and the OKB plans to equip the aircraft with the new Stoopino AV-140 six-bladed props specially developed for the An-140 feederliner. Starting in 1989, the TV7-117A logged 210 hours in 70 flights on the IL-76LL. By 1995 CCCP-06188 was withdrawn from use and still sits at LII minus the propeller and Nos 1 and 3 engines.

IL-76MD 'Falsie' navigation system testbed/geophysical survey aircraft

Candids converted into avionics testbeds are less widely known, since these aircraft were mostly used to test military equipment and hence based at airfields which are off limits to nosey spotters.

In December 1987 the Moscow-based Fine Instruments Research Institute (NIITP – *Naoochno-issledovatel'skiy institoot tochnykh preeborov*) took delivery of a brand-new IL-76MD 'Falsie', CCCP-76753 (c/n 0073481461,

f/n 6206), which was immediately converted into a navigation systems testbed. The aircraft is equipped with an IK-VR centimetre-waveband synthetic-aperture side-looking airborne radar (SLAR); the designation is probably deciphered as *izmeritel'nyy **kompleks** vysokovo razresheniya* – high-resolution measurement complex. The SLAR antennas are located on both sides of the fuselage ahead of the main gear fairings in flattened semi-cylindrical fairings which hinge open fully for maintenance.

Apart from navigation systems testing the aircraft can also be used for geophysical and ecological survey. To this end it is equipped with Malakhit (Malachite), Poisk (Search) and NP-50 infra-red scanners; their sensors are located in square flat projections atop the wing centre section fairing and under the forward fuselage just aft of the emergency exits. An unswept blade aerial is added just aft of the flight deck. The conversion job took the better part of a year and the first post-conversion flight took place on 4th October 1988.

The test equipment is located in a compact cubicle in the forward part of the freight hold, leaving the rest of the hold free, so that the aircraft can carry cargo and generate revenue as well! Reregistered RA-76753, the aircraft was in the static park at the MAKS-95 airshow at Zhukovskiy which is its home base.

IL-76-11 ELINT testbed

NPO Vzlyot (Takeoff), another Moscow-based avionics producer, converted IL-76T 'Falsie' RA-76490 (ex-CCCP-76490, ex-YI-AKO, c/n 093416506, f/n 1307) into an electronic intelligence equipment testbed designated IL-76-11.

The ELINT antennas were housed in a large semi-cylindrical fairing on the starboard side only which blended smoothly into the main gear fairing. The antenna fairing was unpainted and thus plainly visible; it had a cut-off front end to clear the entry door and incorporated three dielectric panels of different size.

The aircraft was first seen at LII in this configuration during MAKS-93. By August 1995 it had been withdrawn from use, sitting engineless at LII. By August 1999 RA-76490 had been reconverted to standard configuration and returned to service with Elf Air, the flying division of NPO Vzlyot.

IL-76MD/IL-76T 'Falsie' SATCOM testbeds

Two *Candid-B*s – IL-76MD CCCP-76790 (c/n 0093496903, f/n 7306) and an unidentified IL-76T 'Falsie' – were converted into satellite communications and data link equipment testbeds for the A-50 AWACS. Both aircraft had a large dielectric fairing over SATCOM antennas ahead of the wing centre section; CCCP-76790 was demilitarised. In 1992 both aircraft were sold to the Yekaterinburg-based airline SPAir; the experimental avionics had been removed by then but the dielectric fairing remained.

Ilyushin/Beriyev A-60 airborne laser laboratory ('IL-76 version 1A')

When President Ronald Reagan announced the Strategic Defense Initiative (SDI) supposed to protect the US from Soviet ICBMs, US weapons makers set to work inventing new weapons systems, including laser weapons. Perhaps it was the laser bit that caused the SDI to be nicknamed Star Wars.

One highly unusual aircraft used in the Star Wars programme was the Boeing NKC-135ALL (Airborne Laser Laboratory) 55-3123 (c/n

Top: **An air-to-air study of IL-76LL CCCP-06188.**
Yefim Gordon

Right: **The unusual shape of the TV7-117A's nacelle is readily apparent in this view.**
Yefim Gordon archive

17239). Photos of this aircraft with its characteristic dorsal canoe fairing and laser turret were sometimes used by the Soviet press for propaganda purposes (to illustrate articles exposing the 'bloody-minded Yankee militarists preparing to unleash war in space'). However, these articles did *not* relate that the Soviet Union had a similar aircraft up its sleeve.

A photograph of the prototype Kamov Ka-32 *Helix* helicopter (CCCP-31000) made by the TASS news agency in Zhukovskiy showed two of the four IL-80 airborne command posts in the background. Having got hold of this photo in June 1991, *Flight International* perceived the apparent similarity of the *Maxdome*'s SATCOM fairing with the NKC-135ALL's superstructure and raised a ballyhoo, claiming a 'Soviet laser experiment revealed'! Of course these aircraft had nothing to do with lasers; in reality the

Soviet laser testbed was a converted IL-76M 'Falsie', CCCP-86879 (c/n 0013430893, f/n 2304).

The aircraft was modified extensively enough to warrant a separate designation, A-60 – indicating the Beriyev OKB had a hand in the matter; another reported designation was 'IL-76 version 1A'. The appearance of the A-60 could easily be described as hair-raising. The weather radar was replaced by a big bulbous fairing reminiscent of the C-135N Apollo Range Instrumentation Aircraft, if rather smaller. This probably housed a target acquisition/tracking antenna dish turning every which way.

The extensive navigator's glazing was almost entirely faired over, leaving only two small windows each side; the result was a vicious scowl instead of the *Candid*'s familiar big grin. Two gas turbine power units identical

to those of the IL-76PP flanked the forward fuselage, resulting in the same structural changes (deletion of the forward emergency exits, relocation of the APU etc.)

The laser gun was installed in a retractable dorsal turret aft of the wings. The cutout was closed by inward-retracting doors made up of several sections. To compensate for this the cargo doors were removed and faired over to add structural stiffness to the rear fuselage; the cargo ramp remained but was non-functional.

Trials began in 1983. Unfortunately no more details are known, as the A-60 was one of the Soviet Union's 'blackest' programmes. Eventually, however, both Russia and the USA abandoned their 'Star Wars' research efforts. The A-60 programme was scrapped; the aircraft is said to have been written off at Chkalovskaya AB after a ground fire.

In the mid-90s, however, the US programme was revived when the Boeing company started work on an airborne laser platform derivative of the Boeing 747-400F freighter. This has now become a fully-fledged weapons system designated AL-1 (for Attack Laser). Serialled 00-0001, a Boeing 747-4G4F (c/n 30201, f/n 1238) was delivered to Boeing Military Aircraft company on 21st January 2000 for conversion as the YAL-1A prototype; it is due to begin tests in 2002 and the USAF has a requirement for seven AL-1As. That said, Russia may answer in kind and develop a new 'flying laser' – possibly based on the IL-76MF.

Left: **IL-76T 'Falsie' CCCP-06188, the final IL-76LL, takes off on 12th August 1992 during MosAeroShow '92. A video camera aimed at the experimental turboprop is just visible aft of the No1 engine.** Yefim Gordon

Left: **IL-76MD 'Falsie' RA-76753 used by the Fine Instruments Research Institute (NIITP) as a testbed for the IK-VR synthetic aperture SLAR and as a geophysical survey aircraft.** Dmitriy Komissarov

Below left: **Close-up of the SLAR fairing on RA-76753.** Dmitriy Komissarov

Below right: **The fairing opens upward for maintenance, revealing the twin antenna array of the IK-VR SLAR.** Dmitriy Komissarov

IL-76MD refuelling tanker

The Iraqi Air Force developed several versions of the IL-76 on its own account. In 1988 one 'true' IL-76MD was converted into a single-point refuelling tanker for the IrAF's Dassault Mirage F1EQ-200 fighter-bombers, as well as Mikoyan MiG-27 *Flogger-D* attack aircraft and Sukhoi Su-22M4 *Fitter-K* fighter-bombers retrofitted locally with Mirage F1 fixed refuelling probes. Unlike the IL-78, the refuelling pod – probably a Douglas D-704 'buddy' refuelling pack, a number of which had been supplied for the Mirages – was carried on the centreline on a pylon fitted to the cargo ramp (!). This obviously required extreme caution on take-off and landing so as to avoid making contact with the runway. The aircraft wore a grey/white air force colour scheme but no IrAF insignia or civil registration.

Baghdad-1 AWACS

Also in 1988 an unidentified IL-76MD 'Falsie' (probably in the YI-AN* registration block) was converted into an AWACS aircraft named *Baghdad-1*. A Thomson-CSF Tigre surveillance radar manufactured locally under French licence was installed under the aft fuselage in a huge GRP fairing supplanting the cargo doors; the cargo ramp remained but was inactive, of course. The aircraft wore standard Iraqi Airways livery but the airline logos and registration were painted out.

Iraqi specialists claimed that the radar, which was manned by four operators, had a scan 'substantially in excess of 180°' and could detect, identify and track targets at up to 350km (190nm) range. Since in its basic form the Tigre is mounted on a semi-trailer, changes had to be made to the radar set for airborne installation in order to reduce ground clutter. Tactical information was transmitted in real time by data link or voice link; the aircraft also featured indigenous radio and radar ESM equipment.

The *Baghdad-1* was actually used operationally in late 1988 during the early stages of the Gulf War (ie, the Iraqi invasion of Kuwait), but there have been no reports of its efficiency.

What *is* certain is that the unconventionally located radar antenna, besides having a limited scan, was extremely vulnerable on take-off and landing.

Adnan-1 (Baghdad-2) and Adnan-2 AWACS

Obviously realising that the *Baghdad-1*'s radar installation left a lot to be desired, the Iraqis fitted another IL-76MD 'Falsie' (probably again ex-YI-AN*) with a conventional rotodome mounted on twin pylons immediately aft of the wings. Despite the apparent similarity to the A-50 and 'aircraft 976', this aircraft also had the Tigre radar; the rotodome was similar in diameter to the Soviet types (some 9 m/29ft 6in) but the metal centre section was much wider and the dielectric portions smaller. Two long trapezoidal splayed strakes were fitted to the aft fuselage sides to compensate for the destabil-

ising effect of the rotodome. It was claimed that the integration and debugging effort had been undertaken entirely in Iraq but Western aviation experts took this with a grain of salt.

Originally known as *Baghdad-2*, the second Iraqi AWACS was soon renamed *Adnan-1* in memory of Defence Minister Gen Adnan Khajrallah Talfah killed in a helicopter crash in May 1988. (Rumour has it that Gen Khajrallah Talfah opposed President Saddam Hussein over some issue and Saddam had the dissenter eliminated.) The aircraft had a grey/white colour scheme but no insignia other than an Iraqi flag on the fin and the inscription *Adnan-1* in Arabic on the nose. It was soon joined by a third AWACS, an identically converted IL-76MD 'Falsie' named *Adnan-2* which wore full Iraqi Air Force insignia and two-tone grey wraparound camouflage but, once again, no serial.

Top: **The only available photo of the bizarre A-60 airborne laser laboratory (CCCP-86879).** Yefim Gordon

Centre: **This view of RA-76490 sitting engineless at LII shows the massive antenna fairing on the starboard side. Unfortunately it was impossible to get an unobstructed view of the aircraft – at least without entering a restricted area and getting busted!** Dmitriy Komissarov

Bottom: **Close-up of the ELINT antenna fairing on the IL-76-11 (IL-76T 'Falsie' RA-76490). Note the soldiers at the foot of the picture; these kept spectators out of restricted areas.** Dmitriy Komissarov

Development projects

IL-96 (first use of designation)

On 1st June 1972 the Ilyushin OKB began development of a convertible passenger/cargo version of the IL-76 designated IL-96. However, this remained a 'paper airplane' and the designation was later reused for the wide-body airliner we know today.

IL-76TD-90 and IL-76MD-90

While the IL-76MF was in the making, the International Civil Aviation Organization (ICAO) toughened its regulations concerning noise and emission levels. The 'sixties-vintage D-30KP turbofan no longer met the stringent requirements; at best this meant big fines and at worst the IL-76 could be barred from international routes. This, of course, was totally unacceptable, since the IL-76 is used a lot for cargo charters in Western Europe and elsewhere (for instance, many *Candids* can be seen at any time

at Sharjah). A European ban on IL-76 operations would bite a big hole in the CIS airlines' trade.

As the next-best thing the Ilyushin OKB proposed upgrading existing IL-76TDs by re-engining them with PS-90A-76 turbofans and updating the avionics. The resulting combination was designated IL-76TD-90; service entry was optimistically planned for mid-1993.

However, the programme was plagued by delays. In February 1994 the would-be prototype, Aeroflot Russian International Airlines' RA-76751 (c/n 0083487610, f/n 6603), finally arrived at Khodynka for conversion at Ilyushin's experimental shop (MMZ No 240). Unfortunately, when it was halfway through the conversion the price of the engines skyrocketed; neither ARIA nor the OKB could afford a complete shipset at that moment, and the work came to a standstill. Eventually ARIA announced its decision to purchase new IL-96T freighters and the IL-76TD-90 was abandoned.

Recently, however, Russian airlines have shown an interest in reviving the project. This is

because new noise regulations (which the old engine no longer meets) will be introduced in 2002, barring the D-30KP-powered versions from flying to Western Europe.

A project designated IL-76MD-90 is also known to exist. This is obviously the military equivalent of the IL-76TD-90 – a *Candid-B* re-engined with PS-90A-76s

'Westernization' projects (IL-76MF-100/IL-76TF-100 etc)

The Soviet Union had had scant success in exporting its commercial and transport aircraft; exports were largely limited to socialist bloc and third-world nations. Politics and the Cold War (which meant maintenance and spares procurement could turn into a major problem) were the main reason, of course, but not the only one. Western customers were unwilling to buy Soviet hardware because of, as Clive Irving (an American aviation writer) put it, 'Russian aviation's serious and persistent handicap – its brutish and appallingly 'dirty' jet engines'.

While Soviet aircraft as such were often regarded as quite capable, sales prospects were crippled by low engine life and mean time between overhauls, poor operating economics and high noise/emission levels. Thus, re-engining was the obvious solution. In the early 1990s the Soviet design bureaux began offering export versions of new commercial aircraft with Western engines and avionics – eg, the Tu-204-120/-130 with Rolls-Royce RB.211-535E4 or Pratt & Whitney PW2040 turbofans respectively, the An-38-100 with Allied Signal TPE331-14GR-801E turboprops and Hartzell M11276NK-3X propellers, the IL-96M/T with PW2337s and so on.

Re-engining existing Soviet aircraft was also considered (eg, Tu-154M with P&W JT8D-217s etc). One such project came up in 1991 when Ilyushin offered a version of the IL-76MD powered by 14,152kgp (31,200lbst) CFM International CFM56-5C2s to the French *Armée de l'Air*. The deal failed to materialise – apparently for political reasons.

(In April 2000, however, the project was revived when Ilyushin and the Uzbek Government signed a memorandum of understanding concerning the delivery of five CFM56-powered IL-76MFs. Ilyushin's General Designer Igor' Katyrev says Western certification will not be sought because the basic Candid was certificated to Soviet NLGS-3 airworthiness regulations and not today's AP-25[45] equivalent of the USA's FAR25 and Europe's JAR25). However, the CFM56-5C4 is a reliable engine and will allow the IL-76MF-100, as the new version is known [or commercial IL-76TF-100], to operate into noise-sensitive airports.)

Later, International Aero Engines picked up the ball, offering to refit the *Candid* with V2500 turbofans. The project was announced at the Aviadveegatel'-93 (Aero Engine-93) exhibition in Moscow in June 1993. This remained a 'paper aeroplane' as well; lack of funding was the reason this time.

IL-76 firebomber

An interesting project was presented by the Aviaspetstrans consortium at the Moscow Aerospace '90 trade fair. It envisaged the use of the IL-76 as a firebomber – literally. The aircraft was to drop capsules filled with a fire retardant which was spread by means of an explosive charge ! A single capsule covered an area of 5m^2 (53.8ft^2) and a full 'bomb load' was enough for 1 hectare (107,600ft^2). The 'bombs' were test-dropped successfully from an An-32 but the project was terminated at the insistence of the Ilyushin OKB. Ilyushin claimed the explosive capsules could injure people in the fire zone. Still, perhaps they were just worried about competition…

IL-76PSD

The sad fate of the IL-76MDPS did not put off the Ilyushin OKB. Future development plans for the *Candid* family include the IL-76PSD project. The D stands for *dahl'niy* (long-range) and longer range is probably obtained by fitting more fuel-efficient Solov'yov PS-90A-76 turbofans. Thus the designation IL-76PSD almost certainly applies to a version of the IL-76MF adapted for SAR duties.

The stretched fuselage enables the IL-76MF to carry two Gagara lifeboats instead of one. By dropping these and inflatable rafts the aircraft can provide for the rescue of up to 1,000 persons at a time. The project also envisages an A-50 style flight refuelling probe; with aerial refuelling from an IL-78 tanker, the aircraft can stay airborne for up to 16 hours and have a 6,000km (3,243nm) operating radius. The

avionics suite may include a Kvitok (Coupon) long-range radio navigation (LORAN) system, a Gori-M[46] integrated navigation system, sea state measurement equipment and an optoelectronic search system.

IL-76Kh cryogenic powerplant technology testbed

On 10th October 1974 the Minister of Aircraft Industry and the Soviet Air Force C-in-C endorsed the **Kholod**-2 (Cold-2) research and development plan for the design bureau led by Vladimir Mikhaïlovich Myasischchev (OKB-23). The objective of this plan was to develop a hypersonic aerospaceplane with a cryogenic powerplant, hence the 'cold' name.

Known at OKB-23 as **tema** *devyatnadtsat'* – Subject (ie, Project) 19, the programme was split into several parts, the first of which, Project 19-1, was concerned with a propulsion technology testbed. It involved fitting an IL-76 transport with an experimental turbojet (a product of the OKB led by Arkhip Mikhaïlovich Lyul'ka) running on liquid hydrogen; the cryogenic tanks would be housed in the freight hold. The aircraft was designated IL-76Kh, the suffix letter referring to the Kholod-2 programme.

Unfortunately, the powers that be intervened; when development was well advanced the Myasischchev OKB was ordered to transfer its know-how to the Tupolev OKB. There the programme bore fruit in the form of the Tu-155 testbed, a much-modified Tu-154 *sans suffixe (Careless)* medium-haul airliner. The aircraft (CCCP-85035, c/n 73A-035) made its first flight on 15th April 1988 with a Kuznetsov NK-89 cryogenic engine in the starboard nacelle.

Fly-by-wire IL-76

In March 1997 the Russian magazine *Ves'nik Vozdooshnovo Flota/Air Fleet Herald* announced that Ilyushin were planning an upgraded version of the IL-76 with fly-by-wire controls, a 'glass cockpit' and a crew of two *(sic)*.

IL-76 rocket launch aircraft

In 1995 TsAGI materials featured a project envisaging the use of the IL-76 for launching small satellites. The aircraft would disgorge the

launch rocket in flight 'head first' by means of a drogue parachute, just like in an ordinary paradrop, whereupon the rocket would fire up and go 'up, up and away'. A similar project designated An-124AK was developed for launching larger rockets. The projects were probably abandoned in favour of the Tu-160SK carrying the Burlak launch vehicle (which still has not progressed beyond the full-scale mockup stage).

IL-76MF drone launcher modification

At the MAKS-95 airshow NPO Mashinostroyeniye unveiled the project of a drone carrier aircraft based on the stretched IL-76MF. The aircraft was to carry a large unmanned aerial vehicle called GLL (**ghiperzvookovaya letayuschchaya laboratoriya** – 'hypersonic flying laboratory', ie, hypersonic research vehicle) piggyback in similar fashion to NASA's Boeing 747SCA shuttle carrier aircraft.

The aircraft could also carry what could be called an 'aerial sandwich' – a suborbital launch system consisting of the same hypersonic UAV which, in turn, carried a single-stage booster rocket that would put satellites into orbit. Curiously, a model of *this* project displayed at MAKS-95 represented a *Candid-B*, not an IL-76MF.

IL-78V and IL-78MK *Midas* refuelling tankers

The Ilyushin OKB is planning further development of the *Midas*. An IL-76 family development plan presented in late 1993 featured the IL-78V tanker equipped with improved UPAZ-MK-32V pods and the IL-78MK tanker/transport (*konverteerooyemyy* – convertible) with a bigger fuel load developed at the request of the VVS. Development was completed in 1993 but the aircraft still has not entered production – solely due to lack of orders, as the Russian Air Force has no money for more tankers.

A model of the proposed drone launcher version of the IL-76MF with the GLL hypersonic research vehicle mounted piggyback. Yefim Gordon

A model of the IL-76MD drone launcher (note tail gunner's station) carrying the two-stage suborbital launch system. Yefim Gordon

Chapter Four

In Action

The trials continued. On 13th November 1973 the first production aircraft (CCCP-76500) was temporarily detached to Artsyz airbase near Odessa to participate in a Red Banner Odessa Defence District military exercise, giving Air Force crews their first acquaintance with the type. The aircraft was captained by G N Volokhov, with P M Fomin as engineer in charge.

A week later the same aircraft commenced combat suitability trials which were part of the manufacturer's test programme. To this end CCCP-76500 was seconded to the 339th VTAP (*voyenno-trahnsportnyy aviapolk*) – military airlift regiment (military airlift wing) in Vitebsk, Belorussian DD. The trials included paradrops of personnel, cargo and vehicles, as well as disgorging troops and vehicles after landing in a simulated airborne assault. This time the aircraft was captained by Aleksandr M Tyuryumin, with V S Krooglyakov as engineer in charge.

On 28th May 1974 a team of Ilyushin OKB operational support specialists under A G Kochkin started work in the 18th VTAD (*voyenno-trahnsportnaya aviadiveeziya* – airlift division, ≅ military airlift group) headquartered in Vitebsk, preparing the ground for re-equipment with the IL-76; this division became the first to master the type. The manufacturer's flight test programme was completed on 9th September 1974 with four aircraft (CCCP-86712, -86711, -76500 and -76501) logging a total of 1,167 hours in 767 flights. Finally, on 15th December the IL-76 completed its State acceptance (= certification) trials; these involved another 197 flights totalling 509 hours.

Whatever doubts the West may have had concerning the capabilities of the IL-76 were dispelled soon enough. Even before the trials programme was completed the first production *Candid* set an impressive series of 25 Class C1m world speed and altitude records in July 1975; 24 of them were officially recognised by the *Fédération Aéronautique Internationale* (FAI) – see Appendix 3. CCCP-76500 was also displayed at the 31st Paris Aerospace Salon in June 1975 with the exhibit code 366.

Meanwhile, IL-76 production at Tashkent was slowly getting under way. By January 1976 the *Candid* had completely replaced the *Cock* on the production line. Ironically, the 66 An-22s built turned out to be all too few; except for three aircraft retained by the Antonov OKB in Kiev, all of them were quasi-civilian and operated by the VTA. Aeroflot requested that An-22A production be resumed for civilian needs, but the Tashkent plant was not in a position to do so, being totally occupied with the IL-76.

Since the IL-76 was conceived as a military freighter we will deal with military operations first. As soon as the State acceptance trials were completed the VTA started taking delivery of the new aircraft. The first eight batches manufactured in 1973-77 consisted almost entirely of military *Candids*; it was not until mid-1977 that production of the commercial version really began.

On 21st April 1976 the Council of Ministers and the Central Committee of the Communist Party issued a directive officially including the IL-76 into the Soviet Air Force inventory. Two months later, on 26th June, CCCP-76500 was demonstrated to representatives of 'friendly nations' at Moscow-Domodedovo airport with a view to attracting foreign orders. The foreign representatives were quick to realise the aircraft's potential, and an order from the Iraqi Air Force followed promptly (see Chapter 6). Depending on how loyal the customer was to the cause of communism, the fly-away price varied from US$ 13 to 39 million.

Operational experience with the *Candid* showed that Ilyushin had been right in following the reputed Soviet design philosophy of 'make it simple, make it strong, but make it work'. The IL-76 earned a good reputation for high reliability and ease of maintenance even in the harshest environments. For instance, the

An early *Candid-B* in landing configuration displays its powerful high-lift devices which enabled the IL-76 to operate into small tactical pads. Yefim Gordon archive

engines were located much lower than on the An-12, which meant lower maintenance platforms could be used. All four engine nacelles were interchangeable and the large cowlings afforded easy access to all engine accessories; if necessary the engine could be completely 'undressed' while still on the wing. Importantly, direct operating costs were reduced almost 50% as compared to the An-12.

Officially Ilyushin stuck to the 'commercial freighter' theory. However, on 5th August 1977 *Krasnaya Zvezda* (Red Star), the Soviet MoD daily, spilled the beans by publishing a photo showing paratroopers lined up behind an IL-76 with the tail guns plainly visible. On 17th August same year a feature in *Komsomol'skaya Pravda* (the Young Communist League daily) on the occasion of Aviation Day[1] was illustrated by a photo of paratroopers boarding five military IL-76s. Thus the aircraft's original military role was tacitly admitted.

The IL-76 *et seq* was operated by VTA units based in Engels (230th APSZ), Ivanovo (12th VTAD/81st VTAP, Ivanovo-Severnyy AB), Klin (Klin-5 AB), Novgorod (3rd VTAD/110th VTAP, Krechevitsy AB), Pskov (334th *Berlinskiy* Red Banner VTAP, Kresty AB),[2] Smolensk, Ukurey and Ul'yanovsk in Russia; Vitebsk (18th VTAD/339th VTAP) in Belorussia; Artsyz (near Odessa), Bel'bek, Dzhankoy, Krivoy Rog (16th VTAP), Melitopol'-1, Melitopol'-2, Uzin (409th SAP) and Zaporozhye (338th VTAP) in the Ukraine (all 7th VTAD); Baku (Nasosnaya AB) and Gyandzha (708th OVTAP)[3] in Azerbaijan; Tartu (18th VTAD/196th VTAP) in Estonia; Kedainiai, Panevezhis (128th VTAP; both 18th VTAD) and Siauliai in Lithuania. After the breakup of the Soviet Union the units in Gyandzha, Tartu, Kedainiai, Siauliai and Panevezhis were transferred to Russia – Taganrog, Tver', Orenburg, Pechora and Shadrinsk respectively – in 1992-93.

Until the mid-80s Soviet Air Force *Candids* ostensibly wore standard Aeroflot colours and civil registrations – and most of them still do. Of course, the tail gunner's station and ECM fairings told too plain a tale; as a Russian aphorism goes, 'if you see 'buffalo' written on a tiger's cage, don't you believe it'. In the late 1980s, however, aircraft with overt military markings began appearing. Usually they retained the blue Aeroflot cheatline, but in 1989-90 some IL-76MDs operated by the airlift regiments in Artsyz and Vitebsk received a white/grey colour scheme *à la* IL-78M and A-50 by the simple expedient of overpainting the cheatline.

Known tactical codes of Soviet/Russian Air Force *Candid-Bs* are 01 Red (ex-RA-78837), 21 Red (ex-CCCP-86643/to RA-76416), 533 Black (ex-CCCP-76533/to RA-76533), 538 Black (ex-CCCP-76538/to RA-76538), 602 Black (ex-CCCP-86602), 626 Black (ex-CCCP-86626/to RA-86626), 629 Black (ex-CCCP-86629/to RA-86629), 632 Black (ex-CCCP-86632), 634 Black (ex-CCCP-86634), 635 Black (ex-CCCP-86635), 644 Black (ex-CCCP-86644/to RA-76418), 645 Black (ex-CCCP-86645), 713 Black (ex-CCCP-

IL-76 final assembly at aircraft factory No 84 in Tashkent. Victor Drushlyakov

A brand-new and shiny IL-76MD is ready for delivery to the VTA. Sergey & Dmitriy Komissarov collection

86713), 716 Black (ex-CCCP-86716), 719 Black (ex-CCCP-86719), 722 Black (ex-CCCP-86722), 725 Black (ex-CCCP-86725), 728 Black (ex-CCCP-86728), 811 Black (ex-CCCP-86811) and 819 Black (ex-CCCP-86819). Aircraft coded 22 Red (ex-CCCP-86898/to RA-86898), 23 Red (ex-CCCP-76560/to UR-76560), 88 Red, 92 Red and 97 Red have also been reported, but these are doubtful.

Speaking of registrations, known Soviet/CIS IL-76s and derivatives are registered -76316 through -76323, -76350 through -76367, -76369 through -76377, -76379 through -76386, -76388 through -76421, -76423 through -76430, -76433 through -76438, -76440 through -76828, -76830 through -76845, -76849, -76900, -78001, -78030, -78129, -78130, -78711, -78731, -78734, -78736,

-78738, -78740, -78743 (?), -78750 through -78854, -78878 (?), -86020 through -86049, -86600 through -86604, -86612, -86621, -86625 through -86647, -86711 through -86749 and -86800 through -86930. (No registration prefixes are given here, since many aircraft were registered new with the various prefixes of the CIS states or changed hands.)

Aircraft registered in the 76*** block can be both commercial and military *Candids* whereas IL-76s registered in the 78*** and 86*** blocks are strictly military versions. The only exceptions are the two civil prototypes (CCCP-86711 and -86712) and IL-76T CCCP-86926. The registrations -76421, -76426, -76492, -76752, -76759, -76767 and -86925 have been used twice. UR-76316 through UR-76323, RA-76372, RA-76382, RA-76383, RA-76388, RA-76389, UR-76390 through UR-76399, CCCP-76408, UR-76412 through UR-76415, RA-76416 through RA-76418, UR-76423, UR-76424, RA-76430, UR-76433, CCCP-76437, UR-76438, UR-76441, CCCP-76443, UR-76444, UR-76759 and UR-76767 are reregistered ex-VVS aircraft.

Mechanics use mobile platforms to service the engines of this *Candid-B*. The tail gunner's station is wrapped in tarpaulins to stop it from turning into a one-man steam bath. A 'cherry picker' based on the Ural-375D 6x6 truck waits in the background. Yefim Gordon

BMD-1 assault fighting vehicles with the VDV (Airborne Forces) badge are loaded into several IL-76s *sans suffixe*, including CCCP-86806,

CCCP-86810 and CCCP-86635 during a military exercise. The wheels on the pallets are for ground handling only. Yefim Gordon archive

Pictured at Klin-5 AB in the summer of 1999, IL-76 *sans suffixe* '713 Black' (ex-CCCP-86713, c/n 043403061, f/n 0206) is one of the few *Candid-Bs* to wear full military markings. Sergey Panov.

Two *Candid-Bs* had non-standard registrations (CCCP-06146 and -06188). Also, some aircraft had temporary non-standard test registrations derived from the 'famous last five' of the c/n; eg, IL-76TD CCCP-76833 (c/n 1023411363, f/n 8501) was test flown as CCCP-11363 (which was really an An-12B).

Interestingly, the registrations CCCP-76457 through CCCP-76493 were previously used for Tu-114 airliners. CCCP-76591 was previously allocated to the first production An-22 (c/n 6340105, to CCCP-08822) and CCCP-76691 to the second production An-22 (c/n 7340106, to CCCP-08837).

The type was well liked by the Air Force, since its capacious freight hold, excellent field performance, high speed and payload, and not least reliability gave the VVS a much-needed boost in strategic airlift capability which the few An-22s could give only in part. The IL-76 could airlift a T-72 main battle tank and drop single loads weighing up to 47 tons (103,615 lb) from an altitude of up to 4,000m (13,123ft) and a load of paratroopers from up to 8,000m (26,246ft). Bulky and heavy loads such as BMD-1 assault fighting vehicles were dropped on P-7 pallets (P = *platforma*). Maximum paradropping speed was 850km/h (459kts) versus 250km/h (135kts) for the An-12. Besides, the IL-76 was easy to fly and very much a 'pilot's airplane'.

New paradropping techniques were gradually developed. On 19th June 1978 CCCP-76500 performed the first drop of four cargo pallets using the so-called 'train technique' (each pallet was extracted by a drogue parachute opened by a rip cord attached to the preceding pallet). This technique jointly developed by the Ilyushin OKB, the Moscow 'Ooniversahl' plant and the Automatic Mechanisms Research Institute (NIIAU – *Na**ooch**no-is**sled**ovatel'skiy insti**toot** avto**mateecheskikh** oo**stroystv**) allowed the cargo to be dropped on a landing zone (LZ) 400m (1,312ft) long.

On 11th February 1981 the same aircraft made the first delivery of a 5-ton palletised load using the low-altitude parachute extraction system (LAPES). The pallet was fitted with special shock absorbers and dropped while the aircraft was flying at 3 to 5m (10 to 15ft). The LAPES technique allowed cargo to be delivered with pinpoint accuracy to an LZ which was too small for the IL-76 to land without risking a bungled paradrop into enemy territory or inaccessible terrain. On 23rd August same year CCCP-76500 dropped a BMD-1 AFV using this technique for the first time.

Finally, on 23rd April 1983 a BMD-1 was paradropped in the normal way (using a multi-canopy parachute system and retro-rockets) but with a crew inside; this included NIIAU employees P M Nikolayev and A L Il'mekeyev. The objective was to test the new Shel'f (Seabed) parachute system. In all cases the aircraft was flown by Aleksandr M Tyuryumin and M N Weinshtein was the engineer in charge.

Quasi-civilian IL-76M/MDs regularly flew

resupply missions for the Soviet forces stationed in East Germany (GSVG[4]) and were used for troop rotation. Usually such flights were made to Falkenberg airbase near Cottbus (also known as Alt-Lönnewitz in the West). Later they were used, along with An-22s and An-124s, to carry personnel and materiel during the Russian withdrawal from Germany in 1990-94. In 1987-89 a pair of A-50 AWACS aircraft was occasionally deployed to East Germany – usually to Köthen AB but occasionally also to Falkenberg and Damgarten (Pütnitz).[5]

Later, IL-76s and freighter-configured IL-78s were used, along with An-12s, An-22s and An-124s, to carry personnel and materiel during the Russian withdrawal from Germany in 1991-94. *Candids* operated to/from the following bases: Allstedt, Altenburg (Nöbitz), Berlin-Schönefeld airport, Brand, Brandis, Cochstedt, Damgarten, Falkenburg, Finow (Eberswalde), Finsterwalde, Großenhain, Jüterbog-Altes Lager, Köthen, Lärz, Mahlwinkel, Merseburg, Neuruppin, Neu-Welzow, Oranienburg, Parchim, Sperenberg, Templin, Tutow, Werneuchen, Wittstock and Zerbst. IL-76M RA-86833 got the distinction of making the final transport flight of the pullout from Berlin-Schönefeld on 9th September 1994.

Apart from regular Air Force aircraft, the operation also involved IL-76TD CCCP-76493 chartered from MAP and three aircraft (IL-76Ts CCCP-76457, CCCP-76780 and IL-76TD CCCP-76781) operated by the Ministry of the

Everybody, say 'cheese'! The Blue Berets, as the Soviet airborne troops are known, pose in front of an IL-76MD (possibly CCCP-76760). This head-on view shows the *Candid*'s characteristic big grin. Yefim Gordon archive

IL-76M CCCP-86851 dropping a BMD-1 – apparently not loaded on a pallet in this case. Yefim Gordon archive

The first production IL-76 was used for a lot of development work, including trials of the LAPES delivery technique. Here, it is seen disgorging a BMD-1 in this fashion. Sergey & Dmitriy Komissarov collection

IL-78M '36 Blue' takes off on a demonstration flight at the MAKS-99 airshow. Yefim Gordon

A-50M '51 Red' during a practice session for an airshow performance with four *Flanker-B*s (01 Blue, 04 Blue, 05 Blue and 06 Blue) from Savostleyka flying escort. Yefim Gordon

Interior. The MoI Candids presumably picked up KGB equipment and materials from Sperenberg.

The collapse of the Soviet Union had its adverse effect on Candid operations. Many VTA units operating the IL-76 were stationed outside Russia – mostly in the Ukraine which was at odds with Russia over the Black Sea Fleet issue and other problems. With tensions between Russia and the Ukraine being the way they were in the early 1990s, spares procurement became a problem. Hence many Ukrainian Candids had to be grounded and cannibalised for spares so as to keep the others flyable. In Russian aviation slang such aircraft are called 'Avrora' (Aurora) – an allusion to the famous Russian Navy cruiser which signalled the beginning of the 1917 October Revolution by firing her nose cannon and was later permanently moored on the Neva River in Leningrad as a museum.

The Ukraine also kept a whole regiment of IL-78 tankers; this came as a severe blow to Russia's strategic air arm which lost a substantial proportion of its tanker fleet. Since the Ukraine did not need a lot of tankers (as it was, the UAF Tu-22 Blinders and Tu-22M3 Backfire-Cs were stripped of flight refuelling capability under the SALT II treaty), most of the IL-78s were converted into transports. They are now used for carrying commercial cargoes, such as Rasputin vodka and Snickers candy!

The Ukraine is known to be a NATO sympathiser (which certainly does not help its relations with Russia), and recently Ukrainian Candids started taking part in NATO exercises. For example, the Co-operative Bear '99 exercise held at Kraków-Balice AB on 25th September to 1st October 1999 under the Partnership for Peace (PfP) programme involved a 321st VTAP IL-76MD, UR-76677, which was the largest aircraft participating (apart from a NAEWF Boeing E-3C). The aircraft was equipped with the Candid's standard medevac equipment kit and the cannons were removed from the tail turret.

Military Candids were regular participants at various airshows – usually as support aircraft for display teams, but sometimes in their own right. For instance, IL-76MD RA-76767 (c/n 0073481436, f/n 6109) was in the static display at the open doors day at Kubinka AB on 14th May 1994. The freight hold was wide open for inspection, but when the cargo doors had to be closed at the end of the day the flight engineer fired up the APU, which sent visitors standing on the port side of the aircraft scattering like roaches – the din of the APU is quite unbearable. Oddly, the freighter sported the Russian

registration prefix on the wings but the old Soviet prefix combined with the Russian flag on the fin. Such a mixture was fairly common in the early days of the CIS; indeed, some Russian quasi-civil aircraft retained the CCCP- prefix even in 1999!

The military parade at Poklonnaya Gora in Moscow on 9th May 1995 featured an unusually large collection of 'Candids and friends'. The first of these was IL-76MD '01 Red' from Ivanovo (c/n 1003401024, f/n 7606) escorted by four Su-27s, followed by two IL-78Ms (30 Blue with a pair of Su-24Ms and 36 Blue with a Tu-95MS) and finally A-50M '51 Red', also with Flanker escort.

Civil operations

Service entry with Aeroflot came soon after the Candid attained initial operational capability with the VTA. On 13th May 1975 IL-76 CCCP-76500 began a series of demonstration flights in the Tyumen' Civil Aviation Directorate (CAD), carrying cargo to the Samotlor oil field and the Nadym gas field in Western Siberia (including several tons of oranges for the workers at Samotlor). The Ilyushin OKB crew was captained by A M Tyuryumin; engineer V V Shkitin was in charge of the demonstration tour.

In December same year the first prototype was loaned to the Tyumen' CAD for evaluation. Except for the blue rudder, the aircraft had by then been repainted in 1973-standard Aeroflot colours. The wing, tail unit and air intake leading edges were painted black for icing visualization during de-icing system tests.

Between 22nd December 1975 and 2nd February 1976 CCCP-86712 made 60 flights from Tyumen' to Nizhnevartovsk, Surgut and Nadym, delivering 1,700 tons (3,747 lb) of assorted cargoes. These included vehicles which were too bulky for the An-12 – 35-ton (77,160 lb) US-built Caterpillar bulldozers, Hungarian Ikarus 250 coaches and West German

Magirus-Deutz 290D-26K dump trucks. 10,000 of these 6 x 4 trucks with an all-up weight of 26 tons (57,319 lb) were delivered to the USSR in the 1970s for use in the construction of the Baikal-Amur railroad.

The aircraft performed excellently in the harsh climate Western Siberia. The service trials often involved operation from snow strips (resulting in terrific snow clouds) and maintenance at temperatures of -40°C (-40°F).

On 22nd December 1976 Aeroflot took delivery of its first IL-76 sans suffixe, CCCP-76502 (c/n 063407206, f/n 0602). The aircraft belonged to the Tyumen' CAD but was initially flown by a GosNII GA crew captained by M S Kuznetsov. Together with CCCP-76503, the second production civil IL-76 sans suffixe (c/n 063408209, f/n 0603), it made 722 flights totalling 1,007 hours during service trials. In the meantime, conversion training of flight and ground crews was organised. Tyumen' United Flight Detachment pilots Boris K Kuznetsov, A I Goorey, A I Pleshakov and A A Dement'yev were the first Aeroflot pilots to master the IL-76.

On 5th April 1977[6] CCCP-76503, by then transferred to Aeroflot's Central Directorate of International Services (TsUMVS – *Tsentrahl'noye oopravleniye mezhdunarodnykh vozdooshnykh so'obschcheniy*), made the first revenue flight outside the Soviet Union, delivering 38 tons (83,774 lb) of fresh vegetables from Sofia. The crew included captain Nikolay I lysenko, first officer Ivan Shoolakov and navigator Anatoliy Koolibaba.

Flown by the same crew, the same aircraft made the type's first visit to Warsaw-Okęcie on 11th May 1978 in order to pick up six Ursus wheeled tractors. These were some of the exhibits of the Sdelano v Pol'she (Made in Poland) trade fair due to open in Alma-Ata, the capital of the Kazakh SSR. When the tractors had been wheeled in and tied down, it transpired that a box with more exhibits was miss-

The first prototype IL-76 (with spin recovery parachute) unloads a tracked excavator during service trials with Aeroflot in the Tyumen' Region. Note the purpose-built ramp placed near the aircraft's cargo ramp.
Yefim Gordon archive

ing. Telephone enquiries revealed that the box had not even arrived in Warsaw yet! The unanimous decision was that the aircraft would depart as planned; the box would have to be delivered by the next scheduled passenger flight if it was not delivered on time.

Imagine the consternation of those concerned when the box, when it finally did arrive, turned out to be a huge container weighing almost a ton (2,200 lb)! The tractor drivers had done their job and left, the vehicles were secured and there was no room for the container. Undaunted by this, the crew deftly unstrapped the rearmost tractor and unloaded it, using the overhead hoists, then loaded the container in the same fashion and loaded the tractor back in. It was just as well that the 'box'

got there in time; there was no way it could have been carried by a passenger jet.

IL-76 CCCP-76500 was displayed again at Le Bourget from 3rd-12th June 1977, this time with the exhibit code 346.

On 26th September 1977 the type began scheduled services with Aeroflot; a further example, CCCP-76504, was delivered in October. Initially the IL-76 *sans suffixe* replaced the An-12 on cargo services in the extreme north, Siberia and the Far East. Soon Aeroflot *Candids* became regular visitors in Western Europe – for example, serving the Yokohama-Nakhodka-Vladivostok-Moscow-Luxembourg route. This was much shorter than the journey by boat via the Indian Ocean, but the big problem was that the An-12 used hitherto could not take a

standard 20' sea/land container. Hence the cargo had to be transferred from the container to the aircraft upon arrival by sea to Nakhodka, which involved considerable risk of damage – or theft. The IL-76 eliminated this problem, delivering the goods in their original container.

On 22nd April 1977 (the anniversary of Vladimir I Lenin's birthday which was a semi-official holiday in the Soviet Union) a group of aircraft industry and civil aviation workers – Radiy P Papkovskiy, Eduard I Kuznetsov, A V Shaposhnikov, V N Sivets, G G Moorav'yov and Pavel A Solov'yov – received the prestigious Lenin Prize for their part in the development and service introduction of the IL-76.

Captained by A M Tyuryumin, IL-76 CCCP-76500 made its third appearance at the Le Bourget airshow from 12-19th May 1979 with the exhibit code 347. Soon afterwards the aircraft received black stripes on the wing leading edges and all-black fin and stabilizer leading edges for icing visualization.

CCCP-76500 was eventually retired at Zhukovskiy and gradually broken up. The fuselage and vertical tail – all that remained by 1992 – could still be seen on the dump at LII during MosAeroShow '92 from 11-16th August. Sure enough, aircraft do not last forever, but this one could, and should, have had a happier fate – like finding a place in a museum.

On 10th July 1979 an Aeroflot (TsUMVS) IL-76 made the type's first Atlantic crossing on a flight to Cuba. The aircraft was flown by two crews captained by V Stroyev and Zh. K Shishkin.

Soviet Air Force IL-76s were often used for civilian tasks as well, including international flights – especially in the early days when the commercial *Candid-A* was still scarce; for example, IL-76M CCCP-86043 carried some of the Soviet exhibits to the 34th Paris Aerospace Salon in May 1981. In such cases the guns were removed, of course. Imagine an armed Soviet aircraft landing in Paris in the Cold War days! It would be pretty hard to convince everyone that World War III had not begun! Iraqi Air Force *Candid-Bs*, too, were often used for commercial flights to Europe until the Gulf War broke loose and sanctions were imposed on Iraq.

GosNII GA kept working on improving operational procedures so as to use the freighter's potential more fully. Normally the IL-76 uses reverse thrust on the outboard engines only, which reduces required runway length by 340m (1,115ft) or allows maximum landing weight to be increased by 8 tons (17,636 lb). GosNII GA devised a method of using reverse

Two Magirus-Deutz 290D-26K dump trucks are driven into the hold of CCCP-76502, the first *Candid-A* delivered to Aeroflot.
Yefim Gordon archive

IL-76 CCCP-76505 after unloading a lumber hauling tractor somewhere in Siberia.
Sergey & Dmitriy Komissarov collection

thrust on all four engines right down to zero speed if necessary. This reduced landing run by a further 150m (492ft), allowing the aircraft to land with a 150-ton (330,687 lb) weight on snow runways where maximum landing weight was previously limited to 135 tons (297,619 lb). In practice this meant the aircraft could take more fuel, which was just as well because fuel was not always available in some northern and Siberian airports.

Consequently changes were made to the flight manual. However, care had to be taken when using full reverse thrust because the jet blast from the inboard engines could damage the cowlings of the outer engines. The IL-76 could even taxi *backwards* by using reverse thrust; the manual expressly forbade this because of the risk of foreign object damage but sometimes pilots had to ignore it.

In the early 1980s someone in the Ministry of Civil Aviation decided that the standard Aeroflot livery was too restrained (putting it mildly) and could use some livening up. Hence an experimental colour scheme was developed and tested on several types operated by Aeroflot and the Soviet Air Force (in Aeroflot colours). This was basically a blue/white version of Aeroflot's 1973-standard red/white polar colours. The cheatline and Aeroflot titles were unchanged but the vertical tail was blue with a broad horizontal white band on which the Soviet flag was superimposed, and sometimes the outer wings were also blue.

Over the years the modified colour scheme was worn by such varied types as the An-3T, An-8, An-12BP, An-12BK, An-24B, An-24RV, An-26, An-72S, An-124, Tu-134A-3, Tu-134AK, Tu-134 Balkany,[7] Tu-134B, Tu-154B-2, Yak-42 – and the IL-76. At least three *Candid-As*, IL-76T CCCP-76462 operated by the West Siberian CAD and IL-76TDs CCCP-76470 and CCCP-76474 operated by TsUMVS, sported blue/white tails for a while. Unfortunately, this clearly more inspiring colour scheme did not gain wide use and is mostly worn by quasi-civil An-72S (*salon*) VIP transports.

On 8th January 1985 the IL-76T/TD was certificated for compliance with ICAO Annex 16, Chapter 3 regulations limiting jet noise.

According to Soviet practice a single aircraft overhaul plant (ARZ – *aviaremontnyy zavod*) would repair all aircraft of a given type, regardless of where they were based (including export aircraft). For the large numbers of *Candids*, however, a single plant was not enough. Also, in post-Soviet times several plants learned to handle new types in the hope of

gaining more orders ('survival of the fattest'!). Thus, ARZ No 402 at Moscow-Bykovo[8] and ARZ No 243 at Tashkent-Toozel' traditionally handle civil IL-76s. Military *Candids* are dealt with by three Russian Air Force plants – ARZ No 123 in Staraya Roossa (near Velikiy Novgorod in northern Russia),[9] ARZ No 325 in Taganrog and ARZ No 360 in Ryazan'. Furthermore, the Air Force plants are now moving into the civil overhaul market, undertaking, among other things, demilitarization work on ex-VVS aircraft (see previous chapter). D-30KP engines are repaired by the Urals Engine Repair Plant in Yekaterinburg and the Air Force's ARZ No 570 in Yeisk (Krasnodar Region).

Aeroflot IL-76s sometimes had to fulfil more or less unusual tasks. IL-76TD CCCP-76498 delivered an IL-114 fuselage (c/n 0104) to Sib-NIA (*Seebeerskiy naoochno-issledovatel'skiy instituut aviahtsii* – the Siberian Aviation Research Institute named after S A Chaplygin) in Novosibirsk for fatigue tests. In September 1988 an Aeroflot *Candid* delivered the wreckage of an Ilyushin DB-3 bomber (c/n 391311) discovered in the taiga 120km (74.5 miles) from Komsomol'sk-on-Amur to the Irkutsk aircraft

factory No 39 which had built the bomber. After painstaking restoration the world's sole surviving DB-3 was donated to the Soviet Air Force Museum in Monino near Moscow on 21st December 1989.

In 1988 TsUMVS IL-76T CCCP-76519 was hijacked in Mineral'nyye Vody by a gang of terrorists led by one G Yashkiyants. In nearby Ordzhonikidze the bandits had captured a school bus full of children going on an excursion; holding the hostages at gunpoint, they demanded several million dollars and an aircraft that would take them to Tel Aviv. The orders were very specific: the aircraft had to be an IL-76 so that the bus could be driven inside.

After lengthy negotiations the terrorists agreed to free the children in exchange for weapons and bulletproof vests; the crew of the freighter offered themselves as hostages. Meanwhile, however, the forces of the law wasted no time contacting the Israeli authorities. When the aircraft landed at Ben Gurion airport, Yashkiyants & Co confidently climbed into a car that was supposed to take them to the finest hotel in town... and found themselves in jail before they could say knife. Later, they were

Plant No 402 at Bykovo is the oldest aircraft overhaul plant handling the *Candid*. Here, Aeroflot Russian International Airlines IL-76TD RA-76482 is seen in one of the plant's hangars on 16th June 2000. Yefim Gordon

A special gantry moving on rails is erected around the tail for tailplane maintenance at Plant No 402. Yefim Gordon

IL-76TD CCCP-76498 loads an IL-114 fuselage at the Ilyushin flight test facility in Zhukovskiy for delivery to SibNIA. Sergey & Dmitriy Komissarov collection

extradited to the Soviet Union and got what was coming to them. The whole story later became the subject of a motion picture called *A Bus Gone Crazy*.

On 20th July 1990 IL-76MD CCCP-86871 owned by the Ilyushin OKB paradropped the heaviest load in Soviet history – a 44,600kg (98,324 lb) dummy spacecraft module used for testing spacecraft parachute recovery systems. On 16th July 1998 Gromov Air IL-76TD 'Falsie' RA-76528 captained by I Cheerkin delivered the earthly remains of the last Russian emperor Nicholas II and his family from Yekaterinburg to St. Petersburg for burial at St. Peter and Paul's Cathedral, the resting place of all Russian monarchs.

Finally, on 24th December 1998 the same IL-76MD (by then reregistered RA-86871) performed the first test drop of the recovery module of the Soyuz-TMA spacecraft at 11,000m (36,089ft). This latest version of the proven Soyuz series will be part of the International Space Station (ISS). The aircraft was flown by Igor' R Zakirov, with A Yurasov as the engineer in charge of the programme.

Many aircraft find their way into museums sooner or later, but no aviation museum can boast an IL-76 so far, and ground instructional airframes at various educational and training establishments are inaccessible to the aviation enthusiast. For example, civil IL-76s *sans suffixe* CCCP-76502 and CCCP-76503 are instructional airframes in Omsk and Ul'yanovsk, IL-76TD RA-76460 at MIIGA (*Moskovskiy institoot inzhenerov grazhdahnskoy aviahtsii* – Moscow Civil Aviation Engineers Institute).

IL-76M CCCP-86834 and IL-76PP CCCP-86889 serve the same purpose at the Irkutsk Military Technical School and IL-76MD CCCP-86912 at the Balashov Higher Military Pilot School where it was relegated after suffering structural damage in a heavy landing during the Afghan War. CCCP-86047, another IL-76M, is used by the Yuriy A Gagarin Air Force Acadamy in Monino near Moscow; the aircraft is in open storage right next door to the Russian Air Force Museum but is of course inaccessible for Monino visitors. In the Ukraine, IL-76T CCCP-76511 became an instructional airframe at KIIGA, IL-76Ms CCCP-86031 and CCCP-86854 at an Air Force technical school in Vasil'kov (Vasil'kiv), and IL-76MDPS CCCP-76621 in Kirovograd.

The *Candid* at war

In 1979-91 the IL-76 proved its worth in combat during the first major conflict in which the Soviet Union openly participated after the Second World War – the Afghan War. From 25-28th December, 1979 Soviet forces entered Afghanistan. During the 47-hour airlift operation the VTA made 343 flights into the country; 77 of these were performed by *Candid-Bs*.

The *Candid* was heavily involved in this war from beginning to end along with the trusted An-12 and the An-22. Quasi-civilian IL-76s *sans suffixe*, 'Ms and 'MDs flew resupply and medevac missions for Soviet forces in Afghanistan (the 40th Army), carrying personnel, heavy equipment, ammunition, fuel and so on. A so-called Composite Flight Detachment (SAO – *Svodnyy aviaotryad*) of the Uzbek CAD operating, among other things, *Candid-Bs* was formed for this purpose at Toozel' airbase near Tashkent. IL-76s also operated into Afghanistan from Khanabad AB near Karshi in south-eastern Uzbekistan and Kokaïdy AB near Termez, right beside the border. Crews from the various *Candid* units were detached to the Afghan group, rotating every month.

The conditions at Khanabad were truly spartan. The ground crews lived in derelict barracks near the airbase; the heating system was out of order and the nights were bitterly cold, forcing the men to sleep with their clothes on. When things got too cold the technicians would take a swig of the pure alcohol issued for cleaning electrical contacts. Incidentally, this helped prevent infectious diseases, as the water was bad in those parts; those crewmen who did not 'take medication' contracted hepatitis after the Afghan tour. The pilots were a lot better off, lodging in a hotel in Karshi which had running water and other adjuncts of civilization.

The crews had to work very hard indeed. First call came at 0300 and pre-flight checks and maintenance began. The aircraft departed at 0500, coming back shortly after noon; by then a convoy of trucks loaded with ammunition or other materiel had arrived and loading for tomorrow's sortie began straight away. Usually the cargo was bombs, rockets for the BM-21 Grad (Hail, pronounced *grahd*), Smerch (Tornado) and Uragan (Hurricane, pronounced *ooragahn*) multiple-launcher rocket systems – or occasionally, *Scud* intermediate-range ballistic missiles. If a malfunction occurred the aircraft's technicians stayed with the ground personnel and worked until the aircraft was fully operational again.

The *Candids* flew fully loaded and with the extra wear and tear on the tyres these had to be changed far more often than usual. Also, the extremely dusty conditions in Afghanistan meant that the engines' oil filters had to be cleaned every 20 to 25 flight hours instead of the usual 50; the all-pervading dust got into the oil tanks and congealed into black slime which clogged up the filters.

Khanabad AB was home to two units – a tactical reconnaissance regiment flying Yak-28R *Brewer-Ds* and Su-17M4R *Fitter-Ks* and a tactical bomber regiment flying Su-24M *Fencer-Ds*. These aided the IL-76 task force in every possible way. The airfield at Khanabad was a real mess, littered with broken ammunition packing crates and spent IRCM flare cases (a huge pit on the edge of the airfield left over from some construction work was filled to the brim with these flare cases!). Intact crates were promptly stolen and sold on the local market by the local ensigns. The canvas covers for the *Scud's* rocket motor nozzles were also valued, as they made capacious and extremely durable bags!

Above: **Close-up of the built-in APP-50s (at bottom of picture) on IL-76TD RA-76781 (ex IL-76MD CCCP-86927).** Yefim Gordon

Left: **Combat losses in Afghanistan led to the development of IRCM equipment for protection against heat-seeking missiles. This IL-76MD carries a full complement of APP-50 chaff/flare dispensers – built-in and strap-on.** Sergey & Dmitriy Komissarov collection

Below: **Close-up of the strap-on APP-50 'suitcases'; note powder stains from flare launches.** Sergey & Dmitriy Komissarov collection

Bottom: **A *Candid-B* fires IRCM flares on final approach to Kabul.** ITAR-TASS

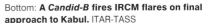

Unfortunately, not all missions ended well. The first loss came on 25th December 1979, the first day of the war. At 0735 Moscow time an IL-76M captained by Capt V V Golovchin (possibly CCCP-86036, c/n 093416500?, f/n 1305) hit a mountain ridge on approach to Kabul. Because of poor weather and scarcity of search and rescue forces the wreckage was not located until five days later. A group of mountain-climbers reached the crash site on 1st January 1980 but found no survivors among the seven crew and 35 troopers. The cause of the crash could not be determined since the flight data recorder (FDR) and cockpit voice recorder (CVR) were lost in the deep snow; the most likely explanation is that the pilots, who were unfamiliar with the approach conditions, had come in too low in darkness.

On 26th November 1984 Afghanistan claimed its next victim. IL-76M CCCP-86739 (c/n 083412354?, f/n 0909) captained by Maj Mikhail F Bondarenko was shot down by Mujahideen guerrillas right over Kabul. A captured 9K32 Strela-2 (SA-7 *Grail*) shoulder-launched surface-to-air missile hit the starboard wing between Nos 3 and 4 engines, causing fuel vapours in the half-filled tank to explode. The wing broke away and the aircraft immediately rolled inverted, disintegrating in mid-air because the airframe was overstressed. The crew had no time to send a distress call or even yell out. Luckily the *Candid* was carrying cargo this time, not personnel; ballpoint pens, notepads, cigarettes and other consumer

goods intended for the local army shop were scattered all over town.

After this tragic event IL-76 flights into Afghanistan were suspended for almost 18 months while countermeasures and new tactics were developed. First, 96-round APP-50 chaff/flare dispensers were built into the aft portions of the main gear wheel fairings; the flares were fired at preset intervals. The APP-50s were installed by the Tashkent plant, starting in 1985, and each aircraft took two months to upgrade. IL-76Ms and 'MDs thus modified include CCCP-76617 (?), -76635, -76641, -76655, -76659, -76677, -76687, -76694, -76697, -76698, -76705 through -76708, -76713, -76736, -76741, -76764, -76767, -86905, -86906, -86915, -86925 No1 and -86927.

A different arrangement was introduced in 1987. Two 96- or 192-round APP-50s were mounted in large streamlined pods on the rear fuselage sides, promptly earning such nicknames as *chemodahny* (suitcases) or *ooshi* (ears). The pods gained much wider use than the built-in version because they could be installed and removed easily if need arose. Aircraft equipped with the strap-on 'suitcases' included CCCP-76650, -76749, -76765, -76771, -76777 through -76779, -78750, -78764, -78772, -78773, -78792, -78799, -78801, -78802, -78807, -78808, -78819, -78820, -78826, -78831, -78837, -78838, -78839, -78842, -78844, -78850, -78853 and -78854. Some IL-76MDs with built-in dispensers (eg, CCCP-76697, -76736, -76764, -86905, -86906 and 86915) were later retrofitted with 96-round pods.

Top left and top right: **The increased stress and strain caused by the special approach technique in Afghanistan caused fatigue cracks to appear in the engine pylons and aft fuselage sides. These were dealt with by riveting on reinforcement plates, as illustrated by IL-76MD RA-78807** (left) **and IL-76 *sans suffixe* CCCP-86631** (right). Sergey Panov

Above left: **On 6th June 1990 IL-76MD CCCP-86905 was damaged beyond repair in a belly landing at Kabul after being hit by a Stinger missile.** Sergey & Dmitriy Komissarov collection

Above right: **Close-up of the missile damage on CCCP-86905. The retracted nosewheels can be seen through the hole.** Sergey & Dmitriy Komissarov collection

The flares were to be launched automatically by the Rifma (Rhyme) system popularly known as *bychiy glahz* (bull's eye).[10] This was an optical sensor which detected the flash when a missile was fired at the aircraft. However, this turned out to be extremely troublesome, reacting to any reflection of the sun, and did not gain wide use; only one IL-76MD of the Composite Flight Detachment in Tashkent had the Rifma kit.

Finally, additional nitrogen bottles for fuel system pressurisation were fitted to complement the inert gas generator which was ineffective during sharp climb or descent. They were installed in the underfloor compartment for storing wheel chocks, stepladders, intake covers and other paraphernalia that went with the aircraft. Of course, relatively new aircraft were the first to be upgraded.

Ironically, IL-76MDs operating into Afghanistan had the guns and ECM equipment (as well as some sensitive avionics items) removed because they were supposed to look like civil aircraft! The tail gunner remained, however, acting as observer and launching IRCM flares after spotting an incoming missile. He also assisted during ground operations.

Despite the addition of ESM equipment, IL-76 crews used a new piloting technique similar to the 'Khe Sanh tactical approach' used by the USAF in Vietnam. The aircraft would stay at about 8,000m (26,246ft) until it entered the air defence zone of Kabul Airport, then descend in a tight spiral to minimise the danger of being fired upon. Climbout on the return trip was also in a tight spiral.

The added stress and strain on the airframe during such violent manoeuvres took its toll on the aircraft. Spoiler actuators leaked; fatigue cracks began appearing in the engine pylon skins and the aft fuselage near the main gear fairings. The cracks were dealt with by riveting on aluminium reinforcement plates; if you see a *Candid* with such 'patches' you can be 95% sure this one has seen action in Afghanistan. 'Six to eight aircraft from every [IL-76] unit – the ones that had been upgraded with the flare packs – were permanently assigned to the Afghan group', an IL-76 crew member recalls. 'We felt sorry for them because the aircraft operated into Afghanistan day after day after day and it wrought havoc with their service life.'

Take-offs and landings of heavy transport aircraft were always covered by a pair of Mi-24 *Hind* gunship helicopters – especially during the pullout phase when the personnel were airlifted out of the country. The Mi-24s also fired IRCM flares and could promptly take out a Mujahideen ambush on the outskirts of the airport Sometimes the choppers got hit by a Stinger missile intended for the transports…

Still, attrition continued. At 1133 Moscow time on 27th March 1990 IL-76MD CCCP-78781 (c/n 0083489670, f/n 6708) crashed on the approach to Kabul on flight AFL-3501. The aircraft, which was delivering jet fuel in its wing tanks, belonged to the Composite Flight Detachment at Toozel' AB and was flown by a civilian crew under contract from Moscow-Sheremet'yevo (at the time crews operating into Afghanistan received combat pay – US$ 240 per person for each flight).

When the aircraft was in the middle of its approach pattern the ATC officer told the crew to hold an altitude of 5,800m (19,028ft) because an Afghan Air Force An-32 was climbing out from Kabul. In so doing the crew was

late in retracting the lift dumpers, causing the airspeed to drop below normal. This was the first in a series of mistakes which ultimately caused the crash.

For unknown reasons the pilots retracted the flaps five seconds after completing the second turn of the landing pattern, which was contrary to the flight manual. The third turn was initiated at 480m (1,574ft) and 360km/h (194kts) IAS; the minimum safe speed in the aircraft's present configuration was 420km/h (227kts). At the same time tailplane trim was increased from -2° to -2.8°, causing the angle of attack (AOA) to increase to 24°, which by far exceeded the prescribed limits. At AOAs around 20° the IL-76 has virtually zero lateral stability and any aileron input may cause the aircraft to stall.

Crews of other VTA aircraft being unloaded at Kabul watched in horror as CCCP-78781 started swaying from side to side like a dry leaf borne on the wind, then spiralled down and impacted 4km (2.5 miles) from the runway threshold, erupting in a fireball. The entire crew of captain Vladimir A Tikhomeerov, first officer Vladimir L Popov, navigator Vladimir G Kononenko, flight engineer Vladimir M Soomenkov, radio operator Anatoliy N Starkov, equipment operators Nikolay V Grooditsyn and Sergey N Chernyshov and mechanics Eskender B Abbasov and Abdusamat T Aliyev died on the spot. Both 'black boxes' were seriously damaged and the cause of the crash could not be determined in full.

On 6th June 1990 another IL-76MD based at Toozel', CCCP-86905 (c/n 0023436054, f/n 2704), was approaching Kabul on flight AFL-3521 with a cargo of 50 tons (110,229 lb) of jet fuel. The crew included captain Aleksandr K Kasatkin, inspector pilot Valeriy S Gres'ko, first officer Anatoliy Z Fomenko, navigator Aleksan-

dr L Krachkov, flight engineer Vladimir I Cheremnykh, radio operator Viktor M Lyutarevich, equipment operators Sergey B Tsooprik and Mirkamol A Mirkhaidarov, and mechanics Aleksandr A Gordoyev and Igor' A Pirogov.

At 0447hr 07sec Moscow time, as the aircraft passed over the Pagman ridge, a Stinger missile struck the fuselage between the flight deck escape hatch and the port entry door. The resulting explosion tore a 2 x 1.5m (6ft 7in x 4ft 11in) hole in the fuselage side, damaging the electrics and main hydraulic system and causing a total failure of the captain's flight instruments, No1 and 2 engine instruments and landing gear position indicator. At the time the aircraft was 34km (21 miles) from Kabul at 7,750m (25,426ft) and the crew did not launch IRCM flares, not expecting to be attacked at altitudes in excess of 7,000m (22,965ft). Normally the flares were launched 14km (8.7 miles) from Kabul.

The aircraft jerked violently to the right as the cabin decompressed; dust and smoke from burning hydraulic fluid poured into the flight deck. The flight engineer shut down Nos 1 and 2 engines, fearing that debris flying from the cabin could be ingested, causing uncontained failure and fire. As he did so, the generators stopped and the radio died; the Russian air traffic controller in Kabul repeatedly but unsuccessfully tried to get in touch with the crew.

The landing gear could not be extended normally because of the hydraulics failure and Kasatkin opted not to use emergency extension since he could not be sure the gear was down and locked. At 0454hr 42sec CCCP-86905 made a wheels-up, flaps-up landing on the old dirt strip and came to rest after 940m (3,084ft), swinging 90° to the right. Nobody was hurt but the aircraft was declared a write-off.

Goin' home. Soviet Army soldiers returning from Afghanistan walk past IL-76MDs CCCP-76736 and CCCP-76749 at Tashkent. Both aircraft are equipped with strap-on chaff/flare dispensers.
ITAR-TASS

There were also minor incidents like the one involving a squadron of Su-24 *Fencer-B* tactical bombers coming home to Khanabad one night after a raid on Kandahar. The lead aircraft burst a tyre on landing and caught fire, blocking the runway, so the remaining bombers were ordered to head for Kokaïdy which was the alternate airfield. With almost zero fuel the *Fencers* landed there, hot on one another's heels. In the ensuing commotion the brake parachutes were left behind on the runway, and one of them was promptly ingested by an IL-76 taxying out for take-off. Of course the sortie had to be cancelled; the transport was grounded for an engine change, and the relationship between the bomber crews and the base commanders was soured.

The IL-76 bore the brunt of the transport operations in Afghanistan. By the end of the 12-year war (December 1991) Soviet Air Force *Candids* had made 14,700 flights into Afghanistan, transporting 786,200 servicemen and 315,800 tons (696,208,112 lb) of cargo – 89% and 74% of the total quantity respectively.

Quasi-Aeroflot *Candid-Bs* put in an appearance in other wars in which the Soviet Union was not formally involved. Between 7th November and 31st December 1977 VTA IL-76Ms were used to airlift supplies to Ethiopia when the Soviet Union supported the Addis Ababa regime in its losing struggle against separatists in the Eritrea and Ogaden provinces. This was the type's first deployment outside the Warsaw Pact nations. The aircraft delivered weaponry, including APCs, artillery and tactical missiles, from military depots in the Urals Defence District, flying over Afghan and Iranian territory. This operation proved the IL-76's considerable potential, demonstrating that the VTA could now airlift at least three army divisions to the Middle East or Africa within some 10 hours.

Soviet Air Force IL-76MDs were also used to extend military support to the pro-Communist Angolan government of José Eduardo dos Santos fighting against UNITA rebels. The support missions did not always go without mishap. In the summer of 1988 IL-76MD CCCP-78768 (c/n 0083487603, f/n 6601) captained by Maj S Mel'nikov was hit by a Stinger shortly after take-off from Luena airbase. With one engine on fire the aircraft made it back to Luena.

On 28th August 1992 IL-76MD CCCP-78780 (c/n 0083489666?, f/n 6707)[11] received a direct hit from an artillery round at Kabul airport where it had arrived together with two other IL-76MDs to evacuate Soviet embassy personnel as Taliban troops attacked Kabul. The aircraft burned

out, injuring two crew members. Another IL-76MD captained by Lt Col A S Kopyrkin interrupted its take-off run to pick up the crew and passengers and took off under fire with the mainwheel tyres shot to pieces. For this operation Lt Col Kopyrkin, Col Ye A Zelenov (regiment CO) and three VDV servicemen received the Hero of Russia title; the remaining participants of the operation were awarded the Personal Bravery Order.

Hostilities in Afghanistan continued after the Soviet withdrawal, and even now the country is torn apart by war as a handful of warlords is fighting for power. In this war Russia supported the anti-Taliban coalition and the Kabul government of Burhanuddin Rabbani. This angered the opposition and on 3rd August 1995 a Taliban MiG-19S *Farmer-C* intercepted IL-76TD RA-76842 (c/n 1033418616, f/n 9104) owned by the Russian airline Airstan, forcing it down in Kandahar 'for customs inspection'. The aircraft, which had been chartered by the UAE-based airline Transavia, was flying from Tirana to Kabul via Sharjah with about 30 tons (66,000 lb) of weapons for the government forces.

When the ammunition was discovered the aircraft was impounded and the crew (captain Vladimir I Sharpatov, first officer Ghazinur G Khairoollin, navigator Aleksandr V Zdor, flight engineer Askhat M Abbyazov, radio operator Yuriy N Vshivtsev and loadmasters Sergey B Bootoozov and Viktor P Ryazanov) were taken hostage. The Talibs demanded the release of Afghan soldiers allegedly held as prisoners of war in Russia and demanded that Russia officially declare its non-involvement in Afghan affairs (read: stop its support of the Kabul government).

Repeated attempts to free the crew via diplomatic channels (including a UN Security Council resolution and an appeal by US President Bill Clinton) gave no results. After lengthy negotiations the Taliban Council promised to release the hostages on 30th December but then refused to do so. However, the Russian authorities contacted the nations bordering on Afghanistan, requesting assistance in case the captives managed to escape. Russian secret services were planning an operation to liberate the crew by force but this was vetoed by the government for fear the hostages might get killed.

For a year the airmen carefully planned their escape, using titbits of information leaked to them by visiting Russian representatives who periodically came to Kandahar to negotiate

Lost and found – Airstan IL-76TD RA-76842 which was captured by the Talibs on 3rd August 1995 and escaped on 16th August 1996.
Peter Davison

Russian Air Force IL-76MDs, including RA-78818 from Migalovo AB, airlifted the Russian KFOR contingent to Kosovo in the summer of 1999.
Yefim Gordon

with the Talibs. 'We decided to escape because we had lost faith in the government', Sharpatov said later. The crew thrice persuaded their captors to give them access to the aircraft in order to maintain it in airworthy condition. On the third occasion (in July 1996) the aircraft even made a short test flight, but there were eight armed guards aboard at the time and the captain decided not to take any chances.

Finally, on 16th August 1996 the Russians were taken to the airport again to perform routine maintenance. They were guarded by two armed Talibs, the chief warden, the chief of the guard and a few more men, including a Pakistani fighter pilot. The latter was the most dangerous of the lot, since he could easily guess the crew's intentions and spoke fairly good Russian into the bargain.

Then the airmen had 'a stroke of luck', as Sharpatov later put it. The APU shut down automatically because of the high ambient temperature. After a while the chief warden, the chief of the guard and the Pakistani pilot left for the control tower, leaving the two armed guards and a unarmed man to guard the crew. Seizing their chance, the crew managed to start the engines, got the plane into the air and made for Iran – taking with them the three guards which were promptly overpowered. The take-off run had to be started from the middle of the runway and the remaining runway length was only just enough to get airborne.

On the ground all hell was let loose. Two cars raced from the control tower to block the runway – too late. Then two Taliban fighters scrambled to intercept but by the greatest good luck one of them burst a tyre and could not take off. The other fighter lost its prey because the pilot expected the freighter to head north for Kabul and thence for Russia, not west. (Another possibility is that the fighter pilot was the same one who had forced the freighter down a year ago. He had taken his flying training in the Soviet Union and had no ill feelings for Russia but had been forced into the Taliban army, the Talibs threatening to kill his family if he refused. The pilot knew Vladimir Sharpatov, and it is just possible that he intentionally let the Russians get away.)

Maintaining radio silence, the IL-76 flew at 50 to 100m (164 to 328ft) to avoid radar detection, raising an almighty dust trail. Using the official air corridors reserved for it, the aircraft landed at Sharjah, making a short hop to Abu Dhabi on the same day. Then the state machinery was brought into play to get the airmen home quickly and safely (crossing the Russian border would otherwise have been a major problem, since the Talibs had taken their passports) and avoid an international ruckus in the unlikely event that Afghanistan accused them of abducting three Afghan citizens. Originally the UAE government insisted that the three Talibs be taken to Moscow together with the Russian pilots, but this issue was quickly solved.

The Russian media had been following the hostage drama closely, and of course the crew's almost miraculous escape created a sensation. On 22nd August 1996 Vladimir Sharpatov and Ghazimur Khairoollin were awarded the Hero of Russia title, the other crewmen receiving the the Personal Bravery Order. Some papers questioned the 'incredible luck' story, claiming that a ransom had been quietly paid for the airmen's lives or they had been exchanged for a supply of weapons.

The IL-76 was actively used in the First Chechen War (1994-96). Russian Air Force *Candid-Bs* delivered troops, equipment and ammunition to Groznyy-Severnyy airport[12] and Mozdok (Ingushetia) from places as far apart as Chkalovskaya AB and Komsomol'sk-on-Amur. Additionally, A-50 AWACS aircraft monitored the airspace over the war zone.

The *Candid* also participated in the Kosovo conflict of 1999 – in more than one way. At least one IL-76T owned by the Latvian airline Inversija (YL-LAK) airlifted NATO war materiel to Tirana during Operation *Allied Force*. A Russian Air Force IL-76MD was reportedly used in April 1999 to deliver the wreckage of Lockheed F-117A Nighthawk 82-0806/'HO' (49th FW/8th FS 'Black Sheep') shot down on 27th March 1999 to Russia for detailed analysis. The F-117A flown by Capt Ken Dwelle had been destroyed by a Yugoslav Air Force MiG-29 *Fulcrum-A* flown by Lt Col Gvozden Djukić about 30km (25 miles) north-west of Belgrade.

Candids airlifted the main part of the Russian contingent of the multinational peacekeeping forces in Kosovo (KFOR) to Prishtina's Slatina airport. On 26th June 1999 IL-76MD RA-78838 became the first aircraft to land there for the past six months – beating an RAF C-130K (Hercules C Mk 3P) to the target by a matter of minutes. Greeted by military top brass (including the Russian KFOR contingent Commander Col Gen Viktor Zavarzin) and numerous TV journalists, the aircraft taxied in, proudly flying the Russian flag from the flight deck roof emergency exit.

During the next day two more IL-76MDs arrived at Slatina, carrying equipment to be used in rebuilding the airport's navaids which had been destroyed and/or pillaged during the war. Three more *Candids* came on 28th June, after which the airport was closed for three days while the equipment was installed.

Then there was a pause because Hungary, which had recently joined the NATO, would not grant an air corridor for Russian aircraft carrying peacekeepers. This prompted a decision to send part of the Russian contingent by sea via Greece, where they would arrive aboard Russian Navy landing ships. On 5th July, however, the air corridor issue was finally settled and next day at 0945 the first Russian Air Force IL-76MD with troops arrived at Slatina. The Russian *Candids* operated out of Tver'-Migalovo AB (224th Flight Detachment aircraft), Ivanovo-Severnyy AB and Pskov-Kresty AB; the aircraft involved included RA-76713 (equipped with strap-on APP-50 chaff/flare dispensers), RA-78809 and RA-78818.

At 1500 on 6th July what was officially presented as the first civil aircraft to land at Slatina after Operation *Allied Force* arrived – again an IL-76MD, this time a Ukrainian Cargo Airways aircraft registered UR-UCS and carrying a humanitarian cargo for the United Nations. The aircraft was duly painted white overall with UN titles on the nose and tail.

The most recent conflict in which the IL-76 participated began in August 1999; it is officially called the anti-terrorist operation in the North Caucasus but has already been dubbed the Second Chechen War by the media. Russian Air Force *Candid-Bs* carried troops and materiel to Mozdok (which, as in the case of the First Chechen War, is the main base of the federal troops) and Makhachkala. Interestingly, at least one aircraft (obviously taken out out of storage) still carried the old Soviet flag and prefix. The IL-76MD Skal'pel'-MT flying hospital (RA-86906) reportedly took part in the war in January 2000 when the battles for Groznyy were at their fiercest, indicating high losses among the federal troops.

North and South

The history of the Ilyushin OKB is closely connected with polar research. Ilyushin aircraft were actively operated by Aeroflot's Polar Directorate from the early 1950s, performing resupply operations for research stations and ice reconnaissance along the Northern Sea Route. The IL-12T and IL-14G freighters had an excellent reputation with Polar Aviation crews for their ability to operate from short semi-prepared runways (including those on ice floes with drifting research stations) and rugged dependability in the harshest environments.

Indeed, the IL-14 earned the ultimate praise – the nickname *Yevo Velichestvo Ledovik Chetyrnadtsatyy* (His Majesty King Iceman the Fourteenth)![13] One example registered CCCP-41808 was preserved at the Soviet Antarctic research station Droozhnaya until wrecked by a hurricane. And now that the IL-14 is long since retired, there is no replacement in sight; the An-74 originally conceived as a polar version of the An-72 turned out to be ill-suited for polar operations (for instance, it has no provision for skis). The king is dead... new king wanted!

The *Candid*'s first polar mission came on 15th September 1982. Two *Candid-Bs* chartered from the VTA – an IL-76 *sans suffixe* captained by Guards Lt Col N P Blinov and an IL-76M captained by Guards Maj V A Borodin – paradropped supplies to the Severnyy Polyus-25 (North Pole-25, or SP-25) drifting ice station in the Arctic Ocean. The mission was led by Col A T Orlenko and Col D K Akhmetzyanov.

On 10th December of the following year IL-76TD CCCP-76473 (then operated by Gos-NII GA) performed another supply mission for SP-25, delivering research equipment and other goods. To ensure accurate cargo delivery the aircraft had to be fitted with an optical bomb sight borrowed from a *Candid-B*. The crew

included captain M S Kuznetsov, first officer V Roolyakov, navigator I Abdulayev and radio operator V Gherasimov. The expedition was led by Zh. K Shishkin.

The objective was to drop the cargo at night on a pad measuring 300 x 600m (984 x 1,968ft); if it missed, finding it among the masses of broken ice surrounding the station would be very hard indeed. Still, the crew did an excellent job. Taking off from Pevek on the coast of the East Siberian Sea, the aircraft made two passes over the station at 150m (492ft), placing the cargo (including two Christmas trees) squarely on the LZ marked by bonfires. On the way home the crew could not resist the temptation to make a pass over the North Pole – for the first time on an IL-76.

With these encouraging results, polar supply operations soon became routine. In early May 1984 two quasi-civil IL-76MDs paradropped 120 200-litre (44 Imperial gallon) drums[14] of diesel fuel on the SP-26 ice station which was then 1,280km (795 miles) from Pevek. One aircraft was flown by captain V A Borodin, first officer Ye. Frolov, navigator V Davidenko, flight engineer A Fil'chenkov, radio operator V Tarabahn'ko, paradrop systems operator S Shelepov and tail gunner V Manyshev, the other crew comprised captain A Maksimov, first officer A Neverov, navigator V Bryklya, flight engineer V Serdyuk, radio operator L Novitskiy, paradrop systems operator V Balagoorov and tail gunner V Minin.

Flying at 600m (1,968ft), each aircraft dropped two P-7 pallets with 30 fuel drums each on a pad measuring 200 x 300m (656 x 984ft). In contrast, the IL-14G can take only five or six fuel drums; this means IL-14s would have to make 20 to 24 flights to SP-26 (with several refuelling stops, note). And consider also that the fuel requirement of an ice station is 500 to 800 fuel drums a year – ie, 100,000 to 160,000 litres (22,000 to 35,200 Imperial gallons).

A few days later, on 15th May, IL-76MD CCCP-76549 captained by Maj A I Maksimov delivered a team of researchers and various cargoes to the newly-established SP-27 ice station. On the Air Force side the operation, named EksPArk-84 (*Ekspeditsiya 'Parashooty nad Arktikoy'* – 'Parachutes over Arctica' Expedition), was led by Col Yuriy A Koba. The 19-man research team included A Z Sidorenko (expedition leader), V Loochshev, V Chizhik, V Prokopov, V Yunok, M Antyukhin, A Kubyshkin, N Selivanov, V Nechipas, A Zagorodnykh, L Zhelonkin, V Dmitriyenko, V Shelopoogin, I Weinshtein etc.

Prefabricated cabins, a DT-75 bulldozer and fuel drums on P-7 pallets were dropped first, followed by an 'airborne assault'. Compared to the traditional delivery method (by ship) the paradropping technique cut costs by more than 60% and reduced mission preparation time by a factor of seven.

In the spring of 1986 the researchers at SP-27 had to turn to the Air Force for help when the ice floe cracked, rendering the station's runway unusable; fuel and new equipment could only be delivered by parachute. Thus on 17th May two IL-76MDs captained by Yuriy Strel'tsov and V A Borodin paradropped fuel drums and six more researchers. Shortly afterwards two more IL-76MDs played a crucial role in the establishment of SP-28.

In November 1986 the State Committee for Hydrological and Weather Research (Goskomghidromet) which operated the ice stations requested urgent assistance. The ice in the Arctic Ocean started shifting rapidly and SP-27 found itself beyond the 83rd parallel, out of reach of the IL-14 normally used for resupply operations. As if that were not enough, the ice floe with station SP-28 broke in two on 10th November, making the runway totally unusable. Hence the EksPArk-86 expedition had to be organised under the leadership of I B Vorob'yov and Nikolay D Talikov.

Again an IL-76MD was used; this time, however, it was not an Air Force machine but an Ilyushin OKB example, CCCP-76623 captained by Stanislav G Bliznyuk. EksPArk-86 was also the first occasion when PGS-500 paradrop-

pable pallets (PGS = *parashootnaya groozovaya sistema* – parachute cargo system) were used in the Arctic. The *Candid*'s P-7 pallets were ill-suited for Arctic operations, being too bulky (4.216 x 3.192 m; 13ft 10in x 10ft 6in) and too heavy (1,100kg/2,425 lb). Worst of all, they were one-piece structures and could not be disassembled for carriage by the IL-14G or An-26, which meant the costly pallets had to be abandoned.

On the other hand, the lightweight PGS-500 pallets equipped with a five-canopy parachute system were standard on the An-12. By then the *Cub* had been almost completely replaced by the IL-76 in the transport role (only specialised ELINT, ECM and SAR versions remained in service) and storage depots were crammed with huge numbers of PGS-500 pallets for which the VTA had no further use.

An immediate problem arose; unlike the An-12, the IL-76 has no powered conveyor belt for 'unloading' the pallets and the track of the fold-away roller conveyors in the freight hold floor does not match the width of the PGS-500. The problem was solved by attaching the roller conveyors to special guide rails which, in turn, were locked into position, using the standard cargo tiedown points. The pallets also had to be adapted for the mission; special stabilising surfaces were mounted on the sides, opening by means of rip cords, and two parachutes (a main canopy and a stabilising parachute) were used instead of five. Ilyushin engineers Nikolay D Talikov, V Belyy, A Lukin, V Arkhipov and A D Yegutko developed these modifications.

The P-7 pallet, of which the *Candid* could take two, accommodated up to 40 standard 200-litre fuel drums, amounting to 80 drums per aircraft. In contrast, 26 PGS-500s with four drums each could be loaded in a double row, totalling 104 drums. With that many pallets extracting them by means of drogue parachutes would be risky, as the parachutes could get entangled. Hence Ilyushin engineers devised a 'dump truck technology'; quite simply, the pilot would begin a steep climb at the right moment and the pallets would roll out of the aircraft under their own weight. The modifications and drop technology were developed in just a month.

In mid-December IL-76MD CCCP-76623 arrived in Tiksi on the Laptev Sea coast. However, poor weather prevented any flights until 23rd December. Operating in *extremely* instrumental meteorological conditions – night, horizontal visibility 50m (164ft), wind speed 15 to 18m/sec (30 to 36kts), cloudbase unknown – the aircraft delivered more than 80 tons (176,366 lb) of fuel and foodstuffs to SP-27 and SP-28. On 28th December the mission had to be aborted when the approaches to the target were suddenly obscured by thick fog. The fifth and final sortie was made on 7th January 1987.

On 15-28th April 1987 two Soviet Air Force IL-76MDs captained by Maj A I Maksimov and Maj S P Ushakov paradropped supplies to ice stations SP-27 and SP-28 and to weather research stations on Wiese Island and Ostrov Uyedineniya (Solitude Island). The mission was led by A Z Sidorenko; Ilyushin engineers A D Yegutko and V S Ponyatoykin took part in the mission.

Operation EksPArk-88 was staged from 22nd April to 5th May 1988. This time IL-76MD CCCP-76623 captained by Stanislav G Bliznyuk delivered fuel to SP-28, which was then in the Laptev Sea 2,125km (1,320 miles) from Khatanga, and the new ice station SP-29. As usual, the mission was led by A Z Sidorenko who 'got off' at SP-28. Mother Nature threw in a challenge once again – visibility deteriorated sharply 20 minutes before arrival; still, navigators V Schchotkin and I Abdulayev unerringly guided the aircraft to the drop zone.

The second sortie of EksPArk-88 took place on 26th April. This time the aircraft overflew the North Pole to greet the ski expedition led by Dmitriy Shparo which passed the Pole that day. A third flight followed on 29th April; by then the aircraft had delivered 70 tons (154,321 lb) of diesel fuel to SP-28 and 25 tons (55,114 lb) to SP-29.

EksPArk-88 was the first operational use of a parachute cargo delivery system developed by V Ponomarenko. Dubbed 'electronic parachutist' by the polar researchers, this consisted of a wing-type parachute, a remote control unit and a servo which hauled on the rigging lines to control the direction of descent. The remote control provided for a landing accuracy margin of 10m (33ft). Ponomarenko personally controlled the 'electronic parachutist' after landing at SP-28.

More action came on 5th November same year when CCCP-76623 was called upon to aid ice station SP-27 which had drifted away to the Canadian sector of the Arctic Ocean (86° north and 2° 30' west). The crew included captain Igor' R Zakirov, first officer A Minchenok, navigators V Schchotkin and I Abdulayev, radio operator V Orlov, engineers M N Weinshtein (Ilyushin OKB) and A Bol'shakov (GosNII GA). Ilyushin CTP Stanislav G Bliznyuk who usually flew EksPArk missions was otherwise engaged at the time, testing the first prototype IL-96-300 (CCCP-96000).

The aircraft was laden with 21 PGS-500 pallets and carried a group of researchers led by A Z Sidorenko. After dropping the cargo on a 300 x 80m (984 x 262ft) pad CCCP-76623 returned to Moscow; the non-stop flight had lasted 10 hours 15 minutes.

Operating from Pevek, IL-76TD CCCP-76481 paradropped 72 tons (158, 730 lb) of diesel fuel to ice stations SP-28, SP-30 and SP-31 and weather research stations on Rudolf Island, Hayes Island, Viktoriya Island and Roosskiy Island on 4-15th January 1989. Despite belonging to GosNII GA, the aircraft was flown by an Ilyushin OKB crew captained by Igor' R Zakirov. This was partly an emergency operation; caught by a strong current, SP-28 was swiftly heading for the Atlantic Ocean where the ice floe would quickly melt. Goskomghidromet had no alternative but to charter the nuclear-powered icebreaker *Rossiya* and evacuate the researchers; nevertheless, supplies had to be delivered.

This time the mission was marred by an incident when the tried and tested PGS-500 parachute system suddenly failed. On 13th January, when the aircraft was making its first 'bombing run' over SP-30, the parachutes on seven pallets out of 18 did not open. Not wanting to risk the rest of the cargo, Zakirov decided to return to Pevek but Weinshtein dissuaded him. Instead, A Romanov parachuted to the ice station and quickly found the cause of the failure while the IL-76 circled overhead. Acting on his instructions, the technicians aboard the aircraft inspected the remaining pallets and found the same fault – the parachutes had been improperly packed. This was quickly corrected and the rest of the cargo dropped normally.

Bad news travels fast; on hearing of the first unsuccessful drop at SP-30 the commander of SP-31 turned down the cargo intended for the station, requesting that only the mail be dropped. Still, the cargo was delivered without mishap this time.

In March 1989 IL-76TD CCCP-76481 was again used in a paradropping operation in the far north – this time for the Ministry of Geology. Operating out of Khatanga, the aircraft delivered two DT-75 bulldozers on P-7 pallets, 200

fuel drums and several liquid propane-butane (LPB) bottles on PGS-500 pallets to the site of an ice runway under construction at 82° 30' north and 165° 30' east. In early October of the same year an IL-76TD (possibly the same aircraft) captained by Distinguished test pilot Boris L'vov paradropped equipment and materials for the Payakhskaya-1 research drilling rig on the Yamal Peninsula.

In mid-December 1989 an IL-76TD flown by test pilots M Chilinyak and M Ptitsyn flew from Moscow to Sredniy Island ('Middle Island'), Severnaya Zemlya Archipelago, via Leningrad and Arkhangel'sk. From there the aircraft delivered fuel, food and equipment to research stations on Ushakov Island, Pravda Island, Cape Chelyuskin and Cape Sterligov. The main part of the cargo (16 tons/35,273 lb) was meant for ice stations SP-30 and SP-31. A special 'airline' called Exparc was established for such operations in post-Soviet times with a fleet of two IL-76TDs (see next chapter).

The *Candid*'s involvement in Antarctic research began a little later, when the need to replace the IL-18Ds carrying personnel to and from the Soviet research stations became acute. The IL-18D offered comfort and long range – both valuable assets, considering how much longer the road to Antarctica is. However, the *Coot* required a long runway with a hard-packed surface which had to be prepared a long time before the aircraft's arrival, and this was a back-breaking job. Besides, the IL-18 had no cargo door and hence could not carry bulky things like bulldozers, and fuel drums. A true freighter was needed, and the IL-76 was the obvious choice.

Two new IL-76TDs – CCCP-76478 and CCCP-76479 – were loaned from TsUMVS in 1985. Both aircraft received Aeroflot's stylish polar colour scheme[15] with red outer wings and horizontal tail (for high definition against white backgrounds in the event of a forced landing),

CCCP-76549

Polar researchers line up un front of IL-76MD CCCP-76549 before departure to the newly-established SP-27 ice station. ITAR-TASS

IL-76MD CCCP-76623 taxies at Zhukovskiy, displaying the Transantarctica international ski expedition badge on the forward fuselage.
Dmitriy Komissarov

days later; it had delivered 170 persons and some 15 tons (33,068 lb) of cargo.

On 14th November 1988 one of the two Polar Aviation IL-76TDs arrived at Molodyozhnaya again, departing two days later. The next flight took place in February 1989. By 1992 both aircraft had been returned to TsUMVS (later transformed into Aeroflot Russian International Airlines), becoming RA-76478 and RA-76479. Initially they retained basic polar colours but, as on most of ARIA's aircraft, the vertical tail was painted grey so that the white upper stripe of the Russian flag would be clearly visible.

On 12th July 1989 IL-76MD CCCP-76623 captained by Stanislav G Bliznyuk took off from Moscow/Sheremet'yevo-1, destination Antarctica. The mission was unusual in several ways. First, this was the first flight to Antarctica in the middle of the polar winter. Second, the passengers were not just an ordinary relief crew for an ice station but the Transantarctica international ski expedition led by Jean-Louis Etienne; the team included Viktor Boyarskiy (USSR), William Steager (USA), Geoffrey Summers (UK), Kitso Funatsu (Japan) and Xing Da-he (China). Hence a badge depicting Antarctica with the proposed route of the expedition surrounded by the flags of the six participating nations was painted on both sides of the fuselage aft of the entry doors. Goskomghidromet and the Ilyushin OKB organised the expedition on behalf of the Soviet Union; Goskomghidromet Vice-Chairman Artur N Chilingarov (HSU) and Nikolay D Talikov were the mission leaders.

Finally, for the first time the route lay to King George Island via North and South America. This was longer than the usual route via the Mediterranean, the Middle East and Africa, but the distance from the tip of South America to Antarctica was just 1,200km (745 miles). In contrast, the final leg of the African route was some 5,000km (3,105 miles) long, and flying over water in those parts was difficult because of the frequent storms which made getting to Antarctica largely a matter of chance.

From Moscow the aircraft headed for Gander, Montreal and Minneapolis where the foreign participants in the expedition boarded the jet and their equipment was loaded, including 42 huskies used for towing sleds with food. Thence the route lay to Miami (CCCP-76623 was the first Soviet aircraft to land there), Havana, Lima, Buenos Aires and Punta Arenas. The Chilean city of Punta Arenas is the southernmost city on earth, being located at 53° south and 71° west.

The final leg of the journey took the aircraft to King George Island, just a stone's throw from the Antarctic Peninsula, where the Chilean Air Force has an auxiliary airfield. This was a daunt-

a red cheatline and black Aeroflot titles. CCCP-76479 had the normal red/white tail with the registration in white on red, whereas CCCP-76478 (the standby aircraft) had a white tail with a black registration.

As mentioned earlier, the IL-76 can carry three 32-seat passenger modules. The Polar division, however, dispensed with the modules so as not to cart useless weight around and use the freight hold more efficiently. The aircraft was fitted with 108 passenger seats in five-abreast configuration (3+2); a galley and a toilet were mounted at the rear of the hold, and baggage was carried on the cargo ramp. This arrangement was specially developed for the Moscow-Antarctica service and evaluated on 17th November 1985 when CCCP-76479 flew from Moscow to Tashkent and back. Of course, the 'cabin' was somewhat claustrophobic, but then, the *Candid* was faster than the *Coot* and the flight would be shorter (to say nothing of the lack of the IL-18's pervasive turboprop roar which reached 100 dB in some parts of the aircraft!).

On 27th January 1986 CCCP-76479 completed a series of tests on a snow-covered strip near Omsk. On 18th February the aircraft flew from Moscow-Sheremet'yevo to Leningrad to pick up a research team led by V Ya. Kiselyov going to ice station Molodyozhnaya (the name means 'Youth Station'). At this stage it was flown by captain Yuriy Golovchenko, first officer Ye. Malakhov, navigator Ye. Ol'chev, flight engineer V Schchipanov and radio operator S Moskvitin.

Then there was a three-day delay caused by bad weather in Antarctica. Finally, on 22nd February the *Candid* departed from Leningrad-Pulkovo to Larnaca on the first leg of flight SU 1453. Now the aircraft was flown by captain Yuriy Yakovlev, first officer L Zaïtsev, navigator G Nikolayenko, flight engineer L Letenkov and radio operator V Roolyakov. The next stop was at Djibouti where the aircraft stopped for the night. On the morning of 23rd February CCCP-76479 landed at Maputo – and got stuck for another 48 hours: Molodyozhnaya was obscured by a storm that showed no intention of moving on. Worse, the temperature at the

station rose and there was considerable risk that the carefully prepared runway would be damaged. The runway and apron constructed in 1980 had a multi-layer covering of hard-packed snow and ice 1m (3ft 3in) thick; the local ground personnel called them 'the slab'.

On 25th February IL-76TD CCCP-76479 finally touched down at Molodyozhnaya, making the type's first landing in Antarctica. The landing was so perfect that many of the passengers missed the touchdown; the entire team of researchers broke out in applause when the din of reverse thrust told them they had arrived.

The entire personnel of the research station poured out to greet the newcomers. The first question addressed to the crew was 'Have you brought the mail?'. This was logical enough; ships and aircraft carrying, among other things, long-awaited letters from home came to Antarctica at *very* long intervals, whereas the ice stations drifting around in the Arctic Ocean were within easy reach and were supplied rather more often.

On 26th February an IL-14G based in Antarctica took off from Molodyozhnaya, carrying a team of experts to ice station Novolazarevskaya, the *Candid*'s next destination, to inspect the runway there and decide whether it was suitable for the IL-76. It looked like a long, long wait for the crew; the slow IL-14 needed five hours to reach Novolazarevskaya, never mind the time needed for inspection. One of the crew members suggested running caterpillar tractors along the runway in order to break up the icy crust, fearing it would be 'too slippery to take-off'. 'Never! – said B Gagarin, an employee of the Leningrad Geological Institute. – It's the top layer of ice that gives the required bearing strength.'

At length a radio message giving the go-ahead came from Novolazarevskaya and soon the IL-76 took off. After circling a couple of times over the Japanese ice station Showa by way of a greeting the aircraft landed at Novolazarevskaya, unloaded the supplies and departed immediately to escape being caught by bad weather. On 1st March CCCP-76479 headed for home, arriving in Moscow three

ing task: the runway at King George Island was just 1,292m (4,238ft) long; until then the biggest aircraft to land there were Chilean Air Force C-130Hs. The runway was covered with wet snow and both ends dropped sharply into the sea (the Drake Passage on one side and the Bransfield Strait on the other). If you landed long, you would be in the drink; if you undershot, the result would be even worse. Therefore the crew of CCCP-76623 had a long discussion with Chilean pilots flying to Antarctica via King George Island.

The aircraft's estimated landing weight would be 140 tons (308,642 lb); at this weight the IL-76's flight manual requires the runway to be at least 1,600m (5,249ft) long. Still, it was not for nothing that the aircraft was flown by Ilyushin's chief test pilot whose job is to take the machine to its limits! The crew used every means of slowing the aircraft down. Tyre pressure was reduced by 50% to increase the contact area and hence wheel brake efficiency. The spoilers were deployed and reverse thrust on the inboard engines applied seconds before touchdown; after touchdown full reverse thrust was applied and the entry doors opened to increase drag.

It worked; the heavy freighter came to a standstill after just 750m (2,460ft)! Some passengers took a stroll to the end of the runway, just to see how deep the plunge would have been if the aircraft had not stopped in time.

The return routing was via Punta Arenas, Buenos Aires, Salvador (Bahia, Brazil), St. Paris Island (sic) and Prague. On 1st August the aircraft returned to Moscow after spending a total of 56 hours in the air and covering a distance of nearly 40,000km (24,844 miles). From August 1989 to May 1990 the Transantarctica expedition crossed the ice continent in a big zigzag, covering 5,986km (3,718 miles) from King George Island to the Soviet ice station Mirnyy on the Davis Sea coast in 220 days.

In July 1991 things were getting out of hand at ice station Molodyozhnaya which hosted two shifts of researchers instead of one – the 35th and 36th Soviet Antarctic expeditions. The old shift could not leave because the oceanographic vessel M/V Akademik Fyodorov which was to take it home suffered two fires and had to call at an African port for repairs. Another research vessel, M/V Mikhail Somov, was sent to the rescue but got into trouble as well – frustratingly, she was trapped by ice just 20km (10.8nm) from the Antarctic coast and started drifting helplessly. Goskomghidromet had no choice but to turn to the Ilyushin OKB for help, requesting that the 35th SAE be airlifted out of Antarctica.

The OKB leaders quickly worked out the details of the mission, and General Designer Ghenrikh V Novozhilov named the crew: captain Stanislav G Bliznyuk, first officer A Kotel'nikov, flight engineer V Volod'ko, navigator Yuriy Yegorov (assisted by two Aeroflot navigators, S Slipchenko and N Knyazev) and technicians V Alfyorov, Yuriy Bliznyuk, V S

Ponyatoykin, A Bol'shov, G Dyboonov and M Alekseyev. The expedition was led by Artur N Chilingarov and Nikolay D Talikov. It included K Zaïtsev, physician Ye. Martynicheva, Arctic & Antarctic Research Institute Director B Krootskikh and Vice-Director S Karpekin, Soviet Antarctic Expeditions Director V Lookin (formerly head of Arctic ice station SP-29), journalist V Ghanichev, photographer M Kharlampiyev and GosNII GA engineer A Bol'shakov who had made many flights to Molodyozhnaya.

The decision to fly was made when it became clear that the Mikhail Somov would be trapped for a long time yet and was unable to pick up the 35th SAE. But then it transpired that Goskomghidromet had no money to pay for the fuel, ATC fees and so on. Undaunted by this, the Ilyushin OKB decided to earn the required sum by flying a cargo charter. There was a cargo in Bangkok destined for Harare which all Western airlines had refused to deliver, as it was totally unsuitable for air freight operations. Its dimensions and weight exceeded the limits set forth in the IL-76's flight manual; still, time was running out and the expedition could not wait until something better turned up. 'Well,' the Ilyushin engineers said to themselves, 'we have considerable experience in carrying unique cargoes; we can handle it'.

On 12th August 1991 IL-76MD 'Falsie' CCCP-76822 departed from Zhukovskiy to Bangkok via Sharjah. The cargo indeed turned out to be unique – or rather uniquely abominable. Loading it took a full day because the sender had not bothered to pack it properly (probably believing that 'the Russian slobs will tolerate anything').

The flight from Bangkok to Harare involved two refuelling stops in Colombo and on Victoria Island in the Seychelles. In Colombo the ground controller directed the aircraft into a dead end by mistake; the pilots had no choice but to taxi backwards, using reverse thrust. In the Seychelles the pilots had to land at night at an unfamiliar airport with a runway extending into the ocean. Of course, the crew hoped to get a good night's rest after two long and tiresome flights. However, the local Aeroflot representative was determined to get rid of the unexpected 'guests' and demanded that the aircraft depart immediately after being refuelled. Ignoring him, the crew contacted the airport authorities who arranged accommodation for everyone on board.

On 16th August the aircraft arrived in Harare, departing to Cape Town after unloading. CCCP-76822 was the first Soviet aircraft to land at Cape Town's D F Malan International airport. The assembled company drove to Cape Town's seaport where the Soviet oceanographic vessel M/V Professor Wiese was moored; she was the expedition's headquarters in the days before the final leg of the flight (the weather at Molodyozhnaya prevented any flying in the next three or four days).

With nothing more to do, the members of the expedition took the opportunity to make a tour

of the city. On 18th August there was a small celebration on occasion of Aviation Day. And next morning the expedition and the crew of the Professor Wiese were in for a shock when they turned on the radio to listen to the news from Moscow. A coup d'état was in progress and the self-appointed National Emergency Committee was addressing the nation with all the usual goodies that come in such cases (curfew, censorship and so on). End of the line… or what?

Understandably enough, everyone was depressed at first. When the members of the expedition had collected their wits, however, the decision was taken: we've got to fly and get the people out of there, coup or no coup. We haven't made the long trip for our own amusement, after all!

On 20th August the weather forecast showed clear weather over Molodyozhnaya in the next two days, and at 0502 local time next day CCCP-76822 took off for Antarctica. The crew was even bigger now, as several South African newspaper reporters had gained permission to join the flight. At 1015 the aircraft overflew M/V Mikhail Somov; the orange-coloured ship covered with black splotches of fuel oil in the middle of the white wilderness was a strange and a sorry sight. Fifteen minutes later the IL-76 made a pass over the runway at Molodyozhnaya and broke to land.

The engines died down and the crew opened the entry door. There was a strong wind on the field, and it was mortifyingly cold! The temperature in Cape Town had been +10°C (50°F); here, the cold was so bitter that the mission planning briefing had to take place in the aircraft which was the warmest place at the station.

170 persons (35th SAE personnel, part of the station's tech staff and part of the Mikhail Somov's crew) and a huge amount of luggage had to be taken home. There was a problem; calculations showed that the aircraft's take-off weight would be 180 to 185 tons (396,825 to 407,848 lb), whereas the runway's design TOW limit was only 170 tons (374,779 lb). Still, splitting the passengers into two groups was impossible: the weather was deteriorating fast and the aircraft had to leave no later than 22nd August, otherwise it would be stuck there for a week. Next day, upon careful consideration, it was decided to airlift all 170 'passengers' at once. Together with the crew, there were 197 persons on board; some of the passengers had to stay on their feet all the way, as there was positively no room to sit down.

Even as the passengers boarded, a blizzard began; the runway shoulder markers were barely visible, to say nothing of the runway threshold. The local helicopter pilots proposed hovering in a Mi-8T Hip-B near the end of the runway to provide a visual reference point. Someone joked that the situation could develop in three possible ways: 'a) if things go wrong nobody will blame us (because we will be dead! – Auth.); b) if things go wrong the survivors will be put to trial; c) if everything works out, no one will even say thanks.' (How *typical* of the Soviet Union...)

The aircraft taxied out to the holding position. Stanislav G Bliznyuk said his customary phrase: 'Well, let's roll, nice and slow' – and the take-off went without a hitch; the perfectly prepared runway had saved the day. Five and a half hours later the *Candid* was back in Cape Town. As soon as the cargo doors opened a crowd of locals rushed to the plane. At first the alarmed crew thought they were hostile and aggressive because of the developments in Moscow. In reality, however, the reason of the commotion was much simpler. The recesses of the cargo ramp were full of Antarctic snow, and the locals, who had never seen snow in their lives, were scrambling to get souvenirs!

On 24th August the newly-repaired *Akademik Fyodorov* docked in Cape Town. Two days later the mayor held a banquet in honour of the Soviet polar researchers and the crews of M/V *Professor Wiese*, M/V *Akademik Fyodorov* and IL-76MD CCCP-76822. The same evening both ships put to sea, carrying the evacuees home (where the coup had fizzled by then). On 29th August the aircraft made for home, too; the return trip went through Johannesburg, Nairobi, Larnaca and Moscow/Sheremet'yevo-1 to Zhukovskiy where the aircraft arrived on 2nd September. In 22 days CCCP-76822 had covered a distance of 43,185km (26,823 miles), spending 52 hours in the air.

The next mission to Antarctica took place from 28th October to 13th November 1991. This time IL-76MD CCCP-78839 (c/n 1003402047, f/n 7702) chartered from the 339th VTAP flew from Moscow to Molodyozhnaya via Leningrad, Larnaca, Nairobi, Antananarivu and Cape Town. P I Zadeerov (Polyus Parachute & Expedition Work Centre) and Col Yuriy M Barinov (339th VTAP) led the expedition. The aircraft was flown by two crews which included pilots A Andronov (NII VVS), Yuriy Klimashin, Yuriy M Barinov and S N Zhbankov, navigators A Smirnov and V Romashkin.

From Molodyozhnaya CCCP-78839 made two flights to other Soviet research stations and for the first time in the history of Antarctic supply operations the cargo had to be paradropped. At Novolazarevskaya the drop was made in the usual way at 600m (1,968ft). Ice station Vostok, however, is located at 3,040m (9,973ft) above sea level, which is probably why the LAPES technique was used – the first use of this technique for civilian needs. The journey home was from Molodyozhnaya to Cape Town, Nairobi and Larnaca to Moscow.

On 20th April 1998 when IL-76MD 'Falsie' RA-76822 captained by N D Kuimov paradropped an international expedition comprising 70 researchers from nine countries on the North Pole. According to some sources, the aircraft had been renamed IL-76TD by then.

The latest use of the *Candid* for polar research was the *Ukraine – North Pole 2000* expedition. On 3rd April An-28 UR-28768 of the O K Antonov Central Airclub flown by Antonov test pilots Anatoliy Khroostitskiy and Ruslan Migoonov departed Kiev for Khatanga via Moscow, Syktyvkar and Noril'sk. On 11th April it was followed by an IL-76MD of the Ukrainian Air Force's Melitopol' Airlift Group captained by Col Konstantin Shoosharin which carried 35 passengers, including TV and newspaper reporters. In Moscow the *Candid* picked up more polar researchers and journalists.

The main action took place on 15th April. First, a Mi-8 *Hip* helicopter with a forward team took off to reconnoiter a landing strip near the Pole for the An-28, which had 'changed' from wheels to skis for the occasion. The team put up a tent and erected the Ukrainian and Russian flags. The the IL-76MD came in to paradrop the main team of researchers, but as it did so the Krassnoyarsk Regional Civil Aviation Directorate inspector coordinating the paradrop was in for a nasty surprise – his radio failed because of the intense cold. Thinking fast, Ruslan Migoonov contacted the crew of the *Candid* by means of the An-28's radio, and all went well on the second try.

Wings of hope

The type was also much used by United Nations peacekeeping forces in 'hot spots' around the world, notably in the former Yugoslavia. IL-76s – usually in all-white UNPF colours – were frequent guests at Sarajevo's Butmir airport which was in 'no man's land' between territories held by the Serbs and the Bosnian Moslems. Most of the aircraft in question were Ukrainian IL-76MDs; these had no guns, nor, curiously, any chaff/flare dispensers, even though there was considerable danger of being fired upon.

UNPF *Candids* in ex-Yugoslavia included IL-76MDs UR-76323, UR-76392, UR-76424, UR-

The *Candid* was actively used by the United Nations Peace Forces. The photo shows Air Service Ukraine IL-76MD UR-76541 in all-white UNPF colours, with BSL Airline Tu-154B-2 UR-85379 (also in UNPF colours) just visible behind. Peter Davison

EMERCOM IL-76TDs RA-76362 and RA-76363 offload supplies at Mozdok during the First Chechen War. The KamAZ-4310 being loaded is an EMERCOM vehicle; the ZiL-131 waiting its turn belongs to the Russian Army. ITAR-TASS

76433, UR-76443 and UR-76630 leased from Atlant-SV, UR-76532 leased from the Ukrainian Air Force, UR-76534 leased from Hoseba, UR-76537, UR-76541 and UR-86924 leased from Air Service Ukraine, and IL-76TDs 76818 and 76819 leased from the Russian airline Exparc. UR-76537 had the distinction of carrying a person of royal blood when Prince Frederik, successor to the Danish throne, came to Sarajevo in March 1994 with the Danish UNPF battalion in Yugoslavia (DANBAT).

Other aircraft used by the United Nations included IL-76TDs UK-76449 leased from Uzbekistan Airways and CCCP-76808 leased from the East Siberian CAD. These aircraft retained basic Aeroflot colours with blue UN titles added rather than having the customary all-white UNPF colour scheme. It is not known where these aircraft were used.

In mid-1992 Sudanese government troops fighting against the National Liberation Army (NLA) rebels were encircled in the El Istwâ'ya region of southern Sudan. All supply routes to the region were cut off and the 300,000 civilians living there faced death from starvation. On 18th July, NLA guerrillas began systematically shelling the city of Jûbâ in the besieged area. Hence the United Nations decided to launch a twice-daily humanitarian airlift programme for Sudan, using chartered cargo aircraft.

On 20th August 1992 an Uzbekiston Havo Yullari IL-76TD made the first flight from Entebbe, Uganda, to Jûbâ, bringing 24 tons (52,910 lb) of corn, wheat and beans and 16 tons (35,273 lb) of medical supplies. The aircraft was chartered for one month via Ecotrends, a US-Russian joint venture. The flight was made in spite of the NLA's threats to shoot down any aircraft operating into the city. These were not just empty threats: the NLA had already shot down three Sudan Airways aircraft, killing about 200 people.

Atlant-SV's IL-76MD UR-76393 was operated by the International Committee of the Red Cross (ICRC). This aircraft was painted white overall with Comité International – Geneve logos on the fuselage and tail. On 16th February 1994 UR-76393 made the 100th Red Cross flight to Sarajevo.

The United Nations High Commission for Refugees (UNHCR) also made use of at least four Candids – IL-76TD RA-76409 leased from the Komsomol'sk-on-Amur aircraft factory (used for evacuating refugees to Burundi during the civil war in Rwanda), demilitarised IL-76 sans suffixe RA-76418, IL-76T RA-76522 and IL-76TD RA-76752. The latter three aircraft were operated by the British Overseas Development Agency on behalf of the UNHCR. At least three more examples – IL-76T RA-76518, 'IL-76T' RA-76372,[16] and IL-76TD 4L-76445 – were operated by the United Nations World Food Programme (WFP) in 1993, 1996 and 2000 respectively.

EMERCOM of Russia IL-76TDs have been used for a variety of tasks. These included the transportation of investigators to the scenes of major air crashes – for example, Baikal Airlines Tu-154M RA-85656 (c/n 89A-801) in Omsk on 3rd January 1994 and Aeroflot Russian International Airlines A310-308 F-OGQS Glinka (c/n 596) near Mezhdurechensk on 22nd March 1994. More often, however, they are used for disaster relief and humanitarian missions all over the world, including former Yugoslavia, Rwanda, Tanzania and Afghanistan (in the latter case after a violent earthquake).

Being a paramilitary agency, EMERCOM also took part in some military operations. In early 1995 RA-76362 and RA-76363 delivered EMERCOM's mobile hospital and flew supply missions to Groznyy and Mozdok for the Russian federal troops during the First Chechen War. During this campaign the hospital treated 13,000 patients, performing over 1,000 surgical operations. The aircraft were also used in the Second Chechen War; for instance, on 28th September 1999 RA-76362 delivered 40 tons (88,183 lb) of humanitarian aid to Ingushetia for refugees fleeing Chechnya.

Also, on 3rd September 1997 IL-76TD RA-76845 and a 25-man Russian team took part in the Co-operative Bear '97 exercise held at Såtenäs AB near Trollhättan, southern Sweden. This was the first time Russia had participated in a Partnership for Peace exercise. The Candid brought EMERCOM's mobile hospital, part of which was deployed, and flew simulated CASEVAC missions from Såtenäs; it was the heaviest aircraft involved.

From 7-30th August 1998 the same aircraft – now named Mikhail Vodop'yanov and configured as an IL-76TDP – participated in a major firefighting operation in Greece. The Greek government had requested assistance under the Black Sea Nations Emergency Co-operation Agreement. Operating from Elefsis AB near Thívai (Thebes), the aircraft was in action against forest fires near Ioánnina, Marathonas, Mesolóngion, Megalópolis and on Crete.

One of the most recent major operations by EMERCOM Candids outside Russia was in August 1999 when a powerful earthquake hit the north-western regions of Turkey, causing massive destruction and a large loss of life. On 18th August IL-76TD RA-76362 Anatoliy Lyapidevskiy delivered a team of rescue workers and their equipment to Gölcuk. It was followed next day by IL-76TDP RA-76840 Nikolay Kamanin which helped extinguish the burning oil refinery in Izmit.

On 28th October 2000 IL-76TD RA-76840 arrived in Dushanbe, Tajikistan, with 30 tons (66,137 lb) of humanitarian cargo for the Northern Alliance (the anti-Taliban coalition in Afghanistan). This was not an unexpected move, since the Taliban militia, which is now getting close to the Tajik border, is seen as a serious threat to the southern CIS republics. Interestingly, by then RA-76840 (and probably the other EMERCOM IL-76s as well) had wooden grids lining the cargo cabin walls to protect the fuselage structure during loading and unloading.

Not only EMERCOM aircraft flew disaster relief missions. From 18-25th December 1997 the Ilyushin OKB's IL-76MD 'Falsie' RA-76822 captained by Igor' R Zakirov fulfilled an emergency supply mission in the remote regions of Yakutia (Sakha), paradropping foodstuffs and commodities on PGS-500 pallets. A similar relief mission (this time by EMERCOM) was undertaken in March 1998 when the cities of Lensk and Yakutsk and numerous smaller settlements were flooded or cut off from the regular supply routes; the flood was caused by a huge ice jam on the Lena river 40km (24.8 miles) downstream from Lensk. Four IL-76TDs delivered 63 tons (138,888 lb) of food, 3 tons (6,613 lb) of medicines, 17 rescue dinghies, 9 diesel generators etc to Mirnyy. Later, two more flights were made to Yakutsk.

Political developments and economic turmoil in the former Soviet Union have slowed the IL-76's production rate considerably. Nevertheless, the Candid looks set to stay in production for quite some time yet, and new advanced versions may still appear. On 7th May 1998 Uzbek President Islam A Karimov paid a visit to the Ilyushin OKB during his trip to Russia. This resulted in the signing of an agreement granting Uzbekistan exclusive production rights for the IL-76 family.

The IL-76 has carved itself a stable niche on the international air cargo transport market thanks to its considerable capabilities and easy availability. The aircraft turned out to be tough and durable, and some examples built in 1975 were still in service in 1999. It should be noted, however, that Candids belonging to civil operators are in urgent need of an upgrade (first and foremost re-engining with 'cleaner' and quieter turbofans).

Upgrading is all very well, but Ilyushin and the Tashkent Aircraft Production Corporation (which markets the IL-76 independently from the OKB) capitalise on new-build aircraft. In particular, they are targeting the Russian Air Force which operates the Candid in substantial numbers and needs a replacement for ageing examples.

Currently the Russian Air Force's acquisition plans include both the IL-76MF (about 100 copies by 2015) and the An-70; the Russian order for the latter has been finally confirmed and the aircraft is due to enter production at the Aviacor factory in Samara. The attitude to these freighters is split approximately 50/50; many top-ranking officers, including Russian Ministry of Defence weapons department chief Col Gen Anatoliy Sitnov, are opposing the An-70 because it is 'definitely NIH' (not invented here). This obviously boils down to the old tensions between Russia and the Ukraine over the Black Sea Fleet and other issues (the critics seem to forget that the IL-76 is also built outside Russia, after all!). On the other hand, Russia is not at odds with Uzbekistan and the IL-76 is originally a Russian design. In any case, the Candid's future with the Russian air arm – as well as with civil operators – looks assured.

Chapter Five

The Candid 'At Home'
(CIS IL-76 Operators)

The IL-76 is operated by most of the CIS republics. In this chapter, for each republic, the air force is analysed first, followed by civil operators in alphabetical order, with each airline's two-letter IATA designator (where applicable) and three-letter ICAO designator. Aircraft no longer operated by the respective carrier are shown in italic script in the fleet lists (except in those cases when the airline itself no longer exists and *all* of its aircraft have been sold or retired).

ARMENIA

The cargo airline **YERAVIA** (Yerevan-Avia) [–/ERV] based at Yerevan-Zvartnots owns two military IL-76s *sans suffixe* registered EK-86724 (c/n 073410284, f/n 0801) and EK-86817 (c/n 063407191, f/n 0508). Both have been demilitarised and are operated by Payam Air of Iran since 1997 as EP-TPZ/86724 and EP-TPO/86817 respectively.

DVIN-AVIA [–/DVN] based at Yerevan-Erebuni operates IL-76TD EK-76446 (c/n 1023412418, f/n 8605). Acquired in September 1999, this aircraft was formerly flown by Altaiskiye Avialinii as IL-76MD 'Falsie' RA-76446 (see below).

AZERBAIJAN

The **AZERBAIJAN AIR FORCE** operates a small fleet of IL-76s based at Nasosnaya AB near Baku (three were reportedly on strength in 2000). Curiously, Azerbaijan has a habit of periodically re-registering its military transports – probably for security reasons or in order to fool other states into thinking it has more *Candids* than it really has.

Registration	Version	C/n	F/n	Notes
AHY-78001 *	*IL-76MD*	*0083489683*	*6801*	*Ex-CCCP-78783, later reregistered AHY-78129*
AHY-78129				Reregistered following damage and repairs.
4K-78030	IL-76MD	?	?	Ex-AHY-78030. Original registration unknown (misquote of 4K-78130?)
4K-78130	IL-76MD	0043454611	4103	Ex-CCCP-76602
RA-86810	IL-76 (mil)	053404094	0304	Reported leased from Russian Air Force (see note below), to be reregistered 4K-86810

* The non-standard AHY- prefix (denoting Azerbaijan Hava Yollari/Azerbaijan Airlines) is one of the tentative registration prefixes rejected by ICAO.

The aircraft retain basic Aeroflot colours with no titles and the Azeri flag on the tail in place of the old Soviet flag (except ex-Al'kor RA-86810, which is white overall with a grey belly) and are occasionally operated by Azerbaijan Airlines.

AZAL AVIA CARGO [–/AHC], the cargo division of Azerbaijan Airlines/Azerbaijan Hava Yollari, operated five IL-76s from Baku-Bina airport.

Registration	Version	C/n	F/n	Notes
4K-AZ11	*IL-76TD*	*1013409280*	*8210*	*Ex-Remex RA-76354, bought 11-98. Sold to unknown operator by 9-99 as S9-BAD*
4K-AZ14	IL-76TD	1023412389	8508	Ex-UK 76447, bought from Avialeasing 11-99 (see below)
UK-76410	*IL-76TD*	*1023412411*	*8603*	*Leased from Avialeasing (Uzbekistan) ?-99 to 3-00*
UK 76447	*IL-76TD*	*1023412389*	*8508*	*Leased from Avialeasing (Uzbekistan) 1998; returned, to 4K-AZ14*
UR-76700	IL-76MD	0063471134	5404	Leased from ATI Airlines 1998
'UR-76752'	'IL-76TD'	0083483519	6310	Leased from ATI Airlines 1998; ex-IL76-MD UR-78752? (see ATI and Kras Air)

IMAIR [IK/ITX], the Baku-based airline, a division of Improtex, operates passenger and cargo aircraft leased from operators in other CIS republics as required. These included three IL-76MDs leased from Veteran Airlines; all three have been returned since.

Registration	Version	C/n	F/n	Notes
4K-76671	IL-76MD	0063465963	5001	Leased 11-95 to ? - ??, ex-/to UR-76671
4K-76677	IL-76MD	0063467005	5102	Leased 10-95 to ? - ??, ex-/to UR-76677
4K-76717	IL-76MD	0073474216	5604	Leased 1995 to ? - ??, ex-/to UR-76717

BELARUS (BELORUSSIA)

TRANSAVIAEXPORT CARGO AIRLINES [AL/TXC], the commercial division of the **Belorussian Air Force**, in post-Soviet times, took over 24 of the 32 IL-76MDs previously operated by the 339th VTAP in Vitebsk. The airline operates them from Vitebsk and Machoolischchi AB near Minsk and leases them to other carriers. Many aircraft have been demilitarised, becoming IL-76TD 'Falsies', and some were even converted into 'true' IL-76TDs. In late 1997, when the Russian Federation and the Republic of Belarus began preparing for integration into a new union, the original red/white 'CIS-style' Belorussian flag carried on the lower part of the fin was replaced by a new red/green flag (strongly reminiscent of the flag of the former Belorussian Soviet Socialist Republic) aft of the flight deck.

Registration	Version	C/n	F/n	Notes
RA-76708	*IL-76MD*	*0063473171*	*5503*	*Leased from Russian Air Force early 1993*
EW-76709	IL-76MD	0063473173	5504	
EW-76710	IL-76MD	0063473182	5506	**Converted to IL-76TD** and leased to Atlant-Soyuz by 8-99
EW-76711	IL-76MD	0063473187	5507	**Converted to IL-76TD** and lsd to Ilavia by 8-99
EW-76712	IL-76MD	0063473190	5508	Ex-Air Service Ukraine UR-76712 (?). **Converted to IL-76TD** and lsd to Ilavia by 8-99
EW-76734	IL-76MD	0073476312	5808	Leased to Air Service Ukraine as UR-76734. **Converted to IL-76TD** and lsd to Ilavia by 8-99
EW-76735	IL-76MD	0073476314	5809	Ex-RA-76735??? **Converted to IL-76TD** 1998; leased to Aero Concept by 8-99
EW-76737	IL-76MD	0073477323	5901	**Converted to IL-76TD** 1998; leased to Volga-Dnepr Cargo Airlines 8-99
EW-78765	IL-76MD	0083486590	6508	
EW-78769	IL-76MD	0083487607	6602	
EW-78779	IL-76MD	0083489662	6706	Demilitarised. Leased to Atlant-Soyuz **as IL-76TD 'Falsie'** 2-98
EW-78787	IL-76MD	0083490698	6805	
EW-78792	*IL-76MD 'Falsie'?*	*0093490718*	*6810*	*Converted to IL-76TD and sold to Ilavia in 1996 as RA-78792*
EW-78799	IL-76MD	0093491754	6909	**Converted to IL-76TD** and leased to East Line by 10-98

EW-78801	IL-76MD	0093492763	7001	**Converted to IL-76TD** and leased to Atlant-Soyuz by 11-98
EW-78808	IL-76MD	0093493794	7009	Demilitarised. Leased to East Line **as IL-76TD 'Falsie'** by 10-98
EW-78819	IL-76MD	0093495883	7301	Demilitarised. Leased to East Line **as IL-76TD 'Falsie'** by 10-98
EW-78826	IL-76MD	1003499991	7508	Demilitarised. Leased to East Line **as IL-76TD 'Falsie'** by 10-98
EW-78827	IL-76MD	1003499997	7510	Demilitarised. Leased to Atlant-Soyuz **as IL-76TD 'Falsie'** by 11-98
EW-78828	IL-76MD	1003401004	7601	Demilitarised (IL-76TD **'Falsie'**?) **Converted to IL-76TD** 1998, lsd to East Line
EW-78836	IL-76MD	0093499986	7507	Out of sequence registration
EW-78839	IL-76MD	1003402047	7702	Demilitarised. Leased to East Line **as IL-76TD 'Falsie'** by 10-98
EW-78843	IL-76MD	1003403082	7801	Demilitarised. Leased to East Line **as IL-76TD 'Falsie'** by 10-98
EW-78848	IL-76MD	1003405159	7910	Demilitarised. Leased to Atlant-Soyuz **as IL-76TD 'Falsie'** by 11-98
EW-78849	IL-76MD	1013405192	8008	

Other *Candids* operated by the **BELORUSSIAN AIR FORCE** (but not **TransAVIAexport**) are:

Registration	Version	C/n	F/n	Notes
CCCP-78761	IL-76MD	0083486570	6503	Ground instructional airframe, Machoolischchi AB?
EW-78763	IL-76MD	0083486582	6506	
EW-78793	IL-76MD	0093490721	6901	Ex-UN-78793??? Reported for TransAVIAexport but not in fleet list 2000, ever as such?
EW-78802	IL-76MD	0093492771	7003	
CCCP-86822	IL-76 (mil)	?	0310A?	Transferred to Belorussian AF 7-92, not seen since. C/n reported as 053405117 (f/n 0310) but this is CCCP-86621 (see Russian AF)
CCCP-86823	IL-76 (mil)	053405124	0401	Ground instructional airframe, Machoolischchi AB since early 1996

In 1992 the charter carrier **BELAIR (BELORUSSIAN AIRLINES)** [–/BLI] based at Minsk-2 airport took delivery of two IL-76TDs – EW-76836 (c/n 1013409305, f/n 8307) and EW-76837 (c/n 1023409316, f/n 8309). The aircraft were painted in the 'CIS-style' Belorussian flag colours of red and white but traces of their former Aeroflot livery were visible upon close inspection.

EW-76836 was wrecked at Sarajevo's Butmir airport on 31st December 1994 while operating for the United Nations. The other aircraft was leased to AZZA Air Transport as ST-APS, then stored for a while and ultimately sold to SAT Airlines (?) for US$ 3.9 million as RA-76837 in late 1996 (see Russian section).

GEORGIA

LASARE AIR [–/LRE] of Tbilisi purchased IL-76TD RA-76445 (c/n 1023410330, f/n 8403) from Novosibirsk Airlines by March 2000. The aircraft was reregistered 4L-76445; this is rather odd, as newly-registered Georgian aircraft have letter-only registrations (some older aircraft are being reregistered in this fashion, too – eg, Georgian Airlines Tu-154B-2 4L-85558 became 4L-AAH). In 2000 the freighter was operated for the UN World Food Programme.

KAZAKSTAN (KAZAKHSTAN)

On 9th September 1995 IL-76MD UN-78793 (c/n 0093490721, f/n 6901) was reported at Rome-Fiumicino in basic Aeroflot colours without titles; this ex-Belorussian Air Force aircraft was presumably operated by the

KAZAKSTAN AIR FORCE. However, by 1998 the aircraft was reported for TransAVIAexport as EW-78793!

AEROSERVICE KAZAKSTAN AVIAKOMPANIYASY [–/AVZ] operated IL-76TD UN-76410 in 1992-97 before selling it to Sayakhat (see below).

AEROSERVICE-SABIT [–/CSM], a sister company of Aeroservis Kazakstan Aviakompaniyasy based in Almaty, flies cargo charters with IL-76s leased from other carriers as required.

AK-KANAT [–/KAN], another airline from Almaty, leases IL-76s from other carriers as required.

KAZAKHSTAN AIRLINES (Kazakhstan Aue Zholy) or **KAZAIR** [K4/KZA] was this Central Asian republic's first flag carrier. Its large fleet consisted almost entirely of passenger aircraft but also included four IL-76TDs. Originally flown in basic Aeroflot colours with the Kazakh flag and 'Kazakhstan Airlines' titles, they received a smart new livery in late 1994 (incidentally, the titles now read 'Kazakstan Airlines', without the 'h').

Registration	Version	C/n	F/n	Notes
UN-76371	IL-76TD	1033414485	8802	
UN-76374	IL-76TD	1033416520	8810	
UN 76435	IL-76TD	1023413428	8607	*Registration applied with no dash after prefix. Crashed near New Delhi 12-11-96*
UN-76810	IL-76TD	1013409282	8301	

On 20th August 1996 Kazakstan Airlines filed for bankruptcy, with total debts of 19 billion tenge (more than US$180 million). Rather than attempt to revive the ailing giant, the government chose to liquidate the airline and establish a new flag carrier called **AIR KAZAKSTAN** [9Y/KZK] which inherited most of Kazair's fleet, including three of the *Candids*. (UN-76435 crashed in November 1996 while still operating under a Kazair flight code, as the reorganization was still in progress at the time. There have been reports that the freighters were transferred to an airline called Chimkentavia but this is incorrect.) UN-76374 was leased to East Line by February 2000.

The other full-time Kazakh *Candid* operator is **SAYAKHAT** [Q9/SAH, later W7/SAH],[1] likewise based in Almaty. Established in 1989 as a cargo carrier, the airline has four IL-76TDs (passenger operations were started later with three Tu-154Ms, as a point of interest).

Registration	Version	C/n	F/n	Notes
UN-76384	IL-76TD	1003401015	7604	Leased to Tesis 1999
UN-76385	IL-76TD	1033416515	8809	
UN-76410	IL-76TD	1023412411	8603	*Sold to Avialeasing (Uzbekistan) 8-97 as UK-76410*
UN-76434	IL-76TD	1023412395	8509	C/n also reported as 1023412392
UN-76442	IL-76TD	1023414450	8703	

Some sources mistakenly reported IL-76TD UN-76834 for Sayakhat. However, this is obvious confusion with UN-76384; this aircraft was never on the Kazakstan register; it 'lived and died' (ie, crashed) as **RA**-76834 (see MAP).

TARAZ WINGS (*Kryl'ya Taraza*) [–/TWC], a regional airline based at Taraz airport, Zhambyl (formerly Dzhamboul), purchased IL-76 *sans suffixe* RA-76496 (c/n 073410301, f/n 0806) from the Kazan' aircraft factory in early 1999. Duly reregistered UN-76496, the aircraft is painted white overall with 'Taraz Wings' titles. The tail gunner's station is intact but it is not known whether the aircraft has been demilitarised.

By May 2000 UN-76496 was sold or leased to an airline called **GST AERO** and reported as an IL-76T 'Falsie'.

Still with Aeroflot titles, an Azerbaijan Air Force IL-76MD sits at Baku. Note that the 'MD' suffix has been painted out. Petr Šebek

IL-76TD EW-78828, seen here at Moscow-Domodedovo in November 1998, is one of 24 *Candids* operated by TransAVIAexport, the commercial division of the Belorussian Air Force. As the registration reveals, this aircraft is a converted IL-76MD. Dmitriy Komissarov

IL-76TD UN-76384 in the livery of Kazakh cargo carrier Sayakhat. The photo was taken shortly after the collapse of the Soviet Union when CIS airlines still operated under Aeroflot flight numbers, as evidenced by the small Aeroflot 'wings' emblem ahead of the entry door. Peter Davison

A lineup of 334th VTAP IL-76Ms and 'MDs at Kresty AB, Pskov. Yefim Gordon

This IL-76T photographed at Moscow-Bykovo (aircraft overhaul plant No. 402) belongs to the Federal Border Guards. Yefim Gordon

KYRGHYZSTAN

KYRGHYZSTAN AIRLINES / KYRGHYZSTAN ABA ZHOLDORU

[K2/KGA], the republic's sole air carrier, operates a single IL-76TD (EX-76815, c/n 1013409310, f/n 8308) based at Bishkek-Manas airport. This is the only known Kyrghyz *Candid*.

MOLDOVA

AEROCOM [–/MCC], a new carrier based in Kishinyov (Chişinău), bought IL-76T RA-76521 (c/n 0003423699, f/n 1805) from Ilavia in 1999; the aircraft was duly reregistered ER-IBV.

Some sources reported that ex-ALLWE Airlines IL-76TD RA-76426 (c/n 1013405184, f/n 8006) was sold to an unidentified Moldovan airline and became ER-ACG, but this is unconfirmed. A possible explanation is that the deal fell through and the registration was allocated but not taken up.

RUSSIA

The **RUSSIAN AIR FORCE** (VVS RF) continues to operate the IL-76 and its derivatives in substantial numbers. The aircraft are in service with the 61st VA *(vozdooshnaya armiya)* – air army (air force) into which the former VTA has been reorganised. This consists of two airlift divisions, each with four or five airlift regiments based in Engels (230th APSZ), Ivanovo (517th VTAP, Severnyy AB), Klin, Orenburg (128th VTAP), Pechora, Pskov (334th *Berlinskiy* VTAP, Kresty AB), Seschcha, Shadrinsk, Smolensk (103rd VTAP), Taganrog (708th OVTAP)[2], Tver' (196th VTAP, Migalovo AB), Ryazan' (Dyaghilevo AB), Velikiy Novgorod (110th VTAP, Krechevitsy AB) etc. Additionally, several *Candids* operated by the **Ministry of the Interior** are based at Nizhniy Novgorod (Strighino airport). 270 IL-76s were reportedly in service with the 61st VA in January 2000; known aircraft are listed below.

Registration	Version	C/n	F/n	Notes
RA-76450	IL-82 ('IL-76VKP')	0053463900	4805	Moscow Defence District, 8th ADON, Chkalovskaya AB
RA-76451	IL-82 ('IL-76VKP')	0053464938	4905	Moscow Defence District, 8th ADON, Chkalovskaya AB
RA-76457	IL-76T	093421621	1606	Ex-CCCP-76457, converted IL-76M CCCP-86925 No1 (see RA-86925 below), built-in chaff/flare dispensers. Federal Border Guards, Moscow/Sheremet'yevo-1
RA-76530	IL-76MD	0023441180	3005	128th VTAP, Orenburg
RA-76533	IL-76MD	0023442205	3102	517th VTAP, Ivanovo-Severnyy AB. Ex-Russian Air Force '533 Black'
RA-76538	IL-76MD	0023442231	3108	Ex-Russian Air Force '538 Black'
RA-76542	IL-76MD	0033443249	3203	334th VTAP, Kresty AB, Pskov
RA-76544	IL-76MD	0033443262	3206	196th VTAP, Migalovo AB, Tver'
RA-76545	IL-76MD	0033443266	3207	196th VTAP, Migalovo AB, Tver'
RA-76546	IL-76MD	0033443272	3208	196th VTAP, Migalovo AB, Tver'
RA-76547	IL-76MD	0033443273	3209	196th VTAP, Migalovo AB, Tver'; operated by Federal Border Guards?
RA-76548	IL-76MD	0033443278	3210	196th VTAP, Migalovo AB, Tver'
RA-76549	IL-76MD	0033444283	3301	196th VTAP, Migalovo AB, Tver'
RA-76550	IL-76MD	0033445306	3307	196th VTAP, Migalovo AB, Tver'
RA-76551	IL-76MD	0033445309	3308	196th VTAP, Migalovo AB, Tver'
RA-76552	IL-76MD	0033445313	3309	517th VTAP, Ivanovo-Severnyy AB
RA-76553	IL-76MD	0033445318	3310	196th VTAP, Migalovo AB, Tver'
RA-76554	IL-76MD	0033445324	3401	128th VTAP, Orenburg
RA-76557	IL-76MD	0033446329	3403	334th VTAP, Kresty AB, Pskov
RA-76558	IL-76MD	0033446333	3404	196th VTAP, Migalovo AB, Tver'
RA-76572	IL-76MD	0033449434	3609	196th VTAP, Migalovo AB, Tver'
RA-76577	IL-76MD	0043449462	3706	334th VTAP, Kresty AB, Pskov
RA-76599	IL-76MD	0043453593	4009	708th OVTAP, Taganrog
RA-76604	IL-76MD	0043454625	4107	128th VTAP, Orenburg
RA-76605	IL-76MD	0043454631	4108	196th VTAP, Migalovo AB, Tver'
RA-76612	IL-76MD	0043455660	4205	708th OVTAP, Taganrog
RA-76613	IL-76MD	0043455664	4206	128th VTAP, Orenburg
RA-76615	IL-76MD	0043455672	4208	196th VTAP, Migalovo AB, Tver'
RA-76632	IL-78	0053459757	4410	Ivanovo. C/n also quoted as 0053459761
RA-76634	IL-76MD	0053459770	4503	128th VTAP, Orenburg
RA-76639	IL-78?	0053460805	4602	Also reported as an IL-76MD!
RA-76640	IL-76MD	0053460811	4603	978th VTAP, Klin-5 AB
RA-76641	IL-76MD	0053460813	4604	978th VTAP, Klin-5 AB
RA-76643	IL-76MD	0053460822	4606	517th VTAP, Ivanovo-Severnyy AB
RA-76648	IL-76MD	0053461848	4702	128th VTAP, Orenburg
RA-76649	IL-76MD	0053462864	4706	708th OVTAP, Taganrog
RA-76668	IL-76MD	0053465946	4907	517th VTAP, Ivanovo-Severnyy AB
RA-76693	IL-76MD	0063470100	5305	708th OVTAP, Taganrog
RA-76708	IL-76MD	0063473171	5503	Leased to Express JSC 1995
RA-76714	IL-76MD	0063474198	5510	128th VTAP, Orenburg
RA-76718	IL-76MD	0073474219	5605	708th OVTAP, Taganrog
RA-76720	IL-76MD	0073475229	5608	708th OVTAP, Taganrog
RA-76722	IL-76MD	0073475242	5701	708th OVTAP, Taganrog
RA-76723	IL-76MD	0073475245	5702	117th VTAP, Orenburg. Crashed at Privolzhskiy AB, Astrakhan', 22-6-2000
RA-76724	IL-76MD	0073475250	5703	708th OVTAP, Taganrog. Also reported as **converted IL-78**/ex-BSL Airline UR-76724 (see below)!
RA-76725	IL-76MD	0073475253	5704	708th OVTAP, Taganrog
RA-76726	IL-76MD	0073475261	5706	708th OVTAP, Taganrog
RA-76731	IL-76MD	0073476290	5803	517th VTAP, Ivanovo-Severnyy AB
RA-76733	IL-76MD	0073476304	5806	110th VTAP, Krechevitsy AB, Velikiy Novgorod
RA-76735?	IL-76MD	0073476314	5809	Reported 4-94, to TransAVIAexport as EW-76735? (possible confusion with RA-76725!)
RA-76739	IL-76MD	0073477332	5903	708th OVTAP, Taganrog
RA-76740	IL-76MD	0073477335	5904	708th OVTAP, Taganrog
RA-76741	IL-76MD	0073478337	5905	978th VTAP, Klin-5 AB
RA-76743	IL-76MD	0073478349	5908	708th OVTAP, Taganrog
RA-76745	IL-76MD	0073479362	6001	708th OVTAP, Taganrog
RA-76746	IL-76MD	0073479374	6004	708th OVTAP, Taganrog
RA-76747	IL-76MD	0073479381	6006	Ex-Eco Patrol UR-76747? 708th OVTAP, Taganrog
RA-76761	IL-76MD	0073479401	6101	196th VTAP, Migalovo AB, Tver'
RA-76762	IL-76MD	0073480406	6102	110th VTAP, Krechevitsy AB, Velikiy Novgorod
RA-76763	IL-76MD	0073480413	6104	110th VTAP, Krechevitsy AB, Velikiy Novgorod
RA-76764	IL-76MD	0073480424	6106	110th VTAP, Krechevitsy AB, Velikiy Novgorod
RA-76765	IL-76MD	0073481426	6107	708th OVTAP, Taganrog
RA-76766	IL-76MDK	0073481431	6108	Gagarin Space Training Centre, Chkalovskaya AB, zero-G trainer
RA-76767	IL-76MD	0073481436	6109	110th VTAP, Krechevitsy AB, Velikiy Novgorod
RA-76768	IL-76MD	0083481448	6202	708th OVTAP, Taganrog
RA-76769	IL-76MD	0073481452	6203	708th OVTAP, Taganrog
RA-76770	IL-76MD	0073481456	6204	110th VTAP, Krechevitsy AB, Velikiy Novgorod
CCCP-76771	IL-76MD	0083482466	6207	978th VTAP, Klin-5 AB/to be RA-reregistered
RA-76772	IL-76MD	0083482472	6208	708th OVTAP, Taganrog
RA-76773	IL-76MD	0083482473	6209	708th OVTAP, Taganrog
RA-76776	IL-76MD	0083482486	6302	110th VTAP, Krechevitsy AB, Velikiy Novgorod
RA-76779	IL-76MD	0083483505	6307	708th OVTAP, Taganrog
RA-76780	IL-76T	0013430901	2306	Ex-CCCP-76780, ex-CCCP-86926 (converted IL-76M?). Federal Border Guards, Moscow/Sheremet'yevo-1
RA-76781	IL-76TD	0023439133	2904	Ex-CCCP-76781, converted IL-76MD CCCP-86927, built-in chaff/flare dispensers. Federal Border Guards, Moscow/Sheremet'yevo-1
RA-76800	IL-76TD	0093493810	7103	FBG, Moscow/Sheremet'yevo-1
RA-76801	IL-76MD	0093495866	7207	Also reported as IL-76TD. MoI, based Nizhniy Novgorod
CCCP-76802	IL-76MD ('Falsie'?)	0093495874	7209	Ministry of the Interior, based Nizhniy Novgorod

Registration	Type	c/n	Line	Notes
RA-76803	IL-76MD 'Falsie'	0093497927	7402	Ministry of the Interior, based Nizhniy Novgorod
CCCP-76804	IL-76MD ('Falsie'?)	0093497931	7403	Ministry of the Interior, based Nizhniy Novgorod
RA-76825	IL-76MD 'Falsie'?	1003404136	7904	Also reported as IL-76TD. MoI, based Nizhniy Novgorod
RA-76826	IL-76MD 'Falsie'	1003404143	7906	Ministry of the Interior, based Nizhniy Novgorod
CCCP-76827	IL-76MD ('Falsie'?)	1003404151	7908	Ministry of the Interior, based Nizhniy Novgorod
RA-76828	IL-76MD 'Falsie'?	1003405164	8001	Also reported as IL-76TD. Moscow DD, Chkalovskaya AB
CCCP-76829	IL-76MD ('Falsie'?)	1003405172	8003	Ministry of the Interior, based Nizhniy Novgorod
RA-76838	IL-76TD	1023411370	8503	FBG, Moscow/Sheremet'yevo-1
RA-76839	IL-76TD	1023411375	8504	FBG, Moscow/Sheremet'yevo-1
RA-78743?	IL-76MD	?	?	Registration doubtful! (misread for RA-76743?)
RA-78750	IL-76MD	0083483510	6308	708th OVTAP, Taganrog
RA-78757	IL-76MD	0083484547	6407	978th VTAP, Klin-5 AB
RA-78762	IL-76MD	0083486574	6504	Based Chelyabinsk
RA-78766	IL-76MD	0083486595	6509	110th VTAP, Krechevitsy AB, Velikiy Novgorod
RA-78768	IL-76MD	0083487603	6601	110th VTAP, Krechevitsy AB, Velikiy Novgorod
RA-78770	IL-76MDK	0083487617	6605	Gagarin Space Training Centre, Chkalovskaya AB, zero-G trainer
RA-78777	IL-76MD	0083489654	6704	110th VTAP, Krechevitsy AB, Velikiy Novgorod
RA-78778	IL-76MD	0083489659	6705	708th OVTAP, Taganrog. To Ukrainian AF as UR-78778?
RA-78782	IL-78	0083489678	6710	230th APSZ, Engels
RA-78784	IL-76MD	0083489687	6802	110th VTAP, Krechevitsy AB, Velikiy Novgorod
RA-78790	IL-76MD	0083490712	6808	196th VTAP, Migalovo AB, Tver'
RA-78791	IL-76MD	0093490714	6809	110th VTAP, Krechevitsy AB, Velikiy Novgorod
RA-78795	IL-76MD	0093491729	6903	110th VTAP, Krechevitsy AB, Velikiy Novgorod
RA-78798	IL-78	0093491747	6907	230th APSZ, Engels
CCCP-78800	IL-78M	0093491758	6910	230th APSZ, Engels
RA-78803	IL-76MD	0093492774	7004	128th VTAP, Orenburg
RA-78804	IL-76MD	0093492778	7005	128th VTAP, Orenburg. Crashed at Abakan 27-11-96
RA-78805	IL-76MD	0093492783	7006	110th VTAP, Krechevitsy AB, Velikiy Novgorod
CCCP-78806	IL-78	0093492786	7007	230th APSZ, Engels; reportedly to 08 Red but this is doubtful!
RA-78807	IL-76MD	0093493791	7008	978th VTAP, Klin-5 AB
RA-78810	IL-76MD	0093493814	7104	128th VTAP, Orenburg
RA-78811	IL-76MD	0093494823	7106	128th VTAP, Orenburg
RA-78812	IL-78	0093494826	7107	230th APSZ, Engels
RA-78813	IL-76MD	0093494830	7108	128th VTAP, Orenburg
RA-78814	IL-78	0093494838	7110	230th APSZ, Engels
CCCP-78822	IL-78M	0093495880	7210	230th APSZ, Engels. Out-of-sequence registration
CCCP-78823	IL-78M	1003496918	7310	230th APSZ, Engels; reported in error as IL-78 sans suffixe
CCCP-78824	IL-78M	1003497947	7407	230th APSZ, Engels; reported in error as IL-78 sans suffixe
CCCP-78825	IL-76MDK-II	1013495871	7208	Gagarin Space Training Centre, Chkalovskaya AB, zero-G trainer. Out-of-sequence registration
RA-78829	IL-76MD	1003401006	7602	
RA-78830	IL-76MD	1003401010	7603	Moscow DD, Chkalovskaya AB. Leased to / jointly operated with Atlant-Soyuz
RA-78845	IL-76MD	1003403095	7804	128th VTAP, Orenburg
RA-78850	IL-76MD 'Falsie'	1013405196	8009	Moscow Defence District, 223rd OSAP, Chkalovskaya AB. Leased to / jointly operated with Atlant-Soyuz
RA-78851	IL-76MD 'Falsie'	1013406204	8101	Sold to Polis Air 1993 as IL-76TD RA-76388
RA-78852	IL-76MD 'Falsie'	1013407212	8103	Sold to Polis Air 1993 as IL-76TD RA-76389
RA-78878?	IL-76MD	?	?	Registration doubtful! Reported built in 1991
RA-86022	IL-76M	083413417	1105	128th VTAP, Orenburg
RA-86023	IL-76M	083413422	1106	128th VTAP, Orenburg
RA-86025	IL-76M	083414433	1109	978th VTAP, Klin-5 AB
RA-86026	IL-76M	083414439	1110	128th VTAP, Orenburg
RA-86027	IL-76M	083415459	1205	128th VTAP, Orenburg
CCCP-86031	IL-76M	083415477	1210	Ground instructional airframe, location unknown
RA-86032	IL-76M	093415482	1301	978th VTAP, Klin-5 AB
RA-86033	IL-76M	093416488	1302	128th VTAP, Orenburg
RA-86034	IL-76M	093416489	1303	334th VTAP, Kresty AB, Pskov
RA-86035	IL-76M	093416494	1304	334th VTAP, Kresty AB, Pskov
RA-86037	IL-76M	093417511	1308	110th VTAP, Krechevitsy AB, Velikiy Novgorod
RA-86038	IL-76M	093417514	1309	334th VTAP, Kresty AB, Pskov
RA-86040	IL-76M	093417521	1401	334th VTAP, Kresty AB, Pskov
RA-86041	IL-76M	093417532	1403	334th VTAP, Kresty AB, Pskov
RA-86042	IL-76M	093417535	1404	110th VTAP, Krechevitsy AB, Velikiy Novgorod
RA-86043	IL-76M	093418539	1405	128th VTAP, Orenburg
RA-86044	IL-76M	093418552	1408	Based Shadrinsk
RA-86045	IL-76M	093418564	1501	Based Shadrinsk
RA-86046	IL-76M	093418565	1502	Based Shadrinsk
CCCP-86047	IL-76M	093418572	1503	GIA at Russian AF Academy, Monino
RA-86048	IL-76M	093419573	1504	978th VTAP, Klin-5 AB
RA-86049	IL-76M	093419580	1505	334th VTAP, Kresty AB, Pskov; named Pskov
CCCP-86601	IL-76 (mil)	033402026	0107	978th VTAP, WFU/stored Klin-5 AB
RA-86612?	IL-76 (mil)	?	?	Mis-sighting for RA-86812? (registration used earlier on a Soviet AF IL-62, c/n 41804). Seschcha AB. RA- prefix but Soviet flag
CCCP-86621	IL-76 (mil)	053405117	0310	Ground instructional airframe, location unknown
RA-86625	IL-76 (mil)	063405130	0403	103rd VTAP, Smolensk
RA-86626	IL-76 (mil)	063405135	0404	Dyaghilevo AB, Ryazan'. Ex-Soviet Air Force '626 Black', ex-CCCP-86626
CCCP-86627	IL-76 (mil)	063405137	0405	Sold to Uralinteravia 10-8-92
RA-86628	IL-76 (mil)	063405144	0406	978th VTAP, Klin-5 AB
RA-86629	IL-76 (mil)	063406148	0407	Dyaghilevo AB, Ryazan'. Ex-Soviet Air Force '629 Black', ex-CCCP-86629
CCCP-86631	IL-76 (mil)	063407202	0601	978th VTAP, WFU/stored Klin-5 AB
CCCP-86636	IL-76 (mil)	063408222	0606	517th VTAP, WFU/stored Ivanovo-Severnyy AB
CCCP-86637	IL-76 (mil)	063409228	0607	517th VTAP, WFU/stored Ivanovo-Severnyy AB
CCCP-86638	IL-76K	073409232	0608	Gagarin Space Training Centre, Chkalovskaya AB, zero-G trainer. Retired/GIA, location unknown
RA-86642	IL-76 (mil)	073409248	0702	Reported as IL-76M but designation doubtful. 517th VTAP, Ivanovo-Severnyy AB
RA-86643	IL-76 (mil)	?	?	Doubtful report! See IL-76 sans suffixe '21 Red'
CCCP-86646	IL-76 (mil)	043402053	0204	978th VTAP, WFU/stored Chkalovskaya AB
CCCP-86715	IL-76 (mil)	053403072	0208	517th VTAP, Ivanovo-Severnyy AB. F/n reported in error as 0203. Sold to Al'kor 16-7-92
CCCP-86717	IL-76 (mil)	063406160	0410	517th VTAP, WFU/stored Ivanovo-Severnyy AB
CCCP-86720	IL-76 (mil)	073409267	0707	Sold to Uralinteravia 10-8-92 as IL-76TD 'Falsie'
CCCP-86723	IL-76K	073410279	0710	Gagarin Space Training Centre, Chkalovskaya AB, zero-G trainer. Sold to Express JSC 1996 as 'IL-76T' RA-76372
CCCP-86729	IL-76K	073410300	0805	Gagarin Space Training Centre, Chkalovskaya AB, zero-G trainer. Sold to Iron Dragonfly 1997 as 'IL-76T' RA-76430
RA-86731	IL-76M	083413391	1008	128th VTAP, Orenburg
RA-86733	IL-76M	083413396	1009	128th VTAP, Orenburg
RA-86734	IL-76M	083413397	1010	128th VTAP, Orenburg
RA-86736	IL-76M	083411342	0906	128th VTAP, Orenburg
RA-86737	IL-76M	083411347	0907	WFU/stored Taganrog
RA-86738	IL-76M	083411352	0908	128th VTAP, Orenburg
RA-86740	IL-76M	083412358	0910	128th VTAP, Orenburg
RA-86741	IL-76M	083412361	1001	128th VTAP, Orenburg
RA-86743	IL-76M	083412369	1003	128th VTAP, Orenburg
RA-86744	IL-76M	083412376	1004	128th VTAP, Orenburg
CCCP-86745	IL-76 (mil)	063407162	0501	Also reported as IL-76M. 517th VTAP, WFU/stored Ivanovo-Severnyy AB
RA-86746	IL-76 (mil)	063407165	0502	Also reported as IL-76M. 103rd VTAP, WFU/stored Smolensk

Registration	Type	C/n	Fuse	Notes
CCCP-86747	*IL-76 (mil)*	*063407170*	*0503*	*Sold to Uralinteravia 10-8-92*
RA-86748	IL-76 (mil)	063407175	0504	Also reported as IL-76M. 103rd VTAP, Smolensk. Active as CCCP- until at least 7-95!
RA-86749	IL-76 (mil)	063407179	0505	Also reported as IL-76M. 103rd VTAP, Smolensk
RA-86805	IL-76 (mil)	053403073	0209	978th VTAP, Klin-5 AB
RA-86806	IL-76 (mil)	053403078	0210	Seschcha AB
CCCP-86807	IL-76 (mil)	053404083	0301	978th VTAP, WFU/stored Klin-5 AB
RA-86809	IL-76 (mil)	?	0303	Seschcha AB
RA-86810	*IL-76 (mil)*	*053404094*	*0304*	*Sold to Al'kor 16-7-92*
RA-86812	IL-76 (mil)	053404103	0306	Reported in error as IL-76M. Seschcha AB
RA-86813	IL-76 (mil)	053404105	0307	Also reported as IL-76M. Seschcha AB
RA-86814	IL-76 (mil)	053405110	0308	Seschcha AB
CCCP-86815	IL-76 (mil)	063407183	0506	517th VTAP, WFU/stored Ivanovo-Severnyy AB
CCCP-86818	IL-76 (mil)	063407194	0509	517th VTAP, WFU/stored Ivanovo-Severnyy AB
RA-86820	IL-76 (mil)	?	?	Seschcha AB
RA-86825	IL-76M	093419581	1506	110th VTAP, Krechevitsy AB, Velikiy Novgorod
RA-86826	IL-76M	093419588	1507	128th VTAP, Orenburg. Active with CCCP-prefix until 7-95!
RA-86827	IL-76M	093419589	1508	978th VTAP, Klin-5 AB
RA-86828	IL-76M	093420604	1601	334th VTAP, Kresty AB, Pskov
RA-86829	IL-76M	0003427798	2010	Based Shadrinsk. Out-of-sequence registration
RA-86830	IL-76M	093421626	1607	110th VTAP, Krechevitsy AB, Velikiy Novgorod
RA-86831	IL-76M	093421642	1701	334th VTAP, Kresty AB, Pskov
RA-86832	IL-76M	0003421646	1702	128th VTAP, Orenburg
RA-86833	IL-76M	0003422650	1703	128th VTAP, Orenburg
CCCP-86834	IL-76M	0003422655	1704	Ground instructional airframe at IVATU, Irkutsk
RA-86835	IL-76M	0003422658	1705	334th VTAP, Kresty AB, Pskov
RA-86836	IL-76M	0003422661	1706	128th VTAP, Orenburg
RA-86837	IL-76M	0003422668	1707	128th VTAP, Orenburg
RA-86838	IL-76M	0003423669	1708	978th VTAP, Klin-5 AB
RA-86839	IL-76M	0003423684	1801	334th VTAP, Kresty AB, Pskov
CCCP-86840	IL-76M	0003423688	1802	Based Shadrinsk
RA-86841	IL-76M	0003423701	1806	128th VTAP, Orenburg
RA-86842	IL-76M	0003423692	1804	334th VTAP, Kresty AB, Pskov
RA-86843	IL-76M	0003423690?	1803?	110th VTAP, Krechevitsy AB, Velikiy Novgorod. Out-of-sequence registration
RA-86844	IL-76M	0003424711	1808	334th VTAP, Kresty AB, Pskov
RA-86845	IL-76M	0003426762	2001	Based Shadrinsk
RA-86847	IL-76M	0003426769	2003	517th VTAP, Ivanovo-Severnyy AB
RA-86849	IL-76M	0003426779	2005	196th VTAP, Migalovo AB, Tver'?
RA-86850	IL-76M	0003427782	2006	196th VTAP, Migalovo AB, Tver'?
RA-86851	IL-76M	0003424715	1809	Out-of-sequence registration. 334th VTAP, Kresty AB, Pskov
CCCP-86852	IL-76M	0003424719	1810	Out-of-sequence registration. Based Shadrinsk
RA-86853	IL-76M	0003424723	1901	Out-of-sequence registration. 334th VTAP, Kresty AB, Pskov
CCCP-86854	IL-76M	0003425728	1902	Out-of-sequence registration. GIA, location unknown
RA-86855	IL-76M	0003425734	1904	Out-of-sequence registration. Migalovo AB, Tver'
CCCP-86856	IL-76M	0003425740	1905	Out-of-sequence registration. Based Shadrinsk
RA-86857	IL-76M	0003425744	1906	Out-of-sequence registration. Based Shadrinsk
RA-86858	IL-76M	0003426751	1908	Out-of-sequence registration. Based Shadrinsk
CCCP-86859	IL-76M	0003426755	1909	Out-of-sequence registration, reported as special-mission aircraft. Based Shadrinsk
CCCP-86860	IL-76M	0003426759	1910	Out-of-sequence registration. Based Shadrinsk
RA-86861	IL-76M	0003427804	2101	978th VTAP, Klin-5 AB
CCCP-86862	IL-76M	0003427806	2102	Based Shadrinsk
RA-86863	IL-76M	0003428809	2103	978th VTAP, Klin-5 AB
CCCP-86864	IL-76M	0003428816	2104	517th VTAP, WFU/stored Ivanovo-Severnyy AB
RA-86866	IL-76M	0003428821	2106	110th VTAP, Krechevitsy AB, Velikiy Novgorod
CCCP-86867	IL-76M	0013428828	2107	Based Shadrinsk
RA-86868	IL-76M	0013428833	2109	334th VTAP, Kresty AB, Pskov
RA-86869	IL-76M	0013428844	2201	
RA-86870	IL-76M	0013429847	2202	110th VTAP, Krechevitsy AB, Velikiy Novgorod
RA-86872	IL-76MD	0013434008	2602	First production aircraft, out-of-sequence registration. 196th VTAP, Migalovo AB, Tver'
RA-86873	IL-76M	0013429850	2203	334th VTAP, Kresty AB, Pskov
RA-86874	IL-76M	0013429853	2204	334th VTAP, Kresty AB, Pskov
RA-86875	IL-76M	0013429859	2205	334th VTAP, Kresty AB, Pskov
RA-86876	IL-76M	0013429861	2206	334th VTAP, Kresty AB, Pskov
CCCP-86877	IL-76M	0013429867	2207	Based Shadrinsk
CCCP-86879	A-60	0013430893	2304	Laser weapon testbed, converted IL-76MD 'Falsie'. WFU Chkalovskaya AB
RA-86880	IL-76M	0013430897	2305	978th VTAP, Klin-5 AB
RA-86881	IL-76M	0013431906	2307	Based Shadrinsk
CCCP-86882	IL-76M	0013431917	2310	Based Shadrinsk
RA-86883	IL-76M	0013431921	2401	Based Shadrinsk
RA-86884	IL-76M	0013431932	2403	978th VTAP, Klin-5 AB
RA-86885	IL-76M	0013431939	2405	103rd VTAP, Smolensk
RA-86886	IL-76M	0013431943	2406	103rd VTAP, Based Shadrinsk
RA-86887	IL-76M	0013431945	2407	110th VTAP, Krechevitsy AB, Velikiy Novgorod?
RA-86888	IL-76M	0013432966	2502	110th VTAP, Krechevitsy AB, Velikiy Novgorod?
CCCP-86889	IL-76PP	0013434009	2603	Out-of-sequence registration. GIA at IVATU, Irkutsk
CCCP-86892	IL-76M	0013432969	2503	517th VTAP, WFU/stored Ivanovo-Severnyy AB
RA-86893	IL-76M	0013432975	2504	Based Shadrinsk
RA-86894	IL-76M	0013432977	2505	517th VTAP, Ivanovo-Severnyy AB
RA-86895	IL-76MD	0013433985	2507	517th VTAP, Ivanovo-Severnyy AB; reported in error as IL-76M
RA-86896	*IL-76MD*	*0013434018*	*2605*	*Sold to Zenit 23-4-94 as IL-76TD 'Falsie'*
RA-86897	IL-76MD	0013434023	2606	517th VTAP, Ivanovo-Severnyy AB;
RA-86898	IL-76MD	0013435028	2607	Ex-Russian AF '22 Red'? 196th VTAP, Migalovo AB, Tver'
86900	IL-76MD	0023435034	2609	196th VTAP, Migalovo AB, Tver'; ever as RA-?
RA-86901	IL-76MD	0023436038	2610	196th VTAP, Migalovo AB, Tver'
RA-86902	IL-76MD	0023436043	2701	196th VTAP, Migalovo AB, Tver'
RA-86906	IL-76MD *Skal'pel'-MT*	0023436064	2706	Moscow Defence District, Chkalovskaya AB, aeromedical
RA-86907	IL-76MD	0023436065	2707	196th VTAP, Migalovo AB, Tver'
RA-86908	IL-76MD	0023437070	2708	334th VTAP, Kresty AB, Pskov
RA-86910	IL-76MD	0023437077	2710	196th VTAP, Migalovo AB, Tver'
CCCP-86912	*IL-76MD*	*0023437099?*	*2805*	*GIA, Balashov Higher Military Pilot School*
CCCP-86913	IL-76MD	0023438108	2807	517th VTAP, WFU/stored Ivanovo-Severnyy AB
RA-86925	IL-76MD	0093492766	7002	Ex-CCCP-86925 No 2. Mol, based Nizhniy Novgorod
01 Red	IL-76MD	1003401024	7606	Ex-CCCP-78837 (callsign RA-78837), 517th VTAP, Ivanovo-Severnyy AB, unit CO's aircraft. Basic Aeroflot c/s, named *Marshal Aviatsii Skripko*
21 Red	*IL-76 (mil)*	*043402041*	*0201*	*Ex-CCCP-86643? Basic Aeroflot c/s. 517th VTAP, Ivanovo-Severnyy AB. Sold to Dobrolyot 29-7-92 as RA-76416*
22 Red?	*IL-76MD*	*0013435028*	*2607*	*Ex-CCCP-86898/to RA-86898? (existence unconfirmed)*
533 Black	*IL-76MD*	*0023442205*	*3102*	*Ex-CCCP-76533, grey/white colour scheme. 517th VTAP, Ivanovo-Severnyy AB. To RA-76533*
538 Black	*IL-76MD*	*0023442231*	*3108*	*Ex-CCCP-76538/to RA-76538*
602 Black	IL-76 (mil)	033402031	0108	Ex-CCCP-86602, grey/white colour scheme. 517th VTAP, Ivanovo-Severnyy AB
626 Black	*IL-76 (mil)*	*063405135*	*0404*	*Ex-CCCP-86626, basic Aeroflot colours. To RA-86626*
629 Black	*IL-76 (mil)*	*063406148*	*0407*	*Ex-CCCP-86629, basic Aeroflot colours. To RA-86629*
632 Black	IL-76 (mil)	073409251	0703	Ex-CCCP-86632, grey/white colour scheme. 103rd VTAP, Smolensk
634 Black	IL-76 (mil)	063408214	0604	Ex-CCCP-86634, 103rd VTAP, Smolensk
635 Black	IL-76 (mil)	063408217	0605	Ex-CCCP-86635, grey/white colour scheme. 103rd VTAP, Smolensk
644 Black	*IL-76 (mil)*	*043402046*	*0202*	*Ex-CCCP-86644, basic Aeroflot colours. Sold to Dobrolyot 29-7-92 as RA-76417*
645 Black	IL-76 (mil)	043402049	0203	Ex-CCCP-86645, grey/white colour scheme. 103rd VTAP, Smolensk
713 Black	IL-76 (mil)	043403061	0206	Ex-CCCP-86713, basic Aeroflot colours. 978th VTAP, Klin-5 AB

Top left: **As in Soviet times, Russian Air Force *Candid-B*s rarely wear overt military markings. Illustrated is one of the few such aircraft, IL-76MD '01 Red' (ex-RA-78837, c/n 1003401024, f/n 7606) based at Ivanovo-Severnyy AB.** Yefim Gordon

Above: **Quasi-civil and overtly military IL-78s in service with the 230th APSZ it Engels, with a Tu-160 in the background.** Yefim Gordon

Left: ***Midas* '41 Red' caught during an unexpected visit to Kubinka AB in early 1997.** Yefim Gordon

Below: **The Russian Air Force also has commercial divisions. Here, RA-78831, one of 31 operated by the 224th Flight Unit State Airline, is unloaded at Moscow/Vnukovo-1 airport on 4th October 2000.** Dmitriy Komissarov

716 Black	IL-76 (mil)	063406156	0409	Ex-CCCP-86716, Seschcha AB
719 Black	IL-76 (mil)	073409263	0706	Ex-CCCP-86719. 103rd VTAP, Smolensk
722 Black	IL-76 (mil)	073410276	0709	Ex-CCCP-86722
725 Black	IL-76 (mil)	073410285	0802	Ex-CCCP-86725, grey/white colour scheme. 517th VTAP, Ivanovo-Severnyy AB
728 Black	IL-76M	073410322	0901	Ex-CCCP-86728, IL-76M prototype
811 Black	IL-76 (mil)	053404098	0305	Ex-CCCP-86811
819 Black	IL-76 (mil)	063407199	0510	Ex-CCCP-86819. 103rd VTAP, Smolensk
30 Blue	IL-78M	1003498959	7410	Grey/white colour scheme. 230th APSZ, Engels
31 Blue	IL-78M	1003402040	7610	Grey/white colour scheme. 230th APSZ, Engels
32 Blue	IL-78M	1003403068	7707	Grey/white colour scheme. 230th APSZ, Engels
33 Blue	IL-78	1013403097	7805	Late version (L-shaped centre HDU pylon), grey/white colour scheme
34 Blue	IL-78	1013404138	7905	Late version (L-shaped centre HDU pylon), grey/white colour scheme
35 Blue (No1?)	IL-78	0043453559	3910	Ex-CCCP-76607, operated by SibNIA?
35 Blue (No 2?)	IL-78M	1013405188	8007	Grey/white colour scheme. 230th APSZ, Engels
36 Blue	IL-78M	1013405197	8010	Grey/white colour scheme. 230th APSZ, Engels
50 Blue	IL-78M	1003403079	7710	Grey/white colour scheme. 230th APSZ, Engels
51 Blue	IL-78M	1003403106	7807	Grey/white colour scheme. 230th APSZ, Engels
52 Blue	IL-78M	1013403119	7810	Grey/white colour scheme. 230th APSZ, Engels
53 Blue	IL-78M	1013407227	8107	Grey/white colour scheme. 230th APSZ, Engels
616 Black	IL-78	0053455676	4209	Ex-CCCP-76616; basic Aeroflot c/s? Ivanovo. Also reported as IL-76 sans suffixe (ex-CCCP-86816, c/n 063407185, f/n 0507)
10 Red	A-50	073409243	0701	First prototype, converted IL-76 sans suffixe (military) CCCP-86641, based Taganrog. Became a ground instructional airframe at Chójna AB (Poland) by 1996, scrapped 1998
15 Red	A-50	073410311	0808	Second prototype, converted IL-76 sans suffixe (military). WFU Taganrog
20 Red	A-50	0013430875	2209A	Third prototype, converted IL-76M? (reported as ex-CCCP-86878 but comment in Chapter 3!) GIA at Taganrog
30 Red	A-50	0023436059	2705	
31 Red	A-50	0053459777	4505	
32 Red	A-50	0063466979	5005	
33 Red	A-50	0043454618	4105	
34 Red	A-50	0043449460	3705	
35 Red	A-50	0063473178	5505	
36 Red	A-50	0073475260	5705	
37 Red	A-50	0073476298	5805	
38 Red	A-50	0033448379	3505	
39 Red	A-50	0043452537	3905	
40 Red	A-50	0083481457	6205	
41 Red	A-50	0083483499	6305	NII VVS, Akhtoobinsk
42 Red	A-50	0083484538	6405	
43 Red	A-50	0073479377	6005	
44 Red	A-50M	0093486579	6505	Prototype, callsign CCCP-78740. Converted to A-50I prototype and supplied to Israel for outfitting 10-99 as RA-78740; to 4X-AGI 1-2000
45 Red	A-50	0093493818	7105	
46 Red (No1)	A-50	0033443258	3205	
46 Red (No 2)	A-50	0043451498	3805	Based Taganrog, TANTK Beriyev test aircraft
47 Red	A-50	0043453577	4005	NII VVS, Akhtoobinsk
48 Red	A-50	0063458738	4405	
49 Red	A-50	0063469057	5205	
50 Red	A-50M	0093496899	7305	
51 Red	A-50M	1003488634	6609	
52 Red	A-50M?	1013491739	6905	
53 Red	A-50M?	0093497940	7405	

On 20th January 2000 334th VTAP IL-76M RA-86049 was christened *Pskov* after the city where it is based, becoming the first Russian Air Force transport to receive a name. The unit was carefully chosen, being the best-trained and best-equipped regiment of the 61st VA. The aircraft

is flown by the unit's best crew captained by Capt Yuriy Rodionov. In June IL-76MD '01 red' operated by the VTA Combat & Conversion Training Centre in Ivanovo was named to honour Air Marshal Nikolay Semyonovich Skripko who devoted 19 years of his life to the VTA (the Centre is also named after him). Another IL-76MD (registration unknown) is named *Gorod-gheroy Smolensk* (Hero City of Smolensk) and a 110th VTAP IL-76M (RA-86037?) is named *Velikiy Novgorod*.

The Russian Air Force also has commercial divisions. The 223rd OSAP (*otdel'nyy smeshannyy aviapolk* – independent composite air regiment), one of the units making up the 8th ADON at Chkalovskaya AB was transformed into an 'airline' called **223RD FLIGHT UNIT STATE AIRLINE** [–/CHD]. Among other things it operates a single IL-76MD, RA-76635 (c/n 0053459775, f/n 4504), in Aeroflot markings. This aircraft is an Afghan War veteran.

Another commercial division of the Russian Air Force is the VTA unit based at Tver'-2 (Migalovo) AB which became the **224TH FLIGHT UNIT STATE AIRLINE** [–/TTF]. The Tver' unit has 30 IL-76MDs (additionally, the 224th Flight Unit operates a number of An-124s based at Bryansk-2 AB). Originally flown in pure Aeroflot colours, some aircraft later received small round blue badges on the tail with the numerals *224*; at least one aircraft received large blue Cyrillic *224-yy Lyotnyy Otryad* (224th Flight Unit) titles on the forward fuselage in mid-1999.

Registration	Version	C/n	F/n	Notes
RA-76592	IL-76MD	0043452555	3909	'224' tail badge
RA-76638	IL-76MD	0053460802	4601	
RA-76650	IL-76MD	0053462865	4707	
RA-76669	IL-76MD	0063465949	4908	Sold or leased to Roos' ?-2000
RA-76686	IL-76MD	0063468045	5202	'224' tail badge
RA-76713	IL-76MD	0063474193	5509	C/n also reported as 0063474191. '224' tail badge
RA-76719	IL-76MD	0073474226	5607	
RA-76738	IL-76MD	0073477326	5902	
RA-78764	IL-76MD	0083486586	6507	
RA-78776	IL-76MD	0083489652	6703	
RA-78788	IL-76MD	0083490703	6806	
RA-78789	IL-76MD	0083490706	6807	Ex-334th VTAP, Kresty AB, Pskov
RA-78794	IL-76MD	0093490726	6902	
RA-78796	IL-76MD	0093491735	6904	
RA-78797	IL-76MD	0093491742	6906	'224' tail badge. Sold to Aerofrakht 10-2000?
RA-78809	IL-76MD	0093493807	7102	'224' tail badge
RA-78815	IL-76MD	0093494842	7201	
RA-78816	IL-76MD	0093495846	7202	C/n also reported as 0093494846
RA-78817	IL-76MD	0093495851	7203	
RA-78818	IL-76MD	0093495858	7205	'224' tail badge
RA-78831	IL-76MD	1003401017	7605	Ex-110th VTAP, Krechevitsy AB, Velikiy Novgorod? '224' tail badge
RA-78833	IL-76MD	1003401025	7607	Ex-334th VTAP, Kresty AB, Pskov
RA-78834	IL-76MD	1003401032	7608	
RA-78835	IL-76MD	1003402033	7609	C/n previously reported in error as 1003401006 (f/n 7602) which is RA-78829
RA-78838	IL-76MD	1003402044	7701	
RA-78840	IL-76MD	1003403056	7704	
RA-78842	IL-76MD	1003403069	7708	'224' tail badge
RA-78844	IL-76MD	1003403092	7803	Ex-128th VTAP, Orenburg; '224' tail badge
RA-78846	IL-76MD	1003403113	7809	C/n also quoted as 1003403115
RA-78847	IL-76MD	1003404132	7903	Ex-110th VTAP, Krechevitsy AB, Velikiy Novgorod
RA-78854	IL-76MD	1013407220	8105	Last IL-76MD delivered to the Soviet Air Force

ATRUVERA AIR TRANSPORT COMPANY [–/AUV], yet another airline under military management, operated five IL-76MDs from Seeverskaya AB near St. Petersburg. The aircraft were reportedly on lease from the Ukrainian Air Force. Atruvera is an acronym for *aviatrahnsportnnye oosloogi v Yevrope i Ahzii* – air transport services in Europe and Asia.

Registration	Version	C/n	F/n	Notes
RA-76588	IL-76MD	0043451530	3903	Not listed in JP Airline-Fleets 1999-2000 (sold to unknown operator?)
RA-76591	IL-76MD	0043452546	3907	Sold to Rosaeroleasing by 3-2000
RA-76659	IL-76MD	0053463908	4807	Leased to Aviacon Tsitotrans, later (1999) lsd to Sukhoi as IL-76TD 'Falsie'; returned by 5-2000
RA-76666	IL-76MD	0053464934	4904	Sold to Aviacon Tsitotrans 2-98; converted to IL-76TD
RA-76672	IL-76MD	0063466981	5006	Sold to Kras Air by 8-99 as IL-76TD 'Falsie'

The Russian **MINISTRY OF EMERGENCY CONTROL (EMER-COM)** [–/SUM] responsible for rescue and relief operations during natural disasters and major accidents has a large paramilitary force at its disposal. Personnel, equipment and humanitarian cargoes are transported by six IL-76TDs fitted with special communications equipment.

Registration	Version	C/n	F/n	Notes
RA-76362	IL-76TD	1033416533	8904	D/D 1993. Named Anatoliy Lyapidevskiy. Leased to / jointly opw Atlant-Soyuz 1996
RA-76363	IL-76TD	1033417540	8905	D/D 1993. Named Vasiliy Molokov. Leased to / jointly opw Atlant-Soyuz 1996
RA-76420	IL-76TD	1023413446	8702	Leased from Almazy Rossii-Sakha 2-98 to ?-98
RA-76429	IL-76TD	1043419639	9110	D/D 1997? Named Sigizmund Levanevskiy. Leased to / jointly opw Atlant-Soyuz 1998
RA-76840	IL-76TD	1033417553	8909	D/D 1994. Named Nikolay Kamanin
RA-76841	IL-76TD	1033418601	9101	D/D 1996. Named Mavrikiy Slepnev. Leased (sold?) to Atlant-Soyuz 1997
RA-76845	IL-76TD	1043420696	9304	D/D 1995. Ex-IL-76MD 'Falsie' (renamed by 3-96)! Named Mikhail Vodop'yanov

The *Candids* are operated by the ministry's flight detachment, Tsentrospas (= Central Rescue Unit) and based at LII. RA-76362 and RA-76363 were delivered in 1993 with red lightning side flashes and orange/blue roundel/triangle markings (the same as, for example, on French *Securité Civile* aircraft). Originally they wore *GKChS Rossii* (*Gosoodahrstvennyy komitet po chrezvychaynym sitooahtsiyam* – State Committee for Emergency Control) and *Tsentrospas* titles. During the next year, however, the committee was transformed into a ministry and the abbreviation changed to *MChS Rossii* (*Ministerstvo po chrezvychaynym sitooahtsiyam*) – probably to avoid associations with the infamous GKChP, the National Emergency Committee that briefly held power during the failed coup of 19th-21st August 1991.

The other four aircraft have a different colour scheme with a kinked orange/blue/orange cheatline, no *Tsentrospas* titles and the familiar roundel markings incorporated into a windrose. In 1998 most of EMERCOM's fleet was christened; like most aircraft, the IL-76s are named after famous Soviet pilots, including the first Heroes of the Soviet Union. (The latter, incidentally, earned this title in a rescue operation, saving the crew and passengers of the research vessel S/S *Chelyuskin* which was crushed by ice in the Arctic Ocean in 1934. It is quite appropriate that EMERCOM's aircraft should be named after these people!)

The *Candid* has proved quite versatile as an SAR aircraft. Firstly, any of the six aircraft can be configured as an IL-76TDP for the firefighting role. Secondly, they can carry EMERCOM's Eurocopter (MBB) Bö 105CBS-5SF and BK117C-1 helicopters used for SAR operations in impassable terrain. Unlike the bigger and heavier Mil' Mi-8MTV-1 *Hip-Hs*, they can be quickly airlifted by the IL-76, saving valuable time.

Thirdly, the IL-76s can be outfitted for carrying 72 stretcher patients on six rows of 12 stretchers. They can also deploy EMERCOM's unique inflatable airmobile hospital which can be paradropped on four P-7 pallets if necessary. When fully deployed, the hospital accommodates 150 patients and can be airlifted anywhere within 12 hours' flying time from Moscow (the IL-76's maximum endurance). The rubberised fabric tents can be used at temperatures ranging from –50° to +50°C (–58° to 122°F).

All six *Candids* are marked 'IL-76TD'. However, RA-76845 has an inert gas generator air intake in the starboard main gear actuator fairing and characteristic covers over chaff/flare pack connectors on the aft fuselage sides, which identifies it as a renamed IL-76MD 'Falsie'; this aircraft can be fitted with a removable upper deck for evacuating up to 225 refugees. All six of EMERCOM's own *Candids* were jointly operated with Atlant-Soyuz Airlines (see below).

ABAKAN-AVIA [–/ABG], a division of the Sobol' (Sable) trade company, is one of two airlines based in Abakan, the capital of the Republic of Khakasia in Southern Central Siberia. Until 1998 Abakan-Avia was a pure cargo carrier, operating two IL-76Ts. In mid-1998 it started passenger operations with two ex-Armenian Tu-154Ms, doubling its freighter fleet at the same time, though one aircraft has been sold since.

Registration	Version	C/n	F/n	Notes
RA-76350	IL-76TD	1023410344	8406	Ex-C-Air, bought 1998; C-Air blue/red cheatline, white tail, English titles
RA-76504	IL-76T	073411328	0902	Converted IL-76 (civil); C-Air style cheatline, grey tail with Russian flag, Cyrillic titles. C/n often reported in error as 073411330
RA-76505	IL-76T	073411331	0903	Converted IL-76 (civil); basic Aeroflot colours, Cyrillic titles
RA-76521	IL-76T	0003423699	1805	Ex-Magadanaerogrooz, bought by 9-98. C-Air style cheatline, white tail, Cyrillic titles. Sold to Ilavia by mid-1999
UR-76687	IL-76MD	0063469051	5203	Leased from Volare Aviation Enterprise 9-99 to 3-2000, English titles

In mid-1999 an airline called **AERO CONCEPT** operated IL-76TD EW-76735 (a converted IL-76MD, c/n 0073476314, f/n 5809) leased from TransAVIAexport.

TsUMVS, the international division of the old Aeroflot based at Moscow/Sheremet'yevo-2, became **AEROFLOT RUSSIAN INTERNATIONAL AIRLINES** (ARIA; *Aeroflot – Rosseeyskiye mezhdunarodnyye avialinii*) [SU/AFL]. The fleet of Russia's new flag carrier included 19 *Candid-As*.

Registration	Version	C/n	F/n	Notes
RA-76460	IL-76T	0013431928	2402	Retired 1995, Ground instructional airframe at MIIGA (Sheremet'yevo-1)
RA-76461	IL-76T	0013431935	2404	Retired 1995
RA-76467	IL-76TD	0023440157	2910	
RA-76468	IL-76TD	0023441195	3009	
RA-76469	IL-76TD	0023444286	3302	Grey tail
RA-76470	IL-76TD	0033445291	3303	
RA-76473	IL-76TD	0033448404	3601	Sold to Ilavia 1995
RA-76474	IL-76TD	0033448407	3602	Sold to Ilavia 1995
RA-76476	IL-76TD	0043451528	3902	Grey tail
RA-76477	IL-76TD	0043453575	4004	Sold to Ilavia 1995
RA-76478	IL-76TD	0053459788	4507	Was operated by Polar Aviation for a while; red/white polar colours, white tail
RA-76479	IL-76TD	0053460790	4508	Was operated by Polar Aviation for a while; red/white polar colours, grey tail
RA-76482	IL-76TD	0053460832	4608	
RA-76488	IL-76TD	0073479371	6003	
RA-76519	IL-76T	093420599	1510	Grey tail. Sold to Ilavia 1996
RA-76750	IL-76TD	0083485561	6501	Grey tail
RA-76751	IL-76TD	0083487610	6603	Grey tail. WFU (see note)
RA-76785	IL-76TD	0093495863	7206	Grey tail
RA-76795	IL-76TD	0093498962	7501	Grey tail

Note: ARIA planned to upgrade its aircraft to IL-76TD-90 standard in order to meet current noise/pollution limits and cut operating costs by reducing fuel consumption. Yet the programme failed to materialise and conversion of the prototype (RA-76751) begun in 1994 was never completed.

Caught by the camera as it takes off on from Zhukovskiy on a disaster relief mission to Turkey, IL-76TD RA-76362 *Anatoliy Lyapidevskiy* illustrates the early livery worn by EMERCOM of Russia *Candids*. Dmitriy Komissarov

Despite the 'IL-76TD' nose titles, RA-76845 was originally an IL-76MD 'Falsie', as revealed by the inert gas generator intake. Dmitriy Komissarov

Seen taxiing at Zhukovskiy, RA-76429 *Sigizmund Levanevskiy* is the newest IL-76TD in EMERCOM's fleet. Note the non-standard cropped chin radome suggesting that a different type of radar is fitted. Yefim Gordon

The airline **AEROFRAKHT** (Aerofreight) [–/FRT] founded in 1998 operated IL-76TD RA-76499 jointly with its owner, Kosmos (see below), in 1998-99. Despite its name, Aerofrakht also operates passenger aircraft (three Tu-134AK executive jets also leased from Kosmos). In October 2000 the airline reportedly bought IL-76MD RA78797 from the Russian Air Force/224th Flight Unit.

The now-defunct airline **AEROTRANS** operated IL-76TD RA-76472 (c/n 0033446350, f/n 3408) in September 1993. It was in full Aeroflot markings with additional Aerotrans titles on the port side. After the airline's demise the aircraft was sold to SVGAL (North-Eastern Cargo Airlines).

AIRSTAN JOINT-STOCK COMPANY [–/JSC] has two IL-76TDs – RA-76369 (c/n 1033414480, f/n 8710) and RA-76842 (c/n 1033418616, f/n 9104) based at Kazan'-International airport. The latter aircraft, which was involved in the much-publicised Afghan hostage drama of 1995-96 (see page 64), wears full red/white Airstan colours, whereas RA-76369 is in basic Aeroflot colours.

The **AIR TRANSPORT SCHOOL** (*Shkola vozdooshnovo trahnsporta*) [–/AIS] operated a demilitarised IL-76T 'Falsie' registered RA-76497 (c/n 073410320, f/n 0810) from Zhukovskiy. The aircraft, an ex-Iraqi machine (ex-YI-AIM?), was painted in basic Aeroflot colours without titles, lacking the company logo composed of the Cyrillic letters ShVT. In 1996 the Air Transport School started doing business as **AIS AIRLINES**. In the following year, however, the airline ceased operations and the aircraft was retired, becoming a ground instructional airframe.

Moscow-based **AIR TROIKA** [–/TKA] operated IL-76s wet-leased from Volga-Dnepr and the Russian Air Force as required; a maximum of three *Candids* was operated at any one time. For instance, RA-86806, a military IL-76 *sans suffixe* (c/n 053403078, f/n 0210), was operated in 1994. Unlike Air Troika's An-24s, An-26s and assorted helicopters (also leased from other carriers) which were operated for the United Nations Peace Forces, the *Candids* were used for ordinary cargo services only.

The charter carrier **ALAK** [J4/LSV] founded in 1992 and based at Moscow-Vnukovo operated three *Candids* until it suspended operations in 1998.[3] The name stands for *aktsionernaya lizingovaya aviakompahniya* (joint-stock leasing airline).

Registration	Version	C/n	F/n	Notes
RA-76405	IL-76TD	1023412402	8601	Leased from LII ?-?? to ?-95
RA-76814	IL-76TD	1013408269	8208	Leased from Rusaeroleasing?
RA-78850	IL-76MD 'Falsie'	1013405196	8009	Leased from Russian Air Force 10-94 to ?-??

The cargo airline **AL'KOR** based in Zhukovskiy operated three *Candid-Bs* – IL-76T 'Falsies' RA-86604 (c/n 043402039, f/n 0110) and RA-86715 (c/n 053403072, f/n 0208) and military IL-76 *sans suffixe* RA-86810 (c/n 053404094, f/n 0304) bought from the Air Force on 16th June 1992. The former two aircraft were in basic Aeroflot colours while RA-86810 was all-white with a grey belly and no titles. In 1996 the airline went bankrupt; RA-86604 and RA-86715 were sold to Air Cess (see next chapter) as EL-RDX and EL-RDT respectively, while RA-86810 was leased to the Azerbaijan Air Force.

Moscow/Vnukovo-based **ALLWE** [–/LWE], one of the many small airlines which appeared in Russia in the early 1990s, operated IL-76TD RA-76426 (ex-UR-76426, c/n 1013405184, f/n 8006) in February-October 1996. After that, the aircraft was sold to Uzbekistan Airways as UK-76426 (see notes on Uzbekistan Airways and Moldova).

ALMAZY ROSSII – SAKHA (Diamonds of Russia – Sakha) [–/DRU], a subsidiary of the identically named diamond mining company based in Mirnyy, has four IL-76TDs. Originally these flew in the basic Aeroflot colours with Cyrillic 'Almazy Rossii – Sakha' titles. By April 2000, however, the airline was rebranded **Alrosa** (a contraction of the original name) and adopted a colour scheme of its own.

Registration	Version	C/n	F/n	Notes
RA-76357	IL-76TD	1033414467	8707	C/n often reported in error as 1023414467
RA-76360	IL-76TD	1033414492	8803	Leased to Samara Airlines by 6-99
RA-76373	IL-76TD	1033415507	8807	
RA-76420	IL-76TD	1023413446	8702	Ex-Vladivostok Air. Leased to Samara Airlines by 10-98

ALTAISKIYE AVIALINII (Altai Airlines) based at Barnaul, formerly part of Aeroflot's Barnaul Air Enterprise, had three IL-76s.

Registration	Version	C/n	F/n	Notes
RA-76445	IL-76MD 'Falsie'	1023410330	8403	Sold to Novosibirsk Airlines 1998 as IL-76TD
RA-76446	IL-76MD 'Falsie'	1023412418	8605	Sold to Dvin-Avia by 9-99 as IL-76TD EK-76446
RA-76833	IL-76TD	1023411363	8501	Lsd to East Line by 9-98; returned by mid-2000

Some Western sources reported that a certain **ALTAI BRANCH DESIGN AND MARKETING CENTRE** operated IL-76TD RA-76466 in January 1994. However, this is almost certainly a misquote, since **CCCP**-76466 was totally destroyed in a fatal crash near Leninakan on 20th October 1989 (see Appendix 2); a second use of this registration appears highly improbable, as the aircraft has not been reported since.

The airline **ANTEX** based in Urai (Tyumen' Region) operated IL-76MD 'Falsie' RA-76445 and IL-76TD RA-76833 in the spring of 1997 jointly with the Polyus Parachute & Expedition Work Centre (which see); the airline were leased from Altaiskiye Availinii. ANTEX suspended operations in the same year.

IL-76TD RA-76419 (c/n 1023414470, f/n 8708) was reportedly operated by **ARKHANGEL'SK AIRLINES** (AVL – *Arkhangel'skiye Vozdooshnyye Linii*) [5N/AUL] which leased it to various third-world companies. The aircraft was ultimately sold to the Algerian Air Force as 7T-WID.

ATLANT-SOYUZ AIRLINES [3G/AYZ] were established on 8th June 1993 as a sister company of the Ukrainian Atlant-SV based in Simferopol'. The airline operates scheduled and charter passenger and cargo services from Moscow (Sheremet'yevo-2 and Domodedovo) and Chkalovskaya airbase, mostly with aircraft leased from other carriers and the Russian, Belorussian and Ukrainian air forces as required. These include numerous *Candids* which come and go, so to say.

Atlant-Soyuz is known as 'the Moscow Government airline' (!) – for more than one reason. First, the Moscow Government has a stake in the airline; second, Moscow Mayor Yuriy M Luzhkov and other government officials, including then State Duma Chairman Ghennadiy N Seleznyov) often made use of the airline's aircraft during trips in Russia and abroad. Hence some Atlant-Soyuz aircraft wear additional Cyrillic *Aviakompahniya pravitel'stva Moskvy* titles, much to the amusement of spotters.

Registration	Version	C/n	F/n	Notes
RA-76362	IL-76TD	1033416533	8904	Leased from / jointly operated with EMERCOM of Russia (1996)
RA-76363	IL-76TD	1033417540	8905	Leased from / jointly operated with EMERCOM of Russia (1996)
RA-76367	IL-76TD	1033414474	8709	Leased from C-Air (bought in 1999). C-Air red/ blue cheatline, Atlant-Soyuz titles and logo
RA-76370	IL-76TD	1033414458	8705	Leased from / jointly operated with Gazpromavia (1999)
RA-76382	IL-76TD 'Falsie'	0023436048	2702	Ex-Hungarian-Ukranian Heavy Lift HA-TCG, ex-Atlant-SV UR-76382, ex-IL-76MD UR-86903. To Atlant Aerobatics 3-2000 as HA-TCG,
RA-76383	IL-76MD	0023437076	2709	Ex-UR-86909, leased from Atlant-SV. To Air Sultan 10-96 as 9L-LBK

Right: **Displaying obvious signs of previous ownership by the defunct C-Air, Abakan-Avia IL-76TD RA-76350 is seen at Moscow-Domodedovo on 3rd November 1998. It is probably the carrier's only aircraft with English titles.** Dmitriy Komissarov

Below: **Abakan-Avia IL-76T with a grey tail and Russian titles. This aircraft was originally built as a civil IL-76 *sans suffixe*.** Dmitriy Komissarov

Above right: **This anonymous-looking IL-76 *sans suffixe*, RA-86810, was operated by the cargo airline Al'kor.** Petr Šebek

Aeroflot Russian International Airlines IL-76TD RA-76750 uses reverse thrust after landing on runway 25L at Moscow-Sheremet'yevo on 26th February 2000. The grey tails were introduced in mid-1993. Dmitriy Komissarov

Lit by the setting sun, Almazy Rossii – Sakha IL-76TD RA-76373 sits at Moscow-Domodedovo in November 1998. Dmitriy Komissarov

Atlant-Soyuz operates a number of constantly shifting *Candids* leased as required. Ex C-Air IL-76TD RA-76367, seen here at Zhukovskiy in September 1999, is one of the few owned examples. Dmitriy Komissarov

Atlant-Soyuz IL-76TD EW-76710, a converted IL-76MD, seen here in a rather incomplete condition at Zhukovskiy on 19th September 1999, retains basic TransAVIAexport colours. Note the 'Moscow Government airline' subtitles. Dmitriy Komissarov

RA-76366, the second of two IL-76TDs operated by Aviaenergo, sits at Moscow-Domodedovo on 3rd November 1998. Dmitriy Komissarov

By 1998 most of Aviatrans's fleet, like IL-76T 'Falsie' RA-76757 photographed at Moscow-Domodedovo in November 1998, had been repainted with Atran titles. Dmitriy Komissarov

IL-76 *sans suffixe* RA-76417 with Dobrolyot's original logo seen at Kubinka AB in April 1997 following retirement. Note the obliterated NSA Soyuz titles. Dmitriy Komissarov

Somewhat anonymous looking Dobrolyot IL-76 *sans suffixe* RA-76418 kicks up a minor snowstorm as it taxies at Moscow-Domodedovo in November 1998; note the different tail logo. The 'man in black' is the airport security guard who accompanied this author – just in case. Dmitriy Komissarov

RA-76389	IL-76TD	1013407212	8103	Leased from Tupolev-Aerotrans 1996; ex-IL-76MD 'Falsie' RA-78852
RA-76401	IL-76TD	1023412399	8510	Leased from Ul'yanovsk Higher Flying School by 3-2000, white overall
RA-76402	IL-76TD	1023413430	8608	Leased from / jointly operated with Gazpromavia (1999)
RA-76409	IL-76TD	1023410355	8409	Leased from KnAAPO 1995. Basic Aeroflot colours, Atlant-Soyuz titles and logo
RA-76423	IL-76MD	0053457720	4310	Ex-UR-76423, ex-CCCP-76423, ex-CCCP-76626, leased from Atlant-SV (dates unknown); returned
RA-76425	IL-76TD	1003405167	8002	Leased from KnAAPO 1995. Basic Aeroflot colours, Atlant-Soyuz titles and logo
RA-76426	IL-76TD	1013405184	8006	Ex-UR-76426, leased from Allwe (dates unknown). Variously reported as reregistered ER-ACG or UK-76426
RA-76429	IL-76TD	1043419639	9110	Leased from / jointly operated with EMERCOM of Russia (1998)
RA-76444	IL-76MD	0063470113	5309	Ex-UR-76444, ex-CCCP-76696, leased from Atlant-SV 1994-97; to Ukrainian Cargo Airways as UR-UCS
RA-76446	IL-76MD 'Falsie'	1023412418	8605	Leased from Altaiskiye Avialinii 5-96 to ?-??
RA-76464	IL-76TD	0023437090	2803	Leased from Kras Air 1998
RA-76465	IL-76TD	0023438101	2806	C/n also quoted as 0023437101. Leased from Kras Air 1998
RA-76471	IL-76TD	0033446345	3407	Leased from Magadanavialeasing ?-98 to ?-99
RA-76472	IL-76TD	0033446350	3408	Leased from SVGAL (North-East Cargo Airlines) ?-99 to ?-2000
RA-76483	IL-76TD	0063468042	5201	Leased from SVGAL 1997 to ?-99
RA-76489	IL-76TD	0083485554	6409	Leased from SVGAL 1997 to ?-99
RA-76493	IL-76TD	0043456700	4305	Leased from VASO (see MAP entry) by 7-2000
RA-76499	IL-76TD	0023441186	3007	Leased from / jointly operated with Kosmos 1996-98, Kosmos colour scheme
UR-76601	IL-76MD	0043454606	4102	Leased from Ukrainian Air Force 11-99 (ex-Atlant-SV)
RA-76666	IL-76TD	0053464934	4904	Leased from Aviacon Tsitotrans 1999, **converted IL-76MD**
EW-76710	IL-76TD	0063473182	5506	**Converted IL-76MD**. Leased from TransAVIA-export by 8-99; TransAVIAexport colours, Atlant-Soyuz/Aviakompahniya pravitel'stva Moskvy titles
RA-76759	IL-76T 'Falsie'	093418543	1406	Demilitarised. Lsd from Sukhoi Design Bureau 1994-97; basic Aeroflot colours, no titles?
RA-76783	IL-76TD	0093498974	7504	Leased from Ul'yanovsk Civil Aviation Higher Flying School 1999. Grey/white c/s, Russian flag on tail, Atlant-Soyuz/Aviakompahniya pravitel'stva Moskvy titles
RA-76787	IL-76TD	0093495854	7204	Leased from SVGAL 1997 to ?-?? Basic Aeroflot colour scheme, Atlant-Soyuz titles and logo
RA-76840	IL-76TD	1033417553	8909	Leased from / jointly operated with EMERCOM of Russia 1996-99
RA-76841	IL-76TD	1033418601	9101	Leased (bought?) from EMERCOM of Russia 1997
RA-76845	IL-76TD	1043420696	9304	Leased from / jointly operated with EMERCOM of Russia 1996-99
EW-78779	IL-76TD 'Falsie'	0083489662	6706	Demilitarised. Lsd from TransAVIAexport 2-98; basic Aeroflot colours, Atlant-Soyuz titles and logo; Aviakompahniya pravitel'stva Moskvy titles added in 2000
EW-78801	IL-76TD 'Falsie'?	0093492763	7001	**Converted IL-76MD**. Lsd from TransAVIAexport by 11-98. Basic Aeroflot colours, Atlant-Soyuz titles and logo
RA-78820	IL-76MD	0093496907	7307	Ex-UR-78820, lsd from Atlant-SV (dates unknown). To Ukrainian Air Force as UR-78820 by 7-96
EW-78827	IL-76TD 'Falsie'	1003499997	7510	Demilitarised. Leased from TransAVIAexport by 11-98; basic Aeroflot colours, Atlant-Soyuz titles and logo
RA-78830	IL-76MD	1003401010	7603	Leased from Russian Air Force 1999
EW-78848	IL-76TD 'Falsie'	1003405159	7910	Demilitarised. Leased from TransAVIAexport by 11-98
RA-78850	IL-76MD 'Falsie'	1013405196	8009	Leased from Russian Air Force 1999

The charter carrier **AVIACON TSITOTRANS JOINT-STOCK COMPANY** [–/AZS] based at Yekaterinburg-Kol'tsovo airport operates IL-76s (mostly leased) since 1996. The name, spelled German-style as Aviacon Zitotrans on the aircraft, is derived from the Latin word *cito* ('quickly' or 'urgently').

Registration	Version	C/n	F/n	Notes
RA-76506	IL-76T	073411334	0904	Converted IL-76 (civil). Ex-Uralinteravia. Retired by 3-2000?
RA-76514	IL-76T	083415433	1204	Ex-Tyumen' Airlines, bought 1998
RA-76659	IL-76MD	0053463908	4807	Leased from Atruvera 1996; returned
RA-76666	IL-76MD/ IL-76TD	0053464934	4904	Lsd from Atruvera 1996 **as IL-76MD** in Atruvera colours. Bought 2-98 and **converted to IL-76TD**, basic Aeroflot colours. Sold to Solair ?-99 as 3C-JJJ?
RA-76783	IL-76TD	0093498974	7504?	Leased from Ul'yanovsk Civil Aviation Higher Flying School 1997-99, white overall
RA-76807?*	IL-76TD	1013405176	8004	Leased from Tyumen' Airlines 1998-99

* Note: RA-76807 was also reported as leased to Atlant-Soyuz during this period!

AVIAENERGO [–/ERG], the Zhukovskiy-based flying division of the 'United Energy System of Russia' Joint-Stock Company (*RAO Yedinaya energheticheskaya sistema Rossii*, the electric power industry), got its first IL-76TD RA-76843 (c/n 1033418584, f/n 9006) in mid-1995. In April 1996 this was joined by another brand-new TD, RA-76366 (c/n 1043418628, f/n 9107). Both aircraft are jointly operated with East Line since 1998.

The Moscow cargo airline **AVIAL' AVIATION COMPANY LTD** [–/RLC] operating from Domodedovo, Sheremet'yevo-1 and Zhukovskiy reportedly had one IL-76TD, RA-76406, in 1994 (see TransSuper). IL-76T 'Falsie' RA-76490 has also been reported for Avial' but this is highly doubtful (see Elf Air!).

AVIALINII CHETYRESTO (Airlines 400) [–/VAZ], the flying division of Aircraft Overhaul Plant No 400 at Moscow-Vnukovo, leased IL-76TD RA-76472 from Magadanavialeasing (which see) in 2000.

The Troitsk-based cargo carrier **AVIAOBSCHCHEMASH** [–/OBM], also referred to as **AOM AIR COMPANY** (not to be confused with the French AOM, Air Outre Mer), operated IL-76TD RA-76494 (c/n 0053465956, f/n 4909) in Aeroflot colours. Aviaobschchemash is not really an airline but the flying division of the former Ministry of General Machinery (MOM – *Ministerstvo obshchevo mashinostroyeniya*, often shortened to Minobschchemash). This weird-sounding name concealed an industry producing launch rockets and other space vehicles. By May 2000 RA-76494 was leased to East Line.

AVIAPRAD [–/VID], a subsidiary of the Urals Engine Overhaul Plant in Yekaterinburg (the name is probably an acronym for **A**viapredpriyahtiye **rem**zavoda **a**via**dvee**gateley – aero engine overhaul plant air enterprise), owns two ex-Uzbekistan Airways IL-76TDs since 1996.

Registration	Version	C/n	F/n	Notes
RA 76352	IL-76TD	1023411378	8505	Ex-UK 76352; basic old Uzbekistan Airways colours, registration painted on with no dash after prefix. Leased to Samara Airlines 4-98
RA 76386	IL-76TD	1033418600	9010	Ex-Uralinteravia, bought 12-96. Ex-UK 76386; basic new Uzbekistan Airways colours, registration painted on with no dash after prefix

An airline called **AVIAST** [–/VVA] (or is it Avia-ST?) operates five *Candids*.

Registration	Version	C/n	F/n	Notes
RA-76485	IL-76TD	0063470088	5302	Leased from Sakha-Avia by 8-2000
RA-76487	L-76TD	0073479367	6002	Leased from Sakha-Avia by 8-2000
RA-76754	IL-76T 'Falsie'	093421637	1610	Ex-CCCP-76754, ex-Iraqi AF IL-76M YI-AKU. Demilitarised. Bought or lsd from Atran by 8-99
RA-76797	IL-76TD	1003403052	7703	Leased from Sakha-Avia by 8-2000
RA-76849	IL-76TD	0023440161?	3001?	Converted IL-76MD (ex-Hoseba UR-86921)? Leased from Sakha-Avia by 8-2000

AVIATRANS CARGO AIRLINES [V8/VAS] established in 1992 operated eight *Candids* from Moscow-Domodedovo and Moscow-Myachkovo. On 1st January 1997 the airline was renamed **ATRAN – AVIATRANS CARGO AIRLINES**.

Registration	Version	C/n	F/n	Notes
RA-76754	IL-76T 'Falsie'	093421637	1610	Ex-CCCP-76754, ex-Iraqi Air Force IL-76M YI-AKU. Demilitarised. Sold or leased to Aviast by 8-99
RA-76755	IL-76T 'Falsie'	0013433984	2506	Ex-CCCP-76755, ex-Iraqi AF IL-76M YI-ALL. Leased to Inversija 1-92, originally as RA-76755, reregistered YL-LAL 10-94 (?)
RA-76757	IL-76T 'Falsie'	0013433990	2508	Ex-CCCP-76757, ex-Iraqi Air Force IL-76M YI-AKX. Demilitarised
RA-76788	IL-76T 'Falsie'	0013433996	2509	Ex-CCCP-76788, ex-Iraqi Air Force IL-76M YI-ALO. Demilitarised. Retired Myachkovo, totally scrapped by 4-97
RA-76789	IL-76T 'Falsie'	0013433999	2510	Ex-CCCP-76789, ex-Iraqi Air Force IL-76M YI-ALP
RA-76809	IL-76TD	1013408252	8203	
RA-76820	IL-76TD	1013409295	8304	Ex-Domodedovo CAPA
RA-86865	IL-76M	0003428817	2105	Leased from the Russian Air Force, dates unknown

BAIKAL AIRLINES [X3/BKL], alias Baikalavia, was the successor of the East Siberian CAD's Irkutsk United Flight Detachment of Aeroflot. Its fleet included seven IL-76T/TDs, the newest of which was built in 1991. In recent years the airline's financial position has been shaky and plans of a merger with Chita-Avia in the hope of improving things were announced in April 1998. The August 1998 bank crisis ruined these plans and Baikal Airlines filed for bankruptcy in September. Subsequent developments, however, show that the airline is not dead after all; currently Baikal Airlines are under outside management and operations were restarted on a small scale in the spring of 1999.

Registration	Version	C/n	F/n	Notes
RA-76458	IL-76T	0013430888	2302	Aeroflot colours. Leased to East Line 1998; sold by 3-2000?
RA-76462	IL-76T	0013432955	2409	Aeroflot colours. Leased to East Line 1998; sold by 3-2000?
RA-76484	IL-76TD	0063469081	5301	Leased to Tesis 1999
RA-76486	IL-76TD	0073476281	5801	Leased (later sold) to Yakutavia (Sakha Avia)
RA-76520	IL-76T	093420605	1602	Retired by 1997
RA-76525	IL-76T	0003427787	2007	
RA-76526	IL-76T	0003427792	2008	
RA-76808	IL-76TD	1013405177	8005	Was leased to United Nations Peacekeeping Forces 1992. Leased to Tesis 1998

IL-76TD RA-76355 (c/n 1023408265, f/n 8207) belonged to the **BERIYEV DESIGN BUREAU** [–/GMB] (TANTK = *Taganrogskiy aviatseeonnyy naoochno-tekhneecheskiy kompleks imeni G M Beriyeva* – Taganrog Aviation Scientific & Technical Complex named after Gheorgiy Mikhaïlovich

Beriyev). In 1997 the aircraft was sold or leased to the Sierra Leonean airline Intalair as 9L-LBO. The company reportedly also has six ex-Soviet Air Force IL-76MDs transferred in August 1992 (see MAP entry).

C-AIR CARGO [–/CEE], a sister company of the Kemerovo Air Enterprise established in 1994, operated two IL-76TDs – RA-76350 (c/n 1023410344, f/n 8406) and RA-76367 (c/n 1033414474, f/n 8709). (The 'cargo' suffix to the airline's name was later dropped when C-Air leased three Antonov An-24RV short-haul turboprops and a pair of Tupolev Tu-154B-2 medium-haul trijets.) The *Candids* had a blue/red cheatline and large 'crowned C' logos on the nose and tail. RA-76350 was sold to Abakan Avia in 1998. The other aircraft was leased to Atlant-Soyuz, which bought it when C-Air went bankrupt in 1999.

The Moscow charter carrier **CONTINENTAL AIRWAYS JOINT-STOCK COMPANY** (*Kontinentahl'nyye Avialinii*) [PC/PVV] operated two IL-76TDs. One, RA-76355, was on lease from the Beriyev Design Bureau in May 1996. The aircraft was white overall with red 'Continental Airways' titles low on the forward fuselage. The other, RA-76498 (c/n 0023442218, f/n 3105), was acquired from the defunct Moscow Airways and flew in full Moscow Airways colours; it was eventually sold to Atlas Air as EP-ALC in 1998.

DACONO AIR [–/DCA] based at Zhukovskiy owned a single IL-76TD, RA-76421 (c/n 1033415504, f/n 8806). It also operated IL-76MD RA-76666 on lease from Atruvera (?) in November 1995 and IL-76TD RA-76808 on lease from Baikalavia in 1995. The airline suspended operations in 1997; some sources say RA-76421 was sold to an unidentified operator and placed on the Liberian register as EL-WTA.

What's in a name? Moscow-based **DOBROLYOT** [–/DOB] is an airline with a famous name. The original Dobrolyot was a passenger carrier, the precursor of Aeroflot, and ceased operations in 1922. Reborn 70 years later as a cargo airline, the new Dobrolyot was the flying division of the Soyuz Production Association, an aerospace industry company. Hence the airline's IL-76s *sans suffixe* – three of the earliest production *Candid-Bs* – had the Soyuz tail logo resembling a bird, a Latin S and a C (ie, Cyrillic 'S') at the same time. Additionally, RA-76416 and RA-76417 briefly wore English 'NSA Soyuz' titles in addition to Cyrillic 'Dobrolyot' titles for a while.

Registration	Version	C/n	F/n	Notes
RA-76388	IL-76TD	1013406204	8101	Leased from Tupolev-Aerotrans by 5-2000; ex-IL-76MD 'Falsie' RA-78851.
RA-76389	IL-76TD	1013407212	8103	Leased from Tupolev-Aerotrans early 1999; ex-IL-76MD 'Falsie' RA-78852
RA-76409	IL-76TD	1023410355	8409	Leased from KnAAPO, dates unknown
RA-76416	IL-76 (mil)	043402041	0201	Ex-Soviet AF '21 Red', ex-CCCP-86643? bought 16-7-92. WFU Kubinka AB by 3-97
RA-76417	IL-76 (mil)	043402046	0202	Ex-Soviet AF '644 Black', ex-CCCP-86644 bought 16-7-92. WFU Kubinka AB by 3-97
RA-76418	IL-76 (mil)	073409237	0610	Demilitarised, no titles. Ex-Soviet Air Force CCCP-86640
RA-76716	IL-76MD	0073474211	5603	Reported as such; leased from Ukrainian Air Force, dates unknown
RA-76753	IL-76MD	0073481461	6206	Leased from NIITP 1999; freighter/avionics testbed/survey aircraft

Unlike Dobrolyot's own aircraft which retain the basic Aeroflot colour scheme, RA-76388 and RA-76389 have the ex-Polis Air brown/white livery and a totally different tail logo.

The all-Ilyushin fleet of **DOMODEDOVO AIRLINES/DOMODE-DOVSKIYE AVIALINII** [E3/DMO], formerly the **Domodedovo Civil Aviation Production Association**, included five IL-76TDs. The new 'Domodedovo Airlines' titles started appearing in mid-1999.

Domodedovo Civil Aviation Production Association IL-76TD RA-76799 at its home base in November 1998. Dmitriy Komissarov

The red-underlined cheatline of East Line IL-76TD RA-76812 seen at Moscow-Domodedovo in November 1998 reveals that the aircraft was leased from the Domodedovo CAPA. Dmitriy Komissarov

Seen at its Domodedovo base in November 1998, IL-76TD UK-76449 _Shenyang_ (named after the destination it usually serves) illustrates the version of East Line's full livery with the green tail. Note the Russian flag (despite the Uzbek registration). Dmitriy Komissarov

IL-76TD RA-76403, one of several to wear full East Line livery, heads a long line of _Candids_ on the cargo apron at Moscow-Domodedovo on 3rd November 1998. The aircraft is named _Igor' Bykov_ in memory of East Line's flight operations director killed in 1997. Dmitriy Komissarov

One of Exparc's IL-76TDs languishing at Moscow/Sheremet'yevo-1 after the airline's demise.
Mikhail Yevdokimov

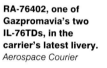

RA-76402, one of Gazpromavia's two IL-76TDs, in the carrier's latest livery.
Aerospace Courier

Demilitarised *Candid-B* CCCP-76528 (ex-YI-AIL) operated by LII, seen here before it became an IL-76T 'Falsie' (the inscription on the nose still reads 'IL-76').
Victor Drushlyakov

Registration	Version	C/n	F/n	Notes
RA-76786	IL-76TD	0093496923	7401	Domodedovo Airlines/Domodedovskiye Avialinii titles. Leased to East Line ?-2000
RA-76799	IL-76TD	1003403075	7709	Leased to East Line ?-2000
RA-76806	IL-76TD	1003403121	7901	Leased to East Line by 7-2000
RA-76812	IL-76TD	1013407230	8108	Leased to East Line ?-2000
RA-76820	*IL-76TD*	*1013409295*	*8304*	*Sold to Aviatrans Cargo Airlines*

EAST LINE [P7/ESL] was established at Moscow-Domodedovo in 1993, initially operating cargo charters with a single IL-76TD. Since then it has grown into a major cargo airline with services to Belgium, China, Greece, India, Italy, South Korea, Pakistan, Turkey and the UAE; passenger services were added later.Until recently the carrier had no fleet of its own, and the many *Candid-A/Bs* it operates are leased from other airlines as required, often in the owner's colours with East Line titles; some IL-76TDs, though, wear East Line's stylish green/white colour scheme.

Registration	Version	C/n	F/n	Notes
RA-76350	*IL-76TD*	*1023410344*	*8406*	*Lsd from C-Air 1997 to 10-98, C-Air colours*
UK-76351	*IL-76TD*	*1023408240*	*8110*	*Lsd from Uzbekistan Airways 2-97 to ?-2000; full Uzbekistan colours plus small East Line titles*
UK-76353	IL-76TD	1023414454	8704	Leased from Uzbekistan Airways 1998; full East Line colour scheme/white tail
UK-76359	IL-76TD	1033414483	8801	Leased from Uzbekistan Airways 1999; full East Line colour scheme/green tail, named *Jinan*
RA-76366	IL-76TD	1043418628	9107	Leased from / jointly operated with Aviaenergo (1998), **no East Line titles**
RA-76369	*IL-76TD*	*1033414480*	*8710*	*Leased from Airstan 12-96 to ?-?? Basic Aeroflot colours, large East Line titles*
UN-76374	IL-76TD	1033416520	8810	Leased from Air Kazakstan by 2-2000. Basic Aeroflot colours, large East Line titles; cheatline broken on nose by Kazakh flag
RA-76381	IL-76TD	1033418596	9009	Ex-Trans Aero Samara, leased 1998 / bought 1999; basic Trans Aero Samara colours, small East Line titles.
RA-76400	IL-76TD	1023413438	8610	Lsd from Vladivostok Air 1998; basic Aeroflot colours, small Vladivostok Air and East Line titles
RA-76403	IL-76TD	1023412414	8604	Leased from Vladivostok Air 1998; full East Line colour scheme/white tail, named *Igor' Bykov*
UK-76448	IL-76TD	1023413443	8701	Leased from Uzbekistan Airways 7-98; full East Line colour scheme/white tail
UK-76449	IL-76TD	1023403058	7705	Leased from Uzbekistan Airways 1998; full East Line colour scheme/green tail, named *Shenyang*
RA-76458	IL-76T	0013430888	2302	Lsd from Baikal Airlines 1998 (bought by 3-2000?); basic Aeroflot colours, large East Line titles
RA-76462	IL-76T	0013432955	2409	Leased from Baikal Airlines 1998; basic Aeroflot colour scheme, large East Line titles; full East Line colours/green tail by 2-2000 (bought?)
RA-76492	IL-76T 'Falsie'	093418548	1407	Demilitarised. Lsd from Vladivostok Air 1998; full Aeroflot colours plus small East Line titles
RA-76494	IL-76TD	0053465956	4909	Leased from Aviaobschchemash by 2-2000, basic Aeroflot colours
UR-76628	IL-76TD 'Falsie'	0053458741	4406	C/n also reported as 0053458743. Leased from Volare by 3-2000
UR-76636	IL-76TD 'Falsie'	0053459781	4506	**Converted IL-78?** Leased from Volare Aviation Enterprise 1998
UR-76727	IL-76TD 'Falsie'	0073475268	5707	Leased from Volare Aviation Enterprise 1998; reported as IL-76MD in 2000!
EW-76734	IL-76TD	0073476312	5808	**Converted IL-76MD.** Lsd from Ilavia by 1-2000; basic Ilavia colours, large East Line titles
UK 76782	*IL-76TD*	*0093498971*	*7503*	*Lsd from Uzbekistan Airways 1997 to ?-2000; full Uzbekistan colours plus small East Line titles*
RA-76786	IL-76TD	0093496923	7401	Leased from Domodedovo Airlines ?-2000, Domodedovo cheatline, small East Line titles and white tail with East Line logo in green circle

RA-76796	IL-76TD	1003499994	7509	Leased from Magadanaerogrooz 1996-98, first IL-76 operated
RA-76799	IL-76TD	1003403075	7709	Leased from Domodedovo Airlines ?-2000, Domodedovo cheatline, small East Line titles and white tail with East Line logo in green circle
UK-76805	IL-76TD	1003403109	7808	Leased from Uzbekistan Intercargo Service 7-99, basic UIS colours, large East Line titles
RA-76806	IL-76TD	1003403121	7901	Leased from Domodedovo Airlines by 7-2000
RA-76812	IL-76TD	1013407230	8108	Lsd from Domodedovo CAPA 1997-98; basic Domodedovo c/s, small East Line titles, Russian flag on tail instead of logo. Lsd again ?-2000, now with East Line logo in green circle
RA-76814	*IL-76TD*	*1013408269*	*8208*	*Leased from Rosaeroleasing 1998-2000; basic Aeroflot colours, large East Line titles*
RA-76817	IL-76TD	1023411387	8507	Ex-Trans Aero Samara, bought 1999; basic Trans Aero Samara colours, small East Line titles
UK 76824	*IL-76TD*	*1013410327*	*8402*	*Lsd from Uzbekistan Airways 1997 to ?-2000; full Uzbekistan colours plus small East Line titles*
RA-76833	*IL-76TD*	*1023411363*	*8501*	*Leased from Altai Airlines by 9-98; returned by 7-2000. Basic Aeroflot colours, large East Line titles*
RA-76843	IL-76TD	1033418584	9006	Leased from / jointly operated with Aviaenergo (1998), **no East Line titles**
EW-78799	IL-76TD	0093491754	6909	**Converted IL-76MD.** Leased from TransAVIA-export 1995; full East Line colours/green tail
EW-78808	IL-76TD 'Falsie'	0093493794	7009	Demilitarised. Leased from TransAVIAexport 1998; basic TransAVIAexport colours, no logo, large East Line titles
EW-78819	IL-76TD 'Falsie'	0093495883	7301	Demilitarised. Leased from TransAVIAexport 1998; basic TransAVIAexport colours, no logo, large East Line titles
EW-78826	IL-76TD 'Falsie'	1003499991	7508	Demilitarised. Leased from TransAVIAexport 1998; basic TransAVIAexport colours, no logo, large East Line titles
EW-78828	IL-76TD	1003401004	7601	**Converted IL-76MD.** Leased from TransAVIAexport 1998; TransAVIAexport colours, **no East Line titles**
EW-78839	IL-76TD 'Falsie'	1003402047	7702	Demilitarised. Leased from TransAVIAexport 1998; full TransAVIAexport colours plus small East Line titles
EW-78843	IL-76TD 'Falsie'	1003403082	7801	Demilitarised. Leased from TransAVIAexport 1998; basic TransAVIAexport colours, no logo, large East Line titles

In May 2000 East Line and Uzbekistan Airways signed an agreement with the Tashkent Aircraft Production Corporation (TAPO) concerning two IL-76TFs. The aircraft will be delivered on a lease-purchase basis to the Uzbek flag carrier, which will then sub-lease them to East Line for ten years; this elaborate scheme turned out to be more profitable than ordering the freighters directly. TAPO urged the airline to order four of the stretched PS-90-powered version; however, East Line's General Director Amiran Koortanidze says two aircraft will be operated initially 'on a trials basis', as the carrier intends to hold a 'flyoff' between the IL-76TF and the IL-96T wide-body freighter built in Voronezh.

In late September 2000 East Line was raided by the Russian secret service, FSB *(Federahl'naya sloozhba bezopahsnosti* – Federal Security Service), on the grounds that the airline was allegedly running a major smuggling operation in order to evade customs duties on goods imported from China. FSB agents confiscated computers and paperwork, leaving East Line's cargo operations paralysed. However, Mr Koortanidze indignantly denies the smuggling charge. Indeed, there are reasons to believe that the raid was instigated by an outfit called the Reconciliation and Accord Foundation which aims to obtain exclusive rights as an air cargo handling agent in Russia and is thus trying to eliminate competitors. The choice of East Line was no chance, since the carrier has a strong position on the lucrative routes to China.

ELF AIR [–/EFR], the commercial flying division of avionics designer NPO Vzlyot, operates a mixed bag of passenger and cargo aircraft from Zhukovskiy, including five IL-76s. (It should be noted that the name has nothing to do with the French oil company Elf-Aquitain.)

Registration	Version	C/n	F/n	Notes
RA-76370	IL-76TD	1033414458	8705	Aeroflot colours. Sold to Gazpromavia 1996
RA-76490	IL-76T 'Falsie'	093416506	1307	Ex-CCCP-76490, ex-Iraqi AF IL-76M YI-AKO, ex-2803. Demilitarised, **IL-76-11 ELINT testbed.** WFU by 8-95; **reconverted to standard** and made airworthy by 8-99. Basic Aeroflot c/s, no titles or flag; titles added by 8-2000
RA-76756	IL-76T 'Falsie'	0013428839	2110	Ex-CCCP-76756, ex-Iraqi Air Force IL-76M YI-AKW. Basic Aeroflot colours, no titles
RA-76819	IL-76TD	1013409274	8209	Ex-Enimex ES-NIT, bought 3-98, basic Enimex colours, operated for Third World Relief Agency. Crashed at Irkutsk-1 airport 26-7-99
RA-76823	IL-76TD 'Falsie' / IL-76TD	0023441189	3008	Ex-Iraqi Air Force IL-76MD YI-ALQ. Demilitarised; **converted to 'true' IL-76TD in 1998.** Basic Aeroflot colours, Elf Air titles

IL-76TD RA-76835 has also been reported for Elf Air but this is doubtful (see Ilavia below). RA-76756 was apparently leased abroad and temporarily reregistered. In August 2000 the aircraft was seen at Zhukovskiy with the registration on the wings only and traces of something overpainted on the aft fuselage; apparently it had been returned from lease, the foreign registration deleted and the Russian one not yet reinstated.

The **EXPARC** [–/EPA] 'airline' was formed in 1992 for providing logistical support of the Russian polar research stations under the EksPArk programme (see Chapter 4) so as not to depend on the Air Force and other *Candid* operators from which aircraft had to be leased. Exparc's two IL-76TDs, RA-76818 (c/n 1013408264, f/n 8206) and RA-76819 (c/n 1013409274, f/n 8209), saw service with the United Nations Peace Forces in ex-Yugoslavia in 1993 as 76818 and 76819. However, the airline was shortlived; it ceased operations in 1994 and the aircraft were placed in storage. RA-76818 ended up with Ilavia, while RA-76819 was sold to the Estonian airline Enimex in September 1995, becoming ES-NIT. The code EPA was reallocated to start-up Express Airways GmbH (Lautzenhausen, Germany) in 1998.

EXPRESS JOINT-STOCK COMPANY [–/PSR] based at Moscow-Domodedovo started operations in 1995 with IL-76MD RA-76708 (c/n 0063473171, f/n 5503) leased from the Russian Air Force; the aircraft is in full Aeroflot colours. In 1996 it was joined by IL-76T RA-76372 (c/n 073410279, f/n 0710). This is not a true IL-76T, since it is nothing less than a former IL-76K zero-G trainer (ex-CCCP-86723)! In late 1998 RA-76372 was operated for the United Nations World Food Programme. By September 1999 it was sold or leased to Express International Cargo Corporation Ltd (São Tomé & Principe) as S9-BOM.

In August 1999 RA-76708 carried stickers advertising the **NOVOLIPETSK IRON & STEEL WORKS** and the **STINOL** refrigerator factory (also located in Lipetsk); Express JSC presumably sub-leased the aircraft to these enterprises.

FAR EASTERN CARGO AIRLINES (*Dahl'nevostochnyye groozovyye avialinii*) [–/FEW] based in Khabarovsk lease IL-76s from other carriers as required.

The large fleet of **GAZPROMAVIA LTD** [–/GZP], the flying division of the powerful Gazprom corporation which controls Russia's natural gas industry, includes two IL-76TDs acquired in 1996 – RA-76370 bought from Elf Air (c/n 1033414458, f/n 8705) and RA-76402 bought from Mostransgaz (c/n 1023413430, f/n 8608). Both aircraft wear Gazpromavia's latest livery and are jointly operated with Atlant-Soyuz since 1999.

GOSNII GA (the State Civil Aviation Research Institute at Moscow/Sheremet'yevo-1) [–/ISP] had a single IL-76TD, RA-76481 (c/n 0053460795, f/n 4509). The aircraft was operated jointly with the **FLIGHT-CHERNOBYL ASSOCIATION** (*Polyot-Chernobyl'*) [–/FCH] in Aeroflot colours. In 1997 RA-76481 was leased to Atlas Air as EP-ALA and ultimately sold to Ramair in November 1998.

The **FLIGHT RESEARCH INSTITUTE NAMED AFTER M M GROMOV (LII)** in Zhukovskiy operated a variety of *Candids* for test and research purposes, mostly in full Aeroflot colours.

Registration	Version	C/n	F/n	Notes
CCCP-06188	IL-76LL5	093421635	1609	Converted IL-76T 'Falsie', demilitarised, TV7-117A development engine. Ex-Iraqi Air Force IL-76M YI-AKQ. WFU 1995
RA-76405	IL-76TD	1023412402	8601	Basic Aeroflot colours / no titles, LII badge. Sold or leased to ALAK; to Yemen AF 11-95 as 7O-ADG
CCCP-76452	'Acft 976'	0063465965	5002	
RA-76453	'Acft 976'	0063466995	5009	LII nose logo
CCCP-76454	'Acft 976'	0063469074	5209	
76455	'Acft 976'	0063471125	5402	Russian flag on tail but no nationality prefix by 8-99
CCCP-76456	'Acft 976'	0073474208	5602	
CCCP-76492	IL-76LL3	0043452549	3908	Converted IL-76MD 'Falsie', PS-90A development engine. WFU 1995? **Registration later reused (see Vladivostok Air)!**
RA-76528	IL-76T 'Falsie'	073410293	0804	Demilitarised. Ex-IL-76 (military) CCCP-76528, ex-Iraqi AF YI-AIL. WFU by 1999, seen being broken up at LII 8-99
RA-76529	IL-76LL4	073410308	0807	Converted IL-76 (mil), demilitarised, D-236T development engine, later D-27 development engine. Ex-CCCP-76529, ex-Iraqi AF YI-AIP. Aeroflot colours with additional LII titles
RA-76623	IL-76MD	0053457705	4307	
RA-78738	IL-76TD 'Falsie'	0033442247	3202	Demilitarised. Ex-CCCP-78738, ex-Iraqi AF IL-76MD YI-ALS. Basic Aeroflot colours, no titles
CCCP-86024	'Acft 776'	083414425	1107	Converted IL-76M. WFU Staraya Roossa by 1995
RA-86600?	IL-76 (mil)	033401022	0106	Based in Zhukovskiy but ownership unconfirmed. Retired by 1999
RA-86603?	IL-76 (mil)	?	0109	Based in Zhukovskiy but ownership unconfirmed. Demilitarised. Retired by 1997
CCCP-86712	IL-76LL	01-01	–	Converted first prototype IL-76 (civil), NK-86 development engine. Scrapped
CCCP-86721	'Acft 676'	073410271	0708	Converted IL-76 (military). WFU Staraya Roossa by 1995
RA-86891*	IL-76LL	093421628	1607A	Converted IL-76M 'Falsie'. D-18T development engine. Aeroflot colours with LII logo on nose. WFU 1997, seen being broken up at LII 8-99

Note: CCCP-86891 was previously reported as ex-YI-AKV **(see Remex, TransSuper and next chapter / Iraqi section).**

RA-76528 and RA-78738 were operated by LII's own airline, **VOLARE AIR TRANSPORT COMPANY** (*Aviatrahnsportnaya kompahniya Volare*) [OP/VLR] founded in 1992. In 1997 this ceased operations[4] and the two aircraft plus RA-76623 were transferred to LII's new airline, **GRO-MOV AIR** [–/LII]. Unlike its two Tu-134AKs (RA-65926 and RA-65927), none of the IL-76s wears Gromov Air titles.

ILAVIA [–/ILV], the Ilyushin Design Bureau's 'house airline' established in 1994, operated 14 IL-76s.

Registration	Version	C/n	F/n	Notes
RA-76473	IL-76TD	0033448404	3601	Ex-ARIA, bought 1995. Leased to Atlas Air 10-98 as EP-ALG
RA-76474	IL-76TD	0033448407	3602	Ex-ARIA, bought 1995. Leased to Atlas Air 9-98 as EP-ALF

Registration	Version	C/n	F/n	Notes
RA-76477	IL-76TD	0043453575	4004	Ex-ARIA, bought 1995. Leased to Atlas Air 9-98 as EP-ALE
RA-76516	IL-76T	093418556	1409	Leased from Kras Air 1997, bought 1998; full colour scheme
RA-76519	IL-76T	093420599	1510	Ex-ARIA, bought 1996 and operated in ARIA c/s for a while; repainted in Ilavia c/s 1998
RA-76521	*IL-76T*	*0003423699*	*1805*	*Ex-Abakan-Avia, bought by 5-99; full colour scheme. Sold to Aerocom 1999 as ER-IBV*
EW-76711	IL-76TD	0063472187	5507	**Converted IL-76MD**, lsd from TransAVIAexport by 8-99; full colours. Returned by 3-2000?
EW-76712	IL-76TD	0063472190	5508	**Converted IL-76MD**, lsd from TransAVIAexport 1998; reported in error by JP Airline-Fleets as RA-76712! Full colour scheme
EW-76734	IL-76TD	0073476312	5808	**Converted IL-76MD**, lsd from TransAVIAexport by 8-99; full colour scheme. Sub-leased to East Line by 1-2000
EW-76735	*IL-76TD*	*0073476314*	*5809*	**Converted IL-76MD**, *lsd from TransAVIAexport 1998;* **reported in error as RA-76735**. *Returned / leased to Aero Concept by 8-99*
EW-76737	IL-76MD	0073477323	5901	Leased from TransAVIAexport 1998; **reported in error as RA-76737**. Returned / leased to Volga-Dnepr by 8-99
RA-76807	IL-76TD	1013405176	8004	Leased from Tyumen' Airlines 1999
RA-76818	*IL-76TD*	*1013408264*	*8206*	*Ex-Exparc, bought 1998. Sold to Roos' JSC ?-99*
RA-76822	IL-76MD 'Falsie' / IL-76TD	0093499982	7506	Aeroflot colour scheme. Repainted in full Ilavia colours by 8-97, then repainted in Ilyushin Aircraft Complex colours **as IL-76TD** by 6-99
RA-76835	IL-76TD	1013408244	8201	Full colour scheme (first aircraft repainted). Not in JP 2000 – sold?
RA-78792	IL-76TD	0093490718	6810	**Converted IL-76MD**. Ex-TransAVIAexport EW-78792, bought 1996; full colour scheme

RA-76835 was displayed at the MAKS-93 airshow configured as an IL-76P firebomber in full Aeroflot colours with additional *AK imeni S V Il'yushina/Ilyushin Aircraft Complex* badges. Other aircraft belonging to the Ilyushin OKB but not included in the Ilavia fleet are:

Registration	Version	C/n	F/n	Notes
RA-76556	IL-78	0033445294	3304	Prototype
RA-76701	IL-78M	0063471139	5405	Prototype. C/n sometimes reported in error as 0063471143. WFU Zhukovskiy by 8-97
RA-86871	IL-76MD	0013434002	2601	Prototype

The now-defunct cargo airline **INTERFREIGHT** operated IL-76TD CCCP-76835 leased from the Ilyushin OKB in 1992. The aircraft was in the static park at MosAeroShow-92 in full Aeroflot colours with additional 'Interfreight' titles on the forward and aft fuselage. From 31st August to 10th October 1992 it was used as a support aircraft for the Paris-Beijing car rally. The aircraft was captained by Ilyushin OKB test pilot Igor' R Zakirov, with A V Manokhin as the engineer in charge and Nikolay D Talikov as the expedition leader.

The Tatar regional airline **IRON DRAGONFLY (IDF)** [–/IDF] based in Kazan' operated three *Candids*.

Registration	Version	C/n	F/n	Notes
RA-76430	*IL-76T 'Falsie'*	*073410300*	*0805*	*Ex-CCCP-86***. Leased to Air Pass (see next chapter); sold to Eco Patrol 13-4-99 as HA-TCI*
RA-76495	IL-76TD 'Falsie'	073410292	0803	Ex-IL-76T 'Falsie', ex-IL-76 *sans suffixe* CCCP-76495, ex-Iraqi AF YI-AIK. Basic Aeroflot colours. Demilitarised; ex-Inversiya, bought 1997
RA-76666	*IL-76MD*	*0053464934*	*4904*	*Leased from Atruvera (?) 2-96 to ?-??*

In June 1993 the Moscow airline **KONVEYER** [EC/TUG], mainly a passenger carrier (which also vanished by 1996), operated IL-76TD RA-76402 in full Aeroflot colours on lease from Mostransgaz. Generally *konveyer* means 'conveyor belt' or 'assembly line' in Russian; when used as an aviation term, however, it refers to a piloting technique called 'touch and go', hence the airline's other name, **TOUCH & GO LTD**. Obviously whoever picked the English name wanted to hint at the carrier's efficiency, with excellent turnaround times ('we barely touch down at all', that is) and was unaware of the expression's *other* meaning. (Speaking of which, the Russian name is not the best choice either, implying the passengers are routinely whisked from A to B without the 'personal touch'.)

The charter airline **KORSAR** [6K/KRS] based at Moscow/Vnukovo-3 operated IL-76TD RA-76499 (c/n 0023441186, f/n 3007) on lease from NPO Energiya, an aerospace corporation responsible, among other things, for the Buran (Snowstorm) space shuttle. The aircraft flew in Aeroflot colours – which was probably just as well, because Korsar's own livery was singularly uninspiring. *Korsar* means 'corsair' in Russian, but the airline's name has nothing to do with pirates; it is derived from the names of its founders, Korovin and Sarzhveladze.

By mid-1996 RA-76499 had been transferred to **KOSMOS AIRCOMPANY** [–/KSM], a division of NPO Energiya, and was given a stylish new colour scheme with a red/white/blue cheatline and a blue tail with a Planet-Earth-cum-orbiting-satellite tail logo. (Some observers have dubbed this livery 'Milky Way', though the 'candy bar' allusion is rather questionable!) The aircraft is still based at Vnukovo-3. By June 2000 it was leased to Sukhoi Airlines.

KRAS AIR (Krasnoyarsk Airlines/*Krasnoyarskiye Avialinii*, or *Krasnoyarskavia*) [7B/KJC] operated 13 IL-76T/TDs. At first they were used only sporadically, but in July 1998 the airline launched its own cargo services programme which reached maximum efficiency by October-December, generating 35 to 37% of the total revenue. Currently Kras Air operates a lot of international cargo charters to Europe, South Korea and China. This and the expanding route network has not only improved efficiency generally but partly offset the effects of the notorious August 1998 bank crisis which almost drove Russia's economy into the ground.

Six or seven of the carrier's *Candids* were operational in mid-1999. Also, Kras Air is working with the Tashkent Aircraft Production Corporation and the Perm Engine Plant on joint operation of the IL-76TF, but these plans are still in the making, since the aircraft has yet to enter production.

Registration	Version	C/n	F/n	Notes
RA-76459	IL-76T	0013430890	2303	
RA-76463	IL-76T	0013432960	2410	
RA-76464	IL-76TD	0023437090	2803	Basic Aeroflot colours, Kras Air titles. Leased to Atlant-Soyuz 1998
RA-76465	IL-76TD	0023438101	2806	C/n also quoted as 0023437101. Leased to Atlant Soyuz 1998
RA-76508	IL-76T	083413412	1103	
RA-76509	IL-76T	083413415	1104	
RA-76515	IL-76T	093417526	1402	
RA-76516	*IL-76T*	*093418556*	*1409*	*Leased to Ilavia 1997; sold 1998*
RA-76517	IL-76T	093418560	1410	
RA-76524	IL-76T	0003425746	1907	Leased to UN / World Food Programme 12-99
RA-76672	IL-76TD 'Falsie'	0063466981	5006	Ex-Atruvera, in service 8-99; basic Aeroflot colour scheme, Kras Air titles
RA-76752	IL-76TD	0093498967	7502	Aeroflot colours, later without titles, still later Kras Air titles. Crashed near Petropavlovsk-Kamchatskiy 5-4-96
RA-76792	IL-76TD	0093497942	7406	Basic Aeroflot colours, Kras Air titles. Was leased to Remex 1997-99, now operated in Remex colours with Kras Air titles

IL-76T RA-76521 is one of several operated by the Ilyushin OKB's own airline, Ilavia. It is seen here immediately after landing at Zhukovskiy in May 1999. The titles are in Russian to port and in English to starboard (compare with EW-76734 on page 18). Yefim Gordon

IL-76T RA-76464 in Kras Air's most basic colour scheme visiting Sharjah in early 1999. Peter Davison

This anonymous-looking IL-76TD photographed at Zhukovskiy in August 1999 was operated by the cargo airline Krylo. Dmitriy Komissarov

IL-76TD 'Falsie' T9-CAC illustrates yet another Ramair/Phoenix colour scheme. Peter Davison

Curiously, the Austrian monthly *Luftfahrt-Journal* keeps reporting 'IL-76TD UR-76752' with the c/n 0093498967 as operated by ATI Airlines more than two years after the crash. The key to this puzzle is that this is almost certainly a mispaint for UR-78752 (thus the aircraft is an IL-76TD 'Falsie', see ATI Airlines). Thus, persons unaware of the crash assume this is the same aircraft – which cannot be true, as RA-76752 was totally destroyed.

The cargo airline **KRYLO** ('wing' in Russian) [–/KRI] based at Moscow-Bykovo and Zhukovskiy operated four IL-76s. Only one of them actually belonged to the airline; this aircraft, delivered new in 1993, looked rather anonymous, with a green cheatline and no titles.

Registration	Version	C/n	F/n	Notes
RA-76379	IL-76TD	1033417569	9003	Sold to Sukhoi Airlines by 2-2000
UK 76427	IL-76TD	1013406207	8102	Leased from TAPO-Avia by 10-99; basic TAPO-Avia colour scheme, Krylo titles and logo
RA-76754	IL-76T 'Falsie'	093421637	1610	Demilitarised. Leased from Atran 1997; returned by mid-1999
UK 76844	IL-76TD	1033416525	8902	Leased from TAPO-Avia by 10-99; basic TAPO-Avia colour scheme, Krylo titles and logo

MAGADANAEROGROOZ (= Magadan Air Cargo) [–/MGG], another cargo airline, operated three *Candid-As* until it went bankrupt in 1998.

Registration	Version	C/n	F/n	Notes
RA-76471	IL-76TD	0033446345	3407	Leased to unidentified Iranian operator 1994 as EP-MKA / RA-76471. Sold to Magadanavialeasing
RA-76521	IL-76T	0003423699	1805	Sold to Abakan-Avia by 9-98
RA-76796	IL-76TD	1003499994	7509	Sold to Atlas Air 1-99 as EP-ALI

Leasing company **MAGADANAVIALEASING** [–/MLZ], has five IL-76s. Until mid-1999 they were mostly operated by SVGAL (see below).

Registration	Version	C/n	F/n	Notes
RA-76471	IL-76TD	0033446345	3407	Basic Aeroflot colour scheme, Cyrillic Magadanavializing titles. Leased to Sukhoi by 8-99
RA-76472	IL-76TD	0033446350	3408	Leased to Avialinii 400 ?-2000
RA-76483	IL-76TD	006348042	5201	Leased to Sukhoi 7-99
RA-76489	IL-76TD	0083485554	6409	Leased to Sukhoi 8-99
RA-76787	IL-76TD	0093495854	7204	C/n sometimes reported in error as 0043451507. Leased to Safiran Airlines by 9-2000 as EP-SFA

IL-76TD CCCP-76817 (c/n 1023411387, f/n 8507) was operated by an airline with the improbable (and certainly not Russian) name of **MALS-DEOGHAR** in 1993-95. The aircraft was based in Zhukovskiy and wore basic Aeroflot colours with a stylised 'MD' tail logo and small Mals Deoghar Cargo titles aft of the flight deck. In 1996 the aircraft was sold to Trans Aero Samara.

The IL-76 was operated by various aircraft factories, divisions of the **MINISTRY OF AIRCRAFT INDUSTRY** (MAP). This was liquidated in 1996, but eventually a successor was formed in 1999 in the shape of the Russian Aerospace Agency (RAKA – *Rosseeyskoye aviatseeonno-kosmicheskoye aghentstvo*). Thus it makes sense to describe all the factories in a single entry. MAP IL-76s were usually operated in standard Aeroflot colours with or without titles.

Registration	Version	C/n	F/n	Notes (see details below)
RA-76409	IL-76TD	1023410355	8409	KnAAPO. Leased to Atlant-Soyuz 1995
RA-76418	IL-76 (mil)	073409237	0610	OAPO (Antey), leased from Dobrolyot 5-99 to ?-2000
RA-76425	IL-76TD	1003405167	8002	KnAAPO. Leased to Atlant-Soyuz 1995

RA-76491	IL-76T 'Falsie'	093421630	1608	UAPK. Ex-CCCP-76491, ex-Iraqi Air Force IL-76M YI-AKP
RA-76493	IL-76TD	0043456700	4305	VASO. **Previously reported as IL-76MD 'Falsie'** (renamed IL-76TD by 1994?) Reported as ex-5A-DNW but this is doubtful! Leased to Atlant-Soyuz by 7-2000
RA-76496	IL-76 (mil)	093421630	0806	KAPO. Ex-CCCP-76496, ex-Iraqi AF YI-AIN (?); sometimes reported in error as IL-76TD. Sold to Taraz Wings 1999 as UN-76496
RA-76834	IL-76TD	1023409319	8310	VASO. Crashed at Anadyr' 25-1-97
RA-86865	IL-76M	0003428817	2105	Parachute Systems Research Institute
CCCP-86890	IL-76MD	0013434013	2604	SibNIA, Novosibirsk

KAPO [–/KAO] = *Kazahnskoye aivatseeonnoye proizvodstvennoye obhedineniye imeni S P Gorboonova* – Kazan' Aircraft Production Association named after Sergey Petrovich Gorboonov (MAP aircraft factory No 22) which built the Tupolev Tu-16 *Badger*, Tu-22 *Blinder*, Tu-22M *Backfire* and Tu-160 *Blackjack* bombers, the IL-62 *Classic* long-haul airliner. Now it produces the Tu-214 medium haul airliner and is set to build the Tu-324 short-haul airliner and Tu-330 civil/military transport.

KnAAPO [–/KNM] = *Komsomol'skoye-na-Amoore aviatseeonnoye proizvodstvennoye obyedineniye imeni Yu A Gagarina* – Komsomol'sk-on-Amur Aircraft Production Association named after Yuriy Alekseyevich Gagarin (MAP aircraft factory No 126) which built the Mikoyan/Gurevich MiG-15bis *Fagot-B* and MiG-17 *Fresco-A* tactical fighters, the Sukhoi Su-7/-17/-20/-22 *Fitter* family of fighter-bombers. Now it produces single-seat versions of the Su-27 *Flanker* tactical fighter (the basic Su-27/Su-27P *Flanker-B*, the shipboard Su-33 (Su-27K) *Flanker-D* and the export Su-27SMK). The factory is also gearing up to build the Beriyev Be-103 six-seat general-purpose amphibian and the Sukhoi S-80 light transport aircraft, a possible successor to the An-26 *Curl*.

OAPO = *Omskoye aviatseeonnoye proizvodstvennoye obyedineniye 'Polyot'* – Omsk Aircraft Production Association 'Flight' (MAP aircraft factory No 166) which built, for instance, the Tupolev Tu-104A *Camel* airliner and now manufactures the Antonov An-74 *Coaler* STOL transport. IL-76 RA-76418 is operated by the factory's flying division, the airline **ANTEY** [–/TEY].

UAPK = *Ool'yanovskiy aviatseeonnyy proizvodstvennyy kompleks* – Ul'yanovsk Aircraft Production Complex, now the **AVIASTAR JOINT-STOCK COMPANY** [–/FUE]. This is the factory building the An-124 Ruslan (*Condor*) heavy transport and the Tu-204 medium-range airliner.

VASO [DN/VSO] = *Voronezhskoye aktseeonernoye samolyotostroitel'noye obschchestvo* – Voronezh Aircraft Production Joint-Stock Company (MAP aircraft factory No 64) which built the Tu-16 *Badger* bomber/naval strike aircraft, the An-10 airliner, the An-12 transport, the IL-86 *Camber* medium-range widebody airliner. It currently produces the IL-96-300 long-range airliner and will build the stretched Pratt & Whitney-powered IL-96M/T derivatives (passenger and all-cargo versions respectively).

Six IL-76MDs are reportedly operated by **TMZD** (*Taganrogskiy mashinostroitel'nyy zavod imeni Gheorgiya Dimitrova* – Taganrog Machinery Plant No 86 named after Gheorgiy Dimitrov) which is closely associated with the Beriyev Design Bureau (which see).

MOSCOW AIRWAYS (aka *Moskovskiye avialinii*) [M8/MSC] established in 1991 and based at Sheremet'yevo-2 owned a single IL-76TD, RA-76498 (c/n 0023442218, f/n 3105). By early 1995 it was joined by IL-76TD RA-76355 leased from the Beriyev Design Bureau. Unlike RA-76498 (which was one of only two aircraft painted in full airline colours), this one was white overall with red Moscow Airways titles.

In 1996 the airline had its licence revoked because of unsatisfactory operational standards.[5] RA-76355 was returned to the lessor, while RA-76498 was sold to Continental Airways. The flight code was reallocated to start-up Med Airlines, SpA [M8/MDS] of Palermo, Italy.

MOSTRANSGAZ, one of the natural gas industry's (initially) many flying divisions, operated IL-76TD RA-76402 in Aeroflot colours. In 1996 the aircraft was sold to Gazpromavia (which see) into which Mostransgaz was integrated in April 1997.

NOVOROSSIYSK AIRLINES (*Novorosseeyskiye avialinii*) [–/NRL] lease IL-76s from other carriers as required.

NOVOSIBIRSK AIRLINES (*Novosibeerskiye avialinii*) [L8/NLB] based at Tolmachovo airport purchased IL-76TD (ex-IL-76MD 'Falsie') RA-76445 (c/n 1023410330, f/n 8403) from Altaiskiye Avialinii in 1998. This was the carrier's sole owned aircraft; Novosibirsk Airlines also operated two Tu-134As and an IL-62 leased from three different carriers. By March 2000, however, the aircraft was sold to Lasare Air as 4L-76445.

The now-defunct cargo airline **PACIFIC EXPRESS** operated *Candids* leased from other carriers as required.

Registration	Version	C/n	F/n	Notes
RA-76408	IL-76MD	0053460820	4605	Leased from Atlant-SV (dates unknown), ex-/to UR-76408
RA-76493	IL-76MD 'Falsie'	0043456700	4305	Leased from VASO, returned by 8-93; **version as reported (see MAP entry)**
RA-76786	IL-76TD	0093496923	7401	Lsd from Domodedovo CAPA, dates unknown
RA-76822	IL-76MD 'Falsie'	0093499982	7506	Leased from Ilyushin Design Bureau, dates unknown

In 1992 the Arkhangel'sk airline **POLIS AIR** [–/PMR] took delivery of IL-76TD RA-76407 (c/n 102341345, f/n 8609) in full Aeroflot colours. Early in the following year it bought two ex-Russian Air Force IL-76MD 'Falsies', RA-78851 (c/n 1013406204, f/n 8101) and RA-78852 (c/n 1013407212, f/n 8103). These were promptly reregistered RA-76388 and RA-76389 respectively and repainted in a brown/white livery as IL-76TDs to match the exterior. In the same year, however, they were sold to Veteran Airline (see below in Russian section). As for RA-76407, it was sold to the Algerian Air Force by March 1995 as 7T-WIG.

The **POLYUS PARACHUTE & EXPEDITION WORK CENTRE** (*Tsentr parashootnykh i ekspeditsionnykh rabot 'Polyus'*) [–/PLB] picked up where Exparc had left off, providing logistical support for polar and other expeditions (*polyus* means 'pole', in the geographical sense). In 1997 it reportedly leased all three Altaiskiye Avialinii *Candids* – IL-76MD 'Falsies' RA-76445 and RA-76446 and IL-76TD RA-76833. The former was jointly operated with Antex until Altaiskiye Avialinii sold it in 1998.

RAMAIR JOINT-STOCK COMPANY (Ramaer) [–/RMY] based in Chelyabinsk and associated with the **PHOENIX FREE ZONE ENTERPRISE** (Sharjah, UAE) had four IL-76s, most of which were bought from Atlas Air in November 1998. All of them had Phoenix titles (not to be confused with Moscow-based Phoenix Airlines, a subsidiary of Incombank) and different paint jobs and were registered in Sudan and Bosnia-Herzegovina as a flag of convenience. In 1999, however, Ramair suspended operations and three of the four *Candids* were sold to Phoenix Aviation (see next chapter).

Registration	Version	C/n	F/n	Notes
ST-AQA	IL-76TD	0023442218	3105	Ex-EP-ALC, ex-Continental Airways RA-76498, basic Moscow Airways colours. To Phoenix Aviation/Trans Attico
ST-AQB	IL-76TD	0053460795	4509	Ex-EP-ALA, ex-GosNII GA RA-76481. To Phoenix Aviation/Trans Attico
T9-QAA	IL-76TD 'Falsie'	0023437076	2709	Demilitarised, grey/white colours. Ex-EP-ALB, ex-Queshmair EP-TQC, ex-Air Sultan 9L-LBK, ex-Atlant-Soyuz RA-76383, ex-Atlant-SV IL-76MD UR-86909. **Reregistered to, see below**
T9-CAC				Ex-T9-QAA. To Phoenix Aviation/BIO Air 1999
T9-QAB	IL-76TD	1023408265	8207	Ex-EP-ALD, ex-Intalair 9L-LBO, ex-Beriyev Design Bureau RA-76355, basic Ramair white/red/blue colours. **Reregistered to, see below**
T9-CAB				To Phoenix Aviation/BIO Air 1999; stored Ostend, Belgium

Moscow-based charter carrier **REMEX** [–/RXM] operated five IL-76s from Zhukovskiy.

Registration	Version	C/n	F/n	Notes
RA-76354	IL-76TD	1013409280	8210	Ex-Aviakompaniya Ural. Aeroflot-style colour scheme with red-underlined cheatline, Remex titles and logo. Leased or sold to AZAL Avia Cargo 11-98 as 4K-AZ11/RA-76354
RA-76485	IL-76TD	0063470088	5302	Leased from Sakha Avia 1997 to ?-2000
RA-76494	IL-76TD	0063465956	4909	Leased from Aviaobschemash by 8-99, returned by 5-2000. Basic Aeroflot colour scheme, Remex titles and logo
RA-76792	IL-76TD	0093497942	7406	Full colour scheme. Leased from Kras Air 1997, returned by 10-99
RA-78731	IL-76T 'Falsie'	0013428831	2108	Ex-CCCP-78731, ex-Iraqi AF IL-76M YI-AKV. Demilitarised. Full colours. Ex-TransSuper, bought 1997. Was leased to Payam Air 1998 to mid-1999 as EP-TPF. Leased to Volga-Dnepr 4-2000

The leasing company **ROSAEROLEASING** (*Rosaerolizing*) [–/KVM] took delivery of IL-76TD RA-76814, leasing it to various operators (currently Sukhoi). In between it was briefly flown in basic Aeroflot colours with black Cyrillic 'Rosaerolizing' titles. Later Rosaeroleasing bought IL-76MD RA-76591 from Atruvera and had it converted to IL-76TD standard.

The airline **ROOS'**[16] **JOINT-STOCK COMPANY** [–/RUR] founded in 1999 operates four IL-76s.

Registration	Version	C/n	F/n	Notes
RA-76591	IL-76TD	0043452546	3907	**Converted IL-76MD.** Leased from Rosaeroleasing ?-99
RA-76669	IL-76MD	0063465949	4908	Leased or bought from 224th Flight Unit State Airline ?-2000
RA-76790	IL-76TD	0093496903	7306	**Converted IL-76TD "Falsie"/IL-76MD.** Ex-Spair RA76790,* bought by 5-2000
RA-76818	IL-76TD	1013408264	8206	Ex-Ilavia, bought ?-99

* The registration was originally painted on like this. It was changed to the normal presentation (RA-76790) after purchase by Roos' and overhaul.

SAKHA AVIA [K7/IKT], formerly Yakutavia, is the national airline of the Republic of Yakutia (Sakha) and one of the biggest Russian air carriers. It is headquartered in Yakutsk and consists of several divisions (air enterprises); the Yakutsk Air Enterprise operated eight IL-76TDs.

Registration	Version	C/n	F/n	Notes
RA-76400	IL-76TD	1023413438	8610	Sold to Vladivostok Air
RA-76403	IL-76TD	1023412414	8604	Sold to Vladivostok Air
RA-76485	IL-76TD	0063470088	5302	Originally flown as 76485 in Aeroflot colours with Yakutavia titles on aft fuselage. Leased to Aviast by 8-2000
RA-76486	IL-76TD	0073476281	5801	Leased (later bought) from Baikal Airlines. Full colour scheme
RA-76487	IL-76TD	0073479367	6002	Full colour scheme; lsd to Aviast by 8-2000
UR-76694	IL-76MD	0063470107	5307	Leased from Veteran Airline 1-94 to 5-94
RA-76785?	IL-76TD	0093495863	7206	Leased from Aeroflot Russian International Airlines (dates unknown)? Possible confusion with RA-76485!
RA-76797	IL-76TD	1003403052	7703	Full colour scheme; leased to Aviast by 8-2000
RA-76849	IL-76TD	0023440161?	3001?	**Converted IL-76MD** (ex-Hoseba UR-86921)? Basic Aeroflot c/s, all-white tail, Sakha Avia titles on aft fuselage (starboard side only). Leased to Aviast by 8-2000

Ramair/Phoenix FZE IL-76TD at Sharjah in January 1999. This aircraft (ex-RA-76355) is on the Bosnian register as T9-QAB. Peter Davison

Remex IL-76TD RA-76792 at the Myasischchev parking area in Zhukovskiy in August 1997. The aircraft has since been returned to Kras Air. Yefim Gordon

Sakha Avia IL-76TD RA-76486 in the Bykovo aircraft overhaul plant's parking area. Yefim Gordon

Samara Airlines operate seven IL-76TDs, including some leased from other carriers, such as Almazy Rossii – Sakha RA-76420 photographed at Moscow-Domodedovo on 25th November 1998. Dmitriy Komissarov

Still in basic Transaero colours, demilitarised IL-76M RA-86726 of Solar Wind is seen in the Ilyushin compound at Zhukovskiy on 22nd August 1995, the opening day of MAKS'95. Dmitriy Komissarov

The Sukhoi Design Bureau's house airline operates several (mostly leased) *Candids*, including IL-76TD RA-76483 seen at Zhukovskiy in August 1999. The aircraft still carries the name of its owner, SVGAL (North-Eastern Cargo Airlines), on the nose. Dmitriy Komissarov

Tesis Airlines IL-76TD RA-76791 pictured at Zhukovskiy in August 1997. The tail was later painted in the same dark shade of blue as the cheatline. Yefim Gordon

Vladivostok Air IL-76TD RA-76400 with additional East Line titles on the forward fuselage rests between flights at Moscow-Domodedovo on 3rd November 1998. Dmitriy Komissarov

SAKHAVIATRANS [–/SVT], the Far Eastern sister company of Atran – Aviatrans Cargo Airlines based in Yuzhno-Sakhalinsk, leases aircraft from Atran as required; these included IL-76T 'Falsie' RA-76757.

SAMARA AIRLINES [E5/BRZ], one of the biggest Russian regional carriers based at Samara-Kurumoch airport, operated ten IL-76TDs.

Registration	Version	C/n	F/n	Notes
RA-76352	IL-76TD	1023411378	8505	Ex-Uzbekistan Airways UK-76352. Leased from Aviaprad 4-98, basic old Uzbekistan colours with Samara titles on aft fuselage
RA-76360	IL-76TD	1033414492	8803	Leased from Almazy Rossii-Sakha by 6-99; Almazy Rossii-Sakha colour scheme plus Samara titles on aft fuselage
RA-76388	IL-76TD	1013406204	8101	Ex-IL-76MD 'Falsie' RA-78851. Leased from Tupolev-Aerotrans, dates unknown
RA-76420	IL-76TD	1023413446	8702	Leased from Almazy Rossii-Sakha by 10-98; Almazy Rossii-Sakha colours plus Samara titles on aft fuselage
RA-76475	IL-76TD	0043451523	3901	Full colour scheme. Leased to Payam Air 2-2000 as EP-TPV
RA-76487	IL-76TD	0073479367	6002	Lsd from Sakha Avia by 8-99, returned; Sakha Avia c/s plus Samara titles on aft fuselage
RA-76791	IL-76TD	0093497936	7404	Basic Aeroflot colours, grey tail, Samara titles. Leased to Tesis 1996, full Tesis colour scheme
RA-76797	IL-76TD	1003403052	7703	Leased from Sakha Avia by 4-2000; returned. Sakha Avia c/s plus Samara titles on aft fuselage
RA-76798	IL-76TD	1003403063	7706	Basic Aeroflot colours. Lsd to Volga-Dnepr 10-94
RA-76817	IL-76TD	1023411387	8507	Leased from Trans Aero Samara 8-99 to ?-2000. C/n often reported in error as 1023412387

IL-76TD RA-76837 (ex-Belair EW-76837, c/n 1023409316, f/n 8309) was reported for **SAT AIRLINES** in December 1996. The name of the carrier is doubtful, however, since SAT Airlines are Sakhalinskiye Aviatrassy (Sakhalin Air Routes, [HZ/SHU]) based in Yuzhno-Sakhalinsk, and this airline has a totally different logo from the one painted on the aircraft. Incidentally, the aircraft was in basic Belair colours, which proves it was indeed ex-EW-76837 and not another aircraft with the same registration. (see also next chapter/Sudanese section).

SIBAVIATRANS [5M/SIB], aka SIAT, was incorporated on 1st February 1995 as a public limited company. The airline is based at Krasnoyarsk-Yemel'yanovo airport and the fleet reportedly includes a single IL-76TD acquired in 1999; unfortunately, no details are known.

A company named **SOLAR WIND** operated Transaero's sole IL-76M (see below) in full Transaero colours but with red 'Solar Wind' titles. The aircraft was based in Zhukovskiy; by 1997 it had been retired, sitting engineless at the Ilyushin compound at LII, and was broken up in 1998.

SPAIR AIR TRANSPORT CORPORATION [–/PAR] (*Aviatrahnsportnaya korporahtsiya Spaer*)[7] based at Yekaterinburg-Kol'tsovo airport and mainly concerned with cargo carriage operated four *Candid-A/Bs*. The letters SP in the carrier's name are derived from the name of its director, Valeriy Spoornov.

Registration	Version	C/n	F/n	Notes
RA-76513	IL-76T	083414451	1203	Crashed near Belgrad-Valjavo airport 19-8-96
RA-76527	IL-76T	0003427796	2009	Was leased from Tyumen' Airlines 1997
RA76790	IL-76MD/ IL-76TD 'Falsie'	0093496903	7306	Demilitarised; **ex-avionics testbed**, renamed IL-76TD soon after purchase. Registration painted on with no dash or space after prefix. WFU Ryazan' by 8-99; sold to Roos' JSC by 5-2000.
RA-?????	IL-76TD 'Falsie'	?	?	Demilitarised; **ex-avionics testbed**

AVIAKOMPANIYA SUKHOI [–/SUH], a subsidiary of the Sukhoi Design Bureau, Russia's famous 'fighter maker', operated eleven *Candids* (mostly leased from other carriers).

Registration	Version	C/n	F/n	Notes
RA-76379	IL-76TD	1033417569	9003	Bought from Krylo by 2-2000
RA-76471	IL-76TD	0033446345	3407	Leased from Magadanavialeasing by 8-99. Basic Aeroflot colours (Russian flag on tail), small Sukhoi titles
RA-76483	IL-76TD	0063468042	5201	Leased from Magadanavialeasing by 7-99. Basic Aeroflot colours, large Sukhoi titles and tail logo, plus ex-SVGAL nose titles
RA-76489	IL-76TD	0083485554	6409	Leased from Magadanavialeasing 8-99
RA-76499	IL-76TD	0023441186	3007	Leased from Kosmos by 6-99, basic Kosmos colour scheme, Sukhoi/Cargo titles
RA-76518	IL-76T	093420594	1509	Leased from Tyumen' airlines 1-2000
RA-76527	IL-76T	003427796	2009	Leased from Tyumen' Airlines 8-99
RA-76659	IL-76TD 'Falsie'	0053463908	4807	Leased from Aviacon Tsitotrans by 8-99. Basic Aeroflot colours, large Sukhoi titles and tail logo. Returned by 5-2000
RA-76759	IL-76T 'Falsie'	093418543	1406	Demilitarised. Ex-CCCP-76759, ex-Iraqi AF YI-AKS, ex-2068. Basic Aeroflot colours, large Sukhoi titles and tail logo
RA-76787	IL-76TD	0093495854	7204	Leased from SVGAL by 6-99. Basic Aeroflot colours, large Sukhoi titles and tail logo. To Magadanavialeasing ?-2000
RA-76814	IL-76TD	1013408269	8208	Leased from Rosaeroleasing by 5-2000; basic Aeroflot colours, large Sukhoi titles and tail logo

RA-76659 and RA-76814 carry the registration on the aft fuselage, Ukrainian-style. On RA-76759 the registration is painted on the aft fuselage to port and on the fin to starboard.

SVGAL (*Severo-vostochnyye groozovyye avialinii* – North-Eastern Cargo Airlines) [–/MGD] based in Magadan and Kent International airport (UK) operated six *Candid-As* until its demise in late 1999, whereupon most of the aircraft went to Magadanavialeasing.

Registration	Version	C/n	F/n	Notes
RA-76361	IL-76TD	1033415497	8805	Sold to Yemenia 11-94 as 7O-ADH
RA-76472	IL-76TD	0033446350	3408	Leased to Atlant-Soyuz by 8-99
RA-76483	IL-76TD	0063468042	5201	Leased to Sukhoi by 8-99
RA-76489	IL-76TD	0083485554	6409	Leased to Atlant-Soyuz 1997
RA-76522	IL-76T	0003424707	1807	Basic Aeroflot colours, no titles. Sold to Inversija as YL-LAK 10-94*
RA-76787	IL-76TD	0093495854	7204	Leased to Sukhoi by 6-99

* JP Airline-Fleets states that YL-LAK was acquired in September 1991. However, the aircraft is confirmed as operated by North-East Cargo Airlines as RA-76522 in 1993.

The Moscow airline **TESIS** [UZ/TIS] operated four IL-76TDs.

Registration	Version	C/n	F/n	Notes
UN-76384	IL-76TD	1003401015	7604	Leased from Sayakhat 1999
RA-76484	IL-76TD	0063469081	5301	Leased from Baikalavia 1999
RA-76791	IL-76TD	0093497936	7404	Leased from Samara Airlines 1996, full colour scheme / light blue tail, registration on tail, later dark blue tail. Sub-leased to Payam Air 3-2000 as EP-TPU No 2 (see ATI Airlines)
RA-76808	IL-76TD	1013405177	8005	Leased from Baikalavia 1998, full colour scheme / dark blue tail, registration on aft fuselage. Sub-leased abroad and temporarily reregistered until early 1999?*

Note: RA-76808 has a dirty patch on both sides of the aft fuselage suggesting the aircraft was temporarily re-registered and later the foreign registration was crudely painted out.

Moscow-based **TRANSAERO** [4J/TSO, later UN/TSO], one of the first new airlines to come into being after the breakup of the USSR and Aeroflot, had a single well-used demilitarised IL-76M – RA-86726 (c/n 083412380, f/n 1005). Transaero's predominantly white livery with the red, white and blue striped tail logo has caused more than one spotter to believe at first sighting that the aircraft was operated by Air France! In 1993 RA-86726 was leased to Solar Wind which operated it 'until (the aircraft's) death did them part'. Additionally, in March 1993 Trans-aero briefly leased IL-76MD UR-76408 (c/n 0053460820, f/n 4605) from Atlant-SV.

Cargo carrier **TRANS AERO SAMARA** [–/TSL] based at Samara-Bezymyanka airport had two IL-76TDs, RA-76381 (c/n 1033418596, f/n 9009) and ex-Mals Deoghar Cargo RA-76817 (c/n 1023411387, f/n 8507) bought in 1996. Despite the similar name, this airline had nothing to do with Transaero. In 1999 the airline ceased operations, selling both aircraft to East Line.

The Moscow-based carrier **TRANS-CHARTER** [–/TCH] operated IL-76TD RA-76832 (c/n 1023410360, f/n 8410) for an unknown period of time before the aircraft was sold to Gulf Aviation Technology & Services (GATS; see page 120).

The Moscow cargo airline **TRANSSUPER** operated two *Candids* – IL-76TD RA-76406 (c/n 1023414463, f/n 8706) and IL-76T 'Falsie' CCCP-78731 (ex-IL-76M YI-AKV, c/n 0013428831, f/n 2108). The latter aircraft was in basic Aeroflot colours, while RA-76406 wore full TransSuper livery with a blue tail and a large white tail logo resembling a stylised V. The airline went bankrupt by 1997; RA-76406 was sold to the Algerian Air Force as 7T-WIE and CCCP-78731 to Remex as RA-78731. *(It should be noted that RA-76406 was reported for Avial' at the time of sighting in TransSuper colours; it was probably leased from Avial'.)*

TUPOLEV-AEROTRANS [–/TUP], a subsidiary of the Tupolev Design Bureau based in Zhukovskiy, bought IL-76TDs RA-76388 and RA-76389 from defunct Veteran Airline in 1997. Originally flown in ex-Polis Air brown/white colours without titles, the aircraft later received Cyrillic 'Tupolev-Aerotrans' titles. RA-76389 is on lease to Dobrolyot since early 1999; RA-76388 followed suit by May 2000.

TYUMEN' AIRLINES/TYUMENSKIYE AVIALINII [7M/TYM] based at Tyumen'-Roschchino airport have seven *Candid-As*.

Registration	Version	C/n	F/n	Notes
RA-76507	IL-76T	073411338	0905	Converted IL-76 *sans suffixe* (civil)
RA-76512	IL-76T	083414447	1202	First production IL-76T? Retired by 3-2000
RA-76514	IL-76T	083415453	1204	Sold to Aviacon Tsitotrans 1998
RA-76518	IL-76T	093420594	1509	Was leased to the United Nations / World Food Programme 10-93, Leased to Sukhoi 1-2000
RA-76523	IL-76T	0003425732	1903	Leased to International Committee of the Red Cross. WFU / stored at Moscow-Bykovo (overhaul plant No 402) since at least 7-99
RA-76527	IL-76T	0003427796	2009	Leased to Sukhoi 8-99
RA-76807	IL-76TD	1013405176	8004	Leased to Ilavia 1999

The **UL'YANOVSK HIGHER CIVIL AVIATION FLYING SCHOOL**[8] (UVLU GA – *Ool'yahnovskoye vyssheye lyotnoye oochilischche grazhdahnskoy aviahtsii*) [–/UHS], which trains both Russian and foreign pilots, has two IL-76TDs, RA-76401 (c/n 1023412399, f/n 8510) and RA-76783 (c/n 0093498974, f/n 7504). Both aircraft are on lease to Atlant-Soyuz since March 2000 and 1999 respectively.

IL-76TD RA-76354 (c/n 1013409280, f/n 8210) was reported for a certain **AVIAKOMPANIYA URAL** (Urals Airline). It wore full Aeroflot colours but the cheatline was underlined in red, not blue. The aircraft was later sold to Remex. (**Note:** Ural Airlines/Ural'skiye Avialinii [–/URW] based at Yekaterinburg-Kol'tsovo have been reported as an IL-76 operator, but no Ural Airlines *Candids* have ever been reported. Also, Ural Airlines' current codes are [U6/SVR].)

The cargo airline **URALINTERAVIA** [–/URA], likewise based at Yekaterinburg, operated five IL-76s. Most were high-time airframes and thus were retired when Uralinteravia ceased operations in November 1996.

Registration	Version	C/n	F/n	Notes
RA 76386	IL-76TD	1033418600	9010	Ex-Uzbekistan Airways UK 76386. Basic new Uzbekistan colours, Uralinteravia titles on starboard side only. Sold to Aviaprad
RA-76506	IL-76T	073411334	0904	Converted IL-76 (civil). Basic Aeroflot colours, grey tail, Uralinteravia titles on starboard side only. Sold to Aviacon Tsitotrans
RA-86627	IL-76 (mil)	063405137	0405	Demilitarised. Full colour scheme. Ex-VVS, bought 10-8-92; WFU Yekaterinburg-Kol'tsovo
RA-86720	IL-76T 'Falsie'	073409267	0707	Ex-IL-76 (military). Ex-VVS, bought 10-8-92; WFU Yekaterinburg-Kol'tsovo?
RA-86747	IL-76 (mil)	063407170	0503	Ex-VVS, bought 10-8-92; WFU Yekaterinburg-Kol'tsovo

VEGA AIRCOMPANY [–/VEG] from Voronezh briefly operated IL-76TD RA-76493 leased from the local aircraft factory.

Zhukovskiy-based **VETERAN AIRLINES** [–/VTN], a sister company of the Ukrainian airline of the same name, operated three *Candids*. The Russian airline suspended operations in 1997

Registration	Version	C/n	F/n	Notes
RA-76388	IL-76TD	1013406204	8101	Ex-IL-76MD 'Falsie' CCCP-78851. Ex-Polis Air, basic Polis Air colours, no tail logo, Veteran Airline (*sic*) titles. Sold to Tupolev-Aerotrans by 1997
RA-76389	IL-76TD	1013407212	8103	Ex-IL-76MD 'Falsie' CCCP-78852. Ex-Polis Air, basic Polis Air colours, no tail logo, Veteran Airline titles, additional Water Bomber titles on aft fuselage. Sold to Tupolev-Aerotrans by 1997
RA-86846	IL-76T 'Falsie'	0003426765	2002	Demilitarised. Ex-Zenit? White with grey belly, no titles. Sold to Air Pass 1997 as 3D-RTA

VIA VIKTOR AIRLINES [–/VKT] from Moscow (renamed Velocity in 1996) leases aircraft from other operators as required. Known IL-76s operated by VIA Viktor Airlines are listed below; all have been returned.

Registration	Version	C/n	F/n	Notes
RA-76355	IL-76TD	1023408265	8207	Lsd from Beriyev Design Bureau, dates unknown
RA-76533	IL-76MD	0023442205	3102	Leased from Russian Air Force 1993
RA-76819	IL-76TD	1013409274	8209	Leased from Exparc, dates unknown

VLADIVOSTOK AIR [XF/VLK], aka Vladivostokavia, had four IL-76s.

Registration	Version	C/n	F/n	Notes
RA-76400	IL-76TD	1023413438	8610	Ex-Sakha Avia. Basic Aeroflot colour scheme, Vladivostok Air titles. Lsd to East Line 1998
RA-76403	IL-76TD	1023412414	8604	Ex-Sakha Avia. Leased to East Line 1998
RA-76420	IL-76TD	1023413446	8702	Sold to Almazy Rossii-Sakha
RA-76492	IL-76T 'Falsie'	093418548	1407	Demilitarised. Ex-Iraqi AF YI-AKT, bought 1994; **second use of registration (see LII for CCCP-76492)**. Aeroflot colours. Lsd to East Line 1998

Veteran Airlines IL-76MD 'Falsie' RA-76389 with additional Zall Trans titles in a brown/white colour scheme left over from its days with Polis Air. This aircraft was later sold to Tupolev-Aerotrans. Yefim Gordon

VIA Viktor Airlines IL-76TD RA-76355 at Prague. Petr Šebek

Fresh from overhaul at Bykovo and resplendent in Volga-Dnepr colours, IL-76TD 'Falsie' RA-76758 sits on the Ilyushin OKB ramp in Zhukovskiy on 22nd August 1999, the closing day of MAKS'99. Curiously, the aircraft has not been demilitarised, retaining the tail gun barbette. Dmitriy Komissarov

Established in 1990 as the first non-Aeroflot specialised cargo carrier in the Soviet Union and later Russia, **VOLGA-DNEPR AIRLINES** [VI/VDA] operates several IL-76s (mostly leased from other operators) on scheduled cargo services to Moscow-Domodedovo, Novosibirsk, Shenyang and Tianjin. Additionally, cargo charters are flown all over the world jointly with London/Stansted-based HeavyLift Cargo Airlines. Volga-Dnepr is a joint-stock company, with the Antonov Design Bureau, the Ul'yanovsk Aviastar aircraft factory and the Motor-Sich aero engine factory as the main stockholders.

Registration	Version	C/n	F/n	Notes
RA-76401	IL-76TD	1023412399	8510	Leased from Ul'yanovsk Higher Flying School 5-95; sub-leased to HeavyLift 7-95 in full colours
RA-76445	IL-76MD 'Falsie'	1023410330	8403	Leased from Altaiskiye Avialinii 7-93 to ?-??
RA-76758	IL-76TD 'Falsie'	0073474203	5601	Was leased to HeavyLift as IL-76MD CCCP- / RA-75758 1-92 to ?-?? in full HeavyLift colours; now full Volga-Dnepr colour scheme
EW-76737	IL-76TD 'Falsie'	0073477323	5901	**Converted IL-76MD**; leased from TransAVIA-export 8-99, white overall with Volga-Dnepr titles and logo
RA-76787	IL-76TD	0093495854	7204	Leased from SVGAL (North-East Cargo Airlines) 1-95 to ?-97. Basic Aeroflot colours, titles unknown
RA-76798	IL-76TD	1003403063	7706	Leased from Samara Airlines 10-94; basic Aeroflot colours, Volga-Dnepr titles and logo
RA-78731	IL-76T 'Falsie'	0013428831	2108	Leased from Remex 4-2000; basic Remex colours, Volga-Dnepr titles and tail logo

ZENIT [–/EZT] owns IL-76TD 'Falsie' RA-86896 (c/n 0013434018, f/n 2605). In December 1998 the aircraft was leased to Atlas Air as EP-ALJ. In 1994 it reportedly also operated IL-76TD 'Falsie' RA-86846 (c/n 0023426765, f/n 2002) which was later sold to Veteran Airline; both aircraft were demilitarised.

IL-76s operated by **UNIDENTIFIED RUSSIAN CARRIERS** include:

Registration	Version	C/n	F/n	Notes
RA-76356	IL-76TD?	?	?	Seen in Bombay 6-1-96
RA-76380	IL-76TD	1033418578	9005	Seen at Moscow-Domodedovo 4-5-94 in full Aeroflot colours; sold to Yemenia 11-94 as 7O-ADF
RA-76404	IL-76 (mil)?	?	?	Seen at Moscow-Sheremet'yevo 27-4-93 in full Aeroflot colours
RA-76440	IL-76TD	1023413423	8606	Seen at Moscow-Sheremet'yevo 20-4-93 in full Aeroflot colours. Sold to Algerian AF as 7T-WIU

TURKMENISTAN

The **TURKMENISTAN AIRLINES CONCERN** – or, to be precise, **AKHAL AIRCOMPANY** [T5/AKH] based in Ashgabat (Ashkhabad) – had eight IL-76TDs. In 1999 the three constituent divisions of the concern (Akhal, Khazar and Lebap) merged into **TURKMENISTAN AIRLINES** [T5/TUA].

Registration	Version	C/n	F/n	Notes
EZ-F421	IL-76TD	1023498978	7505	Reported as ex-CCCP-76421, first use of registration? **(see Dacono Air for RA-76421!)**
EZ-F422	IL-76TD	1023410348	8407	Ex-CCCP-76830
EZ-F423	IL-76TD	1033418608	9102	
EZ-F424	IL-76TD	1033418592	9008	
EZ-F425	IL-76TD	1023410336	8404	Ex-CCCP-76816
EZ-F426	IL-76TD	1033418609	9103	
EZ-F427	IL-76TD	1033418620	9105	
EZ-F428	IL-76TD	1043418624	9106	

THE UKRAINE

The **UKRAINIAN AIR FORCE** (UAF, or VPS – Voyenno-povitryany seely) inherited a substantial number of IL-76MDs and IL-78s from the VTA when the Soviet Union collapsed. One hundred were reportedly in service in November 2000. They are based in Kiev (Kyiv; 1st OSTAP[9]), Artsyz, Dzhankoy, Krivoy Rog (Krivyy Rig; 16th VTAP), Melitopol', Uzin and Zaporozhye (Zaporizhzhya; 338th VTAP). However, as mentioned earlier, funding problems and political complications following the breakup of the Soviet Union and the resulting spares shortage have caused many UAF Candids to be cannibalised for spares. Also, most of the 409th SAP IL-78s at Uzin have been converted to IL-76MDs.

Most Ukrainian IL-76s are operated by numerous 'airlines' under UAF management which help the Air Force generate urgently needed cash (though at times it is hard to tell which airline is civil and which is not!). And even the few Candids that have been seen in overtly military markings carry civil registrations along with UAF roundels and shield-and-trident tail insignia comes in several styles (rounded and angular). A curious trait of Ukrainian IL-76s and IL-78s is that they usually carry the registration on the aft fuselage rather than on the fin, as was customary in Soviet times (and still is in most CIS republics).

Registration	Version	C/n	F/n	Notes
UR-76413	IL-76MD	1013407215	8104	Ex-CCCP-78853. Ex-Busol Airline, Busol cheatline; sometimes reported in error as IL-76TD 'Falsie'
UR-76414	IL-78	0083482478	6210	Ex-CCCP-76774 **Converted to IL-76MD**. Ex-Busol Airline, Busol cheatline; to Ukrainian Cargo Airways 1998 as UR-UCG
UR-76415	IL-78	0083481440	6110	Ex-CCCP-76775 (out-of-sequence), **converted to IL-76MD**. Ex-Busol Airline, Busol cheatline; to Ukrainian Cargo Airways 1998 as UR-UCI
76531	IL-76MD	0023441181	3006	
CCCP-76540	IL-65MD	0023442238	3110	338th VTAP, Zaporozhye
76559	IL-76MD	0033446340	3405	
UR-76560	IL-76MD	0033447363	3406	Ex-Soviet Air Force '23 Red'?, ex-CCCP-76560
76562	IL-76MD	0033447365	3502	
76564	IL-76MD	0033448373	3504	
76565	IL-76MD	0033448382	3506	
76566	IL-76MD	0033448385	3507	
76567	IL-76MD	0033448390	3508	
UR-76574	IL-76MD	0033449441	3701	Ex-Liana Aircompany
76575	IL-76MD	0033449445	3702	
UR-76585	IL-76MD	0043451503	3806	
76596	IL-76MD	0043453583	4006	
76597	IL-76MD	0043453585	4007	
76598	IL-76MD	0043453591	4008	
UR-76601	IL-76MD	0043454606	4102	Ex-Atlant-SV. Leased to Atlant-Soyuz 11-99
UR-76610	IL-78	0043454640	4110	**Converted to IL-76MD**; ex-BSL Airline
UR-76617	IL-76MD	0043455677?	4210	To Avilond TAC as UR-76441
UR-76624	IL-76MD	0053457710	4308	Ex-Polissyaaviatrans
76631	IL-76MD	0053458756	4409	
UR-76633	IL-76MD	0053459764	4501	Ex-ATI Airlines
UR-76646?	IL-78	0053461837	4610	UR- prefix unconfirmed
76653	IL-78	0053462879	4710	Ever flown with UR- prefix? Probably converted to IL-76MD
76657	IL-76MD	0053463896	4804	
76660	IL-78?	0053463910	4808	Also reported as IL-76MD!
76661	IL-76MD	0053463913	4809	
76665	IL-76MD	0053464930	4903	
76675	IL-78	0063466998	5010	Ever flown with UR- prefix? Probably converted to IL-76MD
UR-76677	IL-76MD	0063467005	5102	321st VTAP, Kiev-Borispol'; ex-Veteran Airline, transferred 1999
UR-76680	IL-76MD	0063467020	5105	Ex-Busol Airline. 1st OSTAP, Kiev-Borispol'
UR-76681	IL-76MD	0063467021	5106	Ex-ANTAU
UR-76687	IL-76MD	0063469051	5203	1st OSTAP, Kiev-Borispol'. To Volare Aviation Enterprise 1997

UR-76697	IL-76MD	0063470118	5310	Ex-Veteran Airline
UR-76699	IL-76MD	0063471131	5403	
UR-76700	*IL-76MD*	*0063471134*	*5404*	*1st OSTAP, Kiev-Borispol';*
				registration still on tail. To ATI Airlines 1997
76703	IL-76MD	0063471147	5407	
76736	IL-78	0073476317	5810	
76749	IL-76MD	0073479392	6008	
UR-78778?	IL-76MD	0083489659	6705	Ex-Russian AF RA-78778? Doubtful report
UR-78820	IL-76MD	0093496907	7307	Ex-Atlant-Soyuz RA-78820, returned from
				lease by 7-96
78821	IL-76MD	0093496914	7309	
86028	IL-76M	083415464	1206	
86029	IL-76M	083415465	1207	
86030	IL-76M	083415475	1209	
86031	IL-76M	083415477	1210	Ground instructional airframe at Vasil'kov
				(Vasil'kiv) technical school
86633	IL-76 (mil)	073409256	0704	
86639	IL-76 (mil)	073409235	0609	
86854	IL-76M	0003425728	1902	Ground instructional airframe at Vasil'kov
				(Vasil'kiv) technical school
CCCP-86904	IL-76MD	002346050	2703	WFU Belaya Tserkov' (Bela Tserkva), ex-338th VTAP
CCCP-86911	IL-76MD	0023437093	2804	WFU / stored Belaya Tserkov' (Bela Tserkva),
				ex-338th VTAP
CCCP-86914	IL-76MD	0023438111	2808	WFU / stored Belaya Tserkov' (Bela Tserkva),
				ex-16th VTAP
86915	IL-76MD	0023438116	2809	16th VTAP, Krivoy Rog
UR-86916	IL-76MD	0023438120	2810	Ex-Liana Aircompany
CCCP-86917	IL-76MD	002348122	2901	WFU / stored Belaya Tserkov' (Bela Tserkva),
				ex-16th VTAP
UR-86920	IL-76MD	0023440152	2908	Ex-Liana Aircompany
86922	IL-76MD	0023440168	3002	
86923	IL-76MD	0023441169	3003	

Note: Many IL-76MDs were transferred from one commercial division of the UAF to another. When the ultimate fate of aircraft no longer listed is unknown, these are assumed returned to the UAF.

The now-defunct **AERONAVIGATION AND TRANSPORT AGENCY OF THE UKRAINE (ANTAU)** operated eight IL-76MDs from Melitopol'. All of them except UR-78774 were leased to South African Airways.

Registration	Version	C/n	F/n	Notes
UR-76656	IL-76MD	0053463891	4803	To Azov Avia 1996
UR-76664	IL-76MD	0053464926	4902	To Khors Aircompany by 7-95
UR-76681	IL-76MD	0063467021	5106	Ex-Bel'bek. To Ukrainian Air Force
UR-76705	IL-76MD	0063472158	5410	To Air Ukraine / L'vov Air Enterprise
UR-76706	IL-76MD	0063472163	5501	
UR-76778	IL-76MD	0083483502	6306	To Air Ukraine / L'vov Air Enterprise.
				C/n also reported as 0083482502
UR-78756	IL-76MD	0083484536	6404	To Air Service Ukraine
UR-78774	IL-76MD	0083488643	6701	To Air Service Ukraine

Note: UR-76706 was reported in 1997 as operated by Antey; it is not certain if this was the flying division of the Omsk aircraft factory (see Russia/MAP) or another airline of the same name.

AIR SERVICE UKRAINE [CH/ASG, later 9G/ASG][10] based in Kiev was one of the airlines under UAF management, operating fifteen IL-76MDs until it suspended operations in 1998.

Registration	Version	C/n	F/n	Notes
UR-76537	IL-76MD	0023442225	3107	Operated for UNPF in ex-Yugoslavia (1994)
UR-76541	IL-76MD	0023442241	3201	Operated for UNPF in ex-Yugoslavia (1994)
UR-76622	IL-76MD	0053457702	4306	Ex-Atlant-SV, transferred 1996
UR-76655	IL-76MD	0053463885	4802	Reported as ex-IL-76PP; wingtip antenna pods
				à la 'aircraft 976' and forward ECM aerials à la
				IL-76PP/A-50, no power packs or aft ECM aerials
UR-76658	IL-76MD	0053463902	4806	
UR-76663	IL-76MD	0053464922	4901	To Polissyaaviatrans

UR-76712?	IL-76MD	0063473190	5508	UR- prefix doubtful! To Belorussian Air Force/
				TransAVIAexport as EW-76712
UR-76732	IL-76MD	0073476296	5804	
UR-76734	IL-76MD	0073476312	5808	Ex-/to Belorussian Air Force/TransAVIAexport
				EW-76734, leased 1996 to ?-??
UR-76744	IL-78	0073478359	5910	**Converted to IL-76MD.** Ex-BSL Airline,
				transferred 1997
UR-78756	IL-76MD	0083484536	6404	Ex-ANTAU. To Ukrainian Cargo Airways 1998
				as UR-UCH
UR-78774	IL-76MD	0083488643	6701	Ex-ANTAU, transferred by 9-94. To Ukrainian
				Cargo Airways as UR-UCD
UR-78785	IL-76MD	0083489691	6803	Ex-RA-78785?, ex-Cargo Ukrainian Airlines.
				To Yuzhmashavia 1998
UR-78786	IL-76MD	0093490694	6804	Ex-Atlant-SV, transferred 10-95.
				To Cargo Ukrainian Airlines
UR-86924	IL-76MD	0023441174	3004	Operated for UNPF in ex-Yugoslavia (1994)

AIR UKRAINE CARGO (*Groozovyye Avialinii Ukrainy*) [–/UKC] based in Krivoy Rog operated IL-76MDs of the local airlift regiment. The carrier, which has nothing to do with the 'regular' Air Ukraine (see below) and has also been referred to as **Cargo Ukrainian Airlines**, suspended operations in 1998.

Registration	Version	C/n	F/n	Notes
UR-76555	IL-76MD	0033446325	3402	Leased from Air Ukraine 1994, Air Ukraine
				colours with additional Air Ukraine Cargo titles
UR-76561	IL-76MD	0033447364	3501	
CCCP-76626	IL-76MD	0053457720	4310	To Atlant-SV as CCCP-76423 by 4-93
UR-76628	IL-76MD	0053458741	4406	C/n also reported as 0053458743. To Volare
				Aviation Enterprise 1997
CCCP-76629	IL-76MD	0053458745	4407	To ATI Airlines 1997 as UR-76629
UR-78758	IL-76MD	0083484551	6408	Ex-/to (leased from) ATI Airlines
UR-78772	IL-76MD	0083487627	6607	Ex-/to (leased from) ATI Airlines
RA-78785?	IL-76MD	0083489691	6803	Reported as such but RA- prefix doubtful!
				To Air Service Ukraine by 1997 as UR-78785
UR-78786	IL-76MD	0093490694	6804	Ex-Air Service Ukraine. To Yuzhmashavia 1996

ATI AIRLINES [–/TII] registered in Kiev operated 13 *Candids*.

Registration	Version	C/n	F/n	Notes
UR-76424	IL-76MD	0063470096	5304	Ex-Atlant-SV (ex-CCCP-76692). Crashed at
				Ras al Khaimah 13-7-98
UR-76584	IL-76MD	0043450493	3804	To Altoplan by 3-97
UR-76590	*IL-76MD*	*0043452544*	*3906*	*Ex-Atlant-SV, transferred by 3-96?*
				To Altoplan by 3-97
UR-76629	IL-76MD	0053458745	4407	Ex-Air Service Ukraine
UR-76633	*IL-76MD*	*0053459764*	*4501*	*To Ukrainian Air Force*
UR-76700	IL-76MD	0063471134	5404	Formerly flown in Ukrainian AF markings.
				Leased to AZAL-Avia Cargo 1998
UR-76716	IL-76MD	0073474211	5603	Ex-Liana Aircompany. White overall, logo on nose
UR-76759	IL-78	0083485558	6410	**Ex-CCCP-78759 (painting error, see**
				RA-76759 / Sukhoi)! Converted to IL-76MD
UR-76767	IL-78	0073487598	6510	**Ex-UR-78767 (painting error, see RA-76767/**
				Russian Air Force)! Converted to IL-76MD
UR-76777	IL-76TD	0083482490	6303	Ex-Azov-Avia, transferred 1997
	'Falsie'			
UR-78752	IL-76MD	0083483519	6310	Ex-Air Ukraine/Borispol' United Flight
				Detachment. **Repainted as IL-76TD 'Falsie'**
				UR-76752 in 1998 and leased to AZAL-Avia
				Cargo? (see RA-76752 / Kras Air!)
UR-78758	IL-76MD	0083484551	6408	
UR-78772	IL-76MD	0083487627	6607	

There is some confusion concerning UR-78752. The JP Airline-Fleets International yearbook states the aircraft was transferred to ATI Airlines in 1997 but the aircraft has been reported as operated by Air Ukraine in February 1998!

RA-76798, one of Volga-Dnepr's IL-76TDs, in basic Aeroflot colours awaiting overhaul at Moscow-Bykovo on 16th June 2000. Note the tail servicing gantry slid apart to let the tail pass. Peter Davison

IL-76TD EZ-F421, the first of eight delivered to Turkmenistan/Akhal Airlines. Peter Davison

With stormy skies as a dramatic backdrop, Ukrainian Air Force IL-76MD UR-76413 taxies out at Fairford during RIAT'99; the blue/yellow cheatline reveals previous ownership by Busol Airline. Note the IL-76MF-style wingtips with built-in ECM aerials. Yefim Gordon

Ukrainian Air Force IL-76MD UR-78820 shares the ramp at RAF Fairford with an AFRes KC-135E (57-1479) and a 305th Wing KC-135R during the 1996 Royal International Air Tattoo on 20th July. Writing the registration on the fuselage instead of the tail was common practice for Ukrainian *Candids*. Peter Davison

Simferopol'-based **ATLANT-SV** [–/ATG] was the largest Ukrainian paramilitary operator of the type, operating 44 IL-76MDs. The airline ceased operations in 1997.

Registration	Version	C/n	F/n	Notes
UR-76316	IL-76MD	0043454633	4109	Ex-CCCP-76606. To Liana Aircompany 1995
UR-76317	IL-76MD	0053458733	4404	Ex-CCCP-76627
UR-76318	IL-76MD	0023438127	2902	Ex-CCCP-86918
UR-76319	IL-76MD	0023438129	2903	Ex-CCCP-86919
UR-76320	IL-76MD	0043455686	4302	Ex-CCCP-76619. To Liana Aircompany 1995
UR-76321	IL-76MD	0053457713	4309	Ex-CCCP-76625
UR-76322	IL-76MD	0053462873	4709	Ex-CCCP-76652
UR-76323	IL-76MD	0063466988	5007	Ex-CCCP-76673, operated for UNPF in ex-Yugoslavia
UR-76382	IL-76MD	0023436048	2702	Ex-IL-76MD UR-86903. Leased to Hungarian-Ukrainian Heavy Lift 16-8-96 as HA-TCG
UR-76390	IL-76MD	0043453562	4001	Ex-CCCP-76593
UR-76391	IL-76MD	0043453568	4002	Ex-CCCP-76594
UR-76392	IL-76MD	0043454602	4101	Ex-CCCP-76600. Operated for UNPF in Kenya (1993)
UR-76393	IL-76MD	0043455653	4204	Ex-CCCP-76611. Operated for ICRC in ex-Yugoslavia (1994)
UR-76394	IL-76MD	0063466989	5008	Ex-CCCP-76674. To Polissyaaviatrans 1995
UR-76408	IL-76MD	0053460820	4605	Ex-CCCP-76408, ex-CCCP-76642. Was leased to Pacific Express as RA-76408
UR-76423	IL-76MD	0053457720	4310	Ex-CCCP-76423, ex-CCCP-76626. To Atlant-Soyuz as RA-76423
UR-76424	IL-76MD	0063470096	5304	Ex-CCCP-76692, operated for UNPF. Sold to ATI Airlines
UR-76433	IL-76MD	0053460827	4607	Ex-CCCP-76644, operated for UNPF
UR-76443	IL-76MD	0043452534	3904	Ex-CCCP-76443, ex-CCCP-76589, was operated for UNPF in Kenya (1993)
UR-76444	IL-76MD	0063470113	5309	Ex-CCCP-76696. To Atlant-Soyuz 1994 as RA-76444
UR-76568	IL-76MD	0033448420	3605	
UR-76570	IL-76MD	0033448427	3607	
UR-76571	IL-76MD	0033448429	3608	To Bel'bek 5P by 2-95
UR-76573	IL-76MD	0033449437	3610	
UR-76578	IL-76MD	0043449468	3707	
UR-76579	IL-76MD	0043449471	3708	
UR-76580	IL-76MD	0043450476	3709	To Bel'bek 5P by 3-95
UR-76581	IL-76MD	0043450484	3801	To Air Ukraine/Borispol' United Flight Detachment
UR-76582	IL-76MD	0043450487	3802	
UR-76583	IL-76MD	0043450491	3803	To Air Ukraine/Borispol' United Flight Detachment
UR-76590	IL-76MD	0043452544	3906	To ATI Airlines by 3-96?
UR-76595	IL-76MD	0043453571	4003	
UR-76601	IL-76MD	0043454606	4102	To Ukrainian Air Force
UR-76603	IL-76MD	0043454623	4106	
UR-76614	IL-76MD	0043455665	4207	
UR-76622	IL-76MD	0053457702	4306	To Air Service Ukraine 1996
UR-76630	IL-76MD	0053458749	4408	Operated for UNPF in ex-Yugoslavia. To Polissyaaviatrans 1995 (leased? – see below)
UR-76637	IL-76MD	0053460797	4510	
UR-76683	IL-76MD	0063468029	5108	To Veteran Airline
UR-78786	IL-76MD	0093490694	6804	To Air Service Ukraine 10-95
UR-78820	IL-76MD	0093496907	7307	To Atlant-Soyuz as RA-78820
UR-86903	IL-76MD	0023436048	2702	Reregistered UR-76383 (which see)
UR-86909	IL-76MD	0023437076	2709	To Atlant-Soyuz as RA-76383
86920	IL-76MD	0023440152	2908	Leased from/returned to Liana Aircompany 1997, Liana/Atlant titles

AVILOND TAC [–/LON] of Feodosiya on the Crimea peninsula operated IL-76MDs UR-76441 (ex-UR-76617?, c/n 0043455677?, f/n 4210) and UR-76654 (c/n 0053462884, f/n 4801) from 1995 until its demise in 1998.

AZOV AVIA [–/AZV] operated four IL-76MDs of the Melitopol' airlift regiment. Two of the original aircraft remained by 1999; the rest were replaced by two other *Candid-Bs*.

Registration	Version	C/n	F/n	Notes
76645	IL-76MD	0053461834	4609	New operator unknown
UR-76656	IL-76MD	0053463891	4803	Ex-ANTAU, transferred 1996
UR-76715	IL-76MD?	0073479394?	6009?	Out-of-sequence registration. Reportedly to Ukrainian Cargo Airways as UR-UCA (ex-Busol Airline/**converted IL-78**) but still listed in JP 2000 as IL-76MD!
UR-76777	IL-76TD 'Falsie' ?	0083482490	6303	To ATI Airlines 1997
UR-UCT	IL-76MD	0063470089	5303	Ex-Veteran Airline UR-76691. Lsd from / returned to Ukraine Cargo Airways; all-white, no titles
UR-UCU	IL-76MD	0073476275	5709	Ex-Veteran Airline UR-76729. Leased from Ukraine Cargo Airways, returned?

The airline **BEL'BEK 5P** operated three IL-76MDs until its demise in 1996.

Registration	Version	C/n	F/n	Notes
UR-76571	IL-76MD	0033448429	3608	Ex-Atlant-SV, in service 2-95
UR-76580	IL-76MD	0043450476	3709	Ex-Atlant-SV, in service 3-95
UR-76681	IL-76MD	0063467021	5106	To ANTAU

Kiev-based **BSL AIRLINE** [–/BSL] operated at least nine of the 409th SAP IL-78s from Uzin AB, all of them converted to IL-76MDs, until it suspended operations in 1998.

Registration	Version	C/n	F/n	Notes
UR-76610	IL-76MD	0043454640	4110	To Ukrainian Air Force
UR-76670	IL-76MD	0063465958	4910	
UR-76689	IL-76MD	0063469066	5207	Originally flown as 76689
UR-76690	IL-76MD	0063469080	5210	
UR-76721	IL-76MD	0073475239	5610	
UR-76724?	IL-76MD	0073475250	5703	To Russian Air Force as IL-76MD RA-76724? Possibly a mis-sighting of UR-76742!
UR-76730	IL-76MD	0073476277	5710	WFU 1997?
UR-76742	IL-76MD	0073478346	5907	
UR-76744	IL-76MD	0073478359	5910	To Air Service Ukraine 1997
UR-76760	IL-76MD	0073479400	6010	

BUSOL AIRLINE [–/BUA] (the name, pronounced *boosol*, is Ukrainian for 'stork'), also based in Kiev, operated eight 409th SAP *Candids*. Unlike most UAF IL-76s and IL-78s, they had a cheatline in the national flag colours of blue and yellow and a stork superimposed on a Ukrainian flag on the tail. This airline also vanished in 1998.

Registration	Version	C/n	F/n	Notes
UR-76412	IL-76TD 'Falsie'	0083488638	6610	Ex-IL-76MD CCCP-78773. To Ukrainian Cargo Airways as UR-UCF
UR-76413	IL-76MD	1013407215	8104	Ex-CCCP-78853; sometimes reported in error as IL-76TD 'Falsie'. To Ukrainian Air Force
UR-76414	IL-78	0083482478	6210	Ex-CCCP-76774. **Converted to IL-76MD.** To Ukrainian Air Force
UR-76415	IL-78	0083481440	6110	Ex-CCCP-76775. **Converted to IL-76MD.** To Ukrainian Air Force
UR-76609	IL-78	0043453597	4010	Out-of-sequence registration. **Converted to IL-76MD.** WFU 1998?
UR-76680	IL-76MD	0063467020	5105	To Ukrainian Air Force?
UR-76682	IL-78	0063467027	5107	**Converted to IL-76MD**
UR-76715	IL-78	0073479394	6009	Out-of-sequence registration. **Converted to IL-76MD.** To AzovAvia

UR-76413 is unusual in having IL-76MF-style wingtips with built-in ECM aerials.

Now-defunct **EAST AIR** operated IL-76MD UR-76620 (c/n 0043456692, f/n 4303) and UR-76704 (c/n 0063471150, f/n 5408) in late 1995. Both were later transferred to Volare Aviation Enterprise; however, UR-76704 was leased from / jointly operated with Volare in June 1999.

HOSEBA AIRLINES [–/HOS] based at Kiev-Gostomel' operated six IL-76MDs until liquidated in 1997.

Registration	Version	C/n	F/n	Notes
UR-76532	IL-76MD	0023441201	3101	
UR-76534	IL-76MD	0023442210	3103	Operated for UNPF in ex-Yugoslavia (1994) and Angola (1996)
UR-76535	IL-76MD	0023442213	3104	Ex-Veteran Airline, transferred by 5-94
UR-76539	IL-76MD	0023442234	3109	Crashed at Kinshasa-N'djili 6-6-96
UR-78752	IL-76MD	0083483519	6310	To Volare Aviation Enterprise
UR-86921	IL-76MD	0023440161	3001	Stored Zhukovskiy. Basic Aeroflot colours, no titles. **Converted to IL-76TD** and sold to Sakha-Avia as RA-76849?

KHORS AIRCOMPANY [X6/KHO, later X9/KHO][11] (named after the sun god of the ancient Slavic peoples in pre-Christian times) operated 17 IL-76MDs.

Registration	Version	C/n	F/n	Notes
UR-76395	IL-76MD	0033443255	3204	Ex-CCCP-76543. Sometimes reported in error as ex-CCCP-76595 (see Atlant-SV)
UR-76396	IL-76MD	0043451508	3807	Ex-CCCP-76586
UR-76397	IL-76MD	0043451517	3810	Ex-CCCP-76587
UR-76398	IL-76MD	0083484522	6401	Ex-CCCP-78753. To Ukrainian Cargo Airways 1998 as UR-UCE (see end of table!)
UR-76399	IL-76MD	0083485566	6502	Ex-CCCP-78760. To Ukrainian Cargo Airways 1998 as UR-UCY
UR-76437	IL-76MD	0083484527	6402	Ex-Ecopatrol; ex-CCCP-76437, ex-CCCP-78754. To Ecopatrol (Hungary) as HA-TCJ 29-4-99
UR-76438	IL-76TD 'Falsie'	0083483513	6309	Ex-Ecopatrol (ex-IL-76MD), basic Ecopatrol colour scheme; ex-CCCP-78751. To Ecopatrol (Hungary) as HA-TCH 4-3-99
CCCP-76536	IL-76MD	0023442221	3106	To Veteran Airline as UR-76536 (?)
UR-76651	IL-78	0053462872	4708	Converted to IL-76MD
UR-76664	IL-76MD	0053464926	4902	Ex-ANTAU, transferred by 7-95
UR-78734	IL-76MD	1013409303	8306	Ex-CCCP-78734 #2*. Sold to Hungarian-Ukrainian Heavy Lift as IL-76TD 'Falsie' HA-TCA
UR-78736	IL-76MD	1013408257	8205	Ex-CCCP-78736 #2*. Sold to Hungarian-Ukrainian Heavy Lift as IL-76TD 'Falsie' HA-TCB
UR-78755	IL-76MD	0083484531	6403	To Ukrainian Cargo Airways 1998 as UR-UCJ
UR-78775	IL-76MD	0083489647	6702	To Ukrainian Cargo Airways 1998 as UR-UCC
CCCP-86899	IL-76MD	0023435030	2608	
UR-UCE	IL-76MD	0083484522	6401	Leased from Ukrainian Cargo Airways, 1-2000 (see above!)
UR-UCJ	IL-76MD	0083484531	6403	Leased from Ukrainian Cargo Airways (see above!)

* **Note:** The registration CCCP-78734 was earlier applied to An-26 c/n 4707 which was reregistered CCCP-26215 by May 1989. The registration CCCP-78736 was earlier applied to an An-8 presumably retired by 1991.

LIANA AIRCOMPANY [–/RKS] based in Kiev (called **Lana** by some sources) operated seven IL-76MDs until liquidated in 1998.

Registration	Version	C/n	F/n	Notes
UR-76316	IL-76MD	0043454633	4109	Ex-Atlant-SV, transferred 1995; ex-CCCP-76606

UR-76320	IL-76MD	0043455686	4302	Ex-Atlant-SV, transferred 1995; ex-CCCP-76619. Not current 1997
UR-76574	IL-76MD	0033449441	3701	To Ukrainian Air Force
UR-76618	IL-76MD	0053455682	4301	In service by 2-95
UR-76716	IL-76MD	0073474211	5603	Ex-Dobrolyot RA-76716 (returned from lease)? To ATI Airlines 1997
UR-86916	IL-76MD	0023438120	2810	To Ukrainian Air Force
UR-86920	IL-76MD	0023440152	2908	To Ukrainian Air Force

POLISSYAAVIATRANS (Poles'ye Air Transport) [–/POS] of Zhitomir had five IL-76MDs in its fleet. The airline ceased operations in 1998.

Registration	Version	C/n	F/n	Notes
UR-76394	IL-76MD	0063466989	5008	Ex-Atlant-SV; ex-CCCP-76674
UR-76624	IL-76MD	0053457710	4308	To Ukrainian Air Force
UR-76630	IL-76MD	0053458749	4408	Leased from Atlant-SV? To Ukrainian Cargo Airways 3-98 as UR-UCO
UR-76663	IL-76MD	0053464922	4901	Ex-Air Service Ukraine
UR-76695	IL-76MD	0063470112	5308	

UKRAINIAN CARGO AIRWAYS (UCA, or UATK – *Ookrayins'ka aviatseeyna trahnsportna kompahniya*) [–/UKS] based in Zaporozhye (not to be confused with Cargo Ukrainian Airlines described later!) operated at least 15 IL-76MDs.

Registration	Version	C/n	F/n	Notes
UR-UCA	IL-78	0073479394	6009	**Converted to IL-76MD**, reported as ex-Azov-Avia UR-76715 but has ex-Busol Airline cheatline! In service 3-98
UR-UCC	IL-76MD	0083489647	6702	Ex-Khors Aircompany UR-78775; leased back to Khors 1-2000
UR-UCD	IL-76MD	0083488643	6701	Ex-UR-78774
UR-UCE	IL-76MD	0083484522	6401	Ex-Khors Aircompany UR-76398, ex-CCCP-78753; leased to Khors 1-2000
UR-UCF	IL-76TD 'Falsie'	0083488638	6610	**Converted IL-78**. Ex-Busol Airline UR-76412, ex-UR-78773
UR-UCG	IL-78	0083482478	6210	**Converted to IL-76MD**. Ex-Ukrainian Air Force UR-76414; ex-CCCP-76774
UR-UCH	IL-76MD	0083484536	6404	Ex-Air Service Ukraine UR-78756
UR-UCI	IL-78	0083481440	6110	**Converted to IL-76MD**. Ex-Ukrainian Air Force UR-76415, ex-CCCP-76775. Leased to Air Sofia, crashed Asmara 18-7-98
UR-UCJ	IL-76MD	0083484531	6403	Ex-Khors Aircompany UR-78755. Leased back to Khors 1-2000
UR-UCO	IL-76MD	0053458749	4408	Ex-Atlant-SV (Polissyaaviatrans?) UR-76630
UR-UCR	IL-76MD	0073475270	5708	Ex-Veteran Airline UR-76728
UR-UCS	IL-76MD	0063470113	5309	Ex-Veteran Airline RA-76444. Operated by KFOR 7-99, white overall with United Nations titles
UR-UCT	IL-76MD	0063470089	5303	Ex-Veteran Airline UR-76691
UR-UCU	IL-76MD	0073476275	5709	Ex-Veteran Airline UR-76729, leased to Azov Avia?
UR-UCY	IL-76MD	0083485566	6502	Ex-Khors Aircompany UR-76399, ex-CCCP-78760

VETERAN AIRLINES [–/VPB] operated 17 IL-76MDs belonging to the airlift regiment in Dzhankoy. Originally the aircraft wore basic Aeroflot colours with blue 'Veteran' titles and an all-white tail; it was not until 1997 that some aircraft got a tail logo (a blue circle with a yellow V). The name is oddly appropriate, considering that many of the airline's aircraft are Afghan War veterans. By 2000 all of the airline's *Candids* had apparently been sold off.

Registration	Version	C/n	F/n	Notes
UR-76535	IL-76MD	0023442213	3104	To Hoseba by 5-94
UR-76536?	IL-76MD	0023442221	3106	Ex-Khors. Ever flown with UR- prefix?
				New operator unknown
UR-76647	IL-76MD	0053461843	4701	Not in 1998 fleet list, new operator unknown
UR-76667	IL-76MD	0053465941	4906	New operator unknown
UR-76671	IL-76MD	0063465963	5001	Was leased to Imair as 4K-76671.
				New operator unknown
UR-76676	IL-76MD	0063467003	5101	New operator unknown
UR-76677	IL-76MD	0063467005	5102	Was leased to Imair as 4K-76677.
				To Ukrainian Air Force by 1999
UR-76683	IL-76MD	0063468029	5108	Ex-Atlant-SV. New operator unknown
UR-76684	IL-76MD	0063468036	5109	Not in 1998 fleet list, new operator unknown
UR-76691	IL-76MD	0063470089	5303	To Ukrainian Cargo Airways / Azov Avia 1999
				as UR-UCT
UR-76694	IL-76MD	0063470107	5307	Not in 1998 fleet list, new operator unknown
UR-76697	IL-76MD	0063470118	5310	To Ukrainian Air Force by 2000
UR-76698	IL-76MD	0063471123	5401	Not in 1998 fleet list, new operator unknown
UR-76707	IL-76MD	0063472166	5502	Leased (sold?) to Quick Air Trans 1996
				as HA-TCE
UR-76717	IL-76MD	0073474216	5604	Was leased to Imair as 4K-76717.
				New operator unknown
UR-76728	IL-76MD	0073475270	5708	To Ukrainian Cargo Airways as UR-UCR
UR-76729	IL-76MD	0073476275	5709	To Ukrainian Cargo Airways / Azov Avia 1999
				as UR-UCU

VOLARE AVIATION ENTERPRISE JOINT-STOCK COMPANY

[F7/VRE] was another 'airline' of the regiment based in Krivoy Rog, operating eight IL-76MDs.

Registration	Version	C/n	F/n	Notes
UR-76576	IL-76MD	0033449449	3703	
UR-76620	IL-76MD	0043456692	4303	Ex-East Air
UR-76628	IL-76MD	0053458741	4406	C/n also reported as 0053458743.
				Ex-Air Ukraine Cargo, transferred 1997.
				Leased to East Line by 3-2000
UR-76636	IL-76MD	0053459781	4506	Type uncertain (also reported as IL-78
				converted to IL-76MD). Leased to East Line
				1998 as IL-76TD 'Falsie'
UR-76687	IL-76MD	0063469051	5203	Ex-Ukrainian Air Force, transferred 1997;
				became an IL-76TD 'Falsie' after return from
				lease to Abakan-Avia 3-2000
UR-76704	IL-76MD	0063471150	5408	Ex-East Air; leased to / jointly operated with
				East Air 6-99
UR-76727	IL-76MD	0073475268	5707	Leased to East Line 1998 as IL-76TD 'Falsie'
UR-78752	IL-76MD	0083483519	6310	Ex-Hoseba. To Air Ukraine/Borispol' United
				Flight Detachment 2-98

YUZHMASHAVIA

YUZHMASHAVIA [–/UMK], the flying division of the Southern Machinery Factory (YuMZ, *Yoozhnyy mashinostroitel'nyy zavod*) in Dnepropetrovsk, has two IL-76MDs – UR-78785 (c/n 0083489691, f/n 6803) and UR-78786 (c/n 0083490694, f/n 6804). In 'civvy street' the Southern Machinery Factory is best known for its wheeled tractors, but it is primarily a defence industry enterprise producing ballistic missiles.

AIR UKRAINE/AVIALINÏÏ UKRAÏNY

AIR UKRAINE/AVIALINÏÏ UKRAÏNY [6U/UKR], the Ukrainian flag carrier, leased at least ten IL-76MDs from the Ukrainian Air Force.

Registration	Version	C/n	F/n	Notes
UR-76555	IL-76MD	0033446325	3402	In service 1994/sub-leased to Air Ukraine Cargo
UR-76563	IL-76MD	0033447372	3503	
UR-76581	IL-76MD	0043450484	3801	Ex-Atlant-SV
UR-76583	IL-76MD	0043450491	3803	Ex-Atlant-SV

Registration	Version	C/n	F/n	Notes
UR-76688	IL-76TD	0063469062	5206	Originally operated as IL-76MD
	'Falsie'			
UR-76705	IL-76MD	0063472158	5410	Ex-ANTAU
UR-76748	IL-76MD	0073479386	6007	
76749	IL-76MD	0073479392	6008	
UR-76778	IL-76MD	0083483502	6306	Ex-ANTAU. C/n also reported as 0083482502
UR-78752	IL-76MD	0083483519	6310	Ex-Volare. To ATI Airlines
UR-78772	IL-76MD	0083487627	6607	Operated 11-95. To ATI Airlines

The freighters were operated by the Borispol' United Flight Detachment based at Kiev-Borispol', except UR-76705 and UR-76778 which were (and are) operated by the L'vov Air Enterprise, which has now become an independent carrier, **L'VOV AIRLINES** (*L'vivs'ki avialinii*) [–/UKW].

In 1998 Ukrainian Cargo Airways IL-76MD UR-UCH was seen with small Air Ukraine titles on the forward fuselage. However, it is not clear whether the aircraft was leased as such from UCA, or it had been previously leased from Air Service Ukraine as UR-78756 and already had Air Ukraine titles before being reregistered.

Three IL-76MDs of the UAF's Zaporozhye regiment were operated by the **ECOPATROL** environmental organization (*Mahloye predpriyahtiye Ekopatrool'* – Ecopatrol Small Enterprise) [–/EKP]. In 1997 Ecopatrol 'was swallowed by a horse', ie, merged into Khors Aircompany.

Registration	Version	C/n	F/n	Notes
UR-76437	IL-76MD	0083484527	6402	Ex-Hungarian-Ukrainian Heavy Lift CCCP-76437,
				ex-CCCP-78754
UR-76438	IL-76MD	0083483513	6309	Ex-Khors 76438, ex-CCCP-78751. Became an
				IL-76TD 'Falsie' after transfer to Khors
UR-76747?	IL-76MD	0073479381	6006	UR- prefix doubtful! To Russian Air Force as
				RA-76747

UES-AVIA (YeES-Avia) [–/UES], a subsidiary of the United Energy Systems of Ukraine, operated IL-76TD 'Falsie' UR-78734 bought from HUK Hungarian-Ukrainian Airlines in 1996 (ex-HA-TCA, c/n 1013409303, f/n 8306); the aircraft was promptly leased back to HUK Hungarian-Ukrainian Airlines.

In 1998 UR-78734 was sold to the airline **YOOZHNOYE** [–/UZH] established same year in Krivoy Rog and the lease was terminated. The airline's name is Russian for 'southern'; the neuter gender here apparently implies *Yoozhnoye aviapredpriyahtiye* – Southern Air Enterprise.

Additionally, on 10th March 1993 an IL-76 belonging to an unknown operator overflew the UK using the callsign UR-ALC. It is possible that this registration was fictitious, ie, used only as a callsign and never actually applied.

UZBEKISTAN

The **UZBEKISTAN AIR FORCE** operates five *Candids*, including IL-76TD UK-76364 (plus probably UK-76365, UK-76376 and UK-76377) leased or bought from Avialeasing (see below).

There have also been reports of IL-76MDs registered UK-76552, UK-78783, UK-86901, UK-86913 and UK-86915. However, these are extremely doubtful, since these *Candid-Bs* are now known to be Russian Air Force RA-76552 (a misquote for IL-76TD UK 76352?), Azerbaijan Air Force AHY-78001 (ex-CCCP-78783!), Russian Air Force RA-86901, CCCP-86913 (stored at Ivanovo) and Ukrainian Air Force UR-86915 (UK-86915 was probably a typing error).

AIRSTARS (or, in Russian, Aerostars) leases IL-76TD UK 76831 from TAPO-Avia (see below) by July 2000. The aircraft is in basic TAPO-Avia colours with Airstars (to port) / Aerostars (to starboard) titles and logo.

AVIALEASING AVIATION COMPANY

AVIALEASING AVIATION COMPANY [AD/TWN], an Uzbek/US joint venture based at Tashkent-International (Sergheli) airport, had at least seven IL-76TDs which it leased to other operators.

Registration	Version	C/n	F/n	Notes
UK-76364	IL-76TD	1043419657	9205	Basic Aeroflot colours, no titles. Leased (sold?) to Uzbekistan Air Force
UK-76365	IL-76TD	1043420667	9207	Leased to Uzbekistan Air Force?
UK-76376	IL-76TD	1033417541	8906	Bought 1997. Leased to Uzbekistan Air Force?
UK-76377	IL-76TD	1033417545	8907	Leased to Uzbekistan Air Force?
UK-76410	IL-76TD	1023412411	8603	Ex-Sayakhat UN-76410, bought by 8-97; Sayakhat cheatline, blue Avialeasing titles
UK 76447	IL-76TD	1023412389	8508	Full colour scheme. Leased to AZAL Avia Cargo 1998; reregistered 4K-AZ14 by 11-99
CCCP-76824	IL-76TD	1013410327	8402	Leased, later sold, to Uzbekistan Airways

UZBEKISTAN AIRWAYS

UZBEKISTAN AIRWAYS (Uzbekiston Havo Yullari) [HY/UZB], the Uzbek flag carrier based at Tashkent-International and Samarkand, had 21 IL-76TDs. The airline has a penchant for changing its livery, and the *Candids* have worn three different colour schemes (basic Aeroflot colours with *Uzbekistan* titles and Uzbek flag on the tail; blue/white/green cheatline, grey undersurfaces, Cyrillic *Uzbekiston Havo Yullari* titles and white tail with Uzbek flag; or blue/white/green cheatline, grey undersurfaces, *Uzbekistan* titles and blue tail with stylised bird logo). Most aircraft have the registration painted on with no dash after the prefix.

Registration	Version	C/n	F/n	Notes
UK-76351	IL-76TD	1023408240	8110	Old full colour scheme, later new full c/s
UK 76352	IL-76TD	1023411378	8505	Old full colour scheme. Sold to Aviaprad 1996
UK 76353	IL-76TD	1023414454	8704	Old full colour scheme. Leased to East Line 1998 in East Line colour scheme
UK-76358	IL-76TD	1033410339	8405	
UK-76359	IL-76TD	1033414483	8801	Lsd to East Line 1999 in East Line colour scheme
UK 76386	IL-76TD	1033418600	9010	New full colour scheme. Sold to Uralinteravia 1994 as RA 76386
UK-76426 (1)	IL-76TD	1013405184	8006	Ex-Allwe RA-76426, bought 10-96, basic Aeroflot colours. Sold to unknown operator as RA-76426 by 8-99
UK 76426 (2)	IL-76TD	1043419644	9201	Second active aircraft registered -76426! Registration allocated in error?
UK-76427?	IL-76TD	1013406207	8102	Reported for Uzbekistan Airways 11-94 – never delivered or erroneous report? To Tashkent Aircraft Production Corporation
UK 76428	IL-76TD	1043419648	9202	
UK-76447		1023412389	8508	Basic Aeroflot colours, Uzbekistan titles and Uzbek flag. Leased from Avialeasing 1994 to ?-??

UK-76448	IL-76TD	1023413443	8701	Lsd to East Line 7-98 in East Line colour scheme
UK-76449	IL-76TD	1023403258	7705	Was leased to UNPF. New full c/s. Leased to East Line 1998 in East Line colour scheme*
UK 76782	IL-76TD	0093498971	7503	New full colour scheme. Lsd to East Line 1997-98
UK-76793	IL-76TD	0093498951	7408	
UK-76794	IL-76TD	0093498954	7409	Damaged Peshawar 21-4-93 as CCCP-76794 and repaired. Stored Tashkent-International
UK-76805	IL-76TD	1003403109	7808	C/n also reported as 1003403105. Sold to Uzbekistan Intercargo Services 3-98
UK 76811	IL-76TD	1013407223	8106	New full colour scheme
UK-76813	IL-76TD	1013408246	8202	
CCCP-76824	IL-76TD	1013410327	8402	Leased from Avialeasing in old full colour scheme, later operated as 76824, still later repainted in new full colour scheme as UK 76824. Leased to East Line 1997-98
UK 76831	IL-76TD	1013409287	8302	New full colour scheme. Never delivered? To Tashkent Aircraft Production Corporation 2-92

* After being repainted in East Line colours the aircraft had the registration applied as UK-76449.

In March 2000 Uzbekistan Airways ordered two IL-76TFs (see Russian section/East Line for details).

IL-76TD UK-76805 was sold to newly-established **UZBEKISTAN INTERCARGO SERVICES** in March 1998. By June 1999 the aircraft had been leased to East Line.

TAPO-AVIA

TAPO-AVIA [PQ/CTP, later 4C/TPR],[12] the flying division of the Tashkent Aircraft Production Corporation based at Tashkent-Vostochnyy airfield, has five *Candids*. Besides acting as support aircraft and generating additional revenue by carrying commercial cargo, they help advertise the factory and the aircraft it builds, being painted in the Tashkent Aircraft Production Corporation's smart livery.

Registration	Version	C/n	F/n	Notes
UK-76375	IL-76TD	1033414496	8804	
UK-76427	IL-76TD	1013406207	8102	Ex-Uzbekistan Airways? Leased to Krylo (Russia) by 10-99
UK 76821	IL-76TD 'Falsie'	0023441200	3010	Ex-CCCP-76821, ex-Iraqi Air Force IL-76MD YI-ALR, returned 4-91
UK 76831	IL-76TD	1013409287	8302	Ex-Uzbekistan Airways, bought 2-92; leased to Airstars by 7-2000
UK 76844	IL-76TD	1033416525	8902?	Leased to Krylo by 10-99

From 2nd-7th December, 1997 IL-76TD UK 76844 was displayed at the LIMA'97 airshow (Langkawi airbase, Malaysia). The aircraft was captained by V I Tikhonov; Ghenrikh V Novozhilov headed the Ilyushin OKB delegation at the show.

ATI Airlines IL-78 UR-76759 (ex-UR-78759) with all refuelling equipment removed (note the fuselage illumination lights under the tail). Strictly speaking, this registration cannot be used because there already was an IL-76T 'Falsie' registered RA-76759 at the time. RART

'Adorned' with one of those prolific RIAT stickers, Ukranian Cargo Airways IL-76MD UR-UCH (ex-UR-78756) departs RAF Fairford after taking part in the 1998 Royal International Air Tattoo. Yefim Gordon

Uzbekistan Airways IL-76TDs, such as UK 76428 depicted here, are frequent visitors at Sharjah. Peter Davison

Seen at Moscow-Domodedovo on 25th November 1998, IL-76TD UK 76824 displays one of Uzbekistan Airways' current liveries. The colour scheme may vary subtly from aircraft to aircraft. Note the additional East Line titles. Dmitriy Komissarov

Opposite page: UR-76705 and UR-76778, two of the IL-76MDs operated by the now-defunct Aeronavigation and Transport agency of the Ukraine (ANTAU). Note that the registration is still carried on the fin and not on the fuselage, as per Ukrainian custom. Alfred Matusevich

…and Abroad
(IL-76 Operators outside the CIS)

From the outset the IL-76 obviously had considerable export potential; of the 930 or so examples of the *Candid* family built to date, at least 119 have been delivered new to foreign customers (not counting used aircraft sold after the breakup of the Soviet Union). While this is less than the exports of the Soviet 'bestsellers', the Tu-154 and the An-24/-26/-30/-32 family, it is still an impressive figure, considering that the cargo aircraft market is rather smaller than that for passenger airliners.

Curiously, the Warsaw Pact nations never ordered the *Candid*, probably relying on Big Brother to provide strategic airlift in case of need (despite persistent allegations in the West that the type was operated by the air forces of Poland and Czechoslovakia). Foreign sales were almost entirely limited to the Soviet Union's (and later Russia's) third-world allies. Civil and military deliveries were made to 14 nations in Eastern Europe, Asia, the Middle East, North Africa and the Caribbean. It was also used by civil operators in at least 16 nations on a wet-lease basis.

Non-CIS operators of the IL-76 are listed here on a country-by-country basis. Again, in each country, military users are listed first, followed by civil ones in alphabetical order with IATA/ICAO codes as appropriate.

AFGHANISTAN

BBC TV footage broadcast on 2nd November 1988 showed an IL-76 *sans suffixe* in full Aeroflot colours but wearing the Afghan registration YA-YAA. A plate in the flight deck reportedly read 06146, indicating the registration was really CCCP-06146 – or that the c/n was 063406146. However, no such c/n exists; this could be a misread for 063406148 or 063406149 (f/n 0407 or 0408), which means the aircraft's true identity could be CCCP-86629 or -86630. Other sources state that an IL-76 was loaned by **BAKHTAR AFGHAN AIRLINES** [FG/AFG][1] from Aeroflot in 1986 and this must be the aircraft in question. However, this was almost certainly a Soviet Air Force aircraft masquerading with Afghan markings for appearance's sake – an idea soon dropped. (There have been claims that YA-YAA was really IL-76MD CCCP-86896 (c/n 0023434018, f/n 2605) which returned from Afghanistan on 12th May 1992).

ALGERIA

Starting in 1990, the **ALGERIAN AIR FORCE** (*Force Aérienne Algérienne/al Quwwat al Jawwiya al Jaza'eriya*) took delivery of nine IL-76s. The first three and the last two were factory-fresh examples; the others were used but quite new aircraft. This was something of a breakthrough for the Soviet Union/Russia, as Algeria had not purchased Soviet equipment since the early 1970s when President Col Houari Boumedienne switched allegiance to the West. The order was signed after an IL-76MD captained by Stanislav G Bliznyuk made several demonstration flights in Algeria from 15-25th March 1988.

The IL-76s serve with the 35th Transport Squadron at Boufarik AB,[2] operating alongside Lockheed C-130H and C-130H-30 Hercules. They replaced the last surviving An-12BPs, eight of which (7T-WAA through 7T-WAH) had been delivered in early 1966.[3] Like the *Cubs*, the *Candids* wear civil registrations along with Algerian Air Force insignia; unlike the An-12s, however, they have no military serials and carry Algerian Air Force titles (in Arabic to port and in English to starboard).

Registration	Version	C/n	F/n	Notes
7T-WIA	IL-76MD	0083489674	6709	
7T-WIB	IL-76MD	0093493803	7101	
7T-WIC	IL-76MD 'Falsie'	1003405154	7909	
7T-WID	IL-76TD	1023414470	8708	Ex-Arkhangel'sk Airlines RA-76419
7T-WIE	IL-76TD	1023414463	8706	Ex-TransSuper Airlines RA-76406, bought by 7-96
7T-WIG	IL-76TD	1023413435	8609	Ex-Polis-Air RA-76407
7T-WIP	IL-76TD	1043419636	9109	
7T-WIU	IL-76TD	1023413423	8606	Ex-Arkhangel'sk Airlines RA-76440
7T-WIV	IL-76TD	1043419649	9203	

Note: IL-76TD 7T-WIR was also reported but may have been a mis-sighting of 7T-WIB. The Algerian Air Force reportedly also has six IL-78 tankers also based at Boufarik but no details are known.

ANGOLA

AIR NACOIA EXPLORAÇAO DE AERONAVES [–/ANL] based in Luanda leased IL-76MD UR-76397 (ex-CCCP-76587, c/n 0043451517, f/n 3810) from Khors in March 1994.

BOSNIA-HERZEGOVINA

Two *Candids* – demilitarised IL-76TD 'Falsie' T9-QAA (ex-Atlas Air EP-ALB, c/n 0023437076, f/n 2709) and IL-76TD T9-QAB (ex-EP-ALD, c/n 1023408265, f/n 8207) – were placed on the Bosnian register in November 1998. Soon afterwards they were reregistered T9-CAC and T9-CAB respectively. The aircraft were operated by BIO Air Company [–/BIO], a division of the Bosnian Investment Organization, together with their Russian owner Ramair and, following its demise, Phoenix Aviation. T9-CAB was stored at Ostend. (See previous chapter and UAE section; see also Iranian section/Atlas Air for full details.)

BULGARIA

AIR SYDER BULGARIAN AIRWAYS [B5/SDR] leased IL-76TD CCCP-76819 (c/n 1013409274, f/n 8209) from Aeroflot in 1992.

Additionally, IL-76TD CCCP-76784 was transferred to the Bulgarian register as LZ-INK. However, this was purely a flag of convenience, since the aircraft was operated by Swiss companies (see below).

BURUNDI

Arkhangel'sk Airlines IL-76TD RA-76419 (c/n 1023414470, f/n 8708) was operated by **BURUNDI BCR CHARTER** in July 1993.

CANADA

Toronto-based **SKYLINK AVIATION, INC.** operated IL-76MD UR-76614 (c/n 0043455665, f/n 4207) leased from Atlant-SV in August 1994.

CENTRAL AFRICAN REPUBLIC

CENTRAFRICAIN AIRLINES [GC/CET] established in 1998 bought almost the entire fleet of the defunct Air Pass (see Swaziland section), including all three IL-76T 'Falsies' which were white overall without titles. Two more *Candids* joined the fleet in late 1999. Interestingly, besides Bangui (the capital of the Central African Republic), the airline is also based at Sharjah, UAE – as was Air Cess, a sister company of Air Pass (see Liberian section), which had operated these *Candids* before. It makes you wonder if all three airlines had a common owner and Centrafricain Airlines is simply the successor of Air Cess/Air Pass incorporated under a new name.

Registration	Version	C/n	F/n	Notes
TL-ACN	IL-76T 'Falsie'	053403072	0208	Demilitarised. Ex-3D-RTT, ex-EL-RDT, ex-IL-76 (military) RA-86715. F/n reported in error as 0203. Retired Umm al Quwain 31-1-2000
TL-ACU	IL-76T 'Falsie'	043402039	0110	Ex-3D-RTX, ex-EL-RDX, ex-IL-76 (military) RA-86604
TL-ACY	IL-76T 'Falsie'	0003426765	2002	Ex-3D-RTA, ex-Zenit IL-76M RA-86846. Returned or retired by 2000
TL-ADH	?	?	?	
TL-ADS	IL-76TD	0053464934?	4904?	Ex-Sol Air 3C-JJJ; ex-Aviation Tsitotrans RA-76666, converted IL-76MD?

CHINA

Starting in 1991, **CHINA UNITED AIRLINES** [–/CUA], the commercial division of the **PEOPLE'S LIBERATION ARMY AIR FORCE** (PLAAF, or *Chung-kuo Shen Min Taie-Fang-Tsun Pu-tai*), took delivery of twenty IL-76MDs. The aircraft make up the transport component of this carrier's almost entirely Russian fleet and are based at Fo Shan airbase near Beijing.

Registration	Version	C/n	F/n	Notes
B-4030	IL-76MD 'Falsie'	1013407233	8109	C/n originally reported as 1013409284
B-4031	IL-76MD 'Falsie'	1013408254	8204	C/n originally reported as 1013409288
B-4032	IL-76MD 'Falsie'	1013409289	8303	
B-4033	IL-76MD 'Falsie'	1033416512	8808	
B-4034	IL-76MD 'Falsie'	1033416524	8901	
B-4035	IL-76MD 'Falsie'	1033416529	8903	
B-4036	IL-76MD 'Falsie'	1033417550	8908	
B-4037	IL-76MD 'Falsie'	1033417557	8910	
B-4038	IL-76MD 'Falsie'	1043417567	9002	
B-4039	IL-76MD 'Falsie'	1043418576	9004	
B-4040	IL-76MD 'Falsie'	1053419656	9204	
B-4041	IL-76MD 'Falsie'	1053420663	9206	
B-4042	IL-76MD 'Falsie'	1063418587	9007	
B-4043	IL-76MD 'Falsie'	1063420671	9208	
B-4044	IL-76MD*	?	?	
B-4045	IL-76MD*	?	?	
B-4046	IL-76MD*	?	?	
B-4047	IL-76MD*	?	?	
B-4048	IL-76MD*	?	?	
B-4049	IL-76MD*	?	?	

Note: B-4044 through B-4049 are reportedly used (ex-Russian or ex-Ukrainian) aircraft and thus are very probably 'true' IL-76MDs. *Flight International* mentioned in November 2000 that 'some IL-76/78s' *(sic)* have been converted to refuelling tankers (ie, some used IL-78s may have been acquired?). Furthermore, at Airshow China 2000 held in Ahuhai on 6-12th November 2000 Russia and China negotiated the delivery of 35 more IL-76s.

As noted earlier, in 1994 the PLAAF started negotiations with Russia and Western avionics manufacturers on the conversion of the *Candid* into an AWACS platform, which ultimately resulted in the development of the A-50I equipped with the Elta EL2075 Phalcon surveillance radar. The PLAAF has a requirement for up to four aircraft; the unit price has been quoted as US$250 million.

As early as September 1997 *Flight International* reported that Israel had obtained an IL-76 for the first AWACS conversion. In reality, however, the first A-50I for China with the test and delivery registration RA-78740 (c/n 0093486579, f/n 6505) was not delivered to Israel Aircraft Industries for outfitting until 25th October 1999 (see Israeli section). However, as described in Chapter 3, the USA were displeased with the deal and eventually pressured Israel into cancelling the contract. Now the PLAAF is considering the A-50E export version of the *Mainstay* as the next-best thing.

CONGO-BRAZZAVILLE

An IL-76 (version and identity unknown) was placed on the Congolese register in early 2000 as TN-AFS. Despite its registration, however, the aircraft has been reported as operated by Air Pass (see Swaziland section).

CUBA

The fleet of **CUBANA DE AVIACIÓN** [CU/CUB], the Cuban flag carrier, includes two IL-76MD 'Falsies' originally registered CU-T1258 (c/n 0043454615, f/n 4104) and CU-T1271 (c/n 0053459767, f/n 4502). However, the aircraft were very probably operated on behalf of the **CUBAN AIR FORCE** (FAR – *Fuerza Aérea Revolucionaria*). Little is known of their activities, except that in December 1988 the second aircraft participated in Armenian quake relief flights. In 1996 the *Candids* were reregistered CU-C1258 and CU-C1271 to accentuate their pure freighter role (as were some airliners converted to all-freight configuration). CU-C1271 was apparently withdrawn from use by July 1999..

CZECH REPUBLIC

AIR MORAVIA CZECH CHARTER AIRLINE LTD [–/MAI, later –/MOA] based at Prague-Ruzyne leased IL-76MD 'Falsie' CCCP-76822 (c/n 0093499982, f/n 7506) from the Il'yushin OKB in December 1991 and IL-76T RA-76514 (c/n 083415453, f/n 1204) from Tyumen' Airlines in the mid-1990s.

EGYPT

In 1992 **CAIRO CHARTER & CARGO** bought two factory-fresh IL-76TDs, SU-OAA (c/n 1013409297, f/n 8305) and SU-OAB (c/n 1013409321, f/n 8401). The freighters wore a smart white/green/yellow colour scheme with an eagle and crescent tail logo; curiously, the registration was carried both on the aft fuselage and the outer engine nacelles. In March 1993, however, the airline sold its entire fleet to Mahan Air (Iran) and the *Candids* were reregistered EP-JAY and EP-MAH respectively.

B-4032, one of 15 IL-76MD 'Falsies' operated by the PLAAF/China United Airlines. *Chinese Airliners*

IL-76TD 'Falsie' HA-TCG (ex RA-76382) of Atlant-Aerobatics in early 2000. The aircraft previously wore this registration while with Hungarian-Ukrainian Heavy Lift. RART

K2661/A, the first IL-76MD to be delivered to the Indian Air Force. Peter Davison

Another IAF *Gajraj*, K3000/M. Note the difference in paint jobs. RART

ESTONIA

In September 1995 Tallinn-based cargo carrier **ENIMEX** [–/ENI] bought IL-76TD RA-76819 (c/n 1013409274, f/n 8209) from the defunct Russian airline Exparc. In 1998 it was sold to Elf Air, regaining its previous identity.

EQUATORIAL GUINEA

GATS GUINEA, SA [–/GTS] – see UAE section.

HUNGARY

Two IL-76s are operated by **ATLANT AEROBATICS KFT** [–/ATU], probably a sister company of the Ukrainian Atlant-SV and the Russian Atlant-Soyuz.

Registration	Version	C/n	F/n	Notes
HA-TCG	IL-76TD 'Falsie'	0023436048	2702	Ex-Atlant-Soyuz RA-76382, bought 3-2000; named Szent György (St. George)
HA-TCK	IL-76TD	1013409280	8210	Ex-S9-BAD, ex-AZAL-Avia Cargo 4K-AZ11, ex-Remex RA-76354; bought 10-99

Over the years **HUNGARIAN-UKRAINIAN HEAVY LIFT CO LTD** [–/HUK], a partner of Khors Aircompany (later renamed **HUK HUN-GARIAN-UKRAINIAN AIRLINES CO LTD**), operated at least six IL-76s from Budapest-Budaörs. (Some sources say the carrier was based at Férihegy).

Registration	Version	C/n	F/n	Notes
HA-TCA	IL-76TD 'Falsie'	1013409303	8306	Ex-Khors Aircompany IL-76MD UR-78734, D/D 27-1-94? Sold to UES-Avia* 1996 as UR-78734 / leased back from UES-Avia 1996-98
HA-TCB	IL-76TD 'Falsie'	1013408257	8205	Ex-Khors Aircompany IL-76MD UR-78736. Was leased to UNPF in ex-Yugoslavia (1994). Sold to Hunair ?-99
HA-TCG	IL-76TD 'Falsie'	0023436048	2702	Lsf Atlant-SV 16-8-96 to ?-??, ex-UR-76382 (ex-IL-76MD UR-86903). To Atlant-Soyuz as RA-76382
HA-TCH**	IL-76TD 'Falsie'	0083483513	6309	Ex-Khors Aircompany UR-76438 (ex-IL-76MD), ex-CCCP-78751. Bought 29-4-99, ex-Eco Patrol titles
HA-TCI**	'IL-76T'	073410300	0805	Ex-Air Pass RA-76430, ex-IL-76K CCCP-86729, bought 2-99
HA-TCJ**	IL-76MD	0083484527	6402	Ex-Khors Aircompany UR-76437, ex-CCCP-78754, bought 4-3-99, ex-Eco Patrol titles
CCCP-76437	IL-76MD	0083484527	6402	Ex-CCCP-78754. Leased from Ukrainian AF 12-92; to Eco Patrol by 10-93 as UR-76437

Note: * Some sources report that HA-TCA was sold to Atlant-SV, not UES-Avia; **HA-TCH, -TCI and TCJ were all reported for the already non-existent Eco Patrol in December 1999! This is rather curious, since RA-76430 was never operated by this organisation.

In 1993 the airline became the subject of a major scandal when it came to light that its aircraft were used to smuggle weapons for the Bosnian Moslems during the civil war in ex-Yugoslavia. The scandal broke when 120 tons (264,550 lb) of Chinese weapons – 10,000 Kalashnikov AKM assault rifles, 750,000 rounds of 7.62mm (.50 calibre) ammunition for same, 40 mortars and 1,000 mortar rounds – were discovered at Maribor airport, Slovenia. It turned out that the cargo had been delivered by Hungarian-Ukrainian Heavy Lift IL-76s from Khartoum. Yet the airline's management was probably unaware of this scheme – the weapons had been declared as humanitarian cargo donated by the Sudanese Red Cross and a certain Sudanese national.

In 1999 IL-76TD 'Falsie' HA-TCB was acquired by **HUNAIR HUN-GARIAN AIRLINES CO LTD** [–/HUV] based at Budapest-Férihegy.

QUICK AIR TRANS operated IL-76MD HA-TCE (ex-Veteran Airline UR-76707, c/n 0063472166, f/n 5502) during 1996-98. The ultimate fate of the aircraft is not known but it was most probably returned as UR-76707.

In 1995 **SZER-BON KFT** [–/HSB] intended to lease IL-76MD CCCP-76698 (c/n 0063471123, f/n 5401) from Veteran Airlines as HA-TCD, while **Napkelet Airlines** planned to lease IL-76MD CCCP-76729 (c/n 0073476275, f/n 5709) from the same carrier as HA-TCF. Eventually, however, neither deal materialised and the registrations were only allocated but not applied.

INDIA

The **INDIAN AIR FORCE** (IAF) selected the IL-76MD to meet the HETAC (HEavy Transport AirCraft) requirement. The type replaced the An-12BK which had given sterling service with the IAF but was getting long in the tooth; the decision was speeded by the discovery of fatigue cracks in the wing spars of some An-12s.

In February 1985 No 25 Sqn 'Himalayan Eagles' at Chandigarh and No 44 Sqn 'Mountain Geese' at Agra which had previously operated the *Cub* started taking delivery of IL-76MDs. 24 aircraft were reportedly delivered. However, only 17 have been identified by the c/ns; the rest (K2903/K, K3001 through K3005 and K3015) are a mystery, since they cannot be slotted into the production list! (In contrast, 46 An-12BKs had been delivered.) The aircraft carry Indian Air Force titles in Bengali on the port side and in English on the starboard side; squadron badges and individual letter codes were introduced soon after service entry.

Registration	Version	C/n	F/n	Notes
K2661	IL-76MD	0053458722	4401	Coded 'A'
K2662	IL-76MD	0053458725	4402	Coded 'B', No 44 Sqn
K2663	IL-76MD	0053458731	4403	Coded 'C', No 44 Sqn
K2664	IL-76MD	0053461849	4703	Coded 'D', named Kartika
K2665	IL-76MD	0053462856	4704	Coded 'E', named Rohini
K2666	IL-76MD	0053462857	4705	Coded 'F'
K2878	IL-76MD	0063465970	5003	Coded 'G'
K2879	IL-76MD	0063465973	5004	Coded 'H', No 44 Sqn
K2901	IL-76MD	0073478343	5906	
K2902	IL-76MD	0073478353	5909	Coded 'M'
K2999	IL-76MD	0073480410	6103	Coded 'U'
K3000	IL-76MD	0073480419	6105	Coded 'M'
K3012	IL-76MD	0083487614	6604	
K3013	IL-76MD	0083488629	6608	
K3014	IL-76MD	0093491750	6908	
K3077	IL-76MD	0093496892	7303	Coded 'V'
K3078	IL-76MD	0093496912	7308	Coded 'W', named Nubra

The type soon proved its worth, operating successfully from small airfields in the mountains of Ladakh State. In 1987-88 the IL-76MDs were actively used to airlift personnel and materiel to Sri Lanka during the Indian Peacekeeping Force operation, an attempt to put an end to the prolonged civil war in that country as government forces clashed with the rebel Liberation Tigers of Tamil Eelam (LTTE). Other uses included flights to the UK to pick up spares for the Indian Navy's BAe Sea Harriers. The IAF has a habit of giving popular names to the aircraft it operates – even to those that have one already; the IL-76MD is known locally as Gajraj (King Elephant).

Problems with engine starting were encountered in hot-and-high conditions. Changes had to be incorporated and the aircraft were progressively modified at the Moscow-Sheremet'yevo-1 maintenance base. Some IAF IL-76MDs were reportedly modified as electronic intelligence (ELINT) platforms.

Other members of the *Candid* family have also been considered. As early as 1988 the IAF evaluated and rejected the A-50. At that stage India's Defence Research & Development Organization (DRDO) was already working on its own AWACS. A HAL 748-224 Srs 2[4] serialled H-2175 (c/n K/748/569) was converted into an avionics testbed with a conventionally mounted rotodome called ASP (Airborne Surveillance Platform); upon completion of the trials the system would be installed on the IL-76MD. However, on 11th January 1999 the ASP crashed near Indian Navy Air Station Rajali (Arakkonam) when the rotodome separated in flight, striking the tail, and the future of the programme is now uncertain. This may account for the fact that in April 2000 the IAF leased two A-50s from the Russian Air Force; the *Mainstays* are based at Chandigarh AB.

In July 1996 India started taking delivery of Sukhoi Su-30K and Su-30MKI multi-role fighters having flight refuelling capability which led to a requirement for a refuelling tanker. A single top-up could extend the *Flanker's* range from 3,000km (1,621nm) to 5,200km (2,810nm), allowing it to be used against Pakistan and China with which India had territorial disputes. According to *Jane's Defence Weekly,* senior IAF officials said putting the Su-30s into service without three or four tankers to support them would be tantamount to buying an 'incomplete weapons system'.

The IL-78M was a logical choice, since it meant a common type rating, spares commonality etc with the familiar IL-76MD. Negotiations on buying the *Midas* began in June 1996. According to reports from New Delhi on 27th November 1997, a few days earlier India signed a contract for the purchase of an initial two IL-78Ms, with an ultimate requirement for six. Other reports say the tankers would be leased from the Russian Air Force. Yet so far there is no hard evidence that any *Midases* were actually delivered.

As *Air International* recounted in September 1997, some sources have suggested that the IL-78s could be used as AWACS platforms (!). However, this is obviously nonsense, as it would be impossible to install the AWACS mission equipment and still keep the freight hold fuel tanks, without which the transferable fuel load would be too small.

INDONESIA

Yakutavia IL-76TD CCCP-76797 (c/n 1003403052, f/n 7703) was leased by a Jakarta-based airline with the almost-unprintable name of **PENAS AIR CARGO** [–/PNS] in May 1992. The aircraft carried a Russian flag along with the old Soviet prefix at the time.

IRAN

The **ISLAMIC REPUBLIC OF IRAN AIR FORCE** (IRIAF) reportedly obtained 11 ex-Iraqi Air Force IL-76MDs (mostly 'Falsies') in January 1991 when they fled into neutral Iran at the closing stage of the Gulf War. The transports were impounded and subsequently included into the IRIAF inventory as reparations for damages sustained in the preceding war with Iraq in 1980-88. (Iran also has the IL-76MD 'Falsie' / *Baghdad-1* and *Adnan-1* and/or *-2* AWACS conversions obtained in the same way – see Iraqi section.) In 1993 these were augmented by four IL-76TDs delivered new from Russia as part of a military equipment package. Six of the transports are operated by the **Iranian Revolutionary Guard**.

The *Candids* are based at Teheran and Shiraz and wear a variety of colour schemes (white overall, grey overall and civilian-style à la Algerian Air Force with a white upper fuselage and fin, grey undersurfaces and a wide green cheatline). All of them carry an Iranian flag high on the fin and IRIAF serials ahead of the entry doors. Known Iranian Revolutionary Guard aircraft are serialled 5-2281, 5-2283 and 5-2291, while IRIAF examples identified to date are 5-8203, 5-8205 (the former *Baghdad-1* but now probably called differently!), 5-8206, 5-8207 and 5-8210.

The cargo airline **ATLAS AIR** [–/IRH] based in Tehran operated at least nine IL-76s.

Registration	Version	C/n	F/n	Notes
EP-ALA	IL-76TD	0053460795	4509	Lsf GosNII GA 1997, ex-RA-76481. Sold to Ramair 11-98 as ST-AQB
EP-ALB	IL-76TD 'Falsie'	0023437076	2709	Demilitarised. Bought 2-98, ex-Queshmair EP-TQC, ex-Air Sultan 9L-LBK, ex-Atlant-Soyuz RA-76383, ex-Atlant-SV IL-76MD UR-86909. Sold to Ramair 11-98 as T9-QAA
EP-ALC	IL-76TD	0023442218	3105	Bought 1998, ex Continental Airlines RA-76498, basic Moscow Airways colour scheme. Sold to Ramair 11-98 as ST-AQA
EP-ALD	IL-76TD	1023408265	8207	Ex-Intalair 9L-LBO, ex-Beriyev Design Bureau RA-76355. Sold to Ramair 11-98 as T9-QAB
EP-ALE	IL-76TD	0043453575	4004	Leased from Ilavia 9-98, ex-RA-76477, all-white colour scheme
EP-ALF	IL-76TD	0033448407	3602	Leased from Ilavia 9-98, ex-RA-76474; not in fleet list 2000 – returned?
EP-ALG	IL-76TD	0033448404	3601	Leased from Ilavia 10-98, ex-RA-76473
EP-ALI	IL-76TD	1003499994	7509	Ex-Magadanaerogrooz RA-76796, bought 1-99
EP-ALJ	IL-76TD 'Falsie'	0013434018	2605	Demilitarised. Leased from Zenit 12-98, ex-RA-86896

Note: No information is available on EP-ALH but it is quite possible this was an IL-76 as well – or rather the demilitarised IL-76TD 'Falsie' which later went to Ramair as T9-QAC.

As noted earlier, **MAHAN AIR** [–/IRM] based in Kerman bought the entire fleet of the defunct airline Cairo Charter & Cargo in March 1993, including IL-76TDs EP-JAY (ex-SU-OAA, c/n 1013409297, f/n 8305) and EP-MAH (ex-SU-OAB, c/n 1013409321, f/n 8401). The new owner retained the basic colours of Cairo Charter & Cargo, replacing only the titles and tail logo (an *extremely* stylised bird). EP-MAH was sold to Queshmair by July 2000 as EP-TQI.

PAYAM AIR [–/IRP], aka **PAYAM AVIATION SERVICES CO** (formerly IPTAS – Iran Postal & Telecommunications Aviation Services), based at Karaj-Payam International airport (hence the name) operates *Candids* leased from CIS operators, as required, mostly in basic Aeroflot colours.

Registration	Version	C/n	F/n	Notes
EP-TPD	IL-78	0083485558	6410	UR-76759*, converted to IL-76MD; was to be lsd from ATI Airlines 1997-8, but lease fell through
EP-TPF	IL-76T 'Falsie'	0013428831	2108	Demilitarised. Leased from Remex 1998, ex- / to RA-78731; basic Remex colours
EP-TPO / 86817	IL-76 (mil)	063407191	0508	Demilitarised. Leased from Yer-Avia 7-97, ex-EK-86817
EP-TPU (No1)	IL-78	0073487598	6510	UR-76767*, converted to IL-76MD; was to be lsd from ATI Airlines 1997-8, but lease fell through
EP-TPU (No 2)	IL-78	0093497936	7404	Leased from Tesis 3-2000, ex-RA-76791, basic Tesis colours
EP-TPV	IL-76TD	0043451523	3901	Leased from Samara Airlines by 2-2000, ex-RA-76475, basic Samara c/s (including partial titles – ie 'PAYAM airlines' instead of 'PAYAM AIR')
EP-TPW	IL-76MD	0083487627	6607	UR-78772; was to be leased from ATI Airlines 1997-98 but lease fell through
EP-TPX	IL-76MD	0083484551	6408	UR-78758; was to be leased from ATI Airlines 1997-98 but lease fell through
EP-TPY	IL-76TD 'Falsie'	0083482490	6303	UR-76777; was to be leased from ATI Airlines 1997-98 but lease fell through
EP-TPZ / 86724	IL-76 (mil)	073410284	0801	Demilitarised. Leased from Yer-Avia 1-97, ex-EK-86724

* See comment in previous chapter (Ukrainian section/ATI Airlines).

UR-78772 was initially operated in hybrid markings in December 1996 with ATI Airlines titles above the cheatline, the Iranian flag and Payam Air badge on the tail and Payam Air titles below the cheatline ahead of the entry doors. EP-TPO and EP-TPZ still carry their original registrations (minus prefix) on the aft fuselage.

IL-76 *sans suffixe* EP-TPO (ex-EK-86817), one of several *Candids* leased by Payam Air, being unloaded at Moscow-Domodedovo in November 1998. Dmitriy Komissarov

The airline's name, logo and registration are painted differently on EP-TPO/86817 and EP-TPZ/86724. Both aircraft were frequent visitors to Moscow-Domodedovo in 1998-99. Dmitriy Komissarov

Most Iraqi Air Force *Candids* (illustrated by IL-76 *sans suffixe* YI-AIN) wore standard Iraqi Airways livery. RART

QESHMAIR [–/IRQ], also rendered as Qeshm Air or Qeshm Airlines, operated a single IL-76TD 'Falsie' leased from the Sierra Leonean airline Air Sultan in 1997 and registered EP-TQC (ex-9L-LBK, ex-RA-76383, ex-IL-76MD UR-86909). In February 1998 the aircraft went to Atlas Air as EP-ALB. Another IL-76TD was bought from Mahan Air by July 2000, becoming EP-TQI (ex-EP-MAH); it retains basic Mahan Air colours. Incidentally, Qeshmair has been dubbed *aviakompahniya 'Koshmar'* (Nightmare Airlines, or 'Nightmair') by Russian spotters – for purely phonetic reasons. As you see, etymology is fun!

SAFIRAN AIRLINES [–/SFN], flies cargo charters with aircraft leased as required, including IL-76s. Since September 2000 it operates IL-76TD EP-SFA leased from Magadanavialeasing (ex-RA-76787, c/n 0093495854, f/n 7204). The aircraft was in basic Aeroflot colours with Safiran Airlines titles in Farsi on the nose and English on the aft fuselage and traces of the Russian flag visible underneath the tail logo.

An **UNIDENTIFIED IRANIAN OPERATOR** leased IL-76TD RA-76471 (c/n 0033446345, f/n 3407) from Magadanaerogrooz in 1994. The aircraft received the registration EP-MKA which was carried on the nose in addition to the Russian registration on the tail.

Another **UNIDENTIFIED IRANIAN AIRLINE** operates IL-76 EP-CFA (version unknown). The all-white aircraft with no titles or logo was seen at Sharjah in July 2000.

IRAQ

Iraq was the first – and largest – export customer for the type, taking delivery of the first *Candids* in 1977; at least 41 examples had been delivered by 1990. Though nominally operated by **IRAQI AIRWAYS** [IA/IAW] and usually wearing Iraqi Airways livery, the aircraft were in fact owned by the **IRAQI AIR FORCE** (IrAF, or *al Quwwat al-Jawwiya al-Iraqiya*). Incidentally, the colour scheme was non-standard; Iraqi Airways Boeing 707s and 747s had a dark green top to the fuselage, a leaf green/white cheatline and grey undersurfaces, but on the IL-76 the dark green top colour was replaced by black. Some examples *did* wear overt military markings and a grey/white colour scheme, but such aircraft were rare; most of them later received Iraqi Airways titles and logos while retaining the basic IrAF colour scheme.

Registration	Version	C/n	F/n	Notes
YI-AIK	IL-76 (mil)	073410292	0803	Returned by 1987, to CCCP-76495. Demilitarised; later updated to IL-76T 'Falsie'
YI-AIL	IL-76 (mil)	073410293	0804	Returned by 1987, to LII as CCCP-76528. Demilitarised; later updated to IL-76T 'Falsie'
YI-AIM	IL-76 (mil)	073410320?	0810?	D/D 1-10-77. Returned by 1980, to CCCP-76497? (c/n confirmed for Soviet registration but unconfirmed for Iraqi registration). Demilitarised; later updated to IL-76T 'Falsie'
YI-AIN	IL-76 (mil)	073410301?	0806?	Returned by 1987, to IL-76T 'Falsie' CCCP-76496? (c/n confirmed for Soviet registration but not for Iraqi registration)
YI-AIO	IL-76 (mil)	073410315	0809	Shot down by Iranian fighter near Baghdad-Saddam Hussein International airport 23-9-80
YI-AIP	IL-76 (mil)	073410308	0807	Returned 1980? To LII as CCCP-76529. Demilitarised, **converted to IL-76LL (D-236T with SV-36 prop, later D-27 with SV-27 prop)**
YI-AKO	IL-76M	093416506	1307	Ex-Iraqi AF 2803. Returned to Soviet Union 1988, to NPO 'Vzlyot' as IL-76T 'Falsie' CCCP-76490. Demilitarised, **converted to avionics testbed**
YI-AKP	IL-76M	093421630	1608	Grey/white c/s. Returned by 1989, to MAP (Ul'yanovsk 'Aviastar' aircraft factory) as IL-76T 'Falsie' CCCP-76491
YI-AKQ	IL-76M	093421635	1609	Grey/white c/s. Returned by 1988, to LII as IL-76T 'Falsie' CCCP-06188, demilitarised, **converted to IL-76LL (TV7-117A with SV-34 prop)**
YI-AKS	IL-76M	093418543	1406	Ex-Iraqi AF 2068. Returned to Soviet Union 9-1-87?, to Sukhoi OKB as IL-76T 'Falsie' CCCP-76759, demilitarised
YI-AKT	IL-76M	093418548	1407	Returned 1994, to Vladivostok Air as IL-76T 'Falsie' RA-76492 **(second use of registration, see Russia/LII)**, demilitarised
YI-AKU	IL-76M	093421637	1610	Grey/white c/s. Returned by 1987, to MAP as IL-76T 'Falsie' CCCP-76754, demilitarised
YI-AKV*	IL-76M	0013428831	2108	Returned by 1982, to TransSuper as IL-76T 'Falsie' CCCP-78731
YI-AKW	IL-76M	0013428839	2110	Grey/white c/s. Returned by 1989, to LII as IL-76T 'Falsie' CCCP-76756
YI-AKX	IL-76M	0013433990	2508	Returned 1988? To MAP as IL-76T 'Falsie' CCCP-76757, demilitarised
YI-ALL	IL-76M	0013433984	2506	Ex-Iraqi AF 4600. Returned to Soviet Union 1988? To MAP as IL-76T 'Falsie' CCCP-76755
YI-ALO	IL-76M	0013433996	2509	Ex-Iraqi AF 4660 (also reported as 4214). Returned to Soviet Union 1989? To MAP as IL-76T 'Falsie' CCCP-76788, demilitarised
YI-ALP	IL-76M	0013433999	2510	Ex-Iraqi AF 4601. Returned to Soviet Union 1989? To MAP as IL-76T 'Falsie' CCCP-76789
YI-ALQ	IL-76MD	0023441189	3008	Returned 1991? To NPO 'Vzlyot'/Elf Air as IL-76TD 'Falsie' RA-76823, demilitarised; **converted to 'true' IL-76TD 1998**
YI-ALR	IL-76MD	0023441200	3010	Returned by 2-92, to MAP (Tashkent aircraft factory) as IL-76TD 'Falsie' CCCP-76821
YI-ALS	IL-76MD	0033442247	3202	Returned by 9-91, to LII as IL-76TD 'Falsie' CCCP-78738, demilitarised
YI-ALT**	IL-76MD	0033448393	3509	
YI-ALU**	IL-76MD	0033448398	3510	
YI-ALV**	IL-76MD	0033448409	3603	
YI-ALW**	IL-76MD	0033448416	3604	
YI-ALX**	IL-76MD	0033449455	3704	
YI-ANA	IL-76MD 'Falsie'	0063469055	5204	
YI-ANB	IL-76MD 'Falsie'	0063469071	5208	
YI-ANC	IL-76MD 'Falsie'	0063470102	5306	
YI-AND	IL-76MD 'Falsie'	0063471155	5409	
YI-ANE	IL-76MD 'Falsie'	0073474224	5606	
YI-ANF	IL-76MD 'Falsie'	0073475236	5609	
YI-ANG	IL-76MD 'Falsie'	0073476288	5802	
YI-ANH	IL-76MD 'Falsie'	0073476307	5807	
YI-ANI	IL-76MD 'Falsie'	0073481442	6201	
YI-ANJ	IL-76MD 'Falsie'	0083482481	6301	
YI-ANK	IL-76MD 'Falsie'	0083482495	6304	
YI-ANL	IL-76MD 'Falsie'	0083484542	6406	
YI-ANM	IL-76MD 'Falsie'	0093495886	7302	
YI-ANN	IL-76MD 'Falsie'	0093496894	7304	
YI-ANO	IL-76MD	1003403087	7802	
2068	IL-76M	093418543	1406	Repainted as Iraqi Airways YI-AKS by 3-86
2803	IL-76M	093416506	1307	D/D 21-4-79. Repainted as Iraqi Airways YI-AKO
4600	IL-76M	0013433984	2506	Repainted as Iraqi Airways YI-ALL by 3-82
4601	IL-76M	0013433999	2510	Repainted as Iraqi Airways YI-ALP by 8-82
4660	IL-76M	0013433996	2509	Repainted as Iraqi Airways YI-ALO by 6-82

Note: * YI-AKV was previously reported as c/n 093421628 (f/n 1607A, sold to LII as CCCP-86891; see previous chapter and Chapter 3). However, the new information appears more likely, since CCCP-86891 is an IL-76M 'Falsie' and IL-76s returned from Iraq are usually *Candid-Bs* with 'false' civil designations, not vice versa! Also, it seems rather strange than an IL-76M 'Falsie' should be delivered to Iraq, since all other Iraqi 'Ms (including those delivered later) were 'true' ones;
** Some sources suggest YI-ALT through YI-ALX may also have been returned to Russia.

The Iraqis developed specialised military versions of the *Candid* in the late 1980s as described in Chapter 3 (an IL-76MD refuelling tanker and the *Baghdad-1, Adnan-1* and *Adnan-2* AWACS aircraft). Both *Adnans* were reportedly used against the Allied forces in the closing stages of the Gulf War, operating from Baghdad-Saddam Hussein International airport and designating targets for Iraqi AF MiG-29 *Fulcrum-A* fighters. When Iraq realised it was losing the war, all three AWACS *Candids* and many other Iraqi Air Force aircraft were flown to neighbouring Iran (with which Iraq had conveniently entered a truce in 1988) to save them from destruction by the Allies. There, however, they were impounded and kept by Iran – see Iranian section).

At least half of Iraq's IL-76 fleet (20 aircraft) was returned to the Soviet Union/CIS as foreign debt payments. All but one of the others were flown to Iran and Tunisia at the closing stage of the Gulf War (one of them narrowly escaped being hit by US bombs!). Eleven of these aircraft were retained by Iran; the rest were stored at Tunis in late 2000. On 5th November 2000, however, the sole IL-76MD remaining in Iraq began scheduled domestic passenger services (!) between Baghdad and Basra. The *Candid* and an Antonov An-26 (serving the Baghdad-Mosul route) had to be used because almost the entire Iraqi Airways fleet was stored outside Iraq.

ISRAEL

In January 2000 the A-50I prototype (RA-78740, c/n 0093486579, f/n 6505) delivered to Israel for outfitting to fill a Chinese order was registered to **ELTA ELECTRONICS CO** as 4X-AGI. Following the cancellation of the Chinese contract, however, it is not clear what IAI will do with the aircraft.

LATVIA

INVERSIJA LTD – LATVIAN AVIATION COMPANY [–/INV] operated five leased IL-76s, two of which it later bought. (The airline's name, pronounced *inversiya*, is Russian for 'contrail'.) Originally flown in Aeroflot colours without titles; most of them later received an Aeroflot-style colour scheme with a maroon cheatline, Inversija titles on the tail and Cyrillic (!?) 'IL-76T' nose titles.

Registration	Version	C/n	F/n	Notes
YL-LAJ	IL-76T	083414432	1108	Ex-RA-76510, converted IL-76 (civil); leased from Aeroflot 7-91, bought 10-94
YL-LAK	IL-76T	0003424707	1807	Ex-SVGAL (North-East Cargo Airlines) RA-76522, bought 10-94
YL-LAL	IL-76T 'Falsie'	0013433984	2506	Ex-RA-76755, reregistered 10-94; ex-CCCP-76755, ex-Iraqi Air Force IL-76M YI-ALL. Leased from Atran 1-92 (originally as RA-76755)
CCCP-76495	IL-76 (mil)	073410292	0803	Demilitarised. Ex-Iraqi Air Force YI-AIK. Leased from MAP 1993; reregistered RA-76495 by 9-93. Was sub-leased (?) to SFT 19-3-94 to 4-95 as ST-SFT. Sold to Iron Dragonfly 1997 as IL-76TD 'Falsie'
RA-76788	IL-76T 'Falsie'	0013433996	2509	Ex-CCCP-76788, ex-Iraqi Air Force IL-76M YI-ALO. Demilitarised. Leased from Atran

Note: * See comment in previous chapter (Russia/SVGAL).

LIBERIA

AIR CESS (LIBERIA), INC [–/ACS] obtained two IL-76T 'Falsies' – EL-RDT (ex-Al'kor RA-86715, c/n 053403072, f/n 0208, demilitarised) and EL-RDX (ex-RA-86604, c/n 043402039, f/n 0110) in 1996; both aircraft were white overall without titles. Since the *Candids* were flown by Russian crews, there is good reason to believe they were wet-leased and the Liberian registrations were simply a flag of convenience. Both were transferred to the airline's sister company Air Pass (see Swaziland section) in late 1997, becoming 3D-RTT and 3D-RTX respectively.

An IL-76TD registered EL-WTA[5] in basic Aeroflot colours without titles (some sources say it had 'Ghostbuster' titles!) was seen at Ostend, Belgium, on 17th October 1997. This has been reported as almost certainly ex-Dacono Air RA-76421 (c/n 1033415504, f/n 8806).

Curiously, the IL-76 is pictured on the logo of a Liberian carrier called Air Charter Service [–/ACH], which does not have any *Candids*.

LIBYA

In 1980-85 Libya took delivery of at least 24 IL-76s, including five IL-76Ms. It was much the same story as in Iraq; the *Candid-Bs* wore full **LIBYAN ARAB AIRLINES** [LN/LAA] colours but were operated by the **LIBYAN ARAB REPUBLIC AIR FORCE** (LARAF, or *al Quwwat al-Jawwiya al-Libiya*). In late 1980, however, two IL-76Ms flying supplies to North Yemen reportedly carried full LARAF markings.

The IL-76T/TDs, on the other hand, were operated by **JAMAHIRIAN AIR TRANSPORT**[6] (a commercial division of the LARAF) in an all-white livery with only a Libyan flag on the tail and black titles (in Arabic to port and in English to starboard). Later, however, all the *Candid-As* were also reported as operated by Libyan Arab Airlines! By 1991 Jamahirian Air Transport was renamed **LIBYAN ARAB AIR CARGO** [–/LCR], with minor changes in the colour scheme, and it is this airline which operates the IL-76T/TDs as of this writing.

Registration	Version	C/n	F/n	Notes
5A-DKK	IL-76M	0003423675	1709	WFU Sheba after hard landing in 1985
5A-DLL (No1)	IL-76M	093421612	1603	Destroyed Tripoli 15-4-86 by USAF bombing raid
5A-DLL (No 2)	IL-78E	0093493799	7010	Full Libyan Arab Air Cargo colour scheme
5A-DMM	IL-76M	0003423679	1710	Reported destroyed at Tripoli 15-4-86 by USAF bombing raid
5A-DNA	IL-76TD	0023439140	2905	Stored Moscow-Bykovo since 1992
5A-DNB	IL-76TD	0023437086	2802	
5A-DNC	IL-76TD	0023437084	2801	
5A-DND	IL-76TD	0033445299	3305	
5A-DNE	IL-76T	0013432952	2408	
5A-DNF	IL-76TD	0033445302	3306	Destroyed Tripoli 15-4-86 by USAF bombing raid
5A-DNG	IL-76T	0013432961	2501	
5A-DNH	IL-76TD	0033446356	3409	
5A-DNI	IL-76T	0013430878	2210	
5A-DNJ	IL-76T	0013430869	2208	
5A-DNK	IL-76T	0013430882	2301	
5A-DNL	IL-76T	0033447357	3410	Destroyed Tripoli 15-4-86 by USAF bombing raid
5A-DNO	IL-76TD	0043451509	3808	
5A-DNP	IL-76TD	0043451516	3809	
5A-DNQ	IL-76TD	0043454641	4201	
5A-DNS	IL-76TD	0023439145	2907	
5A-DNT	IL-76TD	0023439141	2906	
5A-DNU	IL-76TD	0043454651	4203	
5A-DNV	IL-76TD	0043454645	4202	
5A-DNW	IL-76TD	0043450479?	3710?	Not in fleet list 1999 – returned to the Soviet Union? (reported as c/n 0043456700, f/n 4305, to CCCP-76493 but this is doubtful!)
5A-DRR	IL-76M	083415469	1208	D/D 15-3-79
5A-DZZ	IL-76M	093416501	1306	Reported destroyed at Tripoli 15-4-86 by USAF bombing raid, not confirmed by Russian sources

Some Iraqi Air Force IL-76Ms which previously wore full military markings had this subdued colour scheme. Note that the Iraqi Airways titles are applied differently to port and starboard. RART

Inversija Airlines IL-76T YL-LAK offloading NATO supplies at Tirana in May 1999 during Operation *Allied Force*. Airzone

Libyan Arab Airlines IL-76TD 5A-DNT at Frankfurt/Main. Libyan *Candid-A*s initially wore this all-white colour scheme. Peter Davison

Seen here at aircraft overhaul plant No. 402 in April 1993, Libyan Arab Air Cargo IL-76TD 5A-DNA was stuck at Moscow-Bykovo for several years due to UN sanctions. Dmitriy Komissarov

Note: Candids registered 5A-DNM, 5A-DNN and 5A-DNR have not been reported to date. Also, IL-76TDs CCCP-76493, -76494, -76498 and -76499 are reported by some sources as ex-Libyan aircraft. Since they have out-of-sequence registrations, there is a remote possibility that they are ex-5A-DNM, 5A-DNN, 5A-DNR and 5A-DNW, though Russian sources do not confirm this.

The LARAF also operates a single IL-78E tanker in Libyan Arab Air Cargo colours (!). This aircraft inherited the registration of an IL-76M destroyed by the USAF (5A-DLL).

On 15th April 1992 the United Nations imposed sanctions on Libya, including a ban on international flights. These were intended to pressure the Libyan government into extraditing the terrorists who blew up Pan American Airlines Boeing 747-121A N739PA Clipper Maid of the Seas over Lockerbie, Scotland, on 21st December 1988 with the tragic death of all 270 on board. Thus the Libyan Candids were theoretically either locked inside the country or stranded outside; for example, 5A-DNA sat for several years at Moscow-Bykovo (aircraft overhaul plant No 402) and 5A-DNG was stored at Khartoum. In reality, however, on at least one occasion a Jamahirian Air Transport IL-76TD (5A-DNS) was seen visiting Paris-Le Bourget in March 1998 in violation of the UN sanctions. The sanctions were finally lifted on 5th April 1999 after the two suspects had been handed over for trial by a Scottish court.

MALAYSIA

This is a case of wishful thinking. The Malaysian regional carrier **SILVERLINE AIRWAYS** intended to operate wet-leased IL-76s in 1996 but operations were never started.

NICARAGUA

GATS, SA [–/GTS] – see UAE section.

NORTH KOREA (People's Democratic Rep of Korea)

In 1990 **CHOSONMINHANG** [JS/KOR], the sole North Korean airline (aka CAAK – Civil Aviation Administration of Korea), took delivery of three IL-76MD 'Falsies' registered P-912 (c/n 1003403104, f/n 7806), P-913 (c/n 1003404126, f/n 7902) and P-914 (c/n 1003404146, f/n 7907). However, these were/are almost certainly operated by the **NORTH KOREAN AIR FORCE.** By 1994 the airline was renamed **AIR KORYO** ('Koryo' is the indigenous name of Korea).

Some sources have mentioned a fourth IL-76 registered P-917; however, this is almost certainly P-912 temporarily 'reregistered' to confuse would-be spies. North Koreans are paranoid about security and are known to alter the registrations on their civil aircraft; for instance, IL-62M P-881 temporarily became P-884.

SÃO TOMÉ & PRINCIPE

EXPRESS INTERNATIONAL CARGO CORPORATION LTD [–/EIC] bought or leased IL-76T RA-76372 (ex-IL-76K CCCP-86723, c/n 073410279, f/n 0710) from Express Joint Stock Company in 1999. The aircraft was placed on the São Tomé register as S9-BOM. Yet this may well be simply a flag of convenience, especially considering the very similar names of the previous and current operators.

By September 1999 an unidentified airline in São Tomé & Principe (possibly **TRANSAFRIK CORPORATION LTD** which also operates in Angola, or **AIR GEMINI**) bought IL-76TD 4K-AZ11 (c/n 1013409280, f/n 8210) from AZAL Avia Cargo; the aircraft was reregistered S9-BAD. In March 2000, however, it was sold to Atlant-Aerobatics as HA-TCK.

SIERRA LEONE

AIR SULTAN LTD [–/SSL] bought IL-76TD 'Falsie' RA-76383 (ex-IL-76MD UR-86909) from Atlant-Soyuz in October 1996. Duly reregistered 9L-LBK, it was promptly leased to the Iranian carrier Queshmair as EP-TQC. In February 1998 the aircraft was sold to Atlas Air as EP-ALB; the registration 9L-LBK was reallocated to a West Coast Airways Let L-410UVP feederliner leased from Ryazan'aviatrans (ex-RA-67434, c/n 831125).[7]

A carrier named **INTALAIR** bought IL-76TD RA-76355 (c/n 1023408265, f/n 8207) from the Beriyev Design Bureau in 1997; the aircraft was reregistered 9L-LBO. Soon, however, it was sold to Atlas Air as EP-ALD.

SOUTH AFRICAN REPUBLIC

In 1992-94 **SOUTH AFRICAN AIRLINES** [SA/SAA] leased nine IL-76MDs from the Ukrainian Air Force. The aircraft wore basic Aeroflot colours without titles but had stickers with the airline's 'winged springbok' logo and the letters SAA-SAL (South African Airlines – Suid-Afrikaanse Lugdiens).

Registration	Version	C/n	F/n	Notes
CCCP-76423	IL-76MD	0053457720	4310	Ex-CCCP-76626. Leased from Atlant-SV 4-93 to ?-??; returned as UR-76423
CCCP-76656	IL-76MD	0053463891	4803	Leased from ANTAU; returned as UR-76656
CCCP-76664	IL-76MD	0053464926	4902	Leased from ANTAU; returned as UR-76664
UR-76681	IL-76MD	0063467021	5106	Leased from ANTAU 5-8-93 to ?-11-93
UR-76688	IL-76MD	0063469062	5206	Leased 10-93. To Air Ukraine after return from lease
CCCP-76705	IL-76MD	0063472158	5410	Leased from ANTAU 4-9-92 to 17-7-94; reregistered 76705, then UR-76705
CCCP-76706	IL-76MD	0063472163	5501	Leased from /ANTAU 4-9-92 to ?-9-93; reregistered UR-76706 during lease (24-4-93)
CCCP-76778	IL-76MD	0083482502	6306	Leased from ANTAU 12-4-93 to ?-??; reregistered UR-76778 during lease
CCCP-78756	IL-76MD	0083484536	6404	Leased from ANTAU 16-1-93 to ?-??; reregistered UR-78756 during lease

SUDAN

The **SUDAN AIR FORCE** (al Quwwat al-Jawwiya as-Sudaniya) operated two IL-76TDs leased from the Russian carrier C-Air in 1997-98. These were registered ST-AIR (ex-/to RA-76367, c/n 1033414474, f/n 8709)[8] and ST-AIY (ex-/to RA-76350, c/n 1023410344, f/n 8406).

AZZA TRANSPORT COMPANY LTD [–/AZZ] operates IL-76TD ST-APS (ex-Belair EW-76837, c/n 1023409316, f/n 8309) in ex-Belair colours without titles since 1996. Or is it ex-RA-76837? The JP Airline-Fleets International yearbook still lists the aircraft as 'ex-EW-76837, leased from Belair' long after the freighter was noted as RA-76837!

SALPA AVIATION CO LTD [–/SLP] operates IL-76s leased from CIS carriers as required. For instance, in May 1993 it leased IL-76TD RA-76752 (c/n 0093498967, f/n 7502) from Kras Air and IL-76TD CCCP-76782 (c/n 0093498971, f/n 7503) from Uzbekiston Havo Yullari. The former aircraft was in Aeroflot colours without titles, while CCCP-76782 had blue SALPA titles; this aircraft was reportedly on lease until 1994 as UK-76782. Interestingly, the operator has also been reported as Salpa Air Transport Russia!

SFT SUDANESE FLIGHT & TRADING SERVICES [–/STF] likewise leases IL-76s from CIS carriers as required. From 19th March 1994 to April 1995 it operated an all-white demilitarised IL-76 *sans suffixe* appropriately registered ST-SFT (ex-RA-76495, c/n 073410292, f/n 0803) – presumably leased from Inversija (which, true enough, is *not* a CIS airline).

The charter airline **SUDANIA** reportedly leased IL-76TD RA-76481 (c/n 0053460795, f/n 4509) from the Russian Civil Aviation Research Institute (GosNII GA) in October 1991. The aircraft was in basic Aeroflot colours without titles.

Two IL-76TDs were placed on the Sudanese register in November 1998 as ST-AQA (ex-Atlas Air EP-ALA, c/n 0053460795, f/n 4509) and ST-AQB (ex-EP-ALC, c/n 0023442218, f/n 3105). They were operated by **TRANS ATTICO** (African Transport, Trading & Investment Co) [–/ETC] jointly with the Russian carrier Ramair and, later, Phoenix Aviation (see previous chapter and UAE section). Hence the aircraft carried Trans ATTICO stickers along with Phoenix titles.

SWAZILAND

Air Pass, a sister company of Air Cess (Liberia),[9] reportedly operated four IL-76s, two of which had been transferred from Air Cess in 1997. 'Pass' is an acronym for Pietersburg Aviation Services & Systems; though nominally a Swazi company, the airline was based at Pietersburg-Gateway International airport, South Africa. In 1998 Air Pass suspended operations, selling almost its entire fleet to Centrafrican Airlines.

Registration	Version	C/n	F/n	Notes
3D-RTA	IL-76T 'Falsie'	0003426765	2002	Demilitarised. Ex-Veteran Airline RA-86846. To Centrafrican as TL-ACY
3D-RTT	IL-76T 'Falsie'	053403072	0208	Demilitarised. Ex-Air Cess EL-RDT, ex-IL-76 (military) RA-86715. F/n reported in error as 0203. To Centrafrican as TL-ACN
3D-RTX	IL-76T 'Falsie'	043402039	0110	Ex-Air Cess EL-RDX, ex-IL-76 (military) RA-86604. To Centrafrican as TL-ACU
RA-76430	IL-76T	073410300	0805	Ex-IL-76K CCCP-86729; leased from Dragonfly. To Exo Patrol as HA-TCI by 4-99

Note: See also Congolese section

SWITZERLAND

Zürich-based **JET AIR CARGO** [–/PJS], a division of Jet Aviation Business Jets established in 1991 as a joint venture with Tyumen' Airlines, operated cargo charters with IL-76s leased from/jointly operated with this Russian carrier.

Registration	Version	C/n	F/n	Notes
CCCP-76484	IL-76	0063469081	5301	Leased 7-91 to ?-?? (returned by 1993)*
CCCP-76486	IL-76	0073476281	5801	Leased 7-91 to ?-?? (returned by 1993)*
CCCP-76807	IL-76	1013405176	8004	Leased from Aeroflot/Tyumen' United Flight Detachment 12-91, reregistered RA-76807 during lease. Operated for UNPF 1991-93

* **Note:** RA-76484 and RA-76486 were later operated by Baikal Airlines (Irkutsk). However, it is possible that they had originally been delivered to the Tyumen' Civil Aviation Directorate.

METRO-CARGO, another Soviet-Swiss joint venture established in November 1990, operated ten *Candid-As* from Luxembourg. With the exception of one IL-76TD which received a Bulgarian registration as a flag of convenience, the freighters retained their Soviet registrations; most of them had basic Aeroflot colours with red Metro-Cargo titles. The airline ceased operations in 1992 – not due to any political complications or rift between the partners but because the customers were, putting it mildly, reluctant to pay!

Registration	Version	C/n	F/n	Notes
CCCP-76481	IL-76TD	0053460795	4509	Leased from GosNII GA 1-91 to 9-91, named *Bern*
CCCP-76484	IL-76TD	0063469081	5301	Leased from Tyumen' CAD/2nd Tyumen' United Flight Detachment (?) 5-91 to 7-91
CCCP-76486	IL-76TD	0073476281	5801	Leased from Tyumen' CAD/2nd Tyumen' United Flight Detachment (?) 1-91 to 7-91, named *Zürich*
CCCP-76514	IL-76T	083415453	1204	Leased from Tyumen' CAD/2nd Tyumen' United Flight Detachment, no titles
CCCP-76522	IL-76T	0003424707	1807	Leased 10-90 to 12-91, named *Ascona*
CCCP-76523	IL-76T	0003425732	1903	Lsd from Tyumen' CAD/2nd Tyumen' United Flight Detachment ?-90 to 7-91, named *Locarno*
CCCP-76782	IL-76TD	0093498971	7503	Leased from Uzbek CAD 1-91 to 9-91, named *Gottardo*
CCCP-76793	IL-76TD	0093498951	7408	Lsd from Uzbek CAD 11-90 to 8-91, named *Ticino*
CCCP-76805	IL-76TD	1003403109	7808	Lsf Uzbek CAD, named *Bellenzona*. C/n also reported as 1003403105
LZ-INK	IL-76TD	0093494835	7109	Ex-CCCP-76784, leased 8-90 to ?-91, named *Lugano*. To Mexair

The Geneva-based airline **MEXAIR, SA** [–/MXC] leased IL-76s from Aeroflot as required. Unfortunately the first *Candid-A* it operated, LZ-INK, crashed near Bakhtaran (Iran) on 24th May 1991 after running out of fuel. Later, in November 1991, Mexair leased IL-76TD RA-76481 from GosNII GA.

SYRIA

In 1979 the **SYRIAN AIR FORCE** (*al Quwwat al-Jawwiya al Arabiya as-Suriya*) took delivery of two quasi-civilian 'true' IL-76Ms registered YK-ATA (c/n 093421613, f/n 1604) and YK-ATB (c/n 093421619, f/n 1605). They sport a civil-style colour scheme with a triple dark blue cheatline and white fin with the Syrian flag. The freighters are nominally operated by **SYRIANAIR** (Syrian Arab Airlines) [RB/SYR], with appropriate titles in English and Arabic on the aft fuselage. (This colour scheme was also worn by some other Syrian Air Force transport aircraft.)

Two years later the *Candid-Bs* were joined by two IL-76M 'Falsies' registered YK-ATC (c/n 0013431911, f/n 2308) and YK-ATD (c/n 0013431915, f/n 2309). These are ostensibly part of Syrianair's fleet and wear the airline's full livery with a single bright blue cheatline (outlined in the same colour) and bright blue tail with stylised bird logo, but are likewise operated on behalf of the Air Force.

THAILAND

From May 1994 to October 1995 Russian Air Force IL-76MD RA-78840 (c/n 1003403056, f/n 7704) was leased to the **PETROLEUM AUTHORITY OF THAILAND**, gaining appropriate titles of the aft fuselage.

TUNISIA

TUBEL AIR (Tunisian Belgian Air SA) [–/TBR] leased two *Candids* from the Russian Air Force / Yuriy A Gagarin Space Training Centre – IL-76MDK-II RA-78825 (c/n 1013495871, f/n 7208) in October 1993 and IL-76MDK RA-76766 (c/n 0073481431, f/n 6108) in April 1994. The former aircraft was in full Aeroflot livery with additional black Tubel Air titles in Arabic, while RA-76766 was white overall without titles (it was repainted in Aeroflot colours after return from lease). The choice of aircraft is surprising, to say the least – why lease specialised zero-G trainers when there are plenty of regular *Candids* around? Additionally, Tubel Air leased IL-76TD 'Falsie' RA-76823 (c/n 0023441189, f/n 3008) from Elf Air at an unspecified date.

Still wearing the basic colours of its original owner (Moscow Airways), Ramair/Phoenix FZE IL-76TD ST-AQA is seen at Sharjah in January 1999. The aircraft was jointly operated with the Sudanese carrier TransATTICO, hence the additional titles. Peter Davison

Safiran Airlines IL-76TD EP-SFA (ex-Magadan-avialeasing RA-76787) parked at Moscow/Vnukovo-1 on 4th October 2000. The Russian flag shows through the hastily-applied Safiran tail logo. Dmitriy Komissarov

Syrian Air Force IL-76M YK-ATA with small Syrianair titles on the aft fuselage. Peter Davison

IL-76M 'Falsie' YK-ATD in full Syrianair livery makes an interesting comparison with the Syrian Air Force's 'true' Ms. RART

Photographed at Chkalovskaya AB on 15th August 1999, the IL-76MDK-II zero-G trainer still wears Arabic 'Tubel Air' titles, but the logo aft of the navigator's glazing and the Tunisian flag on the outer engines have been obliterated. Sergey Komissarov

GATS Airlines IL-76TD
3C-KKF at Moscow-
Domodedovo on 22nd
November 1998 –
apparently after
suffering a minor
technical problem.
The former Nicaraguan
registration YN-CEV
was still visible under
the paint.
Dmitriy Komissarov

HeavyLift Cargo
Airlines IL-76TD
RA-76401 leased from
Volga-Dnepr Airlines.
Milan Cvrkal

UNITED ARAB EMIRATES

AEROCOMPLEX, a Soviet/UAE (later Russian/UAE) joint venture, operated IL-76s leased from Aeroflot as required. These included IL-76TD RA-76367 leased in 1994.

In January 1995 **GATS LTD** (Gulf Aviation Technology & Services) [–/GTS] obtained three IL-76TDs; the aircraft were Russian-registered and based in Moscow. Originally painted in basic Aeroflot colours with blue GATS titles on the nose and tail, they soon received an all-white livery with red titles and the UAE flag aft of the flight deck (despite the Russian registration).

In 1997 the airline was registered in Nicaragua as **GATS, SA** and the aircraft were moved to the Nicaraguan register (probably for tax reasons). A year later the scenario was repeated; this time the airline was incorporated in Equatorial Guinea as **GATS GUINEA, SA** and the aircraft were reregistered accordingly (see table). Despite all these

registration changes, they still carry the UAE flag, lending credibility to the flag-of-convenience theory. Are there more new identities to come?

Registration	Version	C/n	F/n	Notes
RA-76411	IL-76TD	1023411384	8506	To GATS SA 1997 as **YN-CEV**; to GATS Guinea SA 1998 as **3C-KKF**
RA-76436	IL-76TD	1023411368	8502	To GATS SA 1997 as **YN-CEX**; to GATS Guinea SA 1998 as **3C-KKE**
RA-76832	IL-76TD	1023410360	8410	To GATS SA 1997 as **YN-CEW**; to GATS Guinea SA 1998 as **3C-KKG**

Sharjah-based **PHOENIX AVIATION** [–/PHG] a division of the Phoenix Free Zone Enterprise, bought IL-76TDs ST-AQA and ST-AQB and IL-76TD 'Falsie' T9-CAC from the defunct Russian carrier Ramair (see previous chapter) in 1999. The 'true' IL-76TDs are jointly operated with Trans Attico (Sudan) and the 'Falsie' with Bio Air (Bosnia-Herzegovina).

UNITED KINGDOM

AIR FOYLE LTD [GS/UPA] leased IL-76MD UR-78755 (c/n 0083484531, f/n 6404) from Khors Aircompany in January 1994. The aircraft was in full Khors colours with additional blue Air Foyle titles on the outer engine nacelles. It was operated for an organization called Oil Spill Response which used it to transport oil spill control equipment.

HEAVYLIFT CARGO AIRLINES [NP/HLA] operated three *Candids*.

Registration	Version	C/n	F/n	Notes
RA-76401	IL-76TD	1023412399	8510	Leased from Volga-Dnepr 7-95, full HeavyLift colours
CCCP-76758	IL-76TD 'Falsie'	0073474203	5601	Leased from Volga-Dnepr 1-92 to ?-98 in full HeavyLift colours; **reregistered RA-76758 during lease**.
RA-76842	IL-76TD	1033418616	9104	Leased from / jointly operated with Airstan 11-97 to ?-2000; full Airstan colours with additional HeavyLift titles

RA-76758 was operated for an environmental organization called Oil Spill Response while still in full HeavyLift livery.

The **OVERSEAS DEVELOPMENT AGENCY** (ODA), an arm of the British government tasked with overseas aid and development, leased four IL-76s from various Russian carriers. Most of these aircraft carried a large Union Jack on the tail.

Registration	Version	C/n	F/n	Notes
RA-76418	IL-76 (mil)	073409237	0610	Demilitarised, ex-Soviet Air Force CCCP-86640. Leased from Dobrolyot 5-95 to 8-95, operated for UNHCR
RA-76477	IL-76TD	0043453575	4004	Leased from Aeroflot – Russian International Airlines 8-94 to ?-??
RA-76522	IL-76T	0003424707	1807	Leased from SVGAL (North-Eastern Cargo Airlines) 7-94 to 10-94, operated for UNHCR
RA-76752	IL-76TD	0093498967	7502	Leased from Kras Air 21-10-94 to ?-??, operated for UNHCR

YEMEN

The **YEMEN AIR FORCE** had three used IL-76TDs nominally owned by (and jointly operated with **YEMENIA** (Yemen Airways Corporation) [IY/IYE]. However, only one (7O-ADG) was reportedly in service at the end of 1999; the fate of the other two is unknown.

Registration	Version	C/n	F/n	Notes
7O-ADF		1033418578	9005	D/D 11-95, ex-RA76380 (sometimes in error as ex-RA-76360 or RA-76365)
7O-ADG		1023412402	8601	D/D 11-95, ex-RA-76405; sometimes reported in error as ex-RA-76361 (c/n 1033415497, f/n 8805
7O-ADH		1033415497	8805	D/D 11-94, ex-RA-76361 (sometimes reported in error as ex-RA-76380)

ZAIRE

VAC VIRUNGA AIR CHARTER based at Goma (Kivu) leased IL-76TD RA-76419 (c/n 1023414470, f/n 8708) from Arkhangel'sk Airlines in August 1993.

ZIMBABWE

A Harare-based airline called **SOL AIR** operated an IL-76TD registered in Equatorial Guinea as 3C-JJJ in 1999; the aircraft wore basic Aeroflot colours with Sol Air titles. According to some sources (which misspelled the airline's name as 'Colair') the engine covers were marked 666, suggesting the aircraft could be ex-RA-76666 of Aviacon Tsitotrans (c/n 0053464934, f/n 4904). In early 2000 the aircraft was reportedly sold to Centrafricain Airlines as TL-ADS.

OPERATORS FROM UNKNOWN NATIONS

An airline called **ALTOPLAN** operated at least two IL-76MDs, UR-76584 (c/n 0043450493, f/n 3804) and UR-76590 (c/n 0043452544, f/n 3906), leased from the Ukrainian Air Force in March 1997.

EURO ATLANTIC AIR briefly operated IL-76TD RA-76812 (c/n 1013407230, f/n 8108) leased from the Domodedovo Civil Aviation Production Association.

RA-76812 was also leased to **EVA ATLANTIC AIRLINES** (not to be confused with EVA Air, Taiwan).

An airline called **EXPRESS AIR CARGO** leased IL-76T 'Falsie' RA-76788 (c/n 0013433996, f/n 2509) from Aviatrans in July 1994 and IL-76MD RA-76672 (c/n 0063466981, f/n 5006) from Atruvera late in the same year. This cannot be the Russian airline Express JSC because this was established in 1995.

An airline reported as **FINE AIR CARGO SERVICES** leased IL-76TD RA-76464 (c/n 0023437090, f/n 2803) from Kras Air in September 1994. This could be Fine Air [FB/FBF] of Miami, Fla, but this is unconfirmed.

Samara Airlines IL-76TD RA-76798 (c/n 1003403063, f/n 7706) was leased by **JOY AIR CARGO** in April 1992.

Baikalavia IL-76Ts RA-76458 (c/n 0013430888, f/n 2302) and RA-76462 (c/n 0013432955, f/n 2409) were leased to an obscure airline named **PRIDE AFRICAN INTERNATIONAL** in early 1993.

RSC INTERNATIONAL operated IL-76TD 'Falsie' RA-86896 (c/n 0013434018, f/n 2605) leased from Zenit at an unspecified date.

ROMOCO CARGO SA operated IL-76MD UR-76441 (ex-UR-76617?, c/n 0043455677?, f/n 4210) leased from Avilond TAC in August 1995. The 'SA' suffix doesn't give a clue; it could be both *Société Anonyme* and *Sociedad Anonima*, which means the airline could just as easily be, say, Swiss or from some place in Latin America.

Demilitarised IL-76TD 'Falsie' RA-76495 operated by the Latvian airline Inversija was sub-leased to a company named **SCODA** in May 1995.

An airline named **TRAVERSE CARGO** leased IL-76T 'Falsie' RA-76759 (c/n 093418543, f/n 1406) from the Sukhoi Design Bureau between April 1996 and at least August 1997.

ZALL TRANS leased IL-76TDs RA-76388 (c/n 1013406204, f/n 8101) and RA-76389 (c/n 1013407212, f/n 8103) from Polis Air in December 1993. The aircraft continued to wear Zall Trans titles on the nose after Polis Air sold them to Veteran Airline but it is not clear whether they were still on lease.

Chapter Seven

Beneath the Skin

The structural description presented in this chapter is that which applies to the basic Ilyushin IL-76 *sans suffixe*. Details of other versions, where they differ, are included as appropriate in the text.

Type

Four-engined heavy military and commercial transport. The airframe is of all-metal construction.

Fuselage

Semi-monocoque stressed-skin fail-safe structure with frames, longerons and stringers; chemical milling is used on some panels. The riveted fuselage structure is made mainly of D16T duralumin; the milled panels adjacent to the fuselage longerons are made of V95 aluminium alloy. The wing and landing gear attachment mainframes are made of V93 aluminium alloy.

Structurally the fuselage is made up of four sections: the forward fuselage (frames 1 to 18), the centre fuselage (frames 18 to 67), the aft fuselage (frames 67 to 90) and the rear fuselage or tail section (frames 90 to 95). The latter is a simple conical fairing on the commercial *Candid-A* or the tail gunner's station on the military *Candid-B*. All four sections are joined by flanges. The fuselage cross section changes from elliptical with the longer axis vertical (up to frame 18) to circular (frames 18 to 64) to elliptical with the longer axis horizontal (frames 64 to 95). Maximum fuselage diameter is 4.8m (15ft 9in) and maximum cross-section area less main gear fairings is 18.09m² (194.57ft²).

The greater part of the fuselage is pressurized, with a pressure differential of 0.5 ± 0.02kg/cm² (7.14 ± 0.28psi). There are two (on the *Candid-A*) or three independent pressurized compartments: the crew section (frames 1 to 14), the freight hold (frames 14 to 67) and, on the *Candid-B*, the tail gunner's compartment. The hold can be decompressed in flight for paradropping cargo or troops, leaving the crew section and the tail gunner's compartment pressurized. To ensure adequate pressurization the fuselage is sealed in two stages during manufacture. First, U20A elastic sealing tape is placed between the skin and internal structural members (frames and stringers) before they are riveted together; then, two layers of U30-MES-5(k) sealing compound are brushed on over the joint. U20A sealing tape is also used in all rivet joints in the unpressurized areas (eg,

the wing/fuselage fairing and the main gear actuator fairings) to stop water from getting in.

The *forward fuselage (Section F1)* includes the crew section and the foremost portion of the freight hold. The crew section is a double-deck structure with the flight deck above and the navigator's compartment below it. Both are accessed from the freight hold via a passage on the starboard side (with a pressure door and a ladder to the flight deck). The flight deck accommodates the pilots, flight engineer, radio operator and chief technician; the loadmaster and, on the *Candid-B*, the paradrop equipment operator are seated in the hold. A toilet is located on the port side symmetrically to the said passage.

The flight deck and the navigator's station are extensively glazed, with optically-flat bird-proof triplex panes at the front; the curved side panes and the flight deck eyebrow windows are made of plexiglass. The panes immediately ahead of the captain's and first officer's seats are fitted with dual windshield wipers (top and bottom). The flight deck features two sliding windows which can be used as emergency exits on the ground. An inward-opening escape hatch with a window in the flight deck roof (frames 13 to 14) provides access to the inflatable rescue dinghy in the event of ditching and generally to the upper surface of the aircraft for maintenance purposes. Additionally, skin areas between frames 5 to 7 on each side can be chopped out in an emergency.

The forward pressure bulkhead (frame 1) kinked at approximately 80° mounts the weather radar dish covered by a glassfibre radome; a second radome encloses the ground mapping radar antenna mounted under the pressure floor of the navigator's compartment. The space between the forward pressure bulkhead and the flight deck (frames 1 to 3) is occupied by an avionics bay. The nosewheel well is located beneath the navigator's compartment and freight hold between frames 11 to 18. Two forward-hinged (outward-opening) entry doors with circular windows are located at the rear of Section F1 between frames 15 to 17; the port door is deleted on the IL-78M, IL-82 and A-50. An escape hatch with a sloping chute (accessible both from the flight deck and the navigator's station) is provided on the port side between frames 9 to 11; its forward-opening hydraulically-actuated door acts as a slipstream deflector when the crew bails out.

The *centre fuselage (Section F2)* accommodates the freight hold with a titanium floor. The

rear portion is cut away from below, starting at frame 56; the cutout is closed by the cargo ramp which is a continuation of the freight hold floor and extends beyond Section F2 to frame 69. The ramp incorporates a U-shaped tail bumper and a hydraulically-powered circular telescopic support which extends forwards and downwards to prevent the aircraft from falling over on its tail during loading and unloading. Section F2 terminates in a flat rear pressure bulkhead (frame 67) which swings upwards and aft almost entirely for loading and unloading. It features an inward-opening pressure door which serves for access to the tail gunner's station on the *Candid-B*.

The freight hold measures 20.0 x 3.4 x 3.46m (65ft 7in x 11ft 2in x 11ft 4in) excluding the cargo ramp, or 24.5 x 3.4 x 3.46m (80ft 4½in x 11ft 2in x 11ft 4in) with the cargo ramp. The rear loading aperture measures 3.4 x 3.45m (11ft 2in x 11ft 4in). Depending on the type of cargo and its location in the hold the maximum permissible floor loading varies from 1,450 to 3,100kg/m² (297 to 635 lb/ft²); likewise, the maximum axle load for wheeled vehicles varies from 7.5 to 11.0 tons (16,535 to 24,250 lb).

The freight hold features attachment points for a removable upper deck for carrying troops. The upper four attachment points are located on frame 18 and between frames 21 and 22 at stringers 9L and 9R. The lower attachment points (11 on each side) are located between frames 11 to 61 at stringers 18L and 18R. Four emergency exits with circular windows are provided in the hold: two at main deck level ahead of the wings (frames 23 to 24) and two at upper deck level aft of the wings (frames 58 to 60). Additionally, skin areas between frames 19 to 22 and 59 to 61 on each side can be chopped out in an emergency. One more window is provided on each side between frames 50 to 51 (just aft of the wing trailing edge).

Fuselage mainframes 29, 34 and 41 serve as attachment points for the wing centre section's front, middle and rear spars. The wing/fuselage joint is enclosed by a fairing, the front half of which (frames 24 to 29) includes the unpressurized air conditioning system bay. It also houses the slat drive motor (in the ACS bay) and the inflatable rescue dinghy (stowed ahead of the ACS bay). The rear half of the wing/fuselage fairing (frames 41 to 45) includes three unpressurized bays housing the flap drive motor, hydraulic equipment and aileron and spoiler controls.

Two pressurized baggage compartments

are located under the freight hold floor between frames 18 to 35 and 51 to 56; these are used for carrying engine covers, wheel chocks, ladders and other paraphernalia. The forward baggage compartment has two downward-opening ventral access doors hinged on the port side (offset to starboard between frames 22 to 24 and on the fuselage centreline between frames 29 to 31). The space between the luggage compartments (frames 35 to 51) is occupied by the mainwheel wells separated by the fuselage keel beam.

Two elongated fairings of quasi-triangular section are located on the centre fuselage sides between frames 26 to 62, enclosing the main gear attachment points (special projections of fuselage mainframes 37, 41, 45 and 49) and actuators. These fairings accommodate the APU, refuelling panel, DC batteries, liquid oxygen converter, communications and navigation equipment, stabilizer inspection light; on the *Candid-B* they also house the inert gas generator and reconnaissance camera. Two ventral fairings of circular section enclose the mainwheels. The shape and size of all main gear fairings is carefully optimised to reduce drag.

The unpressurized *aft fuselage (Section F3)* is cut away from below; the cutout is closed by three cargo door segments aft of the cargo ramp (the outer segments hinge outwards and the centre segment upwards). The aft fuselage carries the vertical tail attached to mainframes 74, 76, 78, 80, 82, 83, 85 and 86. It terminates in a rear stiffener (frames 80 to 90) – a box-like structure with a walkway through it; the undersurface of this stiffener is level with the freight hold roof.

As already mentioned, the *rear fuselage* or *tail section (Section F4)* is just an unpressurized fairing on commercial versions (and IL-76M/MD 'Falsies') or a tail gunner's station on the *Candid-B*. Once again, it is cut away from below to accommodate the rear end of the centre cargo door segment which is hinged to frame 95. The frames of the tail gunner's station are made of AK-6 aluminium alloy; so are the fin attachment fittings on Section F3.

On military versions the lower part of Section F4 is a pressure compartment accessed from the freight hold by walking up the inside of the cargo door and through a pressure door in the front wall. An emergency door is located on the starboard side, opening forwards hydraulically to act as a slipstream deflector for bailing out. The gunner's station features three rear windows and two side windows; all except the rearmost pane are made of plexiglass. A faired mounting ring for the tail turret (frame 96) is attached to frame 95. The upper part of Section F4 is unpressurized; on the *Candid-B* this is an avionics bay housing the gun ranging radar with a glassfibre radome. (On the IL-78 tanker, Section F4 is a refuelling systems operator's station; hence the tail turret is replaced by a dished fairing and the gun ranging radar is omitted.)

Wings

Cantilever shoulder-mounted monoplane of basically trapezoidal planform, mounted above the fuselage to leave the interior unobstructed; leading-edge sweep constant, trailing-edge sweep increases on outer wings. Sweepback at quarter-chord 25°, anhedral 3° from roots, incidence 3°, camber -3°, aspect ratio 8.5, taper 1.61. The wings utilise TsAGI high-speed airfoils with a high lift/drag ratio throughout the aircraft's speed range; thickness/chord ratio is 13% at root and 10% at tip. Wingspan is 50.5m (165ft 8in) and wing area 300.0m² (3,225.8ft²).

The wings are all-metal, stressed-skin structures made of D16T duralumin. Structurally they are made up of five pieces: the centre section (which is integral with the fuselage), inner wing sections and outer wing sections, plus tip fairings. The wing sections are joined by attachment fittings on the upper surface and splice plates on the undersurface; the joints are located 2.4m (7ft 10½in) and 11.6m (38ft 1in) from the fuselage centreline. The wing/fuselage joint is covered by a fairing (see above).

The centre section and inner wings are three-spar structures, while the outer wings are two-spar structures. The centre section and inner wing ribs (except Nos 10, 11, 17 and 18) are parallel to the fuselage axis, with a pitch of 620 to 650mm (2ft 0.4in to 2ft 1.59in); most of the outer wing ribs are at right angles to the rear spar. The wing skins are chemically milled with integral stringers and incorporate numerous removable access panels for inspection of the integral fuel tanks (located dorsally on the centre section/inner wings and ventrally on the outer wings). The wing leading and trailing edges feature numerous hinged ventral panels for access to control runs, hydraulic and fuel lines, flap and slat drive shafts, electric cables etc.

Two engine pylons are attached to each inner wing at ribs 10 to 11 and 17 to 18. The distance between the inner pylons is 12.7m (41ft 8in) and the distance between the outer pylons 21.2m (69ft 7in), ie, the pylons are respectively 6.35m (20ft 10in) and 10.6m (34ft 9in) from the fuselage centreline. Each outer wing incorporates attachment points for two external stores pylons at ribs 28 and 30.

The wings are equipped with two-section triple-slotted flaps (one section on each inner and outer wing), five-section leading-edge slats (two inboard and three outboard sections), two-section ailerons (see Control system), four-section airbrakes on the inner wings and four-section spoilers/lift dumpers on the outer wings. The flaps move on external tracks enclosed by fairings (four on each inboard flap and three on each outboard flap). Both inboard slat sections on each side have cutouts to clear the engine pylons when fully deployed. Flap settings are 15° or 30° for take-off and 43°/41° (inboard/outboard) for landing; the slats are deployed 14° (at 15° flap) or 25°. Maximum airbrake and spoiler deflection is 40° and 20° respectively.

Tail unit

Cantilever T-tail of all-metal stressed-skin construction made of D16T duralumin. The *vertical tail* consists of a fin and one-piece rudder (see Control system). The fin is a three-spar structure with 20 ribs set at right angles to the rear spar; the spars are attached to aft fuselage mainframes 74, 82 and 86, with five auxiliary fittings in between. Three rudder mounting brackets are located at ribs 10 to 11, 21 to 22 and 33 to 34; an upper rudder support structure extends aft from the rear spar at the top. A small curved root fillet is attached to the centre and aft fuselage (frames 62 to 72). Sweepback at quarter-chord 39°, fin area (less rudder) 50m² (537.63ft²).

The variable-incidence *horizontal tail* is hinged to the fin centre spar and consists of two stabilizers and one-piece elevators (see Control system). Sweepback at quarter-chord 32°, span 17.4m (57ft 1in), stabilizer area (less elevators) 63m² (677.42ft²). Stabilizer incidence +2°/-8°, adjusted by an electric screwjack located on the fin front spar. Each stabilizer has two spars, 22 ribs and a rounded tip fairing; five elevator mounting brackets are located at ribs 6, 10, 14, 18 and 22. The fin/stabilizer joint is enclosed by a large area-ruled bullet fairing with 23 frames; maintenance hatches are provided between frames 6 and 17.

Landing gear: Hydraulically-retractable tricycle type, with free-fall extension in emergency. Five independent units, each with four wheels on a single axle (ie, two pairs each side of the oleo) for soft-field capability. The nose unit has 1,100 x 330mm (43.3 x 13in) KT-159 wheels (KT = *koleso tormoznoye* – brake wheel) and is equipped with a shimmy damper. The four main units are located fore and aft of the aircraft's centre of gravity and have 1,300 x 480mm (51.2 x 18.9in) KT-158 wheels. All wheels have multi-disc brakes.

The nose unit retracts forward, the main units inward into two circular-section ventral fairings. During retraction the mainwheel axles rotate around the oleos by means of mechanical links so that the wheels stow vertically with the axles parallel to the fuselage axis; the axles of the forward pair of main units rotate forward and the axles of the aft pair rotate aft. The main gear fulcrum (main pivot) attachment fittings on fuselage mainframes 37, 41, 45 and 49 are made of VT16 titanium alloy and the side strut attachment fittings of VT22 titanium alloy.

The nosewheel well is closed by two pairs of doors. Each main unit has a large curved main door attached to the fuselage keel beam, small double doors in the lateral main gear fairings near the oleos and a small door segment hinged to the oleo itself. All doors open only when the gear is in transit; this prevents mud, water and slush from entering the wheel wells.

All landing gear struts have oleo-pneumatic shock absorbers and the nose unit has levered suspension. The steerable nose unit can turn ±50° for taxying; steering is assisted by differential braking, enabling the aircraft to make a U-turn on a runway 40m (131ft) wide. Tyre pressure can be adjusted in flight between 2.5 to 5 bars (36 to 73psi) to suit different types of runways (paved or unpaved). Three jacking points are located beneath the front ends of the lateral main gear fairings (at fuselage frame 27) and immediately ahead of the cargo ramp (at frame 55).

Powerplant

The IL-76 *sans suffixe*, IL-76M and IL-76T are powered by four Solov'yov (Aviadvigatel') D-30KP turbofans rated at 12,000kgp (117.7 kN; 26,455 lbst) for take-off, with a cruise rating of 2,750kgp (27 kN; 6,063 lbst) at 11,000m (36,089ft) and Mach 0.8.

The D-30KP is a two-shaft turbofan with a three-stage low-pressure (LP) compressor, 11-stage high-pressure (HP) compressor, cannular combustion chamber, two-stage HP turbine, four-stage LP turbine, fixed-area jetpipe with 16-chute core/bypass flow mixer, and clamshell thrust reverser. Bypass ratio 2.42; overall engine pressure ratio 20 at sea level (engine speed 96%, ie, HP speed 10,460rpm), mass flow at take-off 269kg/sec (593 lb/sec) at LP speed 7,460rpm. Length overall 5.7m (18ft 8in), inlet diameter 1.464m (4ft 10in); dry weight 2,650kg (5,842 lb). Specific fuel consumption (SFC) at take-off rating 0.49kg/kgp · h, cruise SFC 0.7kg/kgp · h.

Construction is mostly of titanium alloy, with steel used for some HP compressor parts. The LP spool rotates in three bearings: a roller bearing in the air intake assembly, a ball bearing in the division casing and a roller bearing in the rear support frame. The HP spool likewise has three bearings: a roller bearing in the division casing, a ball thrust bearing at the rear of the compressor and a roller bearing ahead of the turbine.

The air intake assembly has a fixed spinner and 26 cambered inlet guide vanes (IGVs) de-iced by hot air bled from the 6th or 11th compressor stage; variable IGVs are used on the HP compressor to minimise blade vibration. The division casing is made of magnesium alloy. The combustion chamber has 12 flame tubes, two of which feature igniters; the outer casing and duct shroud are split horizontally for access to the flame tubes. HP turbine blades are cooled by engine bleed air, while LP turbine blades are uncooled.

Two ventral accessory gearboxes (front and rear) are provided, one of which has a constant-speed drive for the AC generator and starter. The lubrication system incorporates a fuel/oil heat exchanger and uses VNII NP-50-1-4F synthetic oil[1] or equivalent. The engine is started by an STV-4 air turbine starter *(startyor vozdooshnyy)* fed by the APU, ground supply or cross-bleed from other engines; time from start to idle is 40 to 80 sec, depending on outside air temperature (operational limits are -60°/+50°C; -76°/+122°F). In-flight starting by windmilling is possible at up to 9,000m (29,527ft).

The engines are mounted in individual nacelles on large forward-swept pylons under the inner wings. Strictly speaking, there are no nacelles as such; each nacelle consists of a one-piece annular forward fairing, four hinged cowling panels and a multi-segment rear fairing. All of these are attached directly to the engine casing, and the nacelle can be disassembled completely or partially, leaving the engine on the wing. The engine attachment lugs are mounted on the division casing and rear support frame.

The IL-76MD, IL-76TD and their derivatives have D-30KP Srs 2 turbofans uprated to 12,500kgp (27,557 lbst) which maintain full power up to ISA +23°C (some sources indicate +27°C) instead of ISA +15°C. These are interchangeable with the D-30KP Srs 1 (see Chapter 3). The engine is manufactured by the Perm' Engine Plant (AO Permskiye Motory).

A Stoopino Machinery Design Bureau TA-6A auxiliary power unit is installed in the front portion of the port main gear fairing for self-contained engine starting, AC/DC ground power supply and air conditioning. The APU has an inward-opening intake door (which opens automatically during APU starting), a one-piece upward-hinged cowling and a lateral exhaust.

Control system

Powered controls with irreversible hydraulic actuators on ailerons, rudder and elevators. Unusually, the actuators are self-contained units, each with its own hydraulic reservoir and electrically-driven pump. There is a manual emergency backup mode with conventional mechanical controls (push-pull rods, cranks and levers). The mechanical control runs are duplicated (except rudder control) and routed along opposite sides of the fuselage for greater survivability; each of the control runs may be disconnected from the control columns or rudder pedals if it jams. An autopilot is fitted.

Roll control is provided by two-section ailerons and four-section spoilers/lift dumpers on the outer wings. The ailerons have trim tabs on the outer sections and servo tabs on the inner sections. Aileron deflection is 28±1° up and 16±1° down, spoiler deflection for roll control 20°.

Pitch control is provided by one-piece elevators; these are single-spar structures with a forward false spar and 61 ribs. Each elevator incorporates a Flettner tab (ribs 1 to 23). Each elevator is hinged on one root support and five brackets located at stabilizer ribs 3, 6, 10, 14, 18 and 22 (corresponding to elevator ribs 0, 8, 18, 29, 40 and 51). Elevator deflection is 21±1° up and 15±1° down

Directional control is provided by a one-piece rudder which has 50 ribs, a forward false spar, a main spar and an auxiliary spar. The rudder features a servo tab (ribs 1 to 36) and a trim tab (ribs 36 to 50). It is is hinged on three brackets located at fin ribs 10, 13 and 17 (corresponding to rudder ribs 10 to 11, 21 to 22 and

33 to 34), plus upper and lower supports located aft of the fin torsion box. Rudder deflection is ±28° 30'.

Fuel system

The wing torsion box (centre section, inner and outer wings) is divided into 12 integral fuel tanks and two vent surge tanks; the latter have pressurization air scoops under the wingtips. The fuel tanks are split into four groups, one for each engine; each group has a service tank from which fuel is fed to the respective engine. All tanks are sealed from within by a coat of sealing compound.

The IL-76 has single-point pressure refuelling; the refuelling panel is located on the port main gear fairing between the main gear units. Operation of fuel transfer and delivery pumps is completely automatic. Fuel grades used are Russian T-1 and TS-1 jet fuel, Western Jet A-1, DERD.2494 and 2498 (NATO F35 and F43) or equivalent.

An inert gas pressurization system is provided on military versions to pressurise the fuel tanks and reduce the hazard of explosion if hit by enemy fire. This includes an inert gas generator in the front portion of the starboard main gear fairing breathing through a small air intake; some IL-76MDs are retrofitted with additional nitrogen bottles in the forward baggage compartment.

Hydraulics

Two separate hydraulic systems which power the landing gear, flaps, slats, airbrakes, spoilers/lift dumpers, cargo ramp/doors, tail support and, if required, entry doors (for paradropping) and escape chute door.

Electrics

AC power supplied by engine-driven generators and APU generator; the electric system includes DC converters. Backup DC power is provided by battery in the starboard main gear fairing. Ground power receptacle under the front end of the starboard main gear fairing.

Oxygen system

Liquid oxygen (LOX) bottles and a LOX converter are installed in one of the main gear fairings to provide breathing oxygen for the crew and troops in the freight hold.

Air conditioning and pressurization system

The crew section, freight hold and, on the *Candid-B*, the tail gunner's compartment are pressurized by engine bleed air to a pressure differential of 0.5 ± 0.02kg/cm² (7.14 ± 0.28psi). Pressurization air is cooled by two heat exchangers located in the forward portion of the wing/fuselage fairing, with elliptical air intakes at the front and efflux gills on the sides.

Fire suppression system

Three groups of fire extinguisher bottles charged with 114V$_2$ grade chlorofluorocarbon extinguishing agent for each engine. The first group is triggered automatically by flame sensors in the engine nacelles; the second and third groups are manually operated. A separate fire extinguisher for the APU bay.

De-icing system
The wing leading edge and engine air intakes are de-iced by engine bleed air. Electric de-icing on the fin and stabilizer leading edges, pitot heads, static ports and flight deck/navigator's station glazing.

Accommodation/cargo handling equipment
Tip-up seats along the freight hold walls. In paradrop configuration a double row of quickly removable seats, back to back, can be installed down the centre of the freight hold on the *Candid-B*. Static line attachments can be configured in different ways, depending on what is to be dropped (cargo or troops) and whether troops are to be dropped through the cargo door, entry doors, or both. A siren and illuminated signs are provided for initiating the drop sequence. In personnel carrier (non-paradrop) configuration a detachable upper deck can be installed on several fittings (see Centre fuselage).

The freight hold floor incorporates four foldaway roller conveyors for container/pallet handling, recessed cargo tiedown points and fittings for special equipment (eg, stretcher supports allowing the aircraft to be configured for the CASEVAC role). Loads are secured by chains and turnbuckles. Removable roller conveyors can be fitted to the cargo ramp. The cargo tiedown points are made of VT5L titanium alloy.

The cargo ramp houses four manually-retractable vehicle loading ramps. These are normally fitted four-abreast with the ramp fully lowered and the tail bumper resting on the ground. If a long vehicle has to be loaded, the cargo ramp is lowered only partially and set at approximately 6° and the vehicle loading ramps are attached consecutively, with auxiliary supports in between. Two LPG-3000A winches developing a force of 3,000kg (6,613 lb) each are installed under the freight hold floor for loading trailers and the like.

Four electric cargo hoists capable of lifting 2,500kg (5,511 lb) each move on rails which run the full length of the freight hold roof, continuing over the rear pressure bulkhead and beyond it (the cargo door centre segment fits between them). This enables the hoists to move 5.65m (18ft 6⅛in) beyond the cargo ramp for straight-in loading of containers etc, weighing up to 10,000kg (22,045 lb) from a truck bed or a trailer. The cargo ramp may also be used to lift loads weighing up to 2.5 tons (5,511 lb), though some sources state 30 tons (66,137 lb); in these cases the retractable support is used (see Centre fuselage).

Armament (*Candid-B*)
One UKU-9K-502-1 tail turret with two Gryazev/Shipoonov GSh-23 double-barrel 23mm (.90 calibre) cannons. The GSh-23 weighs 51kg (112 lb) and fires 200g (7.06 oz) projectiles; rate of fire is 3,200 rounds per minute and muzzle velocity 700m/sec (2,296ft/sec). Ranging and aiming is by means of a PRS-4 Krypton (*izdeliye 4DK*, NATO *Box Tail*) gun ranging radar installed at the base of the rudder above the gunner's station. Two small pylons can be fitted under each outer wing for carrying bombs up to 500kg (1,102 lb) or other stores.

Avionics and equipment
a) navigation and piloting equipment: Full equipment for all-weather day/night operation. The IL-76 features an SAU-1T-2BT automatic flight control system (*sistema avtomateecheskovo oopravleniya*), A DISS-013-S2 or DISS-013-S2M Doppler speed/drift sensor (*doplerovskiy izmeritel' skorosti i snosa*), an RLS-N Groza weather radar in the extreme nose.

The navigation suite comprises a central digital navigation computer, a TKS-P precision compass system (*tochnaya koorsovaya sistema*), a duplex I-P-76 intertial navigation system and an RSBN-7S Vstrecha (Rendezvous) short-range navigation (SHORAN) system. Military aircraft also have an A-723 long-range navigation (LORAN) system with a dorsal strake aerial offset to starboard aft of the wings.

The aircraft is equipped with an instrument landing system permitting ICAO Cat II automatic approach, with Koors-MP-2 and Koors-MP-70 automatic approach systems (*koors* = heading), RV-5 and RV-5M radio altimeters (*rahdiovysotomer*) linked to a Vektor ground proximity warning system (GPWS), an ARK-15M automatic direction finder (*avtomateecheskiy rahdiokompas* – ADF), SD-75 and SDK-67 distance measuring equipment (*samolyotnyy dahl'nomer* – DME).

An RLS-P Koopol ground mapping radar with a 360° field of view is installed under the nose. On the *Candid-B* this is aided by an electro-optical sight at the navigator's station for precision paradropping. An RI-65 automatic voice annunciator (*rechevoy informahtor*) warns the crew of critical failures (fire etc) and dangerous flight modes.

b) Communications equipment: R-855UM, R-855A1 and R-861 UHF radios with dorsal and ventral blade aerials on forward fuselage. Main and backup Mikron (Micron) and Yadro (Core) VHF radios with antennas buried in the fin bullet fairing. R-851 emergency radio beacon for sending distress signals. SPU-8 and SPU-15 intercoms (*samolyotnoye peregovornoye oostroystvo*).

c) IFF system: SRO-2M Khrom (Chromium; NATO *Odd Rods*) IFF transponder (*samolyotnyy rahdiookatseeonnyy otvetchik* – literally, aircraft-mounted radar responder). From approximately 1987 onwards it was replaced by an SRO-1P Parol' (Password, aka *izdeliye 62-01*) IFF transponder on IL-76MDs and other military versions. The IFF aerials are located

The table below lists the cargo containers and pallets used by the commercial IL-76.

Model	Dimensions	Loaded Weight	Qty
UAK-5 air freight container	2,991 x 2,438 x 2,438mm (9ft 10in x 8ft 0in x 8ft 0in)	5,670kg (12,500 lb)	6
UAK-5A air freight container	2,991 x 2,438 x 1,900mm (9ft 10in x 8ft 0in x 6ft 3in)	5,000kg (11,023 lb)	6
UAK-2,5 air freight container	1,456 x 2,438 x 1,900mm (4ft 9in x 8ft 0in x 6ft 3in)	2,500kg (5,511 lb)	12
PA-5,6 rigid pallet	2,991 x 2,438mm (9ft 10in x 8ft 0in)	5,670kg (12,500 lb)	6
PA-2,5 rigid pallet	1,456 x 2,438mm (4ft 9in x 8ft 0in)	2,500kg (5,511 lb)	12
PA-3,6 flexible pallet	2,235 x 2,743mm (7ft 4in x 9ft 0in)	3,630kg (8,002 lb)	6
UAK-10 air freight container	6,046 x 2,438 x 2,438mm (19ft 10in x 8ft 0in x 8ft 0in)	10,000kg (22,045 lb)	4
Standard 20' sea / land container	6,098 x 2,758 x 2,758mm (20ft 0in x 9ft 0in x 9ft 0in)	unknown	3

UAK-5 containers about to be loaded into an IL-76T.
Sergey and Dmitriy Komissarov

ahead of the flight deck glazing and under fuselage section F4, offset to starboard. The aircraft also features SOM-64, SO-70 and SO-72M ATC transponders.

d) Electronic support measures (ESM) equipment: S-3M Sirena-2 radar homing and warning system (RHAWS) with aerials on the forward/aft fuselage sides and wingtips. Active ECM system (*Candid-B* only) with six teardrop antenna fairings (four on the forward fuselage sides and two on the aft fuselage) to give 360° coverage and two small rounded fairings on the navigator's glazing.

Some IL-76MDs have provisions (mounting lugs and electrical connectors) for podded 96- or 192-round APP-50 chaff/flare dispensers on aft fuselage sides firing 50mm (1.96in) magnesium flares or chaff cartridges as a protection against air-to-air and surface-to-air missiles. Some IL-76Ms and 'MDs have 96-round APP-50s built into the aft portions of the ventral main-wheel fairings. The flares are launched at preset intervals, two or four at a time, manually or automatically (by the optional Rifma optical sensor which detects SAM launches). Alternatively, the cannons can fire PRLS rounds filled with chaff and PIKS rounds filled with a termite mixture to decoy radar-guided and IR-homing missiles.

e) Data recording equipment: Standard Soviet Mars-BM flight data recorder (FDR) and MS-61B cockpit voice recorder (CVR).

f) Exterior lighting: Port (red) and starboard (green) navigation lights in wingtips. White tail navigation light on tailcone (*Candid-A*) or under tail turret (*Candid-B*), augmented by amber and green formation/signal lights (used during night paradropping) on the *Candid-B* and IL-76M/MD 'Falsie'. Four retractable landing/taxi lights on forward fuselage sides aft of navigator's station and (on the IL-76 *sans suffixe*, IL-76M and IL-76T) in the middle flap track fairings of the outboard flaps; the IL-76MD and IL-76TD have the wing landing lights moved outboard to the wingtips. Red anti-collision strobe lights on top of wing centre section (offset to starboard) and in the middle of the centre cargo door segment. Faired wing/air intake inspection light on the port side of the forward fuselage (IL-78M, starboard side); buried tail unit inspection light in the rear portion of the port main gear fairing (plus two refuelling pod inspection lights at the same location and one in the starboard fairing on the IL-78/IL-78M). Two floodlights buried in the centre cargo door segment to illuminate the loading area at night. Three 26mm (1.02in) ESKR-46 four-round signal flare launchers low on the starboard side immediately aft of the ground mapping radar.

IL-76 Family specifications

	IL-76	IL-76M/T	IL-76MD/TD	IL-76MF/TF	IL-78 / IL-78M
Wing span, m (ft)	50.5 (165' 8")	50.5 (165' 8")	50.5 (165' 8")	50.5 (165' 8")	50.5 (165' 8")
Wing area, m² (ft²)	300.0 (3,229.2)	300.0 (3,229.2)	300.0 (3,229.2)	300.0 (3,229.2)	300.0 (3,229.2)
Length overall, m (ft)	46.59 (152' 10")	46.59 (152' 10")	46.59 (152' 10")	52.34 (171' 8½")	46.59 (152' 10")
Height on ground, m (ft)	14.76 (48' 5")	14.76 (48' 5")	14.76 (48' 5")	14.45 (47' 5")	14.76 (48' 5")
Freight hold dimensions:					
length including ramp, m (ft)	24.5 (80' 4½")	24.5 (80' 4½")	24.5 (80' 4½")	30.25 (99' 2½")	24.5 (80' 4½")
length excluding ramp, m (ft)	20.0 (65' 7½")	20.0 (65' 7½")	20.0 (65' 7½")	25.75 (84' 6")	20.0 (65' 7½")
width, m (ft)	3.4 (11' 2")	3.4 (11' 2")	3.4 (11' 2")	3.4 (11' 2")	3.4 (11' 2")
height, m (ft)	3.46 (11' 4")	3.46 (11' 4")	3.46 (11' 4")	3.46 (11' 4")	3.46 (11' 4")
Freight hold volume, m³ (ft³)	321 (11,336)	321 (11,336)	321 (11,336)	400 (14,125)	321 (11,336)
Operating empty weight, kg (lb)	n/a	n/a	92,000 (202,821)	104,000 (229,276)	92,000 (202,821)
MTOW, kg (lb)	157,000 (346,120)	170,000 (374,785)	190,000 (418,875)	210,000 (462,963)	190,000 / 210,000 (418,875 / 462,963)
Max landing weight, kg (lb)	135,000 (297,619)	150,000 (330,687)	151,500 (333,995)	n/a	151,500 (333,995)
Fuel load, kg (lb)	n/a	84,840 (187,037)	90,000 (198,412)	90,000 (198,412)	118,000 / 138,000 (260,141 / 304,233)
Max payload, kg (lb)	40,000 (88,186)	48,000 (105,820)	50,000 (110,229)	60,000 (132,275)	85,720 / 105,720 (188,977 / 233,068)
Max axle load (vehicles), kg (lb)			7,500 to 11,000 (16,535 to 24,250)		
Max floor loading, kg/m² (lb/ft²)			1,450 to 3,100 (297 to 635)		
Max wing loading, kg/m² (lb/ft²)	n/a	566.7 (116.05)	633.3 (129.72)	n/a	n/a
Max power loading, kg/kgp (lb/lbst)	n/a	3.54	3.95	n/a	n/a
Top speed, km/h (kts)	850 (459)	850 (459)	850 (459)	850 (459)	850 (459)
Cruising speed, km/h (kts)	750 to 800 (405 to 432)	750 to 800 (405 to 432)	750 to 800 (405 to 432)	750 to 800 (405 to 432)	750 (405)
Unstick speed, km/h (kts)	n/a	210 (114)	n/a	n/a	n/a
Approach and landing speed, km/h (kts)	n/a	220 to 240 (119 to 130)	n/a	n/a	n/a
Normal cruise altitude, m (ft)			9,000 to 12,000 (29,500 to 39,370)		
Absolute ceiling, m (ft)	n/a	15,500 (50,850)	n/a	n/a	n/a
T/O run, m (ft)	n/a	850 (2,790)	1,700 (5,580)	1,800 (5,905)	1,700 / 2,080 (5,580 / 6,825)
Landing run, m (ft)	n/a	450 (1,475)	1,000 (3,280)	900 (2,950)	
Range with max payload, km (nm)	3,650 (1,973)	4,000 (2,162)	4,400 (2,378)	4,200 (2,270)	3,650 (1,973)

Right: **The forward fuselage of IL-76 *sans suffixe* EP-TPO/86817. Note reinforcement ribs on the nose radome, triple signal flare launchers aft of the chin radome, radar homing and warning system antennas over the navigator's station glazing, and traces of the removed ECM antenna blisters ahead of and below the 'IL-76' titles.** Dmitriy Komissarov

Below left: **A flight deck shot of a late-production IL-76TD (RA-76798). Some instruments are missing on the first officer's panel because the aircraft was undergoing an overhaul at the time. Note blind flying hoods.** Yefim Gordon

Below right: **The captain's side control console.** Yefim Gordon

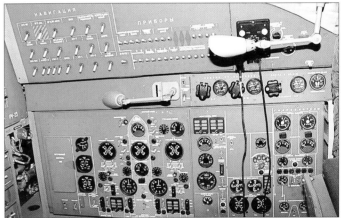

Above left: **The first officer's side control console.** Yefim Gordon

Above right: **The flight engineer's workstation on the port side, with electrics switches for the flight and navigation instruments above it.** Yefim Gordon

Right: **The radio operator's workstation on the starboard side, with a backup set of switches. Note the registration drawn in pencil on the panel.** Yefim Gordon

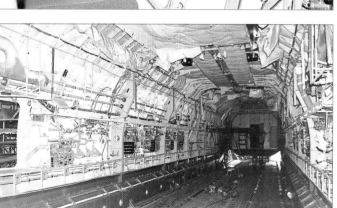

Top left and right: **The main electrics switch panel occupies the entire rear wall of the flight deck.** Yefim Gordon

Above left: **The navigator's station of the IL-76TD with typical Soviet rubber-bladed cooling fan. The yellow circular display to the left on the front panel is the weather radar display; the similar white display to the right is probably for the ground mapping radar.** Dmitriy Komissarov

Above right: **The navigator's port side instrument panel.** Yefim Gordon

Left: **The freight hold of IL-76TD RA-76781. With most of the wall liners removed during an overhaul, the various equipment, control runs and soundproofing/heat-insulating blankets along the walls are clearly visible, as are the roller conveyor stowage recesses in the floor. Note the open door in the rear pressure bulkhead which leads to the gunner's station on the _Candid-B_.** Dmitriy Komissarov

Right: **The retractable support stowed in the cargo ramp; it is extended telescopically to make contact with the ground after extension.** Dmitriy Komissarov

Below left: **The cargo ramp. Part of the skin and the tail bumper have been removed for replacement.** Yefim Gordon

Below right: **The aft fuselage of a *Candid-B*.** Yefim Gordon

Centre left: **The starboard main gear fairing with inert gas generator air intake.** Dmitriy Komissarov

Centre right: **The outer wing panel of IL-76TD RA-76482. The outboard flap (with metal plates indicating the aircraft's c/n) is well visible.** Dmitriy Komissarov

Bottom right: **This view shows the hefty flap tracks, as well as the inner/outer wing joint rib and fittings.** Yefim Gordon

Bottom right: **The port inboard flap.** Dmitriy Komissarov

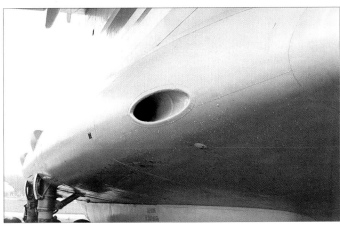

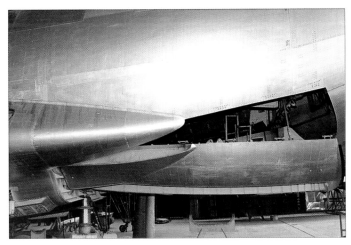

Top left: **The port outboard flap of an early _Candid-B_; note the landing light in the centre flap track fairing typical of early _Candid_ versions.** Dmitriy Komissarov

Top right: **The wingtip of IL-76MD RA-78807, showing vent surge tank air intake and the large aileron. Note landing light position on late IL-76TD/MDs.** Sergey Panov

Above left: **The aft fuselage and tail unit of IL-76MD RA-76577. Note the tail gunner's station emergency door.** Yefim Gordon

Above right: **The horizontal tail, minus front and rear bullet fairings and leading-edge de-icers.** Yefim Gordon

Centre left: **A view of the IL-76's 20-wheel high-flotation landing gear, illustrated in this case by IL-78M '36 Blue'.** Yefim Gordon

Centre right: **The starboard main gear units. Tire pressure can be adjusted in flight to suit different types of runways. The inscription on the gear doors reads DO NOT CLOSE MANUALLY.** Yefim Gordon

Bottom left: **The nosewheel well. Note the scuff-resistant steel liners and the small metal plates with the aircraft's c/n on the inside of the gear doors. The door actuator jacks are held in open position by red safety clamps while maintenance is in progress.** Dmitriy Komissarov

Top right: **This view of IL-76M RA-86884 trestled for landing gear retraction tests shows how the jacks are placed under the aircraft. The extremely weathered finish is noteworthy.** Sergey Panov

Below left: **The starboard mainwheel wells, again with safety clamps on the door actuator jacks.** Dmitriy Komissarov

Below right: **The thrust reverser in deployed position.** Dmitriy Komissarov

Centre left: **The engines can be completely 'undressed' while still on the wing. This view clearly shows the oil tank, the ventral accessories gearboxes and the horizontally split engine casing.** Dmitriy Komissarov

Centre right: **The detachable external stores pylons under the outer wing of a *Candid-B*.** Yefim Gordon

Bottom left: **The TA-6A APU is easily accessed via a large upward-hinging cowling.** Dmitriy Komissarov

Bottom right: **The UKU-9K-502-1 tail turret with twin Gsh-23 cannons and associated PRS-4 Krypton ranging radar.** Yefim Gordon

Production List

Production of the IL-76 family is presented in construction number/fuselage number order. Crashed examples are duly marked with † (RIP cross) followed by the date of the crash (in italics if unconfirmed). The split presentation of c/ns is used for the sake of convenience to show how the numbers accrue. Aircraft certificated later than neighbouring examples and hence having higher 'first three' digits are marked in bold. Manufacture dates are generally obtained from Russian documents,but those obtained from other sources (and hence unconfirmed) are marked with * (asterisk). *d* is used to indicate demilitarised aircraft (with tail gunner's station but no tail turret).

Construction number	Fuselage number	Version	Registration/ tactical code/serial	Manufacture date
01-01	–	IL-76 (civil), IL-76LL	CCCP-86712	
01-02	–	IL-76 (civil)	– (static test airframe)	
01-03	–	IL-76 (civil)	CCCP-86711	
03.34.01.016	0104	IL-76 (civil)	CCCP-76500	
03.34.01.019	0105	IL-76 (military)	CCCP-76501	
03.34.01.022	0106	IL-76 (military)	CCCP-86600, RA-86600	
03.34.02.026	0107	IL-76 (military)	CCCP-86601	
03.34.02.031	0108	IL-76 (military)	CCCP-86602, 602 Black [Russian AF]	
0*.34.02.035?	0109	IL-76 (military) *d*ⁱ	CCCP-86603, RA-86603	
04.34.02.039	0110	IL-76 (military), IL-76T 'Falsie'	CCCP-86604, RA-86604, EL-RDX, 3D-RTX, TL-ACU	
04.34.02.041	0201	IL-76 (military)	CCCP-86643?, 21 Red [Soviet AF], RA-76416	15-11-1973*
04.34.02.046	0202	IL-76 (military)	CCCP-86644, 644 Black [Soviet AF], RA-76417	9-9-1974*
04.34.02.049	0203	IL-76 (military)	CCCP-86645, 645 Black [Russian AF]	
04.34.02.053	0204	IL-76 (military)	CCCP-86646	
04.34.02.060	0205	IL-76 (military)	CCCP-86647, RA-86647	
04.34.03.061	0206	IL-76 (military)	CCCP-86713, 713 Black [Russian AF]	
05.34.03.067?	0207	IL-76 (military)	CCCP-86714 †	
05.34.03.072	0208	IL-76 (military), IL-76T 'Falsie' *d*	CCCP-86715, RA-86715, EL-RDT, 3D-RTT, TL-ACN	
05.34.03.073	0209	IL-76 (military)	CCCP-86805, RA-86805	
05.34.03.078	0210	IL-76 (military)	CCCP-86806, RA-86806	
05.34.04.083	0301	IL-76 (military)	CCCP-86807	
05.34.04.085	0302	IL-76 (military)	CCCP-86808	
05.34.04.091	0303	IL-76 (military)	CCCP-86809, RA-86809	
05.34.04.094	0304	IL-76 (military)	CCCP-86810, RA-86810; 4K-86810?ⁱⁱⁱ	
05.34.04.098	0305	IL-76 (military)	CCCP-86811, 811 Black [Russian AF]	
05.34.04.103	0306	IL-76 (military)	CCCP-86812, RA-86812	
05.34.04.105	0307	IL-76 (military)	CCCP-86813, RA-86813	
05.34.05.110	0308	IL-76 (military)	CCCP-86814, RA-86814	
05.34.05.114	0309	IL-76 (military)	CCCP-86821	
05.34.05.117	0310	IL-76 (military)	CCCP-86621ⁱᵛ	
05.34.05.1**	0310A?	IL-76 (military)	CCCP-86822?	
05.34.05.124	0401	IL-76 (military)	CCCP-86823	
05.34.05.128	0402	IL-76 (military)	CCCP-86824	
06.34.05.130	0403	IL-76 (military)	CCCP-86625, RA-86625	
06.34.05.135	0404	IL-76 (military)	CCCP-86626, 626 Black [Russian AF], RA-86626	
06.34.05.137	0405	IL-76 (military) *d*	CCCP-86627, RA-86627	
06.34.05.144	0406	IL-76 (military)	CCCP-86628, RA-86628	
06.34.06.148	0407	IL-76 (military)	CCCP-86629, 629 Black [Russian AF], RA-86629	
06.34.06.149	0408	IL-76 (military)	CCCP-86630	
06.34.06.156	0409	IL-76 (military)	CCCP-86716, 716 Black [Russian AF]	
06.34.06.160	0410	IL-76 (military)	CCCP-86717	
06.34.07.162	0501	IL-76 (military)	CCCP-86745	
06.34.07.165	0502	IL-76 (military)	CCCP-86746, RA-86746	
06.34.07.170	0503	IL-76 (military)	CCCP-86747, RA-86747	
06.34.07.175	0504	IL-76 (military)	CCCP-86748, RA-86748	
06.34.07.179	0505	IL-76 (military)	CCCP-86749, RA-86749	
06.34.07.183	0506	IL-76 (military)	CCCP-86815	
06.34.07.185	0507	IL-76 (military)	CCCP-86816; 616 Black [Russian AF]?	
06.34.07.191	0508	IL-76 (military) *d*	CCCP-86817, EK-86817, EP-TPO/86817	?-3-1976*
06.34.07.194	0509	IL-76 (military)	CCCP-86818	
06.34.07.199	0510	IL-76 (military)	CCCP-86819, 819 Black [Russian AF]	
06.34.07.202	0601	IL-76 (military)	CCCP-86631	
06.34.07.206	0602	IL-76 (civil)	CCCP-76502	
06.34.08.209	0603	IL-76 (civil)	CCCP-76503	
06.34.08.214	0604	IL-76 (military)	CCCP-86634, 634 Black [Russian AF]	
06.34.08.217	0605	IL-76 (military)	CCCP-86635, 635 Black [Russian AF]	
06.34.08.222	0606	IL-76 (military)	CCCP-86636	
06.34.09.228	0607	IL-76 (military)	CCCP-86637	
07.34.09.232	0608	IL-76 (mil), IL-76K (prototype)	CCCP-86638	

Construction number	Fuselage number	Version	Registration/ tactical code/serial	Manufacture date
07.34.09.235	0609	IL-76 (military)	CCCP-86639, 86639 [Ukrainian AF]	
07.34.09.237	0610	IL-76 (military) *d*	CCCP-86640, RA-76418	
07.34.09.243	0701	IL-76 (mil), A-50 (prototype)	CCCP-86641, 10 Red [Soviet AF]	
07.34.09.248	0702	IL-76 (military)	CCCP-86642, RA-86642	
07.34.09.251	0703	IL-76 (military)	CCCP-86632, 632 Black [Russian AF]	
07.34.09.256	0704	IL-76 (military)	CCCP-86633, 86633 [Ukrainian AF]	
07.34.09.259?	0705	IL-76 (military)	CCCP-86718 †	
07.34.09.263	0706	IL-76 (military)	CCCP-86719, 719 Black [Russian AF]	
07.34.09.267	0707	IL-76 (mil), IL-76T 'Falsie'	CCCP-86720, RA-86720	27-12-1976*
07.34.10.271	0708	IL-76 (mil), aircraft 676	CCCP-86721	
07.34.10.276	0709	IL-76 (military)	CCCP-86722, 722 Black [Russian AF]	
07.34.10.279	0710	IL-76 (mil), IL-76K, 'IL-76T'	CCCP-86723, RA-76372, S9-BOM	?-2-1977*
07.34.10.284	0801	IL-76 (military)	CCCP-86724, EK-86724, EP-TPZ/86724	17-2-1977*
07.34.10.285	0802	IL-76 (military)	CCCP-86725, 725 Black [Russian AF]	
07.34.10.292	0803	IL-76 (mil), IL-76T 'Falsie', IL-76TD 'Falsie' *d*	YI-AIK, CCCP-76495, RA-76495, ST-SFT, RA-76495	
07.34.10.293	0804	IL-76 (mil), IL-76T 'Falsie' *d*	YI-AIL, CCCP-76528, RA-76528	
07.34.10.300	0805	IL-76 (mil), IL-76K, 'IL-76T'	CCCP-86729, RA-76430, HA-TCI	
07.34.10.301	0806	IL-76 (mil); IL-76T 'Falsie'?	YIN-AIN?, CCCP-76496, RA-76496, UN-76496	
07.34.10.308	0807	IL-76 (mil), IL-76LL *d*	YI-AIP, CCCP-76529, RA-76529	
07.34.10.311	0808	IL-76 (mil), A-50 (prototype)	CCCP-86..., 15 Red [Soviet AF]? no code?	
07.34.10.315	0809	IL-76 (military)	YI-AIO † *23-9-1980*	
07.34.10.320	0810	IL-76 (mil), IL-76T 'Falsie' *d*	YI-AIM?, CCCP-76497, RA-76497	15-8-1978
07.34.10.322	0901	IL-76M (prototype)	CCCP-86728, 728 Black [Russian AF]	
07.34.11.328	0902	IL-76 (civil), IL-76T	CCCP-76504, RA-76504	
07.34.11.331	0903	IL-76 (civil), IL-76T	CCCP-76505, RA-76505	25-11-1977
07.34.11.334	0904	IL-76 (civil), IL-76T	CCCP-76506, RA-76506	2-12-1977
07.34.11.338	0905	IL-76 (civil), IL-76T	CCCP-76507, RA-76507	
08.34.11.342	0906	IL-76M	CCCP-86736, RA-86736	
08.34.11.347	0907	IL-76M	CCCP-86737, RA-86737	
08.34.11.352	0908	IL-76M	CCCP-86738, 86738	
08.34.12.354?	0909	IL-76M	CCCP-86739 † *26-11-1984*	
08.34.12.358	0910	IL-76M	CCCP-86740, RA-86740	
08.34.12.361	1001	IL-76M	CCCP-86741, RA-86741	
08.34.12.366?	1002	IL-76M	CCCP-86742 †	
08.34.12.369	1003	IL-76M	CCCP-86743, RA-86743	
08.34.12.376	1004	IL-76M	CCCP-86744, RA-86744	
08.34.12.380	1005	IL-76M *d*	CCCP-86726, RA-86726	
08.34.12.383	1006	IL-76M	CCCP-86727	
08.34.13.388?	1007	IL-76M	CCCP-86732 † *11-12-1988*	
08.34.13.391	1008	IL-76M	CCCP-86731, RA-86731	
08.34.13.396	1009	IL-76M	CCCP-86733, RA-86733	
08.34.13.397	1010	IL-76M	CCCP-86734, RA-86734	
08.34.13.403	1101	IL-76M	CCCP-86020	
08.34.13.405?	1102	IL-76M	CCCP-86021 † *1-2-1990*	
08.34.13.412	1103	IL-76 (civil), IL-76T	CCCP-76508, RA-76508	
08.34.13.415	1104	IL-76 (civil), IL-76T	CCCP-76509, RA-76509	28-8-1978
08.34.13.417	1105	IL-76M	CCCP-86022, RA-86022	
08.34.13.422	1106	IL-76M	CCCP-86023, RA-86023	
08.34.14.425	1107	IL-76M, aircraft 776	CCCP-86024	
08.34.14.432	1108	IL-76 (civil), IL-76T	CCCP-76510, RA-76510, YL-LAJ	28-2-1978*
08.34.14.433	1109	IL-76M	CCCP-86025, RA-86025	
08.34.14.439	1110	IL-76M	CCCP-86026, 86026	
08.34.14.444	1201	IL-76T (prototype)	CCCP-76511	
08.34.14.447	1202	IL-76T	CCCP-76512, RA-76512	22-3-1978*
08.34.14.451	1203	IL-76T	CCCP-76513, RA-76513 † *19-8-1996*	22-3-1978*
08.34.15.453	1204	IL-76T	CCCP-76514, RA-76514	
08.34.15.459	1205	IL-76M	CCCP-86027, RA-86027	
08.34.15.464	1206	IL-76M	CCCP-86028, 86028 [Ukrainian AF]	
08.34.15.465	1207	IL-76M	CCCP-86029, 86029 [Ukrainian AF]	
08.34.15.469	1208	IL-76M	5A-DRR	
08.34.15.475	1209	IL-76M	CCCP-86030, 86030 [Ukrainian AF]	
08.34.15.477	1210	IL-76M	CCCP-86031, 86031 [Ukrainian AF]	

Construction number	Fuselage number	Version	Registration/ tactical code/serial	Manufacture date
09.34.15.482	1301	IL-76M	CCCP-86032, RA-86032	
09.34.16.488	1302	IL-76M	CCCP-86033, RA-86033	
09.34.16.489	1303	IL-76M	CCCP-86034, RA-86034	
09.34.16.494	1304	IL-76M	CCCP-86035, RA-86035	
09.34.16.500?	1305	IL-76M	CCCP-86036 † 25-12-1979?	
09.34.16.501	1306	IL-76M	5A-DZZ † 15-4-1986	
09.34.16.506	1307	IL-76M, IL-76T 'Falsie' d	2803 [Iraqi AF], YI-AKO, CCCP-76490, RA-76490	
09.34.17.511	1308	IL-76M	CCCP-86037, RA-86037 ('Velikiy Novgorod'?)	
09.34.17.514	1309	IL-76M	CCCP-86038, RA-86038	
09.34.17.518	1310	IL-76M	CCCP-86039 †	
09.34.17.521	1401	IL-76M	CCCP-86040, RA-86040	
09.34.17.526	1402	IL-76T	CCCP-76515, RA-76515	10-5-1979
09.34.17.532	1403	IL-76M	CCCP-86041, RA-86041	
09.34.17.535	1404	IL-76M	CCCP-86042, RA-86042	
09.34.18.539	1405	IL-76M	CCCP-86043, RA-86043	
09.34.18.543	1406	IL-76M, IL-76T 'Falsie' d	2068 [Iraqi AF], YI-AKS, CCCP-76759, RA-76759	22-10-1978*
09.34.18.548	1407	IL-76M, IL-76T 'Falsie' d	YI-AKT, RA-76492 (No 2; see 0043452549!)	
09.34.18.552	1408	IL-76M	CCCP-86044, RA-86044	
09.34.18.556	1409	IL-76T	CCCP-76516, RA-76516	
09.34.18.560	1410	IL-76T	CCCP-76517, RA-76517	
09.34.18.564	1501	IL-76M	CCCP-86045, RA-86045	
09.34.18.565	1502	IL-76M	CCCP-86046, RA-86046	
09.34.18.572	1503	IL-76M	CCCP-86047	
09.34.19.573	1504	IL-76M	CCCP-86048, RA-86048	
09.34.19.580	1505	IL-76M	CCCP-86049, RA-86049 'Pskov'	
09.34.19.581	1506	IL-76M	CCCP-86825, RA-86825	
09.34.19.588	1507	IL-76M	CCCP-86826, RA-86826	
09.34.19.589	1508	IL-76M	CCCP-86827, RA-86827	
09.34.20.594	1509	IL-76T	CCCP-76518, RA-76518	26-10-1979
09.34.20.599	1510	IL-76T	CCCP-76519, RA-76519	31-10-1979
09.34.20.604	1601	IL-76M	CCCP-86828, RA-86828	
09.34.20.605	1602	IL-76T	CCCP-76520, RA-76520	
09.34.21.612	1603	IL-76M	5A-DLL No1 † 15-4-1986	
09.34.21.613	1604	IL-76M	YK-ATA	
09.34.21.619	1605	IL-76M	YK-ATB	
09.34.21.621	1606	IL-76M, cvtd to IL-76T	CCCP-86925 No1, CCCP-76457, RA-76457	17-12-1979
09.34.21.626	1607	IL-76M	CCCP-86830, RA-86830	
09.34.21.628	1607A	IL-76M 'Falsie', IL-76LL	CCCP-86891, RA-86891	
09.34.21.630	1608	IL-76M, IL-76T 'Falsie'	YI-AKP, CCCP-76491, RA-76491	17-8-1979?
09.34.21.635	1609	IL-76M, IL-76T 'Falsie', IL-76LL d	YI-AKQ, CCCP-06188	
09.34.21.637	1610	IL-76M, IL-76T 'Falsie' d	YI-AKU, CCCP-76754, RA-76754	
09.34.21.642	1701	IL-76M	CCCP-86831, RA-86831	
000.34.21.646	1702	IL-76M	CCCP-86832, RA-86832	
000.34.22.650	1703	IL-76M	CCCP-86833, RA-86833	
000.34.22.655	1704	IL-76M	CCCP-86834	
000.34.22.658	1705	IL-76M	CCCP-86835, RA-86835	
000.34.22.661	1706	IL-76M	CCCP-86836, RA-86836	
000.34.23.668	1707	IL-76M	CCCP-86837, RA-86837	
000.34.23.669	1708	IL-76M	CCCP-86838, RA-86838	
000.34.23.675	1709	IL-76M	5A-DKK † ?-?-1985	
000.34.23.679	1710	IL-76M	5A-DMM † 15-4-1986?^	
000.34.23.684	1801	IL-76M	CCCP-86839, RA-86839	
000.34.23.688	1802	IL-76M	CCCP-86840	
000.34.23.690	1803	IL-76M	CCCP-86843?, RA-86843?	
000.34.23.692	1804	IL-76M	CCCP-86842, RA-86842	
000.34.23.699	1805	IL-76T	CCCP-76521, RA-76521, ER-IBV	
000.34.23.701	1806	IL-76M	CCCP-86841, RA-86841	
000.34.24.707	1807	IL-76T	CCCP-76522, RA-76522, YL-LAK	17-12-1979*
000.34.24.711	1808	IL-76M	CCCP-86844, RA-86844	
000.34.24.715	1809	IL-76M	CCCP-86851, RA-86851	
000.34.24.719	1810	IL-76M	CCCP-86852	
000.34.24.723	1901	IL-76M	CCCP-86853, RA-86853	
000.34.25.728	1902	IL-76M	CCCP-86854, 86854 [Ukrainian AF]	
000.34.25.732	1903	IL-76T	CCCP-76523, RA-76523	28-1-1980*
000.34.25.734	1904	IL-76M	CCCP-86855, RA-86855	
000.34.25.740	1905	IL-76M	CCCP-86856	
000.34.25.744	1906	IL-76M	CCCP-86857, RA-86857	
000.34.25.746	1907	IL-76T	CCCP-76524, RA-76524	
000.34.26.751	1908	IL-76M	CCCP-86858, RA-86858	
000.34.26.755	1909	IL-76M	CCCP-86859	
000.34.26.759	1910	IL-76M	CCCP-86860	
000.34.26.762	2001	IL-76M	CCCP-86845, RA-86845	
000.34.26.765	2002	IL-76M, IL-76T 'Falsie' d	CCCP-86846, RA-86846, 3D-RTA, TL-ACY	18-4-1980*
000.34.26.769	2003	IL-76M	CCCP-86847, RA-86847	
000.34.26.776	2004	IL-76M	CCCP-86848	
000.34.26.779	2005	IL-76M	CCCP-86849, RA-86849	
000.34.27.782	2006	IL-76M	CCCP-86850	
000.34.27.787	2007	IL-76T	CCCP-76525, RA-76525	29-10-1980
000.34.27.792	2008	IL-76T	CCCP-76526, RA-76526	
000.34.27.796	2009	IL-76T	CCCP-76527, RA-76527	20-11-1980
000.34.27.798	2010	IL-76M	CCCP-86829, RA-86829	
000.34.27.804	2101	IL-76M	CCCP-86861, RA-86861	
000.34.27.806	2102	IL-76M	CCCP-86862	
000.34.28.809	2103	IL-76M	CCCP-86863, RA-86863	29-6-1980*
000.34.28.816	2104	IL-76M	CCCP-86864	
000.34.28.817	2105	IL-76M	CCCP-86865, RA-86865	
000.34.28.821	2106	IL-76M	CCCP-86866, RA-86866	
001.34.28.828	2107	IL-76M	CCCP-86867	
001.34.28.831	2108	IL-76M, IL-76T 'Falsie' d	YI-AKV, CCCP-78731, RA-78731, EP-TPF, RA-78731	29-4-1981
001.34.28.833	2109	IL-76M	CCCP-86868, RA-86868	
001.34.28.839	2110	IL-76M, IL-76T 'Falsie'	YI-AKW, CCCP-76756, RA-76756, ?, RA-76756	
001.34.28.844	2201	IL-76M	CCCP-86869, RA-86869	
001.34.29.847	2202	IL-76M	CCCP-86870, RA-86870	
001.34.29.850	2203	IL-76M	CCCP-86873, RA-86873	
001.34.29.853	2204	IL-76M	CCCP-86874, RA-86874	
001.34.29.859	2205	IL-76M	CCCP-86875, RA-86875	
001.34.29.861	2206	IL-76M	CCCP-86876, RA-86876	
001.34.29.867	2207	IL-76M	CCCP-86877	
001.34.30.869	2208	IL-76T	5A-DNJ	
001.34.30.872?	2209	IL-76M	CCCP-86878?	
001.34.30.875	2209A	A-50 (prototype)	20 Red [Soviet AF]	
001.34.30.878	2210	IL-76T	5A-DNI	
001.34.30.882	2301	IL-76T	5A-DNK	
001.34.30.888	2302	IL-76T	CCCP-76458, 76458, RA-76458	
001.34.30.890	2303	IL-76T	CCCP-76459, RA-76459	14-5-1981
001.34.30.893	2304	IL-76M 'Falsie', A-60	CCCP-86879 †	
001.34.30.897	2305	IL-76M	CCCP-86880, RA-86880	
001.34.30.901	2306	IL-76T	CCCP-76926, CCCP-76780*, RA-76780*^	
001.34.31.906	2307	IL-76M	CCCP-86881, RA-86881	
001.34.31.911	2308	IL-76M 'Falsie'	YK-ATC	
001.34.31.915	2309	IL-76M 'Falsie'	YK-ATD	
001.34.31.917	2310	IL-76M	CCCP-86882	
001.34.31.921	2401	IL-76M	CCCP-86883, RA-86883	
001.34.31.928	2402	IL-76T	CCCP-76460, RA-76460	21-8-1981
001.34.31.932	2403	IL-76M	CCCP-86884, RA-86884	
001.34.31.935	2404	IL-76T	CCCP-76461, RA-76461	
001.34.31.939	2405	IL-76M	CCCP-86885, RA-86885	
001.34.31.943	2406	IL-76M	CCCP-86886, RA-86886	
001.34.31.945	2407	IL-76M	CCCP-86887, RA-86887	
001.34.32.952	2408	IL-76M	5A-DNE	
001.34.32.955	2409	IL-76T	CCCP-76462, RA-76462	6-10-1981
001.34.32.960	2410	IL-76T	CCCP-76463, RA-76463	30-10-1981
001.34.32.961	2501	IL-76T	5A-DNG	
001.34.32.966	2502	IL-76M	CCCP-86888, RA-86888	
001.34.32.969	2503	IL-76M	CCCP-86892	
001.34.32.975	2504	IL-76M	CCCP-86893, RA-86893	
001.34.32.977	2505	IL-76M	CCCP-86894, RA-86894	
001.34.33.984	2506	IL-76M, IL-76T 'Falsie'	4600 [Iraqi AF], YI-ALL, CCCP-76755, RA-76755, YL-LAL	
001.34.33.985	2507	IL-76M, IL-76MD	CCCP-86895, RA-86895	
001.34.33.990	2508	IL-76M, IL-76T 'Falsie' d	YI-AKX, CCCP-76757, RA-76757	10-8-1980*
001.34.33.996	2509	IL-76M, IL-76T 'Falsie' d	4660 [Iraqi AF], YI-ALO, CCCP-76788, RA-76788	
001.34.33.999	2510	IL-76M, IL-76T 'Falsie'	4601 [Iraqi AF], YI-ALP, CCCP-76789, RA-76789	
001.34.34.002	2601	IL-76MD (prototype)	CCCP-86871, RA-86871	
001.34.34.008	2602	IL-76MD	CCCP-86872, RA-86872	
001.34.34.009	2603	IL-76MD, IL-76PP	CCCP-86889	
001.34.34.013	2604	IL-76MD	CCCP-86890	
001.34.34.018	2605	IL-76MD, IL-76TD 'Falsie' d	CCCP-86896, YA-YAA?, CCCP-86896, RA-86896, EP-ALJ	?-11-1981*
001.34.34.023	2606	IL-76MD	CCCP-86897, RA-86897	
001.34.35.028	2607	IL-76MD	CCCP-86898, 22 Red [Russian AF]?, RA-86898	
002.34.35.030	2608	IL-76MD	CCCP-86899	
002.34.35.034	2609	IL-76MD	CCCP-86900, 86900 [Russian AF]	
002.34.36.038	2610	IL-76MD	CCCP-86901, RA-86901	22-2-1982
002.34.36.043	2701	IL-76MD	CCCP-86902, RA-86902	
002.34.36.048	2702	IL-76MD, IL-76TD 'Falsie'	CCCP-86903, UR-86903, UR-76382, HA-TCG, RA-76382, HA-TCG 'Szent György'	
002.34.36.050	2703	IL-76MD	CCCP-86904	
002.34.36.054	2704	IL-76MD	CCCP-86905 † 6-6-1990	25-3-1982
002.34.36.059	2705	A-50	30 Red [Soviet/Russian AF]	
002.34.36.064	2706	IL-76MD Skal'pel'-MT	CCCP-86906, RA-86906	
002.34.36.065	2707	IL-76MD	CCCP-86907, RA-86907	
002.34.37.070	2708	IL-76MD d	CCCP-86908, RA-86908	
002.34.37.076	2709	IL-76MD, IL-76TD 'Falsie' d	CCCP-86909, UR-86909, RA-76383, 9L-LBK, EP-TQC, EP-ALB, T9-QAA, T9-CAC	
002.34.37.077	2710	IL-76MD	CCCP-86910, RA-86910	
002.34.37.084	2801	IL-76TD	5A-DNC	
002.34.37.086	2802	IL-76TD	5A-DNB	
002.34.37.090	2803	IL-76TD	CCCP-76464, RA-76464	17-5-1982
002.34.37.093	2804	IL-76MD	CCCP-86911	
002.34.3*.099	2805	IL-76MD	CCCP-86912	
002.34.38.101	2806	IL-76TD	CCCP-76465, RA-76465	10-6-1982
002.34.38.108	2807	IL-76MD	CCCP-86913	28-6-1982
002.34.38.111	2808	IL-76MD	CCCP-86914	
002.34.38.116	2809	IL-76MD	CCCP-86915, 86915 [Ukrainian AF]	
002.34.38.120	2810	IL-76MD	CCCP-86916, UR-86916	

Construction number	Fuselage number	Version	Registration/ tactical code/serial	Manufacture date
002.34.38.122	2901	IL-76MD	CCCP-86917	
002.34.38.127	2902	IL-76MD	CCCP-86918, 86918, UR-76318	
002.34.38.129	2903	IL-76MD	CCCP-86919, UR-76319	
002.34.39.133	2904	IL-76MD, *cvtd to IL-76TD*	CCCP-86927, CCCP-76781*, RA-76781*	15-8-1982?
002.34.39.140	2905	IL-76TD	5A-DNA	
002.34.39.141	2906	IL-76TD	5A-DNT	
002.34.39.145	2907	IL-76TD	5A-DNS	
002.34.40.152	2908	IL-76MD	CCCP-86920, 86920, UR-86920	
002.34.40.153	2909	IL-76TD	CCCP-76466 † 20-10-1989	8-9-1982
002.34.40.157	2910	IL-76TD	CCCP-76467, RA-76467	
002.34.40.161	3001	IL-76MD; *cvtd to IL-76TD?*	CCCP-86921, UR-86921; RA-76849?	
002.34.40.168	3002	IL-76MD	CCCP-86922, 86922 [Ukrainian AF]	
002.34.41.169	3003	IL-76MD	CCCP-86923, 86923 [Ukrainian AF], unmarked	
002.34.41.174	3004	IL-76MD	CCCP-86924, UR-86924	
002.34.41.180	3005	IL-76MD	CCCP-76530, RA-76530	
002.34.41.181	3006	IL-76MD	CCCP-76531, 76531 [Ukrainian AF]	
002.34.41.186	3007	IL-76TD	CCCP-76499, RA-76499	
002.34.41.189	3008	IL-76MD, IL-76TD 'Falsie' *d*, IL-76TD	YI-ALQ, RA-76823 *cvtd to IL-76TD*	2-12-1982*
002.34.41.195	3009	IL-76TD	CCCP-76468, RA-76468	28-6-1982*
002.34.41.200	3010	IL-76MD, IL-76TD 'Falsie'	YI-ALR, CCCP-76821, UK 76821	
002.34.41.201	3101	IL-76MD	CCCP-76532	
002.34.42.205	3102	IL-76MD	CCCP-76533, 533 Black [Russian AF], RA-76533	
002.34.42.210	3103	IL-76MD	CCCP-76534, UR-76534	
002.34.42.213	3104	IL-76MD	CCCP-76535, RA-76535	
002.34.42.218	3105	IL-76TD	CCCP-76498, RA-76498, EP-ALC, ST-AQA	
002.34.42.221	3106	IL-76MD	CCCP-76536; UR-76536?	
002.34.42.225	3107	IL-76MD	CCCP-76537, UR-76537	
002.34.42.231	3108	IL-76MD	CCCP-76538, 538 Black [Russian AF], RA-76538	
002.34.42.234	3109	IL-76MD	CCCP-76539, UR-76539 † 6-6-1996	31-1-1983
002.34.42.238	3110	IL-76MD	CCCP-76540	
002.34.42.241	3201	IL-76MD	CCCP-76541, UR-76541	
003.34.42.247	3202	IL-76MD, IL-76TD 'Falsie' *d*	YI-ALS, CCCP-78738, RA-78738	
003.34.43.249	3203	IL-76MD	CCCP-76542, RA-76542	
003.34.43.255	3204	IL-76MD	CCCP-76543, UR-76395	
003.34.43.258	3205	A-50	46 Red [Soviet/Russian AF] No1?	
003.34.43.262	3206	IL-76MD	CCCP-76544, RA-76544	
003.34.43.266	3207	IL-76MD	CCCP-76545, RA-76545	
003.34.43.272	3208	IL-76MD	CCCP-76546, RA-76546	
003.34.43.273	3209	IL-76MD	CCCP-76547, RA-76547	
003.34.43.278	3210	IL-76MD	CCCP-76548, RA-76548	
003.34.44.283	3301	IL-76MD	CCCP-76549, RA-76549	
003.34.44.286	3302	IL-76MD	CCCP-76469, RA-76469	
003.34.45.291	3303	IL-76TD	CCCP-76470, RA-76470	
003.34.45.294	3304	IL-78 (prototype)	CCCP-76556, RA-76556	
003.34.45.299	3305	IL-76TD	5A-DND	
003.34.45.302	3306	IL-76TD	5A-DNF † 6-3-1986	
003.34.45.306	3307	IL-76MD	CCCP-76550, RA-76550	20-1-1983*
003.34.45.309	3308	IL-76MD	CCCP-76551, RA-76551	31-5-1983
003.34.45.313	3309	IL-76MD	CCCP-76552, RA-76552	
003.34.45.318	3310	IL-76MD	CCCP-76553, RA-76553	
003.34.45.324	3401	IL-76MD	CCCP-76554, RA-76554	
003.34.46.325	3402	IL-76MD	CCCP-76555, UR-76555	
003.34.46.329	3403	IL-76MD	CCCP-76557, RA-76557	
003.34.46.333	3404	IL-76MD	CCCP-76558, RA-76558	
003.34.46.340	3405	IL-76MD	CCCP-76559, 76559 [Ukrainian AF]	
003.34.46.341	3406	IL-76MD	CCCP-76560, UR-76560	
003.34.46.345	3407	IL-76TD	CCCP-76471, RA-76471, EP-MKA/RA-76471, RA-76471	
003.34.46.350	3408	IL-76TD	CCCP-76472, RA-76472	30-7-1983
003.34.46.356	3409	IL-76TD	5A-DNH	
003.34.47.357	3410	IL-76TD	5A-DNL † 15-4-1986	
003.34.47.364	3501	IL-76MD	CCCP-76561, 23 Red [Soviet AF]?, UR-76561	
003.34.47.365	3502	IL-76MD	CCCP-76562, 76562 [Ukrainian AF]	
003.34.47.372	3503	IL-76MD	CCCP-76563, 76563, UR-76563	
003.34.48.373	3504	IL-76MD	CCCP-76564, 76564 [Ukrainian AF]	
003.34.48.379	3505	A-50	38 Red [Soviet/Russian AF]	
003.34.48.382	3506	IL-76MD	CCCP-76565, 76565 [Ukrainian AF]	
003.34.48.385	3507	IL-76MD	CCCP-76566, 76566 [Ukrainian AF]	
003.34.48.390	3508	IL-76MD	CCCP-76567, 76567 [Ukrainian AF]	
003.34.48.393	3509	IL-76MD	YI-ALT	
003.34.48.398	3510	IL-76MD	YI-ALU	
003.34.48.404	3601	IL-76TD	CCCP-76473, RA-76473, EP-ALG	31-10-1983
003.34.48.407	3602	IL-76TD	CCCP-76474, RA-76474, EP-ALF; RA-76474?	30-9-1983
003.34.48.414	3603	IL-76MD	YI-ALV	
003.34.48.416	3604	IL-76MD	YI-ALW	
003.34.48.420	3605	IL-76MD	CCCP-76568, UR-76568	
003.34.48.421?	3606	IL-76MD	CCCP-76569 † 18-10-1989	
003.34.48.427	3607	IL-76MD	CCCP-76570, UR-76570	
003.34.48.429	3608	IL-76MD	CCCP-76571, UR-76571	
003.34.49.434	3609	IL-76MD	CCCP-76572, RA-76572	
003.34.49.437	3610	IL-76MD	CCCP-76573, UR-76573	
003.34.49.441	3701	IL-76MD	CCCP-76574, UR-76574	
003.34.49.445	3702	IL-76MD	CCCP-76575, 76575 [Ukrainian AF]	
004.34.49.449	3703	IL-76MD	CCCP-76576, UR-76576	
004.34.49.455	3704	IL-76MD	YI-ALX	
004.34.49.460	3705	A-50	34 Red [Soviet/Russian AF]	
004.34.49.462	3706	IL-76MD	CCCP-76577, RA-76577	
004.34.49.468	3707	IL-76MD	CCCP-76578, UR-76578	
004.34.49.471	3708	IL-76MD	CCCP-76579, UR-76579	
004.34.50.476	3709	IL-76MD	CCCP-76580, UR-76580	
004.34.50.479?	3710	IL-76TD?	5A-DNW?	
004.34.50.484	3801	IL-76MD	CCCP-76581, UR-76581	
004.34.50.487	3802	IL-76MD	CCCP-76582, UR-76582	
004.34.50.491	3803	IL-76MD	CCCP-76583, UR-76583	
004.34.50.493	3804	IL-76MD	CCCP-76584, UR-76584	
004.34.51.498	3805	A-50	46 Red [Soviet/Russian AF] No 2? (see 0033443258!)	
004.34.51.503	3806	IL-76MD	CCCP-76585, UR-76585	
004.34.51.508	3807	IL-76MD	CCCP-76586, UR-76396	
004.34.51.509	3808	IL-76TD	5A-DNO	
004.34.51.516	3809	IL-76TD	5A-DNP	
004.34.51.517	3810	IL-76MD	CCCP-76587, UR-76397	
004.34.51.523	3901	IL-76TD	CCCP-76475, RA-76475, EP-TPV	13-4-1984
004.34.51.528	3902	IL-76TD	CCCP-76476, RA-76476	
004.34.51.530	3903	IL-76MD	CCCP-76588, RA-76588	
004.34.52.533	3904	IL-76MD	CCCP-76589, CCCP-76443, UR-76443	
004.34.52.537	3905	A-50	39 Red [Soviet/Russian AF]	
004.34.52.544	3906	IL-76MD	CCCP-76590, UR-76590	
004.34.52.546	3907	IL-76MD, *cvtd to IL-76TD*	CCCP-76591, RA-76591	29-5-1984
004.34.52.549	3908	IL-76MD 'Falsie', IL-76LL	CCCP-76492	
004.34.52.555	3909	IL-76MD	CCCP-76592, RA-76592	
004.34.53.559	3910	IL-78	CCCP-76607; 35 Blue [Russian AF] No 2?	
004.34.53.562	4001	IL-76MD	CCCP-76593, UR-76390	
004.34.53.568	4002	IL-76MD	CCCP-76594, UR-76391	24-2-1984*
004.34.53.571	4003	IL-76MD	CCCP-76595, UR-76595	
004.34.53.575	4004	IL-76TD	CCCP-76477, RA-76477, EP-ALE	6-7-1984
004.34.53.577	4005	A-50	47 Red [Soviet/Russian AF]	
004.34.53.583	4006	IL-76MD	CCCP-76596, 76596 [Ukrainian AF]	
004.34.53.585	4007	IL-76MD	CCCP-76597, 76597 [Ukrainian AF]	
004.34.53.591	4008	IL-76MD	CCCP-76598, 76598 [Ukrainian AF]	
004.34.53.593	4009	IL-76MD	CCCP-76599, RA-76599	
004.34.53.597	4010	IL-78, *cvtd to IL-76MD*	CCCP-76609, UR-76609	14-4-1984
004.34.54.602	4101	IL-76MD	CCCP-76600, UR-76392	
004.34.54.606	4102	IL-76MD	CCCP-76601, UR-76601	
004.34.54.611	4103	IL-76MD	CCCP-76602, 4K-78130	12-6-1984*
004.34.54.615	4104	IL-76MD 'Falsie'	CU-T1258, CU-C1258	
004.34.54.618	4105	A-50	33 Red [Soviet/Russian AF]	
004.34.54.623	4106	IL-76MD	CCCP-76603, UR-76603	
004.34.54.625	4107	IL-76MD	CCCP-76604, RA-76604	
004.34.54.631	4108	IL-76MD	CCCP-76605, RA-76605	
004.34.54.633	4109	IL-76MD	CCCP-76606, UR-76316	
004.34.54.640	4110	IL-78, *cvtd to IL-76MD*	CCCP-76610, UR-76610	
004.34.54.641	4201	IL-76TD	5A-DNQ	
004.34.54.645	4202	IL-76TD	5A-DNV	
004.34.54.651	4203	IL-76TD	5A-DNU	
004.34.55.653	4204	IL-76MD	CCCP-76611, UR-76393	
004.34.55.660	4205	IL-76MD	CCCP-76612, RA-76612	
004.34.55.664	4206	IL-76MD	CCCP-76613, RA-76613	
004.34.55.665	4207	IL-76MD	CCCP-76614, UR-76614	
004.34.55.672	4208	IL-76MD	CCCP-76615, RA-76615	
004.34.55.676	4209	IL-78	CCCP-76616, 616 Black [Russian AF], RA-76616	31-3-1985
004.34.55.677?	4210	IL-76MD	CCCP-76617, UR-76617; UR-76441?	
005.34.55.682	4301	IL-76MD	CCCP-76618, UR-76618	
004.34.55.686	4302	IL-76MD	CCCP-76619, UR-76320	
004.34.56.692	4303	IL-76MD	CCCP-76620, UR-76620	
004.34.56.695	4304	IL-76MDPS (IL-76MD 'Falsie')	CCCP-76621	
004.34.56.700	4305	IL-76MD 'Falsie'?,	IL-76TD CCCP-76493, RA-76493	
005.34.57.702	4306	IL-76MD	CCCP-76622, UR-76622	10-9-1984*
005.34.57.705	4307	IL-76MD	CCCP-76623, RA-76623	
005.34.57.710	4308	IL-76MD	CCCP-76624, UR-76624	
005.34.57.713	4309	IL-76MD	CCCP-76625, UR-76321	
005.34.57.720	4310	IL-76MD	CCCP-76626, CCCP-76423, UR-76423, RA-76423	
005.34.58.722	4401	IL-76MD	K2661/A [Indian AF]	
005.34.58.725	4402	IL-76MD	K2662/B [Indian AF]	21-12-1984*
005.34.58.731	4403	IL-76MD	K2663/C [Indian AF]	
005.34.58.733	4404	IL-76MD	CCCP-76627, UR-76317	
006.34.58.738	4405	A-50	48 Red [Soviet/Russian AF]	
005.34.58.741	4406	IL-76MD, IL-76TD 'Falsie'	CCCP-76628, UR-76628 (also quoted as 0053458743)	
005.34.58.745	4407	IL-76MD	CCCP-76629, UR-76629	
005.34.58.749	4408	IL-76MD	CCCP-76630, UR-76630, UR-UCO	
005.34.58.756	4409	IL-76MD	CCCP-76631, 76631 [Ukrainian AF]	
005.34.59.757	4410	IL-78	CCCP-76632, RA-76632 (also quoted as 0053459761)	

Construction number	Fuselage number	Version	Registration/tactical code/serial	Manufacture date
005.34.59.764	4501	IL-76MD	CCCP-76633, 76633, UR-76633	
005.34.59.767	4502	IL-76MD 'Falsie'	CU-T1271, CU-C1271	?-4-1985*
005.34.59.770	4503	IL-76MD	CCCP-76634, RA-76634	
005.34.59.775	4504	IL-76MD	CCCP-76635, RA-76635	
005.34.59.777	4505	A-50	31 Red [Soviet/Russian AF]	
005.34.59.781	4506	IL-76MD, (?) IL-76TD 'Falsie'	CCCP-76636, UR-76636	
005.34.59.788	4507	IL-76TD	CCCP-76478, RA-76478	
005.34.60.790	4508	IL-76TD	CCCP-76479, RA-76479	14-5-1985
005.34.60.795	4509	IL-76TD	CCCP-76481, RA-76481, EP-ALA, ST-AQB	
005.34.60.797	4510	IL-76MD	CCCP-76637, UR-76637	
005.34.60.802	4601	IL-76MD	CCCP-76638, RA-76638	
005.34.60.805	4602	IL-76MD (IL-78?)	CCCP-76639, RA-76639	
005.34.60.811	4603	IL-76MD	CCCP-76640, RA-76640	
005.34.60.813	4604	IL-76MD	CCCP-76641, RA-76641	
005.34.60.820	4605	IL-76MD	CCCP-76642, CCCP-76408, UR-76408, RA-76408, UR-76408	
005.34.60.822	4606	IL-76MD	CCCP-76643, RA-76643	
005.34.60.827	4607	IL-76MD	CCCP-76644, UR-76433	
005.34.60.832	4608	IL-76TD	CCCP-76482, RA-76482	23-7-1985
005.34.61.834	4609	IL-76MD	CCCP-76645, 76645 [Ukrainian AF]	
005.34.61.837	4610	IL-78	CCCP-76646; UR-76646?	
005.34.61.843	4701	IL-76MD	CCCP-76647, UR-76647	
005.34.61.848	4702	IL-76MD	CCCP-76648, RA-76648	
005.34.61.849	4703	IL-76MD	K2664/D 'Kartika' [Indian AF]	
005.34.62.856	4704	IL-76MD	K2665/E 'Rohini' [Indian AF]	
005.34.62.857	4705	IL-76MD	K2666/F [Indian AF]	
005.34.62.864	4706	IL-76MD	CCCP-76649, RA-76649	
005.34.62.865	4707	IL-76MD	CCCP-76650, RA-76650	12-8-1985
005.34.62.872	4708	IL-76MD (IL-78, cvtd to IL-76MD?)	CCCP-76651, UR-76651	
005.34.62.873	4709	IL-76MD	CCCP-76652, UR-76322	
005.34.62.879	4710	IL-78	CCCP-76653, 76653; UR-76653?	
005.34.62.884	4801	IL-76MD	CCCP-76654, UR-76654	
005.34.63.885	4802	IL-76MD, IL-76PP (?), IL-76MD	CCCP-76655, UR-76655	
005.34.63.891	4803	IL-76MD	CCCP-76656, UR-76656	
005.34.63.896	4804	IL-76MD	CCCP-76657, 76657 [Ukrainian AF]	
005.34.63.900	4805	IL-80	CCCP-76450, RA-76450	
005.34.63.902	4806	IL-76MD	CCCP-76658, UR-76658	
005.34.63.908	4807	IL-76MD, IL-76TD 'Falsie'	CCCP-76659, RA-76659	
005.34.63.910	4808	IL-76MD (IL-78?)	CCCP-76660, 76660 [Ukrainian AF]	
005.34.63.913	4809	IL-76MD	CCCP-76661, 76661 [Ukrainian AF]	
005.34.64.919	4810	IL-78, cvtd to IL-76MD	CCCP-76662, UR-76662	
005.34.64.922	4901	IL-76MD (IL-78?)	CCCP-76663, UR-76663	
005.34.64.926	4902	IL-76MD	CCCP-76664, UR-76664	
005.34.64.930	4903	IL-76MD	CCCP-76665, 76665 [Ukrainian AF]	
005.34.64.934	4904	IL-76MD, cvtd to IL-76TD	CCCP-76666, RA-76666	25-12-1985
005.34.64.938	4905	IL-80	CCCP-76451, RA-76451	
005.34.65.941	4906	IL-76MD	CCCP-76667, UR-76667	
005.34.65.946	4907	IL-76MD	CCCP-76668, RA-76668	
006.34.65.949	**4908**	IL-76MD	CCCP-76669, RA-76669	30-1-1986
005.34.65.956	4909	IL-76TD	CCCP-76494, RA-76494	4-12-1985
006.34.65.958	4910	IL-78, cvtd to IL-76MD	CCCP-76670, UR-76670	
006.34.65.963	5001	IL-76MD	CCCP-76671, UR-76671, 4K-76671, UR-76671	
006.34.65.965	5002	Aircraft 976	CCCP-76452	
006.34.65.970	5003	IL-76MD	K2878/G [Indian AF]	
006.34.65.973	5004	IL-76MD	K2879/H [Indian AF]	
006.34.66.979	5005	A-50	32 Red [Soviet/Russian AF]	
006.34.66.981	5006	IL-76MD, IL-76TD 'Falsie'	CCCP-76672, RA-76672	
006.34.66.988	5007	IL-76MD	CCCP-76673, UR-76323	
006.34.66.989	5008	IL-76MD	CCCP-76674, UR-76394	
006.34.66.995	5009	Aircraft 976	CCCP-76453, RA-76453	28-11-1985*
006.34.66.998	5010	IL-78	CCCP-76675, 76675, UR-76675	
006.34.67.003	5101	IL-76MD	CCCP-76676, UR-76676	
006.34.67.005	5102	IL-76MD	CCCP-76677, UR-76677, 4K-76677, UR-76677	
006.34.67.011	5103	IL-76MD	CCCP-76678	
006.34.67.016?	5104	IL-76MD	CCCP-76679	
006.34.67.020	5105	IL-76MD	CCCP-76680, UR-76680	
006.34.67.021	5106	IL-76MD	CCCP-76681, UR-76681	
006.34.67.027	5107	IL-78, cvtd to IL-76MD	CCCP-76682, UR-76682	
006.34.68.029	5108	IL-76MD	CCCP-76683, UR-76683	
006.34.68.036	5109	IL-76MD	CCCP-76684, UR-76684	
006.34.68.037?	5110	IL-78?	CCCP-76685 †	
006.34.68.042	5201	IL-76TD	CCCP-76483, RA-76483	31-5-1986
006.34.68.045	5202	IL-76MD	CCCP-76686, RA-76686	
006.34.69.051	5203	IL-76MD, IL-76TD 'Falsie'	CCCP-76687, UR-76687	
006.34.69.055	5204	IL-76MD 'Falsie'	YI-ANA	
006.34.69.057	5205	A-50	49 Red [Soviet/Russian AF]	
006.34.69.062	5206	IL-76MD; IL-76TD 'Falsie'?	CCCP-76688, RA-76688	
006.34.69.066	5207	IL-78, cvtd to IL-76MD	CCCP-76689, 76689, UR-76689	
006.34.69.071	5208	IL-76MD 'Falsie'	YI-ANB	
006.34.69.074	5209	Aircraft 976	CCCP-76455	
006.34.69.080	5210	IL-78, cvtd to IL-76MD	CCCP-76690, UR-76690	
006.34.69.081	5301	IL-76TD	CCCP-76484, RA-76484	
006.34.70.088	5302	IL-76TD	CCCP-76485, RA-76485	
006.34.70.089	5303	IL-76MD	CCCP-76691, UR-76691, UR-UCT	
006.34.70.096	5304	IL-76MD	CCCP-76692, UR-76424 † 13-7-1998	
006.34.70.100	5305	IL-76MD	CCCP-76693, RA-76693	
006.34.70.102	5306	IL-76MD 'Falsie'	YI-ANC	
006.34.70.107	5307	IL-76MD	CCCP-76694, UR-76694	
006.34.70.112	5308	IL-76MD	CCCP-76695, UR-76695	
006.34.70.113	5309	IL-76MD	CCCP-76696, UR-76696, RA-76444, UR-UCS	
006.34.70.118	5310	IL-76MD	CCCP-76697, RA-76697?, UR-76697	
006.34.71.123	5401	IL-76MD	CCCP-76698, HA-TCD, UR-76698	
006.34.71.125	5402	Aircraft 976	CCCP-76455, 76455	
006.34.71.131	5403	IL-76MD	CCCP-76699, UR-76699	
006.34.71.134	5404	IL-76MD	CCCP-76700, UR-76700	
006.34.71.139	5405	IL-78M (prototype)	CCCP-76701, RA-76701	
006.34.71.142	5406	IL-76MD	CCCP-76702	
006.34.71.147	5407	IL-76MD	CCCP-76703, 76703 [Ukrainian AF]	
006.34.71.150	5408	IL-76MD	CCCP-76704, UR-76704	
006.34.71.155	5409	IL-76MD 'Falsie'	YI-AND	
006.34.72.158	5410	IL-76MD	CCCP-76705, 76705, UR-76705	
006.34.72.163	5501	IL-76MD	CCCP-76706, UR-76706	
006.34.72.166	5502	IL-76MD	CCCP-76707, UR-76707, HA-TCE	
006.34.73.171	5503	IL-76MD	CCCP-76708, RA-76708	26-6-1986*
006.34.73.173	5504	IL-76MD	CCCP-76709, EW-76709	
006.34.73.178	5505	A-50	35 Red [Soviet/Russian AF]	
006.34.73.182	5506	IL-76MD, cvtd to IL-76TD	CCCP-76710, EW-76710	
006.34.73.187	5507	IL-76MD, cvtd to IL-76TD	CCCP-76711, EW-76711	
006.34.73.190	5508	IL-76MD, cvtd to IL-76TD	CCCP-76712, UR-76712?, RA-76712?, EW-76712	
006.34.74.193	5509	IL-76MD	CCCP-76713, RA-76713 (also quoted as 0063474191)	
006.34.74.198	5510	IL-76MD	CCCP-76714, RA-76714	
007.34.74.203	5601	IL-76MD, IL-76TD 'Falsie'	CCCP-76758, RA-76758	3-7-1986*
007.34.74.208	5602	Aircraft 976	CCCP-76456	
007.34.74.211	5603	IL-76MD	CCCP-76716, RA-76716?, UR-76716	?-2-1987*
007.34.74.216	5604	IL-76MD	CCCP-76717, UR-76717, 4K-76717, UR-76717	
007.34.74.219	5605	IL-76MD	CCCP-76718, RA-76718	
007.34.74.224	5606	IL-76MD 'Falsie'	YI-ANE	
007.34.74.226	5607	IL-76MD	CCCP-76719, RA-76719	
007.34.75.229	5608	IL-76MD	CCCP-76720, RA-76720	
007.34.75.236	5609	IL-76MD 'Falsie'	YI-ANF	
007.34.75.239	5610	IL-78, cvtd to IL-76MD	CCCP-76721, UR-76721	
007.34.75.242	5701	IL-76MD	CCCP-76722, RA-76722	
007.34.75.245	5702	IL-76MD	CCCP-76723, RA-76723 † 22-6-2000	
007.34.75.250	5703	IL-76MD (IL-78, cvtd to IL-76MD?)	CCCP-76724, UR-76724 (?), RA-76724	
007.34.75.253	5704	IL-76MD	CCCP-76725, RA-76725	
007.34.75.260	5705	A-50	36 Red [Soviet/Russian AF]	
007.34.75.261	5706	IL-76MD	CCCP-76726, RA-76726	
007.34.75.268	5707	IL-76MD, IL-76TD 'Falsie'?	CCCP-76727, UR-76727	
007.34.75.270	5708	IL-76MD	CCCP-76728, UR-76728, UR-UCR	15-10-1986*
007.34.76.275	5709	IL-76MD	CCCP-76729, HA-TCF, UR-76729, UR-UCU	20-11-1986*
007.34.76.277	5710	IL-78, cvtd to IL-76MD	CCCP-76730, UR-76730	
007.34.76.281	5801	IL-76TD	CCCP-76486, RA-76486	12-1-1987*
007.34.76.288	5802	IL-76MD 'Falsie'	YI-ANG	
007.34.76.292	5803	IL-76MD	CCCP-76731, RA-76731	
007.34.76.296	5804	IL-76MD	CCCP-76732, UR-76732	
007.34.76.298	5805	A-50	37 Red [Soviet/Russian AF]	
007.34.76.304	5806	IL-76MD	CCCP-76733, RA-76733	
007.34.76.307	5807	IL-76MD 'Falsie'	YI-ANH	
007.34.76.312	5808	IL-76MD, cvtd to IL-76TD	CCCP-76734, EW-76734, UR-76734?, EW-76734	
007.34.76.314	5809	IL-76MD, cvtd to IL-76TD	CCCP-76735, RA-76735?, EW-76735	31-5-1987
007.34.76.317	5810	IL-78	CCCP-76736, 76736 [Ukrainian AF]	
007.34.77.323	5901	IL-76MD, cvtd to IL-76TD	CCCP-76737, RA-76737?, EW-76737	
007.34.77.326	5902	IL-76MD	CCCP-76738, RA-76738	
007.34.77.332	5903	IL-76MD	CCCP-76739, RA-76739	
007.34.77.335	5904	IL-76MD	CCCP-76740, RA-76740	
007.34.78.337	5905	IL-76MD	CCCP-76741, RA-76741	
007.34.78.343	5906	IL-76MD	K2901 [Indian AF]	
007.34.78.346	5907	IL-78, cvtd to IL-76MD	CCCP-76742, UR-76742	
007.34.78.349	5908	IL-76MD	CCCP-76743, RA-76743	
007.34.78.353	5909	IL-76MD	K2902/M [Indian AF]	
007.34.78.359	5910	IL-78, cvtd to IL-76MD	CCCP-76744, UR-76744	
007.34.79.362	6001	IL-76MD	CCCP-76745, RA-76745	
007.34.79.367	6002	IL-76TD	CCCP-76487, RA-76487	
007.34.79.371	6003	IL-76TD	CCCP-76488, RA-76488	29-8-1987
007.34.79.374	6004	IL-76MD	CCCP-76746, UR-76747?, RA-76746	
007.34.79.377	6005	A-50	43 Red [Soviet/Russian AF]	
007.34.79.381	6006	IL-76MD	CCCP-76747, RA-76747	
007.34.79.386	6007	IL-76MD	CCCP-76748, 76748, UR-76748	
007.34.79.392	6008	IL-76MD	CCCP-76749, 76749 [Ukrainian AF]	
007.34.79.394	6009	IL-78, cvtd to IL-76MD	CCCP-76715, UR-76715, UR-UCA	
007.34.79.400	6010	IL-78, cvtd to IL-76MD	CCCP-76760, UR-76760	

Construction number	Fuselage number	Version	Registration/ tactical code/serial	Manufacture date
007.34.79.401	6101	IL-76MD	CCCP-76761, RA-76761	
007.34.80.406	6102	IL-76MD	CCCP-76762, RA-76762	
007.34.80.410	6103	IL-76MD	K2999/U [Indian AF]	
007.34.80.413	6104	IL-76MD	CCCP-76763, RA-76763	
007.34.80.419	6105	IL-76MD	K3000/M [Indian AF]	
007.34.80.424	6106	IL-76MD	CCCP-76764, RA-76764	
007.34.81.426	6107	IL-76MD	CCCP-76765, RA-76765	
007.34.81.431	6108	IL-76MDK	CCCP-76766, RA-76766	
007.34.81.436	6109	IL-76MD	CCCP-76767, RA-76767	
008.34.81.440	6110	IL-78, *cvtd to IL-76MD*	CCCP-76775, 76775, UR-76415, UR-UCI † 18-7-1998	
007.34.81.442	6201	IL-76MD 'Falsie'	YI-ANI	
007.34.81.448	6202	IL-76MD	CCCP-76768, RA-76768	
007.34.81.452	6203	IL-76MD	CCCP-76769, RA-76769	
007.34.81.456	6204	IL-76MD	CCCP-76770, RA-76770	
008.34.81.457	6205	A-50	40 Red [Soviet/Russian AF]	
007.34.81.461	6206	IL-76MD 'Falsie'	CCCP-76753, RA-76753	24-6-1988
008.34.82.466	6207	IL-76MD	CCCP-76771	
008.34.82.472	6208	IL-76MD	CCCP-76772, RA-76772	
008.34.82.473	6209	IL-76MD	CCCP-76773, RA-76773	
008.34.82.478	6210	IL-78, *cvtd to IL-76MD*	CCCP-76774, UR-76414, UR-UCG	
008.34.82.481	6301	IL-76MD 'Falsie'	YI-ANJ	
008.34.82.486	6302	IL-76MD	CCCP-76776, RA-76776	
008.34.82.490	6303	IL-76MD,	CCCP-76777, UR-76777, EP-TPY, UR-76777	?-2-1988*
008.34.82.495	6304	IL-76MD 'Falsie'	YI-ANK	
008.34.83.499	6305	A-50	41 Red [Soviet/Russian AF]	
008.34.83.502	6306	IL-76MD	CCCP-76778, UR-76778	
008.34.83.505	6307	IL-76MD	CCCP-76779, RA-76779	
008.34.83.510	6308	IL-76MD	CCCP-78750, RA-78750	
008.34.83.513	6309	IL-76MD, IL-76TD 'Falsie'	CCCP-78751, 76438, UR-76438, HA-TCH	22-10-1987*
008.34.83.519	6310	IL-76MD; IL-76TD 'Falsie'?	CCCP-78752, UR-78752; UR-76752?	?-3-1988*
008.34.84.522	6401	IL-76MD	CCCP-78753, UR-76398, UR-UCE	
008.34.84.527	6402	IL-76MD	CCCP-78754, CCCP-76437, UR-76437, HA-TCJ	
008.34.84.531	6403	IL-76MD	CCCP-78755, UR-UCJ	
008.34.84.536	6404	IL-76MD	CCCP-78756, UR-78756, UR-UCH	
008.34.84.538	6405	A-50	42 Red [Soviet/Russian AF]	
008.34.84.542	6406	IL-76MD 'Falsie'	YI-ANL	
008.34.84.547	6407	IL-76MD	CCCP-78757, RA-78757	
008.34.84.551	6408	IL-76MD	CCCP-78758, UR-78758, EP-TPX, UR-78758	?-4-1988*
008.34.84.554	6409	IL-76TD	CCCP-76489, RA-76489	31-5-1988
008.34.85.558	6410	IL-78, *cvtd to IL-76MD*	CCCP-78759, UR-76759, EP-TPD, UR-76759	?-8-1988*
			(No 2; see 093418543!)	
008.34.85.561	6501	IL-76TD	CCCP-76750, RA-76750	28-9-1988*
008.34.85.566	6502	IL-76MD	CCCP-78760, UR-76399, UR-UCY	24-2-1988*
008.34.86.570	6503	IL-76MD	CCCP-78761	
008.34.85.574	6504	IL-76MD	CCCP-78762, RA-78762	
009.34.86.579	6505	A-50M, A-50I (prototype)	44 Red [Soviet/Russian AF], RA-78740, 4X-AGI	
008.34.86.582	6506	IL-76MD	CCCP-78763, EW-78763	
008.34.86.586	6507	IL-76MD	CCCP-78764, RA-78764	
008.34.86.590	6508	IL-76MD	CCCP-78765, EW-78765	
008.34.86.595	6509	IL-76MD	CCCP-78766, RA-78766	4-3-1988*
007.34.87.598	6510	IL-78, *cvtd to IL-76MD*	CCCP-78767, UR-76767, EP-TPU No1, UR-76767 (No 2; see 0073481436!)	?-9-1988*
008.34.87.603	6601	IL-76MD	CCCP-78768, RA-78768	
008.34.87.607	6602	IL-76MD	CCCP-78769, EW-78769	
008.34.87.610	6603	IL-76TD	CCCP-76751, RA-76751	
008.34.87.614	6604	IL-76MD	K3012 [Indian AF]	
008.34.87.617	6605	IL-76MDK	CCCP-78770, RA-78770	14-7-1988*
008.34.87.622?	6606	IL-76MD	CCCP-78771 †	
008.34.87.627	6607	IL-76MD	CCCP-78772, UR-78772, EP-TPW, UR-78772	?-10-1988*
008.34.88.629	6608	IL-76MD	K3013 [Indian AF]	
100.34.88.634	6609	A-50M	51 Red [Soviet/Russian AF]	6-9-1990
008.34.88.638	6610	IL-78, *cvtd to IL-76TD 'Falsie'*	CCCP-78773, UR-76412, UR-UCF	
008.34.88.643	6701	IL-76MD	CCCP-78774, UR-78774, UR-UCD	10-7-1988*
008.34.89.647	6702	IL-76MD	CCCP-78775, UR-78775, UR-UCC	
008.34.89.652	6703	IL-76MD	CCCP-78776, RA-78776	
008.34.89.654	6704	IL-76MD	CCCP-78777, RA-78777	
008.34.89.659	6705	IL-76MD	CCCP-78778, RA-78778; UR-78778?	
008.34.89.662	6706	IL-76MD, IL-76TD 'Falsie' *d*	CCCP-78779, EW-78779	
008.34.89.666?	6707	IL-76MD	CCCP-78780 † 28-8-1992	
008.34.89.670	6708	IL-76MD	CCCP-78781 † 27-11-1996	31-10-1988
008.34.89.674	6709	IL-76MD	7T-WIA	
008.34.89.678	6710	IL-78	CCCP-78782, RA-78782	30-12-1988
008.34.89.683	6801	IL-76MD	CCCP-78783, AHY-78001, AHY-78129	31-10-1988
008.34.89.687	6802	IL-76MD	CCCP-78784, RA-78784	
008.34.89.691	6803	IL-76MD	CCCP-78785, RA-78785?, UR-78785	7-9-1988*
008.34.90.694	6804	IL-76MD	CCCP-78786, RA-78786	
008.34.90.698	6805	IL-76MD	CCCP-78787, EW-78787	
008.34.90.703	6806	IL-76MD	CCCP-78788, RA-78788	
008.34.90.706	6807	IL-76MD	CCCP-78789, RA-78789	
008.34.90.712	6808	IL-76MD	CCCP-78790, RA-78790	
009.34.90.714	6809	IL-76MD	CCCP-78791, RA-78791	
009.34.90.718	6810	IL-76MD, *cvtd to IL-76TD*	CCCP-78792, EW-78792, RA-78792	
009.34.90.721	6901	IL-76MD	CCCP-78793, UN-78793?, EW-78793	
009.34.90.726	6902	IL-76MD	CCCP-78794, RA-78794	
009.34.91.729	6903	IL-76MD	CCCP-78795, RA-78795	
009.34.91.735	6904	IL-76MD	CCCP-78796, RA-78796	
101.34.91.739	6905	A-50 (A-50M?)	52 Red [Soviet/Russian AF]	
009.34.91.742	6906	IL-76MD	CCCP-78797, RA-78797	
009.34.91.747	6907	IL-78	CCCP-78798, RA-78798	30-3-1989
009.34.91.750	6908	IL-76MD	K3014 [Indian AF]	
009.34.91.754	6909	IL-76MD, *cvtd to IL-76TD*	CCCP-78799, EW-78799	29-11-1988*
009.34.91.758	6910	IL-78M	CCCP-78800	30-6-1989
009.34.92.763	7001	IL-76MD, *cvtd to IL-76TD*	CCCP-78801, EW-78801	
009.34.92.766	7002	IL-76MD	CCCP-86925 No 2, RA-86925	
009.34.92.771	7003	IL-76MD	CCCP-78802, EW-78802	
009.34.92.774	7004	IL-76MD	CCCP-78803, RA-78803	
009.34.92.778	7005	IL-76MD	CCCP-78804, RA-78804 † 27-11-1996	
009.34.92.783	7006	IL-76MD	CCCP-78805, RA-78805	
009.34.92.786	7007	IL-78	CCCP-78806	30-6-1989
009.34.93.791	7008	IL-76MD	CCCP-78807, RA-78807	
009.34.93.794	7009	IL-76MD, IL-76TD 'Falsie' *d*	CCCP-78808, EW-78808	
009.34.93.799	7010	IL-78E	5A-DLL No 2 (see 093421612!)	
009.34.93.803	7101	IL-76MD	7T-WIB	
009.34.93.807	7102	IL-76MD	CCCP-78809, RA-78809	
009.34.93.810	7103	IL-76TD	CCCP-76800*, RA-76800*	
009.34.93.814	7104	IL-76MD	CCCP-78810, RA-78810	
009.34.93.818	7105	A-50	45 Red [Soviet/Russian AF]	
009.34.94.823	7106	IL-76MD	CCCP-78811, RA-78811	
009.34.94.826	7107	IL-78	CCCP-78812, RA-78812	31-8-1989
009.34.94.830	7108	IL-76MD	CCCP-78813, RA-78813	
009.34.94.835	7109	IL-76TD	CCCP-76784, LZ-INK † 24-5-1991	
009.34.94.838	7110	IL-78	CCCP-78814, RA-78814	30-9-1989
009.34.94.842	7201	IL-76MD	CCCP-78815, RA-78815	
009.34.95.846	7202	IL-76MD	CCCP-78816, RA-78816	
009.34.95.851	7203	IL-76MD	CCCP-78817, RA-78817	
009.34.95.854	7204	IL-76TD	CCCP-76787, RA-76787, EP-SFA	
009.34.95.858	7205	IL-76MD	CCCP-78818, RA-78818	
009.34.95.863	7206	IL-76TD	CCCP-76785, RA-76785	
009.34.95.866	7207	IL-76MD 'Falsie' (IL-76TD?)	CCCP-76801*, RA-76801*	
101.34.95.871	7208	IL-76MDK-II	CCCP-78825, RA-78825	
009.34.95.874	7209		CCCP-76802	
009.34.95.880	7210	IL-78M	CCCP-78822	27-12-1989
009.34.95.883	7301	IL-76MD, IL-76TD 'Falsie' *d*	CCCP-78819, EW-78819	29-9-1989
009.34.95.886	7302	IL-76MD 'Falsie'	YI-ANM	
009.34.96.892	7303	IL-76MD	K3077/V [Indian AF]	
009.34.96.894	7304	IL-76MD 'Falsie'	YI-ANN	
009.34.96.899	7305	A-50M	50 Red [Soviet/Russian AF]	
009.34.96.903	7306	IL-76MD, IL-76TD 'Falsie' *d*	CCCP-76790, RA76790, RA-76790ˣⁱⁱ *converted to IL-76TD*	9-6-1989*
009.34.96.907	7307	IL-76MD	CCCP-78820, RA-78820, UR-78820	
009.34.96.912	7308	IL-76MD	K3078/W 'Nubra' [Indian AF]	
009.34.96.914	7309	IL-76MD	CCCP-78821, 78821 [Ukrainian AF]	
100.34.96.918	7310	IL-78M	CCCP-78823	29-4-1990
009.34.96.923	7401	IL-76TD	CCCP-76786, RA-76786	17-11-1989
009.34.97.927	7402	IL-76MD 'Falsie'	CCCP-76803, RA-76803	
009.34.97.931	7403	IL-76MD ('Falsie'?)	CCCP-76804	
009.34.97.936	7404	IL-76TD	CCCP-76791, RA-76791, EP-TPU No 2 (see 0073487598!)	28-12-1989
009.34.97.940	7405	A-50 (A-50M?)	53 Red [Soviet/Russian AF]	
009.34.97.942	7406	IL-76TD	CCCP-76792, RA-76792	25-12-1989
100.34.97.947	7407	IL-78M	CCCP-78824	29-4-1990
009.34.98.951	7408	IL-76TD	CCCP-76793, UK-76793	
009.34.98.954	7409	IL-76TD	CCCP-76794, UK-76794	30-12-1989
100.34.98.959	7410	IL-78M	30 Blue [Soviet/Russian AF]	31-7-1990
009.34.98.962	7501	IL-76TD	CCCP-76795, RA-76795	
009.34.98.967	7502	IL-76TD	CCCP-76752, RA-76752 † 5-4-1996	
009.34.98.971	7503	IL-76TD	CCCP-76782, UK-76782	31-1-1990
009.34.98.974	7504	IL-76TD	CCCP-76783, RA-76783	
102.34.98.978	7505	IL-76TD	CCCP-76421?, EZ-F421 (see 1033415504!)	
009.34.99.982	7506	IL-76MD 'Falsie', IL-76TD	CCCP-76822, RA-76822	
009.34.99.986	7507	IL-76MD	CCCP-78836, EW-78836	
100.34.99.991	7508	IL-76MD, IL-76TD 'Falsie' *d*	CCCP-78826, EW-78826	28-2-1990
100.34.99.994	7509	IL-76TD	CCCP-76796, RA-76796, EP-ALI	
100.34.99.997	7510	IL-76MD, IL-76TD 'Falsie' *d*	CCCP-78827, EW-78827	
100.34.01.004	7601	IL-76MD *d*, *cvtd to IL-76TD*	CCCP-78828, EW-78828	
100.34.01.006	7602	IL-76MD	CCCP-78829, RA-78829	
100.34.01.010	7603	IL-76MD	CCCP-78830, RA-78830	
100.34.01.015	7604	IL-76TD	CCCP-76384, UN-76384	
100.34.01.017	7605	IL-76MD	CCCP-78831, RA-78831	
100.34.01.024	7606	IL-76MD	CCCP-78837, 01 Red 'Marshal Aviatsii Skripko' [Russian AF] (RA-78837)	
100.34.01.025	7607	IL-76MD	CCCP-78833, RA-78833	22-12-1989*
100.34.01.032	7608	IL-76MD	CCCP-78834, RA-78834	
100.34.02.033	7609	IL-76MD	CCCP-78835, RA-78835	
100.34.02.040	7610	IL-78M	31 Blue [Soviet/Russian AF]	31-8-1990

Construction number	Fuselage number	Version	Registration/ tactical code/serial	Manufacture date
100.34.02.044	7701	IL-76MD	CCCP-78838, RA-78838	
100.34.02.047	7702	IL-76MD	CCCP-78839, EW-78839	
100.34.03.052	7703	IL-76TD	CCCP-76797, RA-76797	
100.34.03.056	7704	IL-76MD	CCCP-78840, RA-78840	
102.34.03.058	7705	IL-76TD	76449, UK-76449 'Shenyang'	31-11-1992
100.34.03.063	7706	IL-76TD	CCCP-76798, RA-76798	
100.34.03.068	7707	IL-78M	32 Blue [Soviet/Russian AF]	30-9-1990
100.34.03.069	7708	IL-76MD	CCCP-78842, RA-78842	29-12-1989*
100.34.03.075	7709	IL-76TD	CCCP-76799, RA-76799	31-7-1990
100.34.03.079	7710	IL-78M	50 Blue [Soviet/Russian AF]	15-11-1990
100.34.03.082	7801	IL-76MD, IL-76TD 'Falsie' d	CCCP-78843, EW-78843	30-6-1990
100.34.03.087	7802	IL-76MD 'Falsie'	YI-ANO	
100.34.03.092	7803	IL-76MD	CCCP-78844, RA-78844	
100.34.03.095	7804	IL-76MD	CCCP-78845, RA-78845	
101.34.03.097	7805	IL-78	33 Blue [Soviet/Russian AF]	30-4-1991
100.34.03.104	7806	IL-78M 'Falsie'	?-912	
100.34.03.106	7807	IL-78M	51 Blue [Soviet/Russian AF]	28-1-1991
100.34.03.109	7808	IL-76TD	CCCP-76805, UK-76805 (also quoted as 1003403105)	
100.34.03.113	7809	IL-76MD	CCCP-78846, RA-78846 (also quoted as 1003403115)	
101.34.03.119	7810	IL-78M	52 Blue [Soviet/Russian AF]	31-3-1991
100.34.03.121	7901	IL-76TD	CCCP-76806, RA-76806	
100.34.04.126	7902	IL-76MD 'Falsie'	?-913	
100.34.04.132	7903	IL-76MD	CCCP-78847, RA-78847	
100.34.04.136	7904	IL-76MD 'Falsie' (IL-76TD?)	CCCP-76825, RA-76825	
101.34.04.138	7905	IL-78	34 Blue [Soviet/Russian AF]	29-6-1991
100.34.04.143	7906	IL-76MD 'Falsie'	CCCP-76826, -76826, RA-76826	
100.34.04.146	7907	IL-76MD 'Falsie'	?-914	
100.34.04.151	7908	IL-76MD ('Falsie'?) CCCP-76827		
100.34.05.154	7909	IL-76MD 'Falsie'	7T-WIC	
100.34.05.159	7910	IL-76MD	CCCP-78848, EW-78848	
100.34.05.164	8001	IL-76MD 'Falsie' (IL-76TD?)	CCCP-76828*, RA-76828*	
100.34.05.167	8002	IL-76TD	CCCP-76425, RA-76425	?-3-1991*
100.34.05.172	8003	IL-76MD ('Falsie'?)	CCCP-76829	
101.34.05.176	8004	IL-76TD	CCCP-76807, RA-76807	23-5-1991
101.34.05.177	8005	IL-76TD	CCCP-76808, RA-76808, ?, RA-76808	
101.34.05.184	8006	IL-76TD	CCCP-76426, UR-76426, RA-76426, ER-ACG?, UK-76426 No1 (see 1043419644!), RA-76426	10-2-1990*
101.34.05.188	8007	IL-78M	35 Blue [Soviet/Russian AF]	30-9-1991
101.34.05.192	8008	IL-76MD	CCCP-78849, EW-78849	
101.34.05.196	8009	IL-76MD 'Falsie'	CCCP-78850, RA-78850	
101.34.05.197	8010	IL-78M	36 Blue [Soviet/Russian AF]	30-11-1991
101.34.06.204	8101	IL-76MD 'Falsie', IL-76TD	CCCP-78851, RA-78851, RA-76388	15-3-1992*
101.34.06.207	8102	IL-76TD	06207, CCCP-76427, UK 76427	
101.34.07.212	8103	IL-76MD 'Falsie', IL-76TD	CCCP-78852, RA-78852, RA-76389	
101.34.07.215	8104	IL-76MD	CCCP-78853, UR-76413	
101.34.07.220	8105	IL-76MD	CCCP-78854, RA-78854	
101.34.07.223	8106	IL-76TD	CCCP-76811, 76811, UK 76811	
101.34.07.227	8107	IL-78M	53 Blue [Soviet/Russian AF]	
101.34.07.230	8108	IL-76TD	CCCP-76812, RA-76812	
101.34.07.233	8109	IL-76MD 'Falsie'	B-4030	
102.34.08.240	8110	IL-76TD	UK 76351	
101.34.08.244	8201	IL-76TD	CCCP-76835, RA-76835	
101.34.08.246	8202	IL-76TD	CCCP-76813, UK-76813	
101.34.08.252	8203	IL-76TD	CCCP-76809, RA-76809	9-6-1991*
101.34.08.254	8204	IL-76MD 'Falsie'	B-4031	
101.34.08.257	8205	IL-76MD, IL-76TD 'Falsie'	CCCP-78736, UR-78736, HA-TCB	
101.34.08.264	8206	IL-76TD	CCCP-76818, 76818, RA-76818	27-9-1991*
102.34.08.265	8207	IL-76TD	RA-76355, 9L-LBO, EP-ALD, T9-QAB, T9-CAB	
101.34.08.269	8208	IL-76TD	CCCP-76814, RA-76814	15-8-1991*
101.34.09.274	8209	IL-76TD	CCCP-76819, 76819, RA-76819, ES-NIT, RA-76819 † 26-7-1999	30-11-1991
101.34.09.280	8210	IL-76TD	CCCP-76354, RA-76354, 4K-AZ11, S9-BAD, HA-TCK	
101.34.09.282	8301	IL-76TD	CCCP-76810, UN-76810	
101.34.09.287	8302	IL-76TD	CCCP-76831, UK 76831	
101.34.09.289	8303	IL-76MD 'Falsie'	B-4032	
101.34.09.295	8304	IL-76TD	CCCP-76820, RA-76820	
101.34.09.297	8305	IL-76TD	SU-OAA, EP-JAY	20-11-1991*
101.34.09.303	8306	IL-76MD, IL-76TD 'Falsie'	CCCP-78734, UR-78734, HA-TCA, UR-78734	
101.34.09.305	8307	IL-76TD	CCCP-76836, EW-76836 † 31-12-1994	
101.34.09.310	8308	IL-76TD	CCCP-76815, EX-76815	
102.34.09.316	8309	IL-76TD	CCCP-76837, EW-76837, ST-APS, RA-76837, ST-APS	
102.34.09.319	8310	IL-76TD	CCCP-76834, RA-76834 † 25-1-1997	
101.34.09.321	8401	IL-76TD	SU-OAB, EP-MAH	
102.34.10.327	8402	IL-76TD	CCCP-76824, 76824, UK 76824	21-4-1992
102.34.10.330	8403	IL-76MD 'Falsie'?, IL-76TD CCCP-76445, RA-76445, 4L-76445		
102.34.10.336	8404	IL-76TD	CCCP-76816, EZ-F425	
103.34.10.339	8405	IL-76TD	UK 76358	
102.34.10.344	8406	IL-76TD	CCCP-76350, RA-76350, ST-AIY, RA-76350	19-11-1992
102.34.10.348	8407	IL-76TD	CCCP-76830, EZ-F422	31-3-1992*
103.34.10.351	8408	? (izdeliye 1076)		
102.34.10.355	8409	IL-76TD	CCCP-76409, RA-76409	22-9-1992*
102.34.10.360	8410	IL-76TD	CCCP-76832, RA-76832, YN-CEW, 3C-KKG	
102.34.11.363	8501	IL-76TD	CCCP-11363, CCCP-76833, RA-76833	
102.34.11.368	8502	IL-76TD	CCCP-76436, RA-76436, YN-CEX, 3C-KKE	
102.34.11.370	8503	IL-76TD	CCCP-76838*, RA-76838*	30-5-1992
102.34.11.375	8504	IL-76TD	CCCP-76839*, RA-76839*	30-4-1992
102.34.11.378	8505	IL-76TD	UK 76352, RA 76352	23-11-1992*
102.34.11.384	8506	IL-76TD	CCCP-76411, RA-76411, YN-CEV, 3C-KKF	
102.34.11.387	8507	IL-76TD	CCCP-76817, RA-76817	
102.34.12.389	8508	IL-76TD	CCCP-76447, 76447, UK 76447, 4K-AZ14	22-5-1992*
102.34.12.395	8509	IL-76TD	CCCP-76434, UN-76434	30-4-1992*
102.34.12.399	8510	IL-76TD	CCCP-76401, RA-76401	6-5-1992*
102.34.12.402	8601	IL-76TD	CCCP-76405, RA-76405, 7O-ADG	
102.34.12.408	8602	IL-76MD Skal'pel'-MT		
102.34.12.411	8603	IL-76TD	UN-76410, UK 76410	
102.34.12.414	8604	IL-76TD	CCCP-76403, RA-76403 'Igor' Bykov'	30-6-1992
102.34.12.418	8605	IL-76MD 'Falsie'?, IL-76TD	CCCP-76446, RA-76446, EK-76446	
102.34.13.423	8606	IL-76TD	RA-76440, 7T-WIU	
102.34.13.428	8607	IL-76TD	CCCP-76435, UN 76435 † 12-11-1996	
102.34.13.430	8608	IL-76TD	RA-76402	
102.34.13.435	8609	IL-76TD	RA-76407, 7T-WIG	
102.34.13.438	8610	IL-76TD	RA-76400	
102.34.13.443	8701	IL-76TD	76448, UK-76448	30-9-1992
102.34.13.446	8702	IL-76TD	RA-76420	29-1-1993
102.34.14.450	8703	IL-76TD	CCCP-76442, UN-76442	
102.34.14.454	8704	IL-76TD	76353, UK 76353	13-12-1992*
103.34.14.458	8705	IL-76TD	CCCP-76370, RA-76370	
102.34.14.463	8706	IL-76TD	RA-76406, 7T-WIE	
103.34.14.467	8707	IL-76TD	RA-76357	26-2-1993
102.34.14.470	8708	IL-76TD	RA-76419, 7T-WID	
103.34.14.474	8709	IL-76TD	RA-76367, ST-AIO, RA-76367	30-3-1993
103.34.14.480	8710	IL-76TD	RA-76369	15-3-1993
103.34.14.483	8801	IL-76TD	UK-76359 'Jinan'	
103.34.14.485	8802	IL-76TD	UN-76371	1-2-1993*
103.34.14.492	8803	IL-76TD	RA-76360	27-4-1993
103.34.14.496	8804	IL-76TD	UK 76375	
103.34.15.497	8805	IL-76TD	RA-76361; 7O-ADH?	
103.34.15.504	8806	IL-76TD	RA-76421; EL-WTA? (see 1023498978!)	1-3-1993*
103.34.15.507	8807	IL-76TD	RA-76373	30-6-1993
103.34.16.512	8808	IL-76MD 'Falsie'	B-4033	
103.34.16.515	8809	IL-76TD	UN-76385	?-3-1993*
103.34.16.520	8810	IL-76TD	UN-76374	
103.34.16.524	8901	IL-76MD 'Falsie'	B-4034	
103.34.16.525	8902	IL-76TD	UK 76844	
103.34.16.529	8903	IL-76MD 'Falsie'	B-4035	
103.34.16.533	8904	IL-76TD	RA-76362 'Anatoliy Lyapidevskiy'	
103.34.17.540	8905	IL-76TD	RA-76363 'Vasiliy Molokov'	30-7-1993
103.34.17.541	8906	IL-76TD	UK-76376	
103.34.17.545	8907	IL-76TD	UK 76377	
103.34.17.550	8908	IL-76MD 'Falsie'	B-4036	
103.34.17.553	8909	IL-76TD	RA-76840 'Nikolay Kamanin'	
103.34.17.557	8910	IL-76MD 'Falsie'	B-4037	
105.34.17.563	9001	IL-76MF (prototype)	17563, IS 76900, RA-76900	26-11-1993
104.34.17.567	9002	IL-76MD 'Falsie'	B-4038	
103.34.17.569	9003	IL-76TD	17569, RA-76379	
104.34.18.576	9004	IL-76MD 'Falsie'	B-4039	
103.34.18.578	9005	IL-76TD	RA-76380, 7O-ADF	
103.34.18.584	9006	IL-76TD	RA-76843	17-1-1995
106.34.18.587	9007	IL-76MD 'Falsie'	B-4042	
103.34.18.592	9008	IL-76TD	EZ-F424	
103.34.18.596	9009	IL-76TD	RA-76381	
103.34.18.600	9010	IL-76TD	UK 76386, RA 76386	30-9-1993*
103.34.18.601	9101	IL-76TD	RA-76841 'Mavrikiy Slepnev'	
103.34.18.608	9102	IL-76TD	EZ-F423	
103.34.18.609	9103	IL-76TD	EZ-F426	
103.34.18.616	9104	IL-76TD	RA-76842	25-11-1993*
103.34.18.620	9105	IL-76TD	EZ-F427	26-11-1993*
104.34.18.624	9106	IL-76TD	EZ-F428	
104.34.18.628	9107	IL-76TD	RA-76366	
104.34.19.632	9108	IL-76TD		
104.34.19.636	9109	IL-76TD	7T-WIP	
104.34.19.639	9110	IL-76TD	RA-76429 'Sigizmund Levanevskiy'	?-4-1997*
104.34.19.644	9201	IL-76TD	UK 76426 No.2 (! – see 1013405184)	
104.34.19.648	9202	IL-76TD	UK 76428	
104.34.19.649	9203	IL-76TD	7T-WIV	
105.34.19.656	9204	IL-76MD 'Falsie'	19656, B-4040	
104.34.19.657	9205	IL-76TD	UK-76364	
105.34.20.663	9206	IL-76MD 'Falsie'	B-4041	
104.34.20.667	9207	IL-76TD	UK-76365	
106.34.20.671	9208	IL-76MD 'Falsie'	B-4043	
106.34.20.673	9209	IL-76TD		
106.34.20.680	9210	IL-76TD		

Construction number	Fuselage number	Version	Registration/ tactical code/serial	Manufacture date
106.34.20.681	9301	IL-78?		
106.34.20.685	9302	IL-78?		
106.34.20.689	9303	IL-76TD		
104.34.20.696	9304	IL-76MD 'Falsie', IL-76TD	RA-76845 'Mikhail Vodop'yanov'	22-3-1995
106.34.20.697	9305	IL-76TD		
106.34.21.704	9306	IL-76TD		
106.34.21.708	9307	IL-76TD		
106.34.21.709	9308	IL-76TD		
106.34.21.716	9309	IL-76TD		
106.34.21.717	9310	IL-76TD		
106.34.21.724	9401	IL-76MF (prototype)		
106.34.21.727	9402	IL-76TD		
106.34.21.730	9403	IL-76TD		
106.34.21.736	9404	IL-76TD		
106.34.21.737	9405	IL-76TD		
106.34.22.743	9406	IL-76TD		
107.34.22.748	9407	IL-76TD		
107.34.22.752	9408	IL-76TD		
107.34.22.753	9409	IL-76TD		
107.34.22.760	9410	IL-76TD		

Construction number	Fuselage number	Version	Registration/ tactical code/serial	Manufacture date
107.34.22.761	9501	IL-76TD		
107.34.22.768	9502	IL-76TD		
107.34.22.772	9503	IL-76TD		
107.34.22.773	9504	IL-76TD		
107.34.23.780	9505	IL-76TD		
107.34.23.784	9506	IL-76TD		
107.34.23.785	9507	IL-76TD		
107.34.23.789	9508	IL-76TD		
107.34.23.793	9509	IL-76TD		
107.34.23.800	9510	IL-76TD		
106.34.23.801	9601	IL-76MF (IL-76TF?)		
106.34.23.808	9602	IL-76MF (IL-76TF?)		
106.34.24.812	9603	IL-76MF (IL-76TF?)		
106.34.24.815	9604	IL-76MF (IL-76TF?)		
106.34.24.819	9605	IL-76MF (IL-76TF?)		
106.34.24.824	9606	IL-76MF (IL-76TF?)		
106.34.24.825	9607	IL-76MF (IL-76TF?)		
106.34.24.829	9608	IL-76MF (IL-76TF?)		
106.34.24.836	9609	IL-76MF (IL-76TF?)		
106.34.24.840	9610	IL-76MF (IL-76TF?)		

i The manufacture date is the date when the aircraft is formally accepted by the customer.

ii Demilitarised (with tail gunner's station but no tail turret).

iii Registrations preceded by a semi-colon are unconfirmed

iv The registration CCCP-86621 was also quoted for an IL-62 *sans suffixe* likewise built in 1975 (c/n 52005, later changed to 3520556 which basically means the same). IL-76 CCCP-86621 has been reported as a misread for CCCP-86821 but, firstly, was quoted in official lists with this c/n; secondly, photoproof exists!

v 5A-DMM is listed as destroyed by Western sources but Russian official lists do not confirm this.

vi IL-76T/TDs marked with an asterisk are quasi-civilian, despite being unarmed civil versions.

vii CCCP-76636 has also been reported as an IL-78 later converted to a pure freighter.

viii The registration was applied with no dash or space after the Russian prefix when the aircraft was an IL-76TD 'Falsie'. It was changed to the standard presentation after conversion to 'true' IL-76TD and repaint.

Most of the Belorussian *Candids* operated by East Line, such as IL-76TD 'Falsie' EW-78826 seen here taking off from Zhukovskiy in May 1999, flew in basic TransAVIAexport colours. Yefim Gordon

Accident Attrition

Unfortunately the IL-76 has had its share of accidents (though the accident rate was nowhere near as high as with some other types), and most of the aircraft involved were military *Candids*. As of this writing, 33 fatal and non-fatal accidents resulting in 29 total hull losses are known to have happened. In most cases, however, human error was the cause of the loss. Additionally, seven aircraft were lost and three more damaged due to hostile action.

In 1979 a Soviet Air Force IL-76M captained by Capt Panfilov crashed near its home base in Vitebsk. The cause was traced to a flap drive failure – one of the type's teething troubles; asymmetric flap deflection had caused the aircraft to lose control and crash on approach.

As already mentioned, a Soviet Air Force IL-76M (possibly CCCP-86036, c/n 093416500, f/n 1305) crashed on approach to Kabul at 19:35 Moscow time on 25th December 1979, the day when Soviet forces entered Afghanistan (see Chapter 4).

On 23rd September 1980, a few days after the eight-year Iran-Iraq war had begun, Iranian McDonnell Douglas F-4E Phantom IIs raided Baghdad's Saddam Hussein International airport. A quasi-civilian 'Iraqi Airways' IL-76 registered YI-AIO (c/n 073410315, f/n 0809) was on short finals at that moment, inbound from Paris-Orly, and it just happened to be at the wrong place at the wrong time. On sighting the Iraqi aircraft the Phantom pilots (who were tipped off by an Iran Air crew which saw the aircraft departing Paris) shot it down; the freighter blew up in mid-air and crashed short of the runway. *À la guerre comme à la guerre…*

As noted earlier, on 26th November 1984 IL-76M CCCP-86739 (c/n 083412354?, f/n 0909) was shot down with a shoulder-launched surface-to-air missile over Kabul (see Chapter 4).

Sometime in 1985 Libyan Arab Republic Air Force IL-76M 5A-DKK (c/n 0003423675, f/n 1709) was damaged beyond repair in a hard landing at Sheba.

On the night of 15th April 1986 three Libyan examples were 'killed in action' when the USA decided to teach Col Muammar Qaddafi a sharp lesson. General Dynamics FB-111As deployed to RAF Mildenhall raided Tripoli, dropping their bombs squarely on the presidential palace; Qaddafi was unhurt because he was hiding in a bunker deep underground. But the bombers also raided the airport, knocking out (among other things) LARAF IL-76M 5A-DLL (c/n 093421612, f/n 1603) and Jamahirian Air Transport IL-76Ts 5A-DNF (c/n 0033445302, f/n 3306) and 5A-DNL (c/n 0033447357, f/n 3410). The weapons used must have been cluster bombs packed with pellets because the aircraft were so full of holes they looked like sieves. Ironically, the abbreviation *DNF* used in sports event protocols means *did not finish*. Talk about bad omens!

On 2nd April 1987 two Melitopol' airlift regiment IL-76MDs captained by Maj N S Kastur and Maj V N Pakhomov collided in mid-air near Dzhankoy on the Crimea peninsula during a night paradropping practice sortie. One of the pilots made an error when changing formation and the aircraft's wing hit the tail of the other freighter; both *Candids* immediately became uncontrollable, crashing into the Sivash Gulf with the tragic loss of all on board. The search effort went on for a week but turned up nothing. Then the cosmonaut group's SAR detachment was put on the job and one of the chopper pilots got lucky, spotting the wreckage a few feet below the surface. No bodies or 'black boxes' could be recovered, however, as the place was one huge swamp (Sivash means Rotten Sea in Tatarian).

In the summer of 1988 Soviet Air Force IL-76MD CCCP-78768 (c/n 0083487603, f/n 6601) detached to Angola was hit by a Stinger missile shortly after take-off from Luena airbase. With one engine on fire the aircraft made an emergency landing at Luena (see Chapter 4).

When a disastrous earthquake hit Armenia in December 1988, killing 25,000 and flattening the cities of Kirovakan and Spitak, rescue teams and humanitarian aid came to the stricken region from all over the world. Much of it was airlifted by *Candids* – mostly quasi-Aeroflot IL-76M/MDs. On 11th December 1988 IL-76M CCCP-86732 (c/n 083413388?, f/n 1007) captained by Capt N P Brilyov hit a hill during a night approach to Leninakan, killing all on board – nine crew and 69 rescue workers. The pilots had set the atmospheric pressure (QNH) incorrectly, causing the altimeters to give incorrect readings. The aircraft was completely destroyed, only the aft fuselage and tail unit remaining relatively intact.

On 21st March 1989 a Soviet Air Force IL-76MD was reportedly shot down by UNITA rebels near Menongue AB, Angola.

On 10th August 1989 an IL-76M captained by Capt Zastavnyuk crashed 32km (19.8 miles) from Krechevitsy AB near Novgorod during a thunderstorm, killing the entire crew.

At 1838 Moscow time on 18th October 1989 IL-76MD CCCP-76569 (c/n 0033448421?, f/n 3606) crashed near Nasosnaya AB 40km (24.8 miles) from Baku while attempting an emergency landing. Five minutes after take-off at 1827 No1 engine disintegrated and caught fire. The fire extinguishers failed and the fire began spreading; three minutes later the stricken engine broke away. The landing gear would not extend properly because of hydraulics damage, forcing the crew to use emergency extension.

The wreckage of IL-76 *sans suffixe* CCCP-86732 which crashed on approach to Leninakan on 11th December 1988. ITAR-TASS

The port wing's flaps were on fire and the captain made the unprecedented decision to make a flaps-up landing. Yet the wing structure failed 6km (3.7 miles) from the runway threshold; the aircraft rolled to port and crashed into the Caspian Sea in shallow water 700m (2,296ft) from the shore, killing all on board – Col Aleksandr Kalmykov, first officer Lt (sg) Valeriy Vologhin, flight engineer Lt (sg) Yevgeniy Andreyev, navigator Lt Col Faskhaddin Zakirov, radio operator Maj Yuriy Gavrikov, gunner Ens. Aleksandr Andriyash, loadmaster Lt (sg) Aleksandr Pesterev, engineer Maj Igor' Krayookhin and mechanic Lt (sg) Aleksey Gashimov – and 48 interior troops soldiers detached to Armenia to aid in reconstruction work after the earthquake.

Analysis of the wreckage revealed that the low pressure turbine bearing of the No1 engine – a weak spot of the D-30KP – had failed on take-off, causing the LP turbine shaft to break; the turbine overspeeded and disintegrated, the fragments puncturing the wing tanks. The resulting massive fire could not be extinguished because turbine fragments had severed the fire extinguisher control wires. This caused the entire *Candid* fleet to be grounded for engine checks and measures were taken by the engine's manufacturer.

Two days later disaster struck again. On 20th October IL-76TD CCCP-76466 (c/n 0023440153, f/n 2909) crashed 18km (11 miles) from Leninakan, killing the crew and 8 passengers. The aircraft belonging to the Ul'yanovsk Higher Flying School was on a quake relief flight from Ul'yanovsk with a load of construction materials. It was the same story as with CCCP-86732 two years earlier: the altimeter had been set incorrectly and the aircraft hit a hillside at 0132, exploding on impact and burning out completely.

On 1st February 1990 IL-76M CCCP-86021 (c/n 083413405?, f/n 1102) flown by trainee Lt (sg) O V Kooklin and instructor Lt Col V P Pankratov crashed near Panevezhis, Lithuania, when making a go-around after a failed runway approach. The aircraft impacted 3700m (2.3 miles) beyond the runway, killing all on board.

At 1133 Moscow time on 27th March 1990 IL-76MD CCCP-78781 (c/n 0083489670, f/n 6708) stalled and spun in on final approach to Kabul, killing all on board (see Chapter 4).

On 6th June 1990 IL-76MD CCCP-86905 (c/n 0023436054, f/n 2704) was written off in a crash-landing at Kabul after being hit by a Stinger missile on long finals (see Chapter 4).

During the same year IL-76MD CCCP-78711 (c/n unknown) was damaged beyond repair at the Novaya Zemlya archipelago in the Barents Sea, undershooting on landing; luckily, all occupants of the aircraft were unhurt.

On 24th May 1991 IL-76TD LZ-INK (ex-CCCP-76784, c/n 0093494835, f/n 7109) operated by the Swiss airline Mexair crashed 10km (6.2 miles) south of Bakhtaran, Iran, while attempting a forced landing. The aircraft, which flew with a mixed Soviet-Bulgarian crew, was chartered to deliver humanitarian aid to Kurdish refugees. The cause was quadruple engine failure due to fuel starvation; four crew members were killed in the crash and six others injured.

On 28th August 1992 IL-76MD CCCP-78780 (c/n 0083489666?, f/n 6707) was destroyed by shelling at Kabul airport as Taliban troops attacked the city (see Chapter 4).

On 21st April 1993 Uzbekistan Airways IL-76TD UK-76794 (c/n 0093498954, f/n 7409) overran the runway during an emergency landing at Peshawar, Iran, colliding with airport structures and damaging the wings and landing gear. The aircraft was repaired and is still in service as of this writing.

At 2047 Moscow time on 8th July 1993 a 334th VTAP IL-76M captained by Maj V V Toodin crashed on short finals to Kresty AB, Pskov, after a paradrop training sortie. Fire had broken out in the aft fuselage and the aircraft impacted 3,400m (2.1 miles) short of the runway, killing the seven crewmen, instructor and three trainees.

On 20th September 1994 Azerbaijan Air Force IL-76MD AHY-78001 (c/n 0083489683, f/n 6801) was attacked and damaged on the ground at an unspecified location by an Armenian fighter during the fighting over the disputed Nagornyy Karabakh enclave. The damage proved to be minor, the aircraft was repaired and reregistered AHY-78129.

On 31st December 1994 IL-76TD EW-76836 (c/n 1013409305, f/n 8307) owned by the Belorussian airline Belair was substantially damaged on landing at Sarajevo. The aircraft, which was chartered by UNPF in Bosnia-Herzegovina, was inbound on flight UN-188 from Luxembourg with 35,690kg (78,680 lb) of humanitarian cargo. This particular flight was *not* in the contract and was made at the insistence of the customer's representative.

The weather conditions at Butmir airport were below minima, with the cloudbase at 130 m/426ft (the required minimum was 214 m/702ft) and a tailwind gusting up to 12.7 m/sec (25kts); still the crew continued the approach, expecting an improvement in the weather. The temperature was 4°C (39°F) and the runway was flooded but the approach controller did not inform the crew of this until four seconds before touchdown. The aircraft overran on the slippery runway and careered over trenches dug by UNPF soldiers, collapsing the nose gear and smashing the ground mapping radar. The crew (captain Yuriy V Koorganov, first officer Oleg N Pologovskiy, flight engineer Ivan M Pekhota, instructor navigator Aleksandr A Shavrin, trainee navigator Yevgeniy S Tereschchenko, radio operator Artur G Gvardiyan and operators A A Tkachenko and V V Tarasov) and three passengers were unhurt but the aircraft had to be abandoned because the activity of snipers rendered repairs impossible.

Flight International stated that an Angolan Air Force IL-76MD had been damaged by UNITA ground fire on 19th July 1994, making a forced landing at an unspecified location. However, there are no reports of IL-76 deliveries to Angola, so if the incident *did* take place this was obviously a CIS aircraft.

At 0544 Moscow time on 5th April 1996 Kras Air IL-76TD RA-76752 (c/n 0093498967, f/n 7502) went missing on approach to Petropavlovsk-Kamchatskiy's Yelizovo airport. The aircraft, which was bound from Novosibirsk on a charter flight for the Poseidon fishing company, was carrying 57 tons (125,661 lb) of frozen meat, which is 7 tons (15,432 lb) over the IL-76TD's design limit. This and unexpectedly strong headwinds caused it to use up fuel faster than anticipated. Realising they were running out of fuel, the crew requested permission to leave the air route and make a short cut. The ATC said no but the pilots disobeyed. The result was predictable: 40km (24.8 miles) from the airport the aircraft smacked into the Vashkazhech volcano 890m (2,920ft) above sea level and was totally destroyed. The wreckage was located five days later; there were no survivors among the 19 occupants.

At 15:40 UTC on 6th June 1996 IL-76MD UR-76539 (c/n 0023442234, f/n 3109) crashed on take-off from Kinshasa-N'djili airport on a flight to Athens. The unloaded aircraft, which belonged to the Ukrainian airline Hoseba, was bound for Athens after delivering a cargo from Cairo. The crew was forced to use reverse thrust when taxying out from the parking space (there was no towbar on board and available towbars at Kinshasa were incompatible with the IL-76); also, the ATC kept urging the crew to take-off as quickly as possible. As a result, the flight engineer forgot to extend the flaps and slats, going perfunctorily through the checklist.

With no high-lift devices, UR-76539 stalled immediately after take-off, striking the runway with the aft fuselage at 22° AOA and turning 10° to starboard. Then the aircraft left the runway 3,800m (12,467ft) from the holding point and became airborne again at 260 to 265km/h (140 to 143kts), rolling to the right, out of control. A second tailstrike followed 140m (459ft) later; then the *Candid* hit the side of a ravine, rolled inverted and exploded 180m (590ft) beyond the runway threshold. The airport's fire brigade took an hour (!) to get to the scene. Needless to say that all ten occupants of the aircraft (captain Mikhail I Zavadskiy, first officer Bogdan S Ghirenko, flight engineer Vladimir L Fofanov, navigator Vladimir S Savchuk, radio operator Vladimir N Krivenko, equipment operators Oleg Yu Starchenko and Mikhail A Remzhin, mechanics V V Bogdan and A D Sharapa, and cargo operations manager D Yu Il'chenko) were dead by then…

On 19th August 1996 SPAir IL-76T RA-76513 (c/n 083414451, f/n 1203) crashed near Belgrade's Valjavo airport. The aircraft had taken off at 00:05 local time bound for Malta; 30 minutes later when the aircraft was 96km (60 miles) from the airport, the pilots radioed that they had lost all electric and hydraulic power and were attempting to return. For three hours the freighter circled, burning off fuel; the pilots were flying the big jet manually at the limit of their physical strength because of the enormous control forces. Finally, a visual approach was attempted but since all flight instruments had failed the pilots misjudged their altitude. RA-76513 hit the ground in a wheat field and exploded, killing the crew of ten and two passengers. Within minutes the aircraft was consumed by flames, only the tail unit remaining relatively intact.

An incredibly acrid stench spread from the burning wreckage, forcing the police to evacuate the local population. Speculation immediately arose that the aircraft's cargo had been ammunition and that SPAir was involved in illegal arms trafficking. An airline spokesman insisted next day that the cargo had been 14.5 tons (31,966 lb) of car tyres and 500kg (1,102 lb) of signal flares.

On 31st October 1996 IL-76TD RA-76783 (c/n 0093498974, f/n 7504) operated by the Ulyanovsk Higher Civil Aviation School overran at Rostov-on-Don, collapsing the nose gear. The aircraft was repaired and is still in service.

The fourth-gravest accident in the history of aviation happened near New Delhi on 12th November 1996. Kazakstan Airlines IL-76TD UN 76435 (c/n 1023413428, f/n 8607) was approaching Indira Gandhi International airport in poor visibility. Unknown to its crew a Saudi Arabian Airlines Boeing 747-168B (HZ-AIH, c/n 22748, f/n 555) had taken off from New Delhi on flight SV763 to Jeddah via Dhahran. The Boeing was cleared for flight level 140 (14,000ft/4,267 m) and the IL-76 for FL 150 (15,000ft/4,572 m). For reasons still unknown as of this writing the 747 collided head on with the Candid 72km (45 miles) west of the airport as it made a gentle left turn. Both aircraft immediately became uncontrollable, crashing in a field near the village of Charkhi Dadri. All 39 persons on the IL-76 were killed; incredibly, two of the 312 aboard the 747 survived.

What came next defies description. The ATC became aware of the crash only when the press descended on the scene and live TV footage was broadcast. The local populace, however, wasted no time in plundering the wreckage strewn over the field.

Predictably, Indian authorities blamed the Kazakh crew, claiming it had misunderstood the approach controller and the IL-76 had descended below its cleared flight level. The local press jumped with glee at this statement, calling Russian aircraft 'flying coffins' and claiming their crews barely spoke English and never obeyed ATC commands. However, India has become notorious for its horrible flight safety standards and obsolete, worn-out airport equipment.

On 27th November 1996 128th VTAP IL-76MD RA-78804 (c/n 0093492778, f/n 7005) was making a flight from Chkalovskaya AB near Moscow to Petropavlovsk-Kamchatskiy with a load of New Year presents for children of the Primor'ye region; officially the payload was 30 tons (66,137 lb). After making a refuelling stopover in Abakan the aircraft climbed out with an abnormally flat gradient. At 2349hr 42sec local time RA-78804 crashed into a hill 14km (8.7 miles) beyond the runway with 15° bank and blew up, killing the crew of ten and 13 passengers, including two children.

The hill, which has been stated by different sources as being 247 to 350m (810 to 1,148ft) high, was not considered a dangerous obstacle; normally the IL-76 should have climbed to at least 420m (1,377ft) at that point. The cause of the accident is not known; it could have been icing (it was snowing heavily at the time of the crash), fuel contamination or simply overloading. The air traffic controller had no way of knowing RA-78804 was below the glide path because the aircraft's ATC transponder indicating true altitude was out of order.

At 1453 local time on 25th January 1997 IL-76TD RA-76834 (c/n 1023409319, f/n 8310) owned by the Voronezh aircraft factory stalled immediately after taking off from Anadyr' on a flight to Moscow and sank back on its belly, crashing through a weather observation station and coming to rest 270m (885ft) beyond the runway threshold. Poor crew discipline was the reason this time; quite simply, the pilots had forgotten to set the flaps and tailplane trim to take-off position, being all too busy discussing personal matters. Only two of the 21 occupants received minor injuries but the aircraft was damaged beyond economical repair.

On 17th June 1998 EMERCOM of Russia forces were called upon to help extinguish a fire in an ammunition dump near Yekaterinburg. Using a water-bomber was the only option because exploding ammunition prevented firemen from getting within a couple of miles from the blaze. Hence IL-TD RA-76840 (c/n 1033417553, f/n 8909) was quickly fitted out with a VAP-2 firefighting module and filled up with water, departing from Zhukovskiy at 1800 Moscow time. The aircraft was flown by captain Valeriy Drobinskiy, first officer Leonid Filin, flight engineer Aleksandr Markov, navigator Dmitriy Vladimirov, radio operator Aleksandr Apollonov and loadmaster Vladimir Sakhno. Also aboard was an EMERCOM group consisting of Lt Gen Sergey Salov, Viktor Kuznetsov, Aleksandr Kutakov and camera operator Vasiliy Yoorchuk.

At 1825 the rear pressure bulkhead failed just as the aircraft was climbing through 6,800m (22,310ft). The result was an instant explosive decompression which ripped away the greater part of the pressure bulkhead, the centre and starboard cargo door segments; indeed, it was only the water tanks which prevented the people sitting in the freight hold from being, pardon the expression, gone with the wind.

Drobinskiy executed an emergency descent and made for home, requesting an emergency landing. Now, however, the VAP-2 module filled with 40 tons of water put the crew at a disadvantage. With the water on board, the aircraft's landing weight would exceed the limit stated in the flight manual. Yet dumping the water was dangerous, too, as the aircraft's CG position changes perceptibly in the process; no one knew the actual extent of the damage and this CG shift could cause the aircraft to break up in mid-air. Therefore, Drobinskiy chose to land with full water tanks. After circling the airfield for some time to burn off fuel the Candid made a perfect landing at 2033. An hour later another EMERCOM IL-76TD firebomber with the same crew took off from Zhukovskiy and headed for Yekaterinburg. It says a lot for the crew that they decided to accomplish the mission after just having had such a narrow escape; a fire won't wait, after all! As for the unlucky RA-76840, the aircraft was repaired and returned to service.

On 10th July 1999 the captain of East Line IL-76TD 'Falsie' EW-78843 (c/n 1003403082, f/n 7301) ordered the engines shut down after taxiing in at Krasnoyarsk-Yemel'yanovo airport before the parking brake was on or the DC batteries confirmed on line. As a result, all electric and hydraulic power was lost when the inboard engines were shut down; unrestrained by brakes, the Candid rolled forward and collided head on with a warehouse. The damage to the fuselage nose looks horrendous but the aircraft is considered repairable.

At 1910 local time on 13th July 1998, ATI Airlines IL-76MD UR-76424 (c/n 0063470096, f/n 5304) caught fire and crashed into the Red Sea six minutes after departing Ras al Khaimah, UAE, killing all eight crew. The aircraft was bound for Nikolayev, the Ukraine, on flight TII 2570 with an undisclosed commercial cargo. Eyewitnesses gave contradictory evidence; some said it was an engine fire while others claimed the fire was in the centre fuselage. The latter sounds plausible, considering that the cargo may have contained automobiles (CIS residents often shop for used cars in the UAE). With air temperatures approaching 40°C (104°F), a leaky tank would have quickly filled the cargo hold with gasoline fumes, and then the tiniest spark would have been enough to trigger an explosion.

Five days later, on 18th July, Ukrainian Cargo Airways IL-76MD UR-UCI (ex-IL-78 UR-76415, ex-CCCP-76775, c/n 0083481440, f/n 6110) chartered by the Bulgarian cargo airline Air Sofia crashed near Asmara, Eritrea, inbound from Sofia. The cause of the crash was cited as CFIT (controlled flight into terrain). The aircraft was probably carrying military materiel, since hostilities had resumed between Eritrea and Ethiopia.

On 26th July 1999 IL-76TD RA-76819 of Elf Air (c/n 1013409274, f/n 8209) captained by Dmitriy Yu Sorokin crashed on take-off at Irkutsk International (Irkutsk-1) airport where it had made a refuelling stop on a charter flight from Shenyang to Moscow (the next stop was to be in Perm'). Seconds after lift-off the aircraft sank down on its belly, crashed through the concrete perimeter fence, ploughed through some trees and came to rest in a field adjacent to the airport, turning 90° to port and bursting into flames. All seven crew members escaped, only two of them sustaining injuries, but the aircraft was totally destroyed by the fire. Overloading has been cited as a possible cause, though other sources state the payload was 30 tons (66,137 lb) which is well within the IL-76's design limits. The aircraft was operated by the Third World Relief Agency at the time of the crash.

Finally, on 22nd June 2000 117th VTAP IL-76MD RA-76723 (c/n 0073475245, f/n 5702) captained by Lt Col Andrey Zh Zelenko suffered technical problems 23 minutes after take-off from Privolzhskiy AB near Astrakhan', where it had made a refuelling stop en route from Makhachkala to Khabarovsk. At 17:30 Moscow time the fuel system malfunctioned at 6,100m (20,997ft), then one of the hydraulic systems failed, rendering the high-lift devices inoperative, and a fire broke out in the port wing. At 17:50 the aircraft returned to the base but, landing fast, it overran and crashed through the perimeter fence, bursting into flames in a field 200m (656ft) beyond the runway. The 232 people aboard (main and relief crews, 210 conscripts and 11 accompanying officers) evacuated the aircraft in under two minutes; no one was killed or seriously injured but the *Candid* was totally destroyed by the fire. On 9th August Lt Col Zelenko was awarded the Hero of Russia title; the other crewmen received the Personal Bravery Order.

There were also accidents where the IL-76 was indirectly involved. On 16th January 1987, Yak-40 CCCP-87618 of the Uzbek CAD (c/n 9131918) crashed on take-off at Tashkent's Youzhnyy airport at 0511 Moscow time, killing all four crew and five passengers. The aircraft had hit wake turbulence from an International Air Services Directorate IL-76TD (CCCP-76482, c/n 0053460832, f/n 4608) which had departed 1 minute 6 seconds earlier. Normally the diminutive trijet would have passed between the *Candid*'s wingtip vortices without any trouble, but, as luck would have it, there was a crosswind at 15 to 20m (49 to 65ft) which moved the turbulence squarely into the path of the feederliner. The Yak-40 rolled sharply to the left, impacting 13m (42.6ft) beyond the runway with 70° left bank and exploding.

On another occasion, however, the crew of a *Candid* was directly responsible for a major accident. On 12th December 1995 the Roosskiye Vityazi display team was coming home to Kubinka from Langkawi AB, Malaysia, where it had performed at the LIMA'95 airshow. The formation was led by an IL-76MD support aircraft (RA-78847, c/n 1013404132, f/n 7903) captained by Maj Gen V Grebennikov. A Su-27 *Flanker-B* flown by Maj V Koval'skiy and a Su-27UB *Flanker-C* trainer (10 Blue) flown by Maj A Lichkoon and Maj S Klimov was on the *Candid*'s port wing; two more single-seaters flown by Lt Col Nikolay V Grechanov and Lt Col Nikolay T Kordyukov plus another Su-27UB flown by Col Boris M Grigor'yev and Lt Col Aleksandr V Syrovoy were on the freighter's starboard wing.

The return trip included a refuelling stopover at Cam Ranh – a Russian Naval Aviation base in southern Vietnam (Thành Hoa province). The base was virtually inactive and in a sorry state, as locals had pillaged everything they could lay their hands upon.

108km (58nm) from Cam Ranh the flight leader requested permission to land. ATC officer Lt Col A Matushkin checked the weather conditions and gave clearance for descent to 2,900m (9,514ft). After passing the outer marker beacon the group was cleared to descend to 1,500m (4,921ft) and enter a right-hand landing pattern.

The approaches to Cam Ranh were obscured by layer upon layer of clouds; the cloudbase was 150 to 200m (492 to 656ft) and it was raining. Visibility was poor and the group had to keep close formation in order to maintain visual contact and avoid getting separated. At 0627 Moscow time (1027 local time) Grebennikov lost radio contact with his three right-hand wingmen as he was making the turn for final approach. It was later established that the flight leader had dropped way below the glide path. At the time of the accident the group was flying at only 600m (1,968ft) instead of the prescribed minimum of 1,500m (4,921ft).

When the ground proximity warning system (GPWS) horn sounded, Grebennikov was late in ordering the whole group to climb urgently. The formation was making a right turn and the right-hand wingmen were flying a little lower than the rest – just a few dozen feet too low. The three *Flankers* crashed into the wooded slope of a 722m (2,368ft) hill, killing the crews instantly. The other aircraft climbed to a safe altitude and the two remaining fighters diverted to Phan Rang 40km (21.6nm) south of the base; the IL-76MD managed to land at Cam Ranh after prolonged but fruitless attempts to get in touch with the missing wingmen. The wreckage was located in the jungle by a Vietnamese search group ten days later.

The investigation took more than two years. Grebennikov was tried and found guilty of criminal negligence in early 1998. He was sentenced to six years in prison but amnestied in view of his prior merits.

On 26th July 1997 Yuzhmashavia IL-76MD UR-78785 (c/n 0083489691, f/n 6803) had a narrow escape at Ostend, Belgium, when an Extra 300 competition aerobatic aircraft of the Royal Jordanian Air Force's *Royal Falcons* display team crashed on the flightline right next to it (apparently due to pilot error), killing the pilot and ten spectators. The *Candid* was fully fuelled and could have caused a tremendous fire with, no doubt, more fatalities as a result.

The remains of Elf Air IL-76TD RA-76819 which crashed at Irkutsk on 26th July 1999. The landing gear strut in the foreground shows that the aircraft was sliding sideways before it came to rest. Courtesy CIS Interstate Aviation Committee

Records Galore

CCCP-76500, the first production civil IL-76, used during the record breaking flights described below.
The Le Bourget '75 exhibit code 366 is visible in this in-flight photograph . Yefim Gordon archive

The first world record in which the IL-76 was involved was not established by the aircraft itself. On 24th April 1975 a team of skydivers set a daytime group skydiving record in Akhtoobinsk, using the *Candid-B* prototype (CCCP-76501). They left the aircraft at 15,300m (50,197ft), opening their parachutes at 800m (2,624ft).

On 4th July 1975 IL-76 CCCP-76500 flown by captain Aleksandr M Tyuryumin, first officer Stanislav G Bliznyuk, flight engineer V P Gorovoy, navigator V A Schchotkin, radio operator L Ya. Vinogradov and test engineers I B Vorob'yov and V V Shkitin averaged 856.607km/h (463.03kts) over a 2,000km (1,242 miles) closed circuit with payloads of 35, 40, 45, 50, 55 and 60 tons (77,160; 88,183; 99,206; 110,229; 121,252; 132,275 lb).

On the same day another crew – captain Yakov I Vernikov (Distinguished Test Pilot, HSU), first officer A M Tyuryumin, flight engineer I N Yakimets, navigator Schchotkin, radio operator I S Kondaoorov and test engineers Vorobyov and Shkitin set an altitude record, reaching 11,875m (38,959ft) with payloads of 60, 65 and 70 tons (132,275; 143,298; 154,321 lb). In this flight the IL-76 also set a payload record, lifting a 70,121kg (154,587.74 lb) load to an altitude of 2,000m (6,561ft).

On 7th July 1975 the same aircraft captained by Tyuryumin averaged 857.657km/h (463.598kts) over a 1,000km (621 miles) closed circuit, establishing nine records with payloads of 30, 35, 40, 45, 50, 55, 60, 65 and 70 tons (66,137; 77,160; 88,183; 99,206; 110,229; 121,252; 132,275; 143,298; 154,321 lb).

On 10th July 1975 Tyuryumin's crew completed a 5,000km (3,105 miles) closed circuit on CCCP-76500 with an average speed of 815.968km/h (441.06kts), claiming records with payloads of 15, 20, 25, 30, 35 and 40 tons (33,069; 44,091; 55,114; 66,137; 77,160; 88,183 lb).

On 26th October 1977 a team of female skydivers established two world records. Again, CCCP-76500 was the aircraft in question; it was captained by A M Tyuryumin and the flight was made from Artsyz AB. First, E Fomichova made a solo jump from 15,496m (50,840ft), falling 14,800m (48,556ft) before opening her parachute. Then a group consisting of N Pronyushkina, L Fisher, N Gritsenkova. N Vasil'kova, Ye. Yegorova, P Boorlaka, M Chernetskaya, V Bookhtoyarova, Z Vakarova and Z Salmina left the aircraft at 14,846m (48,707ft), executing a free fall of 14,246m (46,739ft).

IL-76 Family Cutaway and Drawings

Ilyushin Il-76MD/TD *Candid-B*
Cutaway Drawing Key

1 Nose radome
2 Groza weather radar scanner
3 Front pressure bulkhead
4 Lower nose compartment glazing
5 Retractable landing/taxying lamp
6 Ventral radome
7 Koopol navigational and ground mapping radar
8 Lower deck navigator's and communications officer's stations
9 Navigation instrument panels
10 Flight deck floor level
11 Rudder pedals
12 Instrument panel
13 Control column
14 Instrument panel shroud
15 62-01 IFF antenna
16 Windscreen panels
17 Cockpit eyebrow windows
18 Overhead systems switch panel
19 Co-pilot's seat
20 Centre control pedestal
21 Direct vision opening side window panel
22 Pilot's seat
23 Dual pitot heads
24 Flight deck escape hatch (there should be no steps)
25 Engineer's station
26 Flight engineer's instrument panels
27 Communications aerials
28 Crew rest area and loadmaster's seat (two)
29 Avionics equipment racks
30 Toilet compartment
31 Wing/air intake inspection light (port side only)
32 Crew escape hatch
33 Underfloor equipment stowage racks
34 Nosewheel doors (closed after cycling of undercarriage)
35 Levered-suspension nose undercarriage leg strut
36 Four-wheel steerable nose bogie (forward retracting)
37 Lower communications aerials
38 Main cabin door/paratroop door (port and starboard)
39 Fuselage frame and stringer construction
40 Forward overhead cargo rails
41 Cabin wall soundproofing lining
42 Folding roller conveyor tracks
43 Main cargo loading deck
44 Emergency exit window hatch (port and starboard)
45 Wing/fuselage attachment main frame
46 Fold-away paratroop seating
47 Wing root leading-edge fillet
48 Air conditioning system ram air intake
49 Heat exchangers
50 Heat exchanger spill air louvres
51 Engine bleed air supply duct
52 Air conditioning equipment bay
53 Central leading-edge slat hydraulic drive motor
54 Anti-collision light
55 Wing centre-section spar box

56 Wing centre-section fuel tank (total fuel capacity 18,000 Imp gals/ 81,830 litres)
57 Bolted wing root attachment joint
58 Inner wing panel integral fuel tank
59 Leading-edge slat drive shaft
60 Inboard leading-edge slat segments (two)
61 Nacelle pylons
62 Starboard inner engine nacelle
63 Starboard outer engine nacelle
64 Side cowling panels (open)
65 Outer wing panel joint rib
66 Slat guide rails
67 Slat screw jacks
68 Outboard leading-edge slat segments (three)
69 Outer wing panel integral fuel tank
70 Starboard navigation light
71 Wing-tip fairing
72 Starboard aileron
73 Outboard triple-slotted flap segment (extended)
74 Outboard roll control spoilers (open)
75 Inboard spoilers/lift dumpers (open)
76 Inboard triple-slotted flap segment (extended)
77 Flap screw jacks
78 Flap drive shaft
79 Central flap drive hydraulic motor
80 Wing root trailing-edge fillet
81 Flush aerial panels
82 Cabin air distribution ducting
83 Emergency exit window hatches (port and starboard)
84 Fuselage skin panelling
85 Cargo compartment overhead loading rails
86 Rear pressure bulkhead
87 Motorised travelling cargo hoist (four)

93 Nose radomes
94 Flight refuelling probe
95 Satellite communications and navigation antenna
96 Rotodome antenna fairing
97 Rotodome pylons
98 Avionics cooling air intake
99 Rear ECM antenna
100 Tail radomes

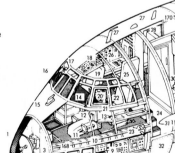

88 Aft folding pressure bulkhead door (open)
89 Central rear cargo door (open position)
90 Fin root fillet
91 A-50 AEW&C *Mainstay* airborne early warning and control variant
92 Forward ECM antenna (with wing/intake inspection light on starboard side)

101 Leading-edge thermal de-icing
102 Tailfin spar box construction
103 Tailplane bullet fairing
104 All-moving tailplane control jack
105 Starboard tailplane
106 Starboard elevator
107 Elevator tabs
108 Tailcone aft fairing
109 Port elevator
110 Port all-moving tailplane

111 Leading-edge thermal de-icing
112 Rudder
113 PRS-4 Krypton (box tail) gun ranging radar (military transport *Candid-B* variant only), observer's station in IL-78 *Midas* tanker variant
114 Tail gunner's compartment
115 2 x 23-mm GSh-23 cannon
116 UKU-9K-502-1 tail gun turret

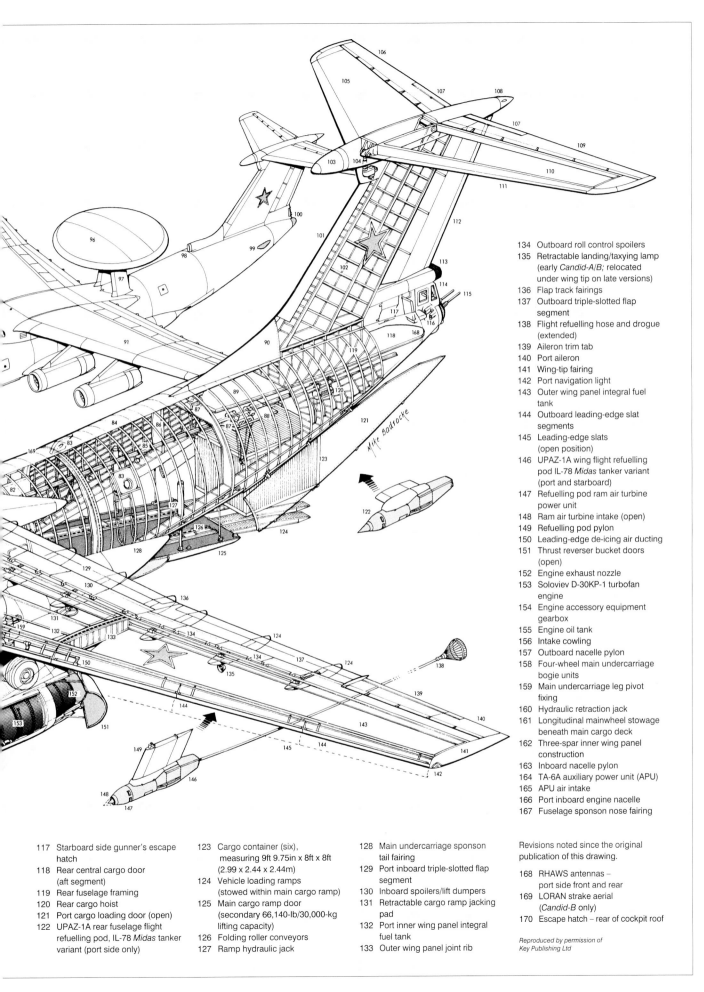

134 Outboard roll control spoilers
135 Retractable landing/taxying lamp (early *Candid-A/B*; relocated under wing tip on late versions)
136 Flap track fairings
137 Outboard triple-slotted flap segment
138 Flight refuelling hose and drogue (extended)
139 Aileron trim tab
140 Port aileron
141 Wing-tip fairing
142 Port navigation light
143 Outer wing panel integral fuel tank
144 Outboard leading-edge slat segments
145 Leading-edge slats (open position)
146 UPAZ-1A wing flight refuelling pod IL-78 *Midas* tanker variant (port and starboard)
147 Refuelling pod ram air turbine power unit
148 Ram air turbine intake (open)
149 Refuelling pod pylon
150 Leading-edge de-icing air ducting
151 Thrust reverser bucket doors (open)
152 Engine exhaust nozzle
153 Soloviev D-30KP-1 turbofan engine
154 Engine accessory equipment gearbox
155 Engine oil tank
156 Intake cowling
157 Outboard nacelle pylon
158 Four-wheel main undercarriage bogie units
159 Main undercarriage leg pivot fixing
160 Hydraulic retraction jack
161 Longitudinal mainwheel stowage beneath main cargo deck
162 Three-spar inner wing panel construction
163 Inboard nacelle pylon
164 TA-6A auxiliary power unit (APU)
165 APU air intake
166 Port inboard engine nacelle
167 Fuselage sponson nose fairing

117 Starboard side gunner's escape hatch
118 Rear central cargo door (aft segment)
119 Rear fuselage framing
120 Rear cargo hoist
121 Port cargo loading door (open)
122 UPAZ-1A rear fuselage flight refuelling pod, IL-78 *Midas* tanker variant (port side only)

123 Cargo container (six), measuring 9ft 9.75in x 8ft x 8ft (2.99 x 2.44 x 2.44m)
124 Vehicle loading ramps (stowed within main cargo ramp)
125 Main cargo ramp door (secondary 66,140-lb/30,000-kg lifting capacity)
126 Folding roller conveyors
127 Ramp hydraulic jack

128 Main undercarriage sponson tail fairing
129 Port inboard triple-slotted flap segment
130 Inboard spoilers/lift dumpers
131 Retractable cargo ramp jacking pad
132 Port inner wing panel integral fuel tank
133 Outer wing panel joint rib

Revisions noted since the original publication of this drawing.

168 RHAWS antennas – port side front and rear
169 LORAN strake aerial (*Candid-B* only)
170 Escape hatch – rear of cockpit roof

Reproduced by permission of Key Publishing Ltd

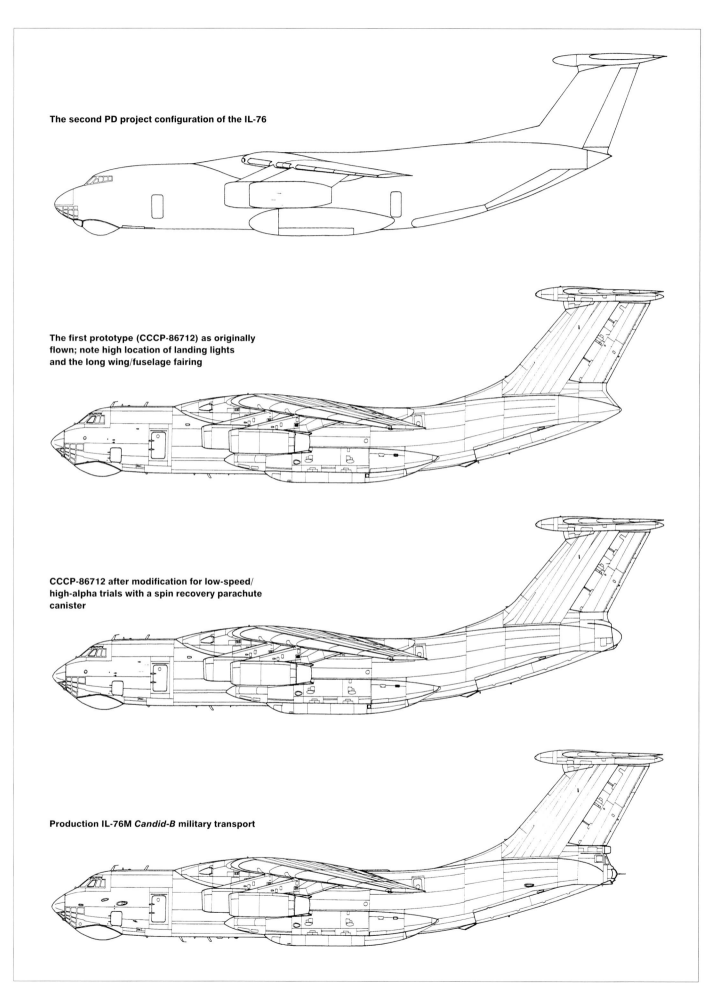

The second PD project configuration of the IL-76

The first prototype (CCCP-86712) as originally
flown; note high location of landing lights
and the long wing/fuselage fairing

CCCP-86712 after modification for low-speed/
high-alpha trials with a spin recovery parachute
canister

Production IL-76M *Candid-B* military transport

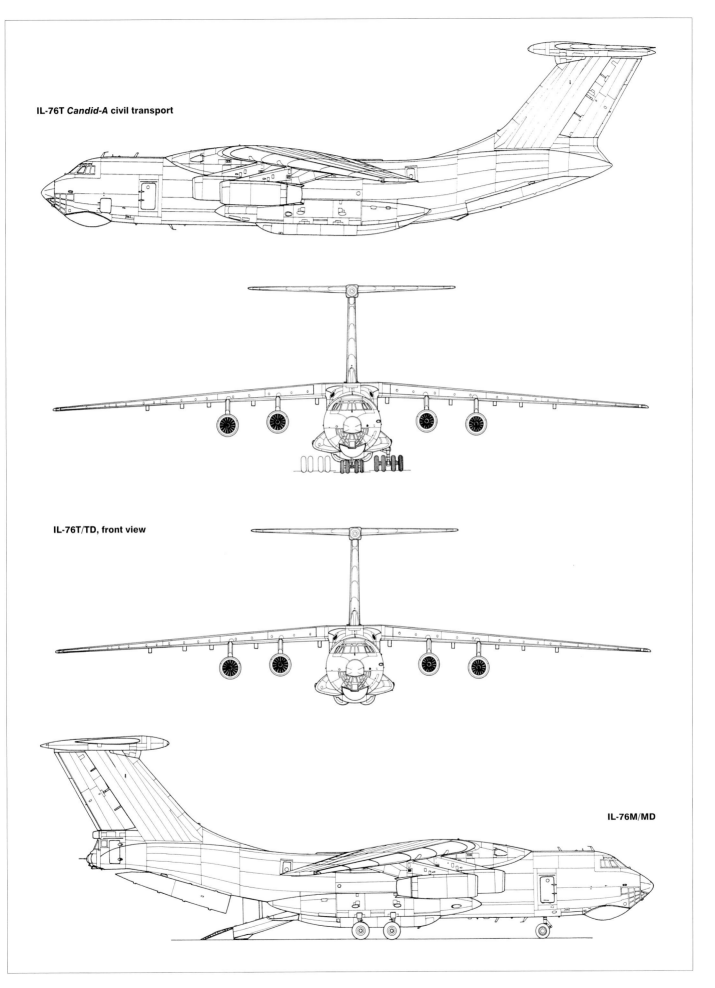

IL-76T *Candid-A* **civil transport**

IL-76T/TD, front view

IL-76M/MD

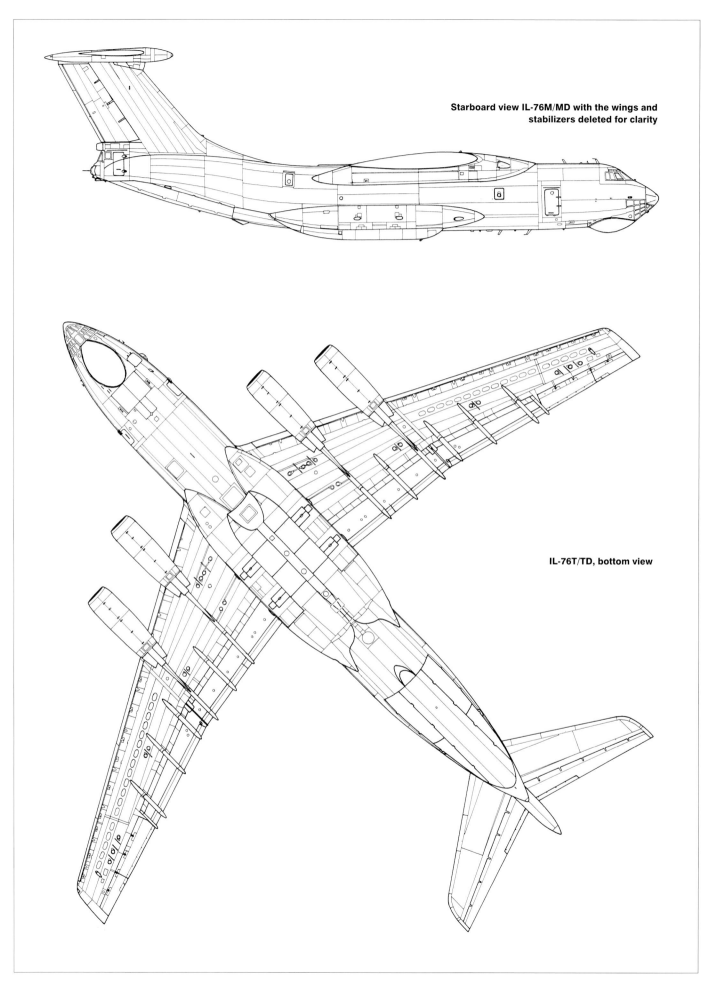

Starboard view IL-76M/MD with the wings and stabilizers deleted for clarity

IL-76T/TD, bottom view

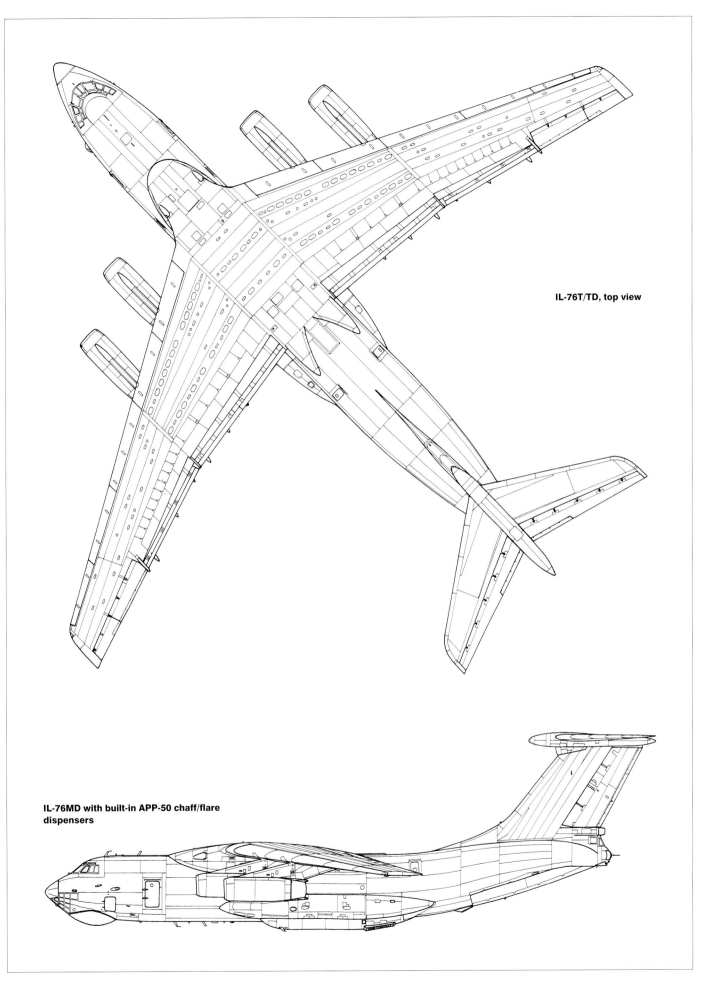

IL-76T/TD, top view

IL-76MD with built-in APP-50 chaff/flare dispensers

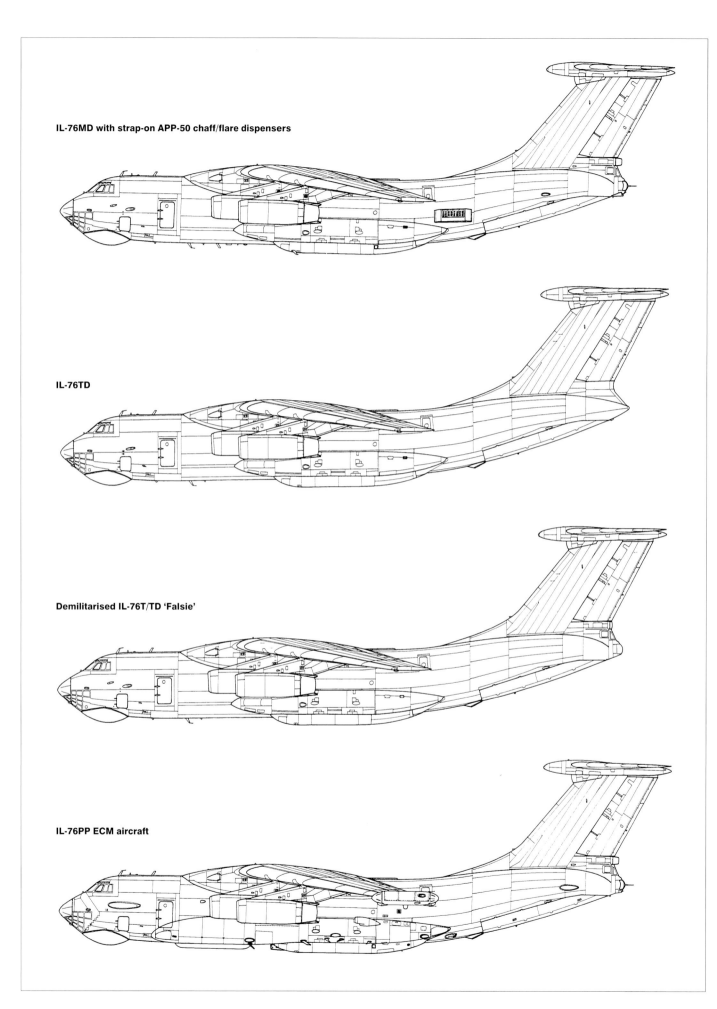

IL-76MD with strap-on APP-50 chaff/flare dispensers

IL-76TD

Demilitarised IL-76T/TD 'Falsie'

IL-76PP ECM aircraft

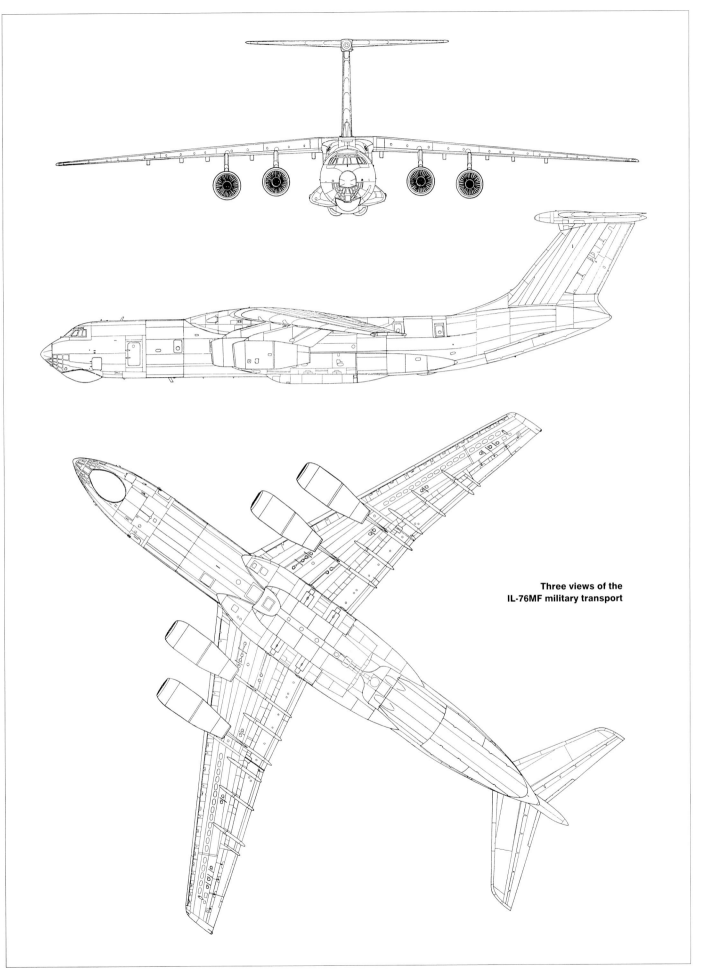

**Three views of the
IL-76MF military transport**

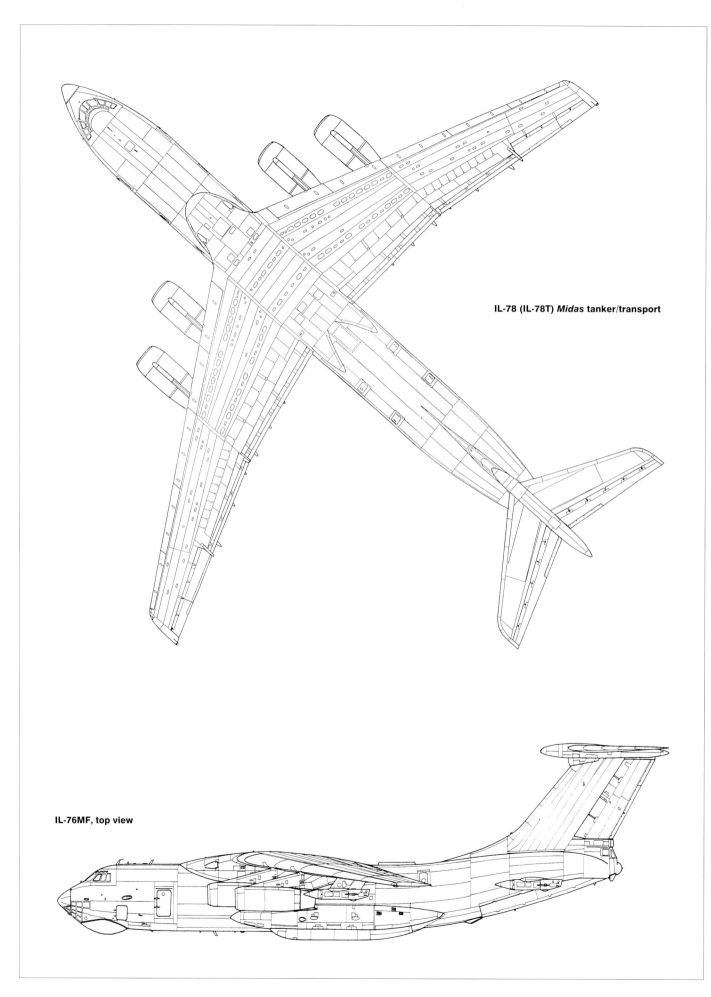

IL-78 (IL-78T) *Midas* **tanker/transport**

IL-76MF, top view

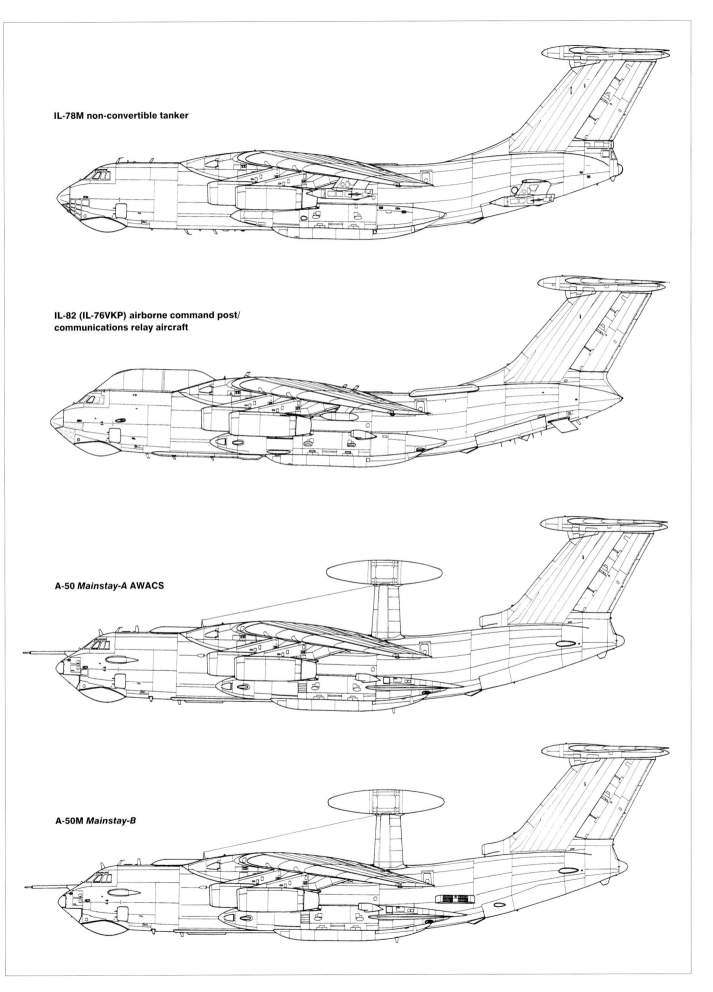

IL-78M non-convertible tanker

**IL-82 (IL-76VKP) airborne command post/
communications relay aircraft**

A-50 *Mainstay-A* AWACS

A-50M *Mainstay-B*

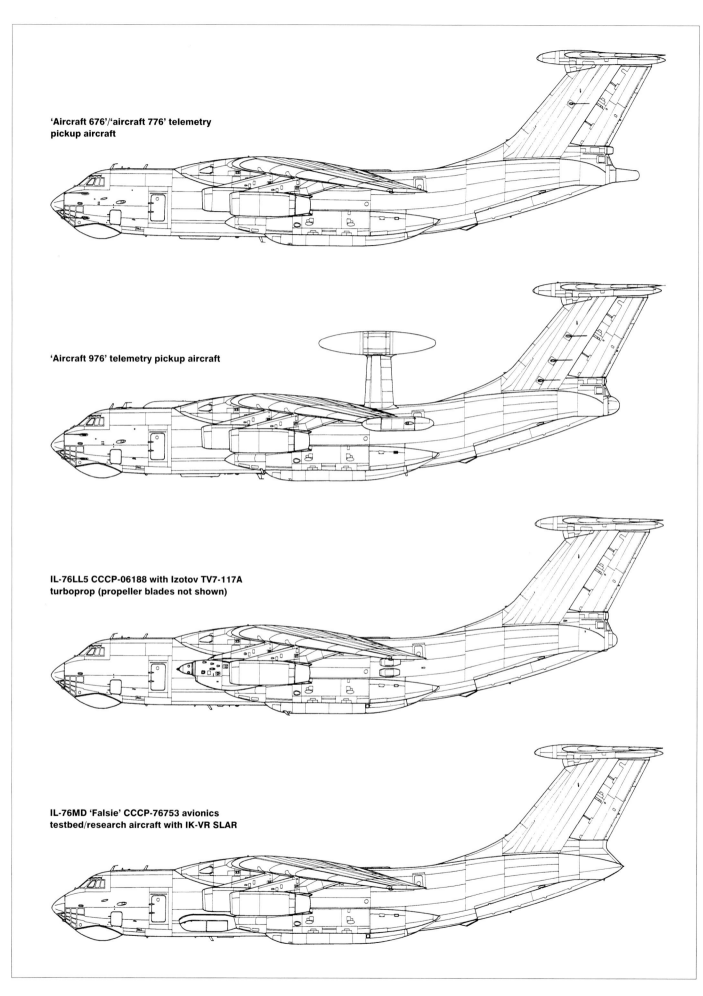

'Aircraft 676'/'aircraft 776' telemetry pickup aircraft

'Aircraft 976' telemetry pickup aircraft

IL-76LL5 CCCP-06188 with Izotov TV7-117A turboprop (propeller blades not shown)

IL-76MD 'Falsie' CCCP-76753 avionics testbed/research aircraft with IK-VR SLAR

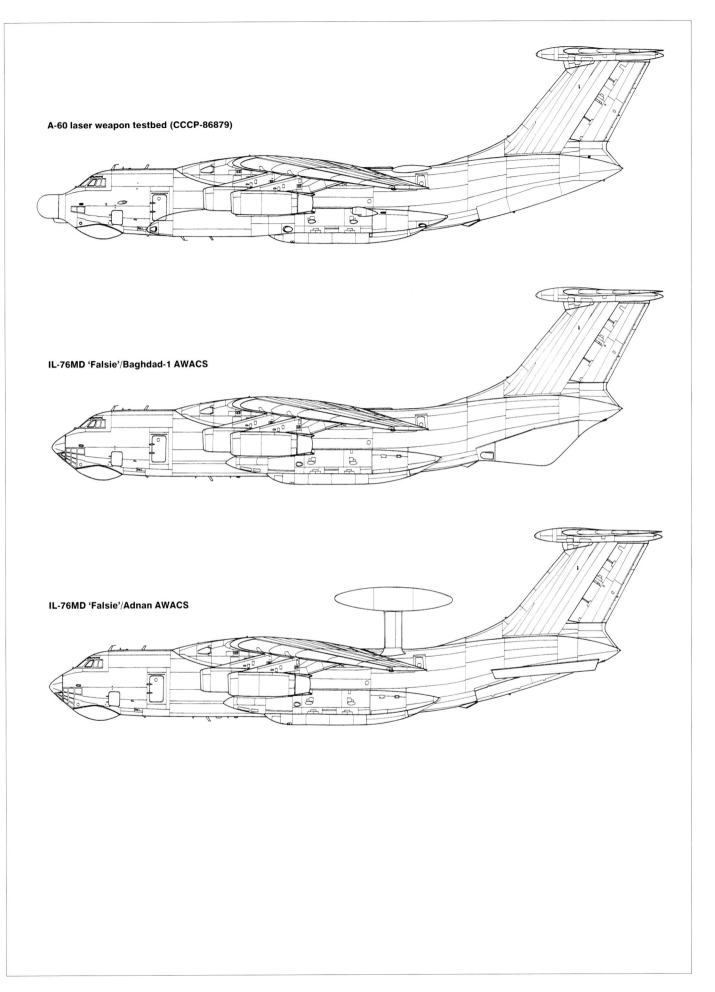

A-60 laser weapon testbed (CCCP-86879)

IL-76MD 'Falsie'/Baghdad-1 AWACS

IL-76MD 'Falsie'/Adnan AWACS

End Notes

Introduction
1 The number is a code allocated for security reasons.
2 PRS = *preetsel rahdiolokatseeonnyy, strelkovyy* – gunner's radar sight.

Chapter One
A New Machine
1 Now called the Aviadvigatel' (= Aero Engine) Production Association.
2 LNPO = *Leningrahdskoye naoochno-proizvodstvennoye obyedineniye* – Leningrad scientific and production association. LNPO Leninets is currently known as Leninets Holding Co.
3 NII = *naoochno-issledovatel'skiy institoot* – research institute.
4 Including loading ramp 4m (13ft 1½in) long.
5 Now NPP Aerosila (= Aeropower Scientific & Production Enterprise)
6 MMZ = *Moskovskiy mashinostroitel'nyy zavod* – Moscow Machinery Plant.

Chapter Two
A First Flight from Downtown
1 ie, SSSR-86712 in Cyrillic characters. This rendering of the Soviet registration prefix (as actually applied) is used throughout.
2 This town was often erroneously referred to as Ramenskoye in the West. Ramenskoye is located further south from Moscow and was the nearest town to the LII airfield until the town of Zhukovskiy was built.
3 Now called MAPO, *Moskovskoye aviatseeonnoye proizvodstvennoye obyedineniye* – the Moscow Aviation Production Association named after Pyotr V Dement'yev (former Minister of Aircraft Industry).
4 Currently Russia State Transport Company.
5 Now called TAPO (*Tashkentskoye aviatseeonnoye proizvodstvennoye obyedineniye* – Tashkent Aircraft Production Association named after Valeriy P Chkalov).
6 At least one batch (No16) contained *eleven* aircraft. Extra aircraft 'inserted' in the middle of a batch have fuselage numbers with suffix letters – eg, CCCP-86891, c/n 093421628, f/n 1607A.

Chapter Three
Versatility
1 UKU = *oonifitseerovannaya kormovaya oostanovka* – standardised tail [gun] installation. The same turret and gun ranging radar are fitted to the Tu-22M1/M2 *Backfire-B* and Tu-95MS *Bear-H* bombers.
2 Pronounced *izdeliye* – 'product', a term often used for coding Soviet military hardware items.
3 Now the Ukraine State Flight Academy (DLAU – *Derzhavna lyotna akademiya Ookrayiny*).
4 84,840kg (187,037 lb) has also been quoted (equals 110,474 litres or 24,304 Imperial gallons).
5 Some sources state CCCP-76504 as the prototype and CCCP-76511 as the first production IL-76T.
6 Some sources indicate +27°C (80°F).
7 SRO = *samolyotnyy rahdiolokatseeonnyy otvetchik* – aircraft-mounted radar [IFF] responder.
8 AgitAB = *aghitatseeonnaya aviabomba* – propaganda (ie, psychological warfare) bomb.
9 APP = *apparaht postanovki pomekh* – lit. 'interference emitting device'.
10 The registration -76492 has been reused – see IL-76LL section below.
11 This name was also used for the An-26M Skal'pel' (*Curl*); M = *meditsinskiy* – medical.
12 Doctor Aibolit (lit. 'ouch, it hurts!') is a children's book character created by Korney Chookovskiy – the Russian equivalent of Dr. Doolittle.
13 Pronounced *fregaht*. The name comes from the model of lifeboat carried by the aircraft.
14 MKS = *mnogokoopol'naya [parashootnaya] sistema* – multi-canopy [parachute] system.
15 VPS = *vytyazhnaya parashootnaya sistema* – parachute extraction system.
16 SKB = *spetsiahl'noye konstrooktorskoye byuro* – 'special' (ie, specialised) design bureau.
17 Soviet Navy ship.

18 Lockheed used the same principle for the MAFFS (Modular Airborne Fire-fighting System) fitted to the C-130, while MBB developed a similar system for the Transall C.160 in 1976 and Aeritalia for the G.222PROCIV. This only shows that engineers in different countries faced with the same problem often come to the same solution.
19 A Russian source refers to the aircraft in both cases as 'IL-76MD RA-86646' but this is obviously an error, as this aircraft is a military IL-76 *sans suffixe* (not an MD) and never received the RA- prefix.
20 Unlike Western military aircraft which have **serials** allowing positive identification, Soviet (Russian) military aircraft have two-digit **tactical codes** since 1955. As a rule, these are simply the aircraft's sequence number in the unit operating it, making positive identification impossible. Three- or four-digit tactical codes are rare and are usually worn by development aircraft only, in which case they still tie in with the c/n or f/n. On military *transport* aircraft, however, three-digit codes are usually the last three of the former civil registration.
21 In the case of the Tu-104AK the K means [*dlya podgotovki*] *kosmonahvtov* – for cosmonaut training. With the Tu-134AK, however, the K stands for [*povyshennyy*] *komfort* – enhanced comfort. Since the Tu-134K already existed (it was a VIP version of the original short Tu-134 *sans suffixe*), the zero-G trainer had to be designated Tu-134LK, ie, [*dlya podgotovki*] *lyotchikov-kosmonahvtov* – 'for pilot/cosmonaut training'. This *lyotchik-kosmonahvt* appellation was quite logical, since one has to qualify as a pilot before becoming an astronaut!
22 IL-76MD CCCP-76769 (c/n 0073481452, f/n 6203), IL-76MD 'Falsie' CCCP-78750 (c/n 1013405196, f/n 8009) and IL-76M CCCP-86825 (c/n 093419581, f/n 1506) have also been reported as IL-76MDKs but the former report is doubtful (probably a mis-sighting for CCCP-76766) and the latter two are obviously wrong.
23 The aircraft is designated IL-96MO (*opytnyy* – experimental).
24 Interestingly, the c/n is stencilled on the rear pressure bulkhead as **105**3417563, whereas the plates on the vehicle loading ramps read **104**3417563, showing that construction dropped way behind schedule.
25 UPAZ = *oonifitseerovannyy podvesnoy agregaht zaprahvki* – 'standardized suspended (ie, external) refuelling unit' or HDU. The 'standardized' part of the name means it can also be used as a 'buddy' refuelling pack by tactical aircraft – eg, the Su-24M, Su-30 and Su-33 (Su-27K).
26 Some sources say 400 to 600km/h (216 to 324kts).
27 RSBN = *rahdiotekhneecheskaya sistema blizhney navigahtsii* – short-range radio navigation system.
28 Later repainted in a desert camouflage scheme with the low-visibility tactical code 709 Black outline.
29 VPU = *vozdooshnyy poonkt oopravleniya* – airborne command/control post. The aircraft has also been referred to as IL-86VKP.
30 The designation IL-70 had been used in 1961 for a projected 24-seat regional airliner powered by two Tumanskiy R19M-300 turbojets; development was discontinued in 1963.
31 This has been reported as ex-IL-76M CCCP-86878; however, the latter was probably c/n 0013430872 (f/n 2209).
32 A quotation from Aleksandr S Pushkin's poem *The Prophet*.
33 Both aircraft were eventually withdrawn from use at the Russian Air Force's aircraft overhaul plant No123 in Staraya Roossa.
34 There were two Tu-4LLs, seven Tu-16LLs and two Tu-142LLs, all of them with different engines.
35 A sixth aircraft, IL-76T 'Falsie' CCCP-76528 (c/n 073410293, f/n 0804), was set aside for conversion but never converted.
36 This aircraft was originally reported as ex-YI-AKV; see Chapter Six – Iraqi section.
37 ZMKB = *Zaporozhskoye motorno-konstrooktorskoye byuro 'Progress'* – 'Progress' Zaporozh'ye Engine Design Bureau.
38 MGS = *mnogotselevoy groozovoy samolyot* – multi-role cargo aircraft.
39 A derivative of the Tu-204 airliner. The **real** Tu-214 is a high gross weight version of the Tu-204 built by the Kazan'

Aircraft Production Association named after Sergey P Gorboonov (aircraft factory No 22); curiously, in Ul'yanovsk this aircraft is built under its original designation, Tu-204-200.
40 Now known as MKB 'Trood', the 'Labour' Engine Design Bureau.
41 The registration was reused for IL-76T 'Falsie **RA**-76492 (ex-YI-AKT, c/n 093418548, f/n 1407) in 1994.
42 Also called Yak-42E (*eksperimentahl'nyy*).
43 Production IL-114s are powered by the 2,500eshp (1,840kW) TV7-117S (*sertifitseerovannyy* – certificated).
44 The original S-80 project envisaged TV7-117A engines. However, the first prototype built in late 1999 is powered by General Electric CT7-9B turboprops with Hamilton Standard propellers.
45 AP = *aviatseeonnyye prahvila* – aviation rules.
46 Gori is the name of a city in Georgia.

Chapter Four
In Action
1 Celebrated on the second Sunday of August.
2 The honorary appellation *Berlinskiy* was granted for the unit's gallantry in the taking of Berlin in 1945; however, the 334th was probably a bomber unit then.
3 OVTAP = *otdel'nyy voyenno-trahnsportnyy aviapolk* – independent military airlift regiment.
4 *Grooppa sovetskikh voysk v Ghermahnii* – Group of Soviet Forces in Germany; renamed ZGV (*Zahpadnaya grooppa voysk* – Western Group of Forces) in 1989.
5 NATO and the Soviet command often used different names for the same East German airbases. In such cases the Soviet name comes first with the NATO name following in parentheses.
6 The date has been quoted by Western sources as 5th April *1978* but Russian sources state 1977.
7 The Tu-134AK is a VIP version of the Tu-134A identifiable by the extra entry door in front of the port engine which is missing on regular 'As (including those converted to VIP configuration). The Tu-134 Balkany is an airborne command post derivative of the Tu-134AK often erroneously referred to as 'Tu-135' (which was really a bomber project of 1963) and identifiable by the HF aerial 'sting' under the APU exhaust and four small additional blade aerials.
8 Now called Bykovo Air Services Company (BASCO).
9 Now called Velikiy Novgorod ('Great Novgorod') to differentiate it from Nizhniy Novgorod ('Lower Novgorod', ie, 'the one down south' on the Volga River).
10 This was merely an allusion to appearance, *not* meaning a direct hit (the Russian equivalent to the idiom 'bull's eye' is totally different).
11 Some sources claim the aircraft in question was again CCCP-78768 but this has been reported several times as RA-78768, ie, **not** destroyed!)
12 Later renamed Sheikh Mansour International airport by the Chechens.
13 A pun on King Louis XIV, called *Lyudovik Chetyrnadtsatyy* in Russian (from the Latin spelling of his name, Ludovicus).
14 Roughly equivalent to the standard American 55 US gal. drum.
15 The red/white version of Aeroflot's 1973-standard colours was worn not only by Polar Aviation aircraft but also by many passenger and cargo aircraft flying scheduled services in the East Siberian, West Siberian and Far Eastern CADs.
16 See previous chapter (IL-76K section).

Chapter Five
The Candid 'At Home' (CIS IL-76 Operators)
1 The flight code Q9 was reallocated to Interbrasil Star [Q9/ITB]; for some obscure reason this airline and Sayakhat had the same code until 1999!
2 Possibly transformed to the 610th Training Centre.
3 Even before that (in 1997) its flight code was reallocated to Buffalo Airways Ltd [J4/BFL] of Hay River, North-Western Territories, Canada.
4 The flight code OP was reallocated to Chalk's International Airlines (Miami, Florida).
5 The crash of An-32B RA-26222 at Kinshasa-N'dolo on 8th January 1996 when the aircraft ploughed through the adjacent Simba Zikita market, killing some 260 people, was

the last straw. Some sources, however, claim that Moscow Airways' licence **had already been suspended at the time of the crash** and the aircraft had no business being there in the first place!

6 This is an old poetic-style name of Russia.

7 The name has also been rendered as SP Air and Spaero (not to be confused with Spaero JSP, see Ukrainian section).

8 Formerly the COMECON Civil Aviation Centre (*Tsentr grazhdahnskoy aviahtsii SEV*). COMECON (aka CMEA) = Council for Mutual Economic Assistance (*Sovet ekonomicheskoy vzaimopomoschchi*), the Soviet Union and its satellites' equivalent of the European Economic Council.

9 OSTAP = *otdel'nyy smeshannyy trahnsportnyy aviapolk* – independent composite airlift regiment. The 1st OSTAP at Kiev-Borispol' airport was formerly the 16th OSAP.

10 For some reason the original flight code was used by Bemidji Airlines [CH/BMJ] of Bemidji, Minnesota, at the same time. However, the new code was also a duplication, being assigned to Caribbean Air [9G/CRB] of Roatan, Honduras!

11 The new flight code is also assigned to Omni Air International [X9/OAE] of Tulsa, Oklahoma.

12 The PQ flight code was reassigned to Tropical International Airways (Basseterre, St. Kitts & Nevis). However, the new flight code is also used by AIRES Columbia [4C/ARE].

Chapter Six
...and Abroad (IL-76 Operators outside the CIS)

1 Now renamed back to Ariana Afghan Airlines.

2 The name has also been spelled 'Bourfarik'.

3 Some sources claim that the three An-12s were traded in for used IL-76TDs, while others indicate they were sold to Angolan carrier ALADA (Empresa de Transportes Aéreos, Lda).

4 A British Aerospace 748 built under licence by Hindustan Aeronautics Ltd.

5 This registration was later reused for an Air Cess An-24RV (ex-RA-47197, c/n 27307701) which later became 3C-KKH.

6 The name is derived from the full official name of the country, Socialist People's Libyan Arab Jamahiriya. The airline is often referred to as 'Jamahiriya Air Transport', but the actual titles on the aircraft read 'Jamahirian Air Transport'.

7 There is some confusion regarding 9L-LBK, as some sources indicate the L-410 had this registration first!

8 Some sources say RA-76367 became ST-AIO. This registration was later reused for a Cessna U206F Stationair of Blue Bird Aviation Co Ltd (ex-5Y-HSP, c/n U20602107).

9 Air Pass was just a trading name; the official name was Air Cess (Swaziland), Ltd.

Chapter Seven
Beneath the Skin

1 VNII NP = *Vsesoyoozznyy naoochno-issledovatel'skiy institoot nefteprodooktov* – All-Union Petroleum Products Research Institute.

Russian AF/224th Flight Unit IL-76MDs, like RA-78764 pictured here, are frequent visitors at Moscow-Domodedovo's cargo terminal. Note that the last three digits of the registration are repeated on the navigator's glazing.
Dmitriy Komissarov

The probe-equipped MiG-29SD prototype (c/n 2960536034, f/n 4808) prepares to take on fuel from IL-78 CCCP-78782 during manufacturer's flight tests. Arthur Sarkisyan/MAPO

An Indian Air Force IL-76MD takes off from Leh airfield in the Himalayas, 3,505m (11,500ft) above sea level. Wing Commander A P Mote

Quasi-civil IL-76Ms lined up at Kabul during the Afghan War. DAZ Press Bureau

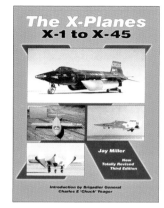

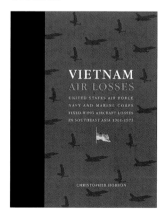

In 1982, American author Jay Miller published his first major book, the 'AeroGraph' on the F-16. Since then there has been a steady flow of widely acclaimed books from the Aerofax line.

After many years acting as European distributors, Midland Publishing Limited acquired the rights to the Aerofax name and have since commissioned many new titles for the series. Some will continue to be produced for Midland by Jay Miller in the USA, others will be originated by a talented team of internationally known authors.

The previous categories of AeroGraph, DataGraph, MiniGraph, and Extra are no longer used; all new titles are simply published as 'Aerofax' books.

These softback volumes are full of authoritative text, detailed photographs, plus line drawings. They also contain some colour, and cockpits, control panels and other interior detail are well illustrated in most instances.

Some of the more recent titles are outlined alongside, whilst a listing of the others in the series that are still in print, plus details of newly announced titles, is available upon request.

Aerofax
MIKOYAN-GUREVICH MiG-15
Yefim Gordon

In this Aerofax, compiled from a wealth of first-hand Russian sources, there is a comprehensive history of every evolution of the Soviet Union's swept-wing fighter and its service. Notably in this volume, there are tables listing intricate details of many individual aircraft, a concept which would have been unthinkable in any publications only a few years ago.

There is extensive and detailed photo coverage, again from Russian sources, almost all of which is previously unseen.

Softback, 280 x 215 mm, c176 pages
c250 b/w photos, plus colour section, and colour drawings/side-views
1 85780 105 9 **c£17.95/US $27.95**

Aerofax
TUPOLEV Tu-95/Tu-142 'BEAR'
Yefim Gordon and Vladimir Rigmant

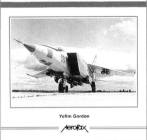

During the 'Cold War' Tupolev's Tu-95 'Bear' strategic bomber provided an awesome spectacle. It was the mainstay of the USSR's strike force, a reliable and adaptable weapons platform. Additional roles included electronic/photographic reconnaissance and maritime patrol, AEW and command and control.

The author has had unparalleled access to the Tupolev OKB archives, taking the lid off a story previously full of speculation to produce the most comprehensive study to date.

Softback, 280 x 216 mm, 128 pages
236 b/w, 24 col photos, 12 diagrams
1 85780 046 X **£14.95/US $24.95**

Aerofax
MIG-25 'FOXBAT' and MIG-31 'FOXHOUND'
Yefim Gordon

This book takes a detailed, informed and dispassionate view of an awesome aeronautical achievement – the titanium and steel MiG-25 – which became the backbone of the USSR defensive structure. Its follow-on was the similar-looking MiG-31 'Foxhound', very much a new aircraft designed to counter US cruise missiles and in production from 1979. Includes a large amount of previously unpublished material plus extensive and lavish illustrations.

Softback, 280 x 216 mm, 96 pages
110 b/w and colour photos plus 91 line and colour airbrush illustrations
1 85780 064 8 **£13.95/US $21.95**

Aerofax
BOEING KC-135
More Than Just a Tanker
Robert S Hoskins III

This book, written by a former USAF RC-135 crew commander, follows the development and service use of this globe-trotting aircraft and its many and varied tasks. Every variant, and sub-variant is charted, the histories of each and every aircraft are to be found within; details of the hundreds of units, past and present, that have flown the Stratotanker are given. This profusely illustrated work will interest those who have flown and serviced them as well as the historian and enthusiast community.

Softback, 280 x 216 mm, 224 pages
210 b/w and 46 colour photos
1 85780 069 9 **£24.95/US $39.95**

Aerofax
CONVAIR B-58 HUSTLER
The World's First Supersonic Bomber
Jay Miller

Instantly recognisable with its delta wing and 'coke bottle' area-ruled fuselage the B-58 was put into production for the US Air Force in the 1950s.

First published, in 1985, this is a revised edition, which takes a retrospective in-depth look at this significant aircraft, from design studies, through its development and comparatively short service life, to and beyond retirement. It includes yet more amazing material and 80 new illustrations, bringing the story up to date.

Softback, 280 x 216 mm, 152 pages
462 b/w, 15 colour, 100 line illusts.
1 85780 058 3 **£16.95/US $27.95**

Aerofax
McDONNELL DOUGLAS DC-10 AND KC-10 EXTENDER
Arthur A C Steffen

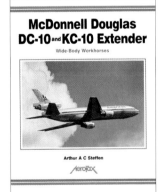

From 1970 to 1988 McDonnell Douglas built 446 DC-10s of all models and they are at work around the clock carrying passengers and freight. The central part of this book gives details of each DC-10 operator, including illustrations of all major colour schemes. The United States Air Force has 60 of the KC-10A Extender tanker/transport version, a very capable addition to the inventory.

The illustrations are almost totally full colour, to show to best advantage the wide range of schemes and operators.

Softback, 280 x 216 mm, 128 pages
276 colour, 14 b/w photos, 11 line dwgs
1 85780 051 6 **£19.95/US $34.95**

Aerofax
McDONNELL DOUGLAS MD-11
Arthur A C Steffen

McDonnell Douglas' follow-on to the DC-10 proved less successful in terms of numbers produced and has fallen casualty to the Boeing takeover. However it has been service with many airlines worldwide and is entering a second phase of existence as a pure freighter conversion.

Again, this book details each and every aircraft and operator. The illustrations are almost totally full colour, to show to best advantage the wide range of schemes and operators.

Softback, 280 x 216 mm, 128 pages
c230 mostly colour photos, 19 drawings
1 85780 117 2 **£19.95/US $34.95**

Above: **IL-76TD 76819 was operated for the United Nations Peace Forces in ex-Yugoslavia in 1993.** Petr Šebek

Below: **An A-50M completes its landing run.** Yefim Gordon